land of plenty

FUCHSIA DUNLOP

land of plenty

a treasury of authentic sichuan cooking

W. W. NORTON & COMPANY   New York   London

First published in Great Britain in 2001 by Michael Joseph Ltd, the Penguin Group,
under the title *Sichuan Cookery*

First American edition 2003

Manufacturing by The Haddon Craftsmen, Inc.
Book design by Carole Goodman
Production manager: Andrew Marasia

Library of Congress Cataloging-in-Publication Data

Dunlop, Fuchsia.
Land of plenty : a treasury of authentic Sichuan cooking / Fuchsia
Dunlop.— 1st American ed.
p. cm.
Includes bibliographical references and index.
ISBN 0-393-05177-3 (hardcover)
1. Cookery, Chinese. I. Title.
TX724.5.C5D86 2003
641.5951—dc21
2003002213

W. W. Norton & Company, Inc., 500 Fifth Avenue, New York, N.Y. 10110
www.wwnorton.com

W. W. Norton & Company Ltd., Castle House, 75/76 Wells Street, London W1T 3QT

1 2 3 4 5 6 7 8 9 0

For my mother, Carolyn

I never raise my chopsticks without remembering my dear Sichuan.

—Lu You

contents

a note on transliteration

The standard pinyin transliteration system for Chinese characters has been used throughout this book. Many of the vowels and consonants are pronounced almost as they are in English, with the following main exceptions:

q	pronounced	"ch"
x	pronounced	"sh"
z	pronounced	"dz"
c	pronounced	"ts"
zh	pronounced	"j"
ai	pronounced	"i" as in "kite"
ei	pronounced	"ay" as in "hay"
ao	pronounced	"ow" as in "cow"
ia	pronounced	"ee-ar"
iu	pronounced	"ee-o"
ian	pronounced	"ee-en"
ua	pronounced	"oo-ar"
uo	pronounced	"oo-or"
uai	pronounced	"oo-i" ("i" as in "kite")
ui	pronounced	"oo-ay" ("ay" as in "hay")

preface

In 1994 I moved to the Sichuanese capital, Chengdu, to take up a British Council Scholarship at Sichuan University. It wasn't my first visit to the province, and I have to admit that my choice of university was heavily influenced by Sichuan's gastronomic reputation. On two previous trips to the region I had been bowled over by the rich flavors and warm colors of the local food, and I knew I wanted to find out more about it. When I'd been in Chengdu for a couple of months, sampling the street snacks and the folk cuisine, drinking in the colors of the open markets, I decided with a German friend to make inquiries about cooking classes. One sunny October afternoon we cycled across the city in search of the famous provincial cooking school.

We could hear from the street that we had arrived. Fast, regular chopping, the sound of cleavers on wood. Upstairs, in a plain white room, dozens of apprentice cooks in white overalls were engrossed in learning the art of sauces. Chiles and fresh ginger were being pulverized with pairs of cleavers on wooden cutting boards, Sichuan peppercorns ground to a fine brown powder, and the students scurried around mixing oils and spices, fine-tuning the flavors of the rich dark liquids in their crucibles. The air hummed with a gentle rhythmic pounding, the sound of china spoons in china bowls. On long parallel tables sat bowls of ingredients; pools of soy sauce and oil, piles of sugar and salt. Notebooks scribbled with Chinese characters lay around on the tables amid the blood-red chiles and scattered peppercorns. The light streamed in through open windows. We decided immediately that this was where we had to study.

My friend Volker and I took private classes at the Sichuan Institute of Higher Cuisine over the next two months. Our teacher was the brilliant Gan Guojian, and the school's English tutor, Professor Feng Quanxin, was at hand to help us decipher the Sichuan dialect and explain the unfamiliar culinary terms. With this foundation, and a knowledge of a small repertoire of classic Sichuan dishes, I was able to talk to chefs and restaurateurs, and to spend fascinating days of study in several local restaurants.

Some months later, when I had finished my course at Sichuan University and was thinking about returning home to England, I dropped in at the cooking school to say hello. To my surprise, the principal of the school invited me to enroll as a regular student in a professional training course. This was a particular privilege, as no foreigner had ever done this before. Naturally I leapt at the opportunity, enrolled and paid my modest fees, and was promptly issued my own chef's overalls and Chinese cleaver.

For the next three months I studied cooking every day with forty-five young Sichuanese men and two young women. Mornings were spent in the classroom studying cooking theory—the selection of raw ingredients, the mixing of flavors, the control of the temperature of the fire and oil, and the different cooking methods—and then we would all move over to the demonstration room. There, we would gather around to watch our teachers, Long Qingrong and Lu Maoguo, prepare examples of home cooking and banquet delicacies with ease and artistry. The highlight of the morning was always, inevitably, the sampling. In the afternoons it was our turn to try. In teams of ten we prepared our raw ingredients, killing and cleaning fish, washing and chopping vegetables, collecting dried spices and pickled chiles from the nearby storeroom. Then each of us would have a turn at the wok, our classmates gathering around to tease and criticize. The finished dishes were all presented to the teacher, who would assess them for color, taste, and texture.

Once a week we studied pastry-making with the famous pastry chef Li Daiquan. Mr. Li acquired his skills as an apprentice to one of the great Sichuanese chefs of the twentieth century, Kong Daosheng, and his "rippled-silk fried dumplings" (bo si you gao) are celebrated all over the province. From him we learned to make different kinds of dumpling wrappers; to prepare stuffings sweet and savory; to fold, pinch, and tuck; and to steam, fry, and boil all kinds of mouthwatering snacks.

On my days off I would cycle around Chengdu, learning about street food and researching raw ingredients. I was also lucky enough to be allowed to study in the kitchens of several restaurants, including the traditional snack specialist Long Chao Shou and the magical Shufeng restaurant. Exploring Chengdu was a never-ending pleasure. I recall sitting with an old roast duck vendor in a narrow back street that meandered among the wooden courtyard houses in the center of town, discussing the food of the past and watching the life of the teeming city flow by. Fruit vendors passed, bearing bamboo baskets laden with cherries or "dragon-eye" fruit dangling from either end of their bamboo shoulder poles. A sharp metal clink heralded the arrival of the knife sharpener, bearing two cleaver blades and a pair of round-handled Chinese scissors.

In the quieter alleys, home-cured bacon and sausages hung from the eaves in midwinter; in summer they were decked with pieces of radish, citrus peel, and cabbage hung out to dry. Someone would be tinkering with a bicycle, a group of old people playing mahjong on a makeshift table, clattering the tiles. Dried foods would lie soaking in preparation for an evening meal; somewhere a pot would be bubbling away on a charcoal burner. Brightly colored clothes hung on lines crisscrossing the lanes. Elderly people sat back in bamboo chairs, watching their grandchildren play.

Since those first days, I have returned to Chengdu every year, sometimes for months at a time, to continue my research and to collect more recipes. Each visit has opened up new paths of culinary exploration, and I never cease to be amazed by the diversity and dynamism of Sichuanese cuisine.

Since I began my research, I have entertained countless friends and relatives with Sichuanese meals, and the reception has often been ecstatic. These dishes are simply so different from any Chinese food most people have tasted. They may have eaten Chinese dumplings before, but they've never had Sichuan's famous Zhong dumplings, with their delicious sweet, salty, spicy, garlicky sauce. They've eaten stir-fried dishes, but never a cold cucumber stir-fry with the merest, tantalizing rumor of spice and sesame. And they think they know what bean curd tastes like, but they've never tasted real *ma po dou fu*, with its fiery red sauce and scattering of ground beef and dark, leafy greens.

Sichuanese cuisine ranges from street snacks to banquet cooking, its ingredients from seasonal vegetables to rare delicacies. A few of the recipes in this book require unusual materials or complex cooking methods; most do not. All of them have been tested in my London kitchen, on an ordinary gas stove, with ingredients that are locally available. I have tried to offer a glimpse of the diversity and sophistication of Sichuanese cuisine, but the emphasis of this collection of recipes is firmly on the folk cooking of the region, on the wonderful dishes that my Sichuanese friends make at home or in their restaurants, and that I lived on, with great delight, for more than two years of my life.

Fuchsia Dunlop
London

introduction

Sichuanese cooking is one of the great unknown cuisines of the world. It is legendary in China for its sophistication and amazing diversity, but known in the West only by a few famous dishes and its "hot-and-spicy" reputation. Chinese people say that "China is the place for food, but Sichuan is the place for flavor," and local gourmets claim the region boasts five thousand different dishes. Chinese poets have glorified Sichuanese food for the last thousand years. The Sichuanese themselves are particularly obsessed with food, even given the strong competition in this respect from other parts of China. Surly taxi drivers wax lyrical as they describe their favorite dumplings; travelers sigh, dewy-eyed, when they stop to think of the pickled vegetables they are leaving behind; office workers slurping a quick bowl of noodles on their lunch break recount stories of the legendary chefs of the 1930s.

In the West, strangely, Chinese cuisine is almost always treated as one great tradition, with a few regional variations. Viewed from the outside, perhaps it is the unifying themes that leap to mind: the use of chopsticks, the consumption of rice, bread, or noodles with shared dishes of meat and vegetables, the technique of stir-frying in a wok, the use of soy sauce as a flavoring. Viewed from inside, however, it is the differences that seem to matter, the differences among the fresh, natural flavors of the south, the sweeter, oilier cooking of the eastern coastal areas, and the spicy western diet; between the wheaten staples of the north and the southern use of rice. Outsiders often forget that China is more of a continent than a country: its vast territory encompasses deserts and rain forests, high mountains and fertile plains, salt lakes and rolling grasslands. Sichuan is as large as France, with a population nearly twice the size of Britain's. It has its own dialect, its own operatic style, a unique teahouse culture and, of course, an outstanding culinary tradition.

The real Sichuan cuisine is quite unlike the Cantonese, eastern, or northern styles, and quite unlike any other outside China. Its most famous characteristic, which it shares with the cooking of nearby Hunan and Guizhou provinces, is its fiery spiciness, derived from the liberal use of red chiles and numbing Sichuan pepper.

In the Sichuan countryside, red chiles are strung up in enormous bunches from the eaves of the wood-frame farmhouses (like the strings of scarlet firecrackers that are detonated for the Chinese New Year). Dried in the sun, blood red and lustrous, or pickled bright scarlet in salt and wine, chiles are at the heart of Sichuanese cooking. Sichuanese people have an extraordinary appetite for chiles, which tend to find their way into at least some of the dishes served at every breakfast, lunch, and dinner. Because of this, the Sichuanese have a reputation for being a little bit spicy themselves, and local women are even known as "spice girls" (*la mei zi*). The spicy local diet is so notorious that Chinese people will invariably ask outsiders on their way to Sichuan whether or not they are "afraid of chile heat" (*pa la*).

Chiles are used in many local dishes, but they are used so inventively that their taste never palls. Dried chiles, sizzled in oil, give the "scorched chile flavor" that is the base of Gong Bao (Kung Pao) chicken and innumerable stir-fried vegetable dishes; combined with Sichuan pepper, they are used in the "hot-and-numbing" dishes that are so notoriously fiery. Milder chiles pickled in brine and spices yield a more subtle heat, the base of the sensational "fish-fragrant flavor" with its mix of salty, sweet, sour, and spicy tastes. Chili and fava bean paste is the dominant taste in "homestyle" dishes; and ground chiles and chili oil are used in a myriad of cold dishes, most famously the "strange-flavor" concoctions that combine salty, sweet, numbing, hot, sour, and nutty tastes. The heat of chiles is never meant to overwhelm the flavors of the other ingredients, however, but to heighten sensation and to open up the palate to a rich variety of tastes.

Despite the emphasis on chiles in Sichuan's gastronomic reputation, hot and spicy food certainly isn't all the region has to offer. In fact, the most salient characteristic of Sichuanese cooking is its audacious combinations of several different flavors in a single dish. Some of these compound flavors are hot and spicy, many others, such as sour, sweet, melting "lychee flavor," boozy "fragrant wine flavor," and fresh, light "ginger juice flavor," are not. So those who do *pa la*, fear chiles, as they say, will still find plenty to entice them within the pages of this book.

The other famous Sichuan spice is Sichuan pepper (*hua jiao*), known variously as flower pepper, brown peppercorns, prickly ash, or (erroneously) fagara. It is one of the most ancient Chinese spices, and a Sichuan specialty. It has an extraordinary, heady aroma that carries hints of wood, citrus peel, and the languid scents of summer, and it produces a weird numbing effect on the lips and tongue. This tingling sensation is known in Chinese as *ma*, which also means "anesthetic" and "pins-and-needles." Despite the initial strangeness of this spice, its taste and fragrance are incomparable, and I have seen most of my friends and relatives succumb quickly to its aromatic charms. One folk explanation for the widespread use of this pepper in Sichuanese cooking is, curiously, that its numbing effects allow people to consume more chiles than would otherwise be humanly possible!

The finest Sichuan pepper in China is grown in Hanyuan county in the mountains of western Sichuan. Local people say its fragrance is so strong that you can rub the raw spice onto your palm and still smell it on the back of your hand, through skin and bone. Hanyuan Sichuan pepper was used as a scent before it became a cooking spice, and it was so highly prized that it was offered in tribute to the emperors of China. During the Han period, the spice was actually mixed into the mud walls of the residences of imperial concubines, which became known as "pepper houses" (*jiao fang*), a term that survived into the late imperial era, although the practice didn't. According to Sichuanese scholars, the custom arose not only because of its fragrance, but because the Sichuan pepper plant bears many seeds and is thus a traditional symbol of fertility. Sichuan pepper and peanuts are still thrown over brides and grooms at weddings in rural areas.

Most local people ascribe the spiciness of Sichuanese cooking to the muggy climate. In Chinese medicine, dampness is seen as dangerously unhealthy, for it impairs the yang energy of the body and causes sluggishness. The best way to restore a healthy equilibrium is to eat foods that drive out moisture and dispel the cold, which makes heating foods like chiles, ginger, and Sichuan pepper part of the perfect local diet. Sichuanese people feel obliged to eat plenty of chiles not only during the winter, when they conquer the creeping dampness that penetrates every layer of clothing, but also at the height of summer, when they aid perspiration and dispel humidity. (Incidentally, several Sichuanese friends, reared on stereotypes of rainy, foggy London, have remarked on the suitability of Sichuanese food for the English climate!)

Sichuan is also famous for its mistiness, for the gray moistness that for much of the year shrouds trees and rivers, blotting out the sunlight. Clear skies are famously rare, so much so that they say Sichuanese dogs bark at the sight of the sun (*shu quan fei ri*). But against all this dismal weather, picture the colors of a typical Sichuanese meal: the chili-oil dressing on a bowlful of fresh fava beans, the scarlet pickled chiles resplendent on a braised fish, the cool pinks of aromatic boiled meats, the dusky red of Sichuan pepper. The local cooking not only restores the body, its rich autumn colors also soothe the heart and offer a fitting rebuke to the perennial grayness of the sky.

THE DEVELOPMENT OF SICHUANESE CUISINE

The Sichuan region has long been famous for its cooking. As far back as the fifth century A.D., a historian, Chang Qu, remarked on local people's liking for interesting flavors and hot-and-fragrant dishes (*shang zi wei, hao xin xiang*). By about the sixth century A.D. the regional cuisine was embarking on a period of great development, and by the Song Dynasty (tenth to thirteenth centuries) it was becoming known all over China. In the early days, however, the intense, spicy tastes of the region's cooking came not from chiles, but from flavorings like ginger, betel nuts, and, later, pepper.

It was only in the sixteenth century, the late Ming period, that chiles first arrived in China from the Americas and contemporary botanical sources described them as "barbarian peppers" (*fan jiao*). These early sources presented the chile as an ornamental plant, and it was another century before its use to flavor food was documented.

By the mid-eighteenth century, chiles were widely eaten in the lower Yangtze region, but it wasn't until the early nineteenth century that their cultivation became common in Sichuan. One can only imagine how readily they were adopted by the local people, who had long been accustomed to seasoning their food boldly to counter the unhealthy humors of the climate. Their use spread during the reign of the Qing emperors, China's last imperial dynasty, and Sichuanese food became ever more famous for its strong, intense tastes and intriguing use of hot and numbing spices. These days, chiles are an indispensable part of the Sichuanese diet, but their dialect name, *hai jiao* ("sea peppers"), remains as a reference to their foreign origins. (Strangely, the use of chiles has all but disappeared in the coastal parts of China that first encountered them.)

People sometimes ascribe the distinctiveness of Sichuan's culture to geographical isolation. Look at a topographical map of China and you'll see why: the green, fertile Sichuan basin is ringed by forbidding mountains, with the vast Tibetan plateau rising to its west. The only way out is along the path of the Yangtze River, which snakes its way through treacherous gorges to central China and, finally, the sea. Before the advent of railways and modern transport, reaching Sichuan was something of an ordeal—not for nothing did the poet Li Bai describe the way there as more difficult than the road to heaven.

Actually, however, Sichuan has not had a history of isolation. More than two thousand years ago, the forces of China's great unifying emperor, Qin Shihuang (the one who was buried with the terracotta army), defeated the ancient western kingdoms of Ba and Shu and brought the Sichuan basin under central control. His followers, migrating to the region from the central Chinese plains, are thought to have brought with them some of their own eating customs, beginning a long process of cultural exchange between the Sichuan region and the rest of China.

In times of peace, the Sichuan region often closed in on itself, retreating behind its geographical fortifications, the inward flow of immigrants slowing to a trickle. Each period of war or dynastic upheaval, however, saw great waves of immigrants entering the province. The most dramatic influx occurred in the late Ming and early Qing dynastic periods, around the seventeenth century. The dying days of the Ming had seen conflict and chaos all over China, and war, pestilence, and natural disasters had decimated the population of the Sichuan region. Vast areas of valuable farmland had fallen into disuse. As the new Qing rulers worked to restore food production and bring about stability, they encouraged large-scale immigration into the fertile Sichuan basin. As a result, the following century saw a huge influx of outsiders from about a dozen other Chinese provinces. Most of the population of today's Chengdu are thought to be descendants of outsiders.

Centuries later, during the Japanese invasion of China in the 1930s, millions of people from northern and coastal areas sought refuge in inland Sichuan, and Chongqing, Sichuan's second city, became the wartime capital of the Nationalist government.

Every wave of immigration has brought new cultural and culinary influences. Sichuanese food, like Sichuanese opera and the local dialect, may have a very distinctive local character, but today's "traditional" culinary repertoire incorporates many outside influences: most notably chiles from South America, but also roasting and smoking techniques that originated in the imperial kitchens in Beijing, "red-braising" from the eastern provinces, an interest in deep-frying that is said to have come from Americans supporting the war effort in 1930s Chongqing, and all kinds of dumplings and snacks that came from northern and coastal areas.

These days the pace of change is inevitably faster, and local cooks are beginning to experiment with Japanese wasabi, all kinds of fresh seafood, and Korean-influenced barbecues, to name just a few. Sichuanese people are beginning to learn about Western food and wine, so there's no doubt that more and more foreign ingredients will work their way into the local diet and cuisine. Few local chefs or gourmets see this as a threat: such is their confidence in Sichuanese cooking skills that they are merely excited at the prospect of having so many new ingredients and techniques to play with. New dishes spring up every day, such as air-freighted fresh sea crabs cooked with chiles by the traditional "dry-braising" method, or Sichuanese "mustard-flavor" sauces made with green wasabi instead of the common yellow mustard.

THE LAND OF PLENTY

Sichuan is known in China as "the land of plenty" (*tian fu zhi guo*) because of its agricultural wealth. The fertile soil of the Sichuan basin, its warm climate, and its abundance of rain and river water create ideal conditions for farming. The region has been a center of food production for more than two millennia: as early as the third century B.C., an imperial official, Li Bing, supervised the harnessing of the rivers near Chengdu with the enormous Dujiangyan irrigation project, which you can still see today.

From the rich Sichuan earth spring forth all kinds of fruits and vegetables, all year round: local specialties include various types of mandarin oranges, pomeloes, apples and pears, lychees and longans, peaches and loquats, Chinese chives, many varieties of bamboo shoot, celery, eggplants, lotus leaves and stems, water spinach, and gourds and melons of all shapes and sizes. Exceptionally fine tea leaves grow in the mountains, and wild vegetables such as fiddlehead ferns (*jue cai*), *Houttuynia cordata* (*ze'er gen*), and the spring shoots of the Chinese toon tree (*chun ya*) are also enjoyed. Sichuan is crisscrossed by rivers and streams, once the habitat of a multitude of fish. The surrounding mountains, forests, and grasslands teem with wildlife: exotic fungi, wild frogs, and all kinds of medicinal roots and herbs. To the eyes of Chinese gourmets, the entire Sichuan region, with its mountains, forests, rivers, and plains, is one extraordinary pantry filled with the stuff of gastronomic dreams.

Sichuanese well salt is another celebrated local product. It is made by heating bittern extracted from salt mines deep within the earth and is prized for its purity of flavor. Salt has been mined in the area for more than two millennia, and the salt mines founded by irrigation expert Li Bing in the third century B.C. are among the oldest in the world. By the the Tang Dynasty there were nearly five hundred salt mines in the area, and the center of salt production, today's Zigong, became known as the "salt capital" (*yan du*). If you visit Zigong today, you can still see the Qing Dynasty halls of the old Salt Administration, which now house a local salt industry museum.

Of course it's not only the raw materials that contribute to the diversity of Sichuanese cuisine. Local people have developed an extraordinarily sophisticated culinary tradition, with a whole armory of skills for processing and cooking their ingredients. Sichuanese chefs are well known for their cutting skills, for their subtle control of heat, and most of all for their inspired flavoring techniques, which are quite unmatched in Chinese and possibly in global cooking. The combination of all these crafts can transform even a limited range of ingredients into a banquet—with the resources available to the official cooks of the great mansions of the past and the expert chefs of the present day, the possibilities are almost infinite.

Chinese scholarship has a long-standing love of detailed classification, which is also reflected in Chinese food culture. Sichuanese cooks use a highly complex culinary vocabulary, much of which is almost impossible to translate into English. Recipe books identify fifty-six distinct cooking methods, their differences minutely analyzed (see page 358). There are different terms for every type of slice and chunk (see page 32 on cutting), and twenty-three "official" Sichuanese flavoring combinations (see page 353). Subtle gradations of texture or "mouth-feel" (*kou gan*) are recognized and labeled. Professional cooking manuals preface every recipe with a note on the flavor category, cooking method, and special characteristics (*te dian*) of the dish in question—the latter might include its appearance, fragrance, and texture and is usually expressed in a catchy, formulaic "four-character" phrase. Each dish is also somewhat bureaucratically ranked according to its class or function—it might be, for example, a high-level banquet dish, a middle-ranking banquet dish, or a "convenient dish for the masses" (*da zhong bian can*).

Scholars and officials throughout Chinese history have written about the pleasures of eating, and an appreciation of fine food was one of the traditional accomplishments of the Confucian gentleman. Some of China's most famous food writers were officials whose political careers had been thwarted. Food scholars suggest they may have tried to drown their professional sorrows in gastronomy. Whatever their motivations, the interest of the educated elite in eating, if not generally in cooking, must have been a key factor in the development of such a very sophisticated culinary culture.

CHENGDU AND CHONGQING

Chengdu, the ancient capital of the Shu kingdom, is in many ways the capital of Sichuanese cuisine. It has been a center of silk production and brocade weaving for two millennia, and its wealthy merchants long ago developed a taste for the luxuries of life. Chengdu's mellow climate and plentiful produce made life there easier than in many parts of China, and the local population earned a reputation for being idle pleasure-lovers, never happier than when they were playing cards or mahjong in a teahouse or devouring some of the delicious local food. Chengdu has changed out of all recognition in the last decade, but if you visit the remaining old teahouses and the nicer restaurants, you can still find glimpses of the sensibility that created a cup of tea that can last for a whole afternoon, and a hotpot you can mull over from dusk to midnight.

To the east of Chengdu lies Chongqing, formerly Sichuan's second city and now a separate municipality. Chongqing is a mountain city, clinging to the steep banks of the Yangtze River. Before the railways, this river was Sichuan's most important transportation link with the rest of China; and Chongqing is still a crucial river port, sending boats downstream through the Three Gorges to Shanghai and the sea. The Chongqing climate is even steamier than Chengdu's; in fact so overwhelming is the summer heat that it's known as one of China's "furnace cities" (*huo lu*). Predictably, the response of the local people to this heat and humidity is to eat even more chiles and Sichuan pepper than their Chengdu neighbors, so Chongqing folk cooking can be quite fiendishly hot and numbing.

The steep hills and busy port give Chongqing a much brisker atmosphere than Chengdu, and this fast pace is reflected in its culinary culture. Chongqing has traditionally been a rich source of new food trends and a dynamic innovator. It is a melting pot as well as a furnace, the point at which Sichuan meets the outside world. Many of Sichuan's most famous dishes rose to prominence in Chongqing—most notably the Sichuan hotpot, and in recent years fish soup with pickled mustard greens (*suan cai yu*). Chongqingers traditionally look down on the people of Chengdu for being lazy and out-of-date in their eating habits. The inhabitants of Chengdu habitually retort that while Chongqing people may know how to invent a good dish, their food is coarse and crude and needs the refining touch of Chengdu chefs before it can become really great cuisine.

DIFFERENT FOOD TRADITIONS

HOMESTYLE COOKING

Homestyle cooking is where you'll find the soul of Sichuanese cuisine. This is the hearty, economical cooking of homes and informal restaurants, the kind of dishes that make Sichuanese people dreamy with nostalgia when they're away from home. Old favorites like twice-cooked pork (*hui guo rou*), pock-marked Mother Chen's bean curd (*ma po dou fu*), and Gong Bao (Kung Pao) chicken with peanuts (*gong bao ji ding*), all scrumptious and easy to prepare; simple stir-fried vegetables, tossed in the wok with a few chiles or Sichuan pepper husks; homemade pickled vegetables, served with a drizzling of chili oil and a scattering of sugar; the traditional feast dishes of rural Sichuan—ducks, chickens, or pork belly steamed for hours in earthenware bowls and turned out onto serving platters when the guests arrive.

Sichuanese homestyle cooking lacks the refinement of banquet cuisine: its flavors are strong and robust, its ingredients seasonal and local. It is in this style of cooking that Sichuanese food lives up to its hot-and-spicy reputation, through the widespread use of dried and pickled chiles, chili bean paste, and Sichuan pepper. The sour spiciness of pickled vegetables is another characteristic note. Homestyle dishes are not all devilishly hot, however: ordinary meals, like banquets, should offer a variety of flavors, with mild, simple dishes to counterbalance the rich and fiery.

Chinese gourmets have a long tradition of idealizing rustic cooking and the simple peasant diet. Today, Chengdu's discerning diners-out, veterans of many exotic banquets, still insist that there is nothing to beat the hearty simplicity of Sichuanese home cooking.

STREET FOOD

Sichuan in general, and Chengdu in particular, are famous for their street snacks—the dumplings, noodles, and other delicious nibbles that are known collectively as "little eats" (*xiao chi*). Almost every town has its own specialty— a kind of leaf-wrapped dumpling, perhaps, or a cold-dressed meat dish, or a style of noodles. These delicacies were originally sold on the streets by itinerant vendors who each specialized in one particular snack. Some can still be bought this way, although it's more common now to eat the snacks in noodle shops or restaurants that specialize in them. (For a more detailed description of *xiao chi*, see page 85.)

BANQUET COOKING

A Sichuanese banquet can be an astonishing display of exotic dishes and virtuoso cooking skills, far beyond the home cook in terms of scale and elaboration. Banquet menus usually feature expensive ingredients such as dried seafood, as well as rare wild delicacies from the mountains and forests that surround the Sichuan basin. (These are known collectively as "treasures from the mountains and the seas," *shan zhen hai wei*.) One of Sichuan's most famous banquet dishes is duck with caterpillar fungus (*chong cao ya zi*). The duck is stewed with *Cordyceps sinensis*, a fungus from the Tibetan grasslands that invades the bodies of caterpillars and grows inside them, until nothing is left of the creatures but their outer shells. When they are harvested, the fungi look exactly like caterpillars, which makes for a very interesting duck soup. The fungus is prized as a medicine and has been used in Sichuanese cooking for around three hundred years.

Sichuanese cooks also use distinctive regional cooking methods to prepare some universal Chinese delicacies such as shark's fin; the most extravagant banquets would also include dishes made with parts of wild animals, most famously bear's paw, but the listing of endangered species in recent years has outlawed many of these legendary delicacies.

Banquet cooking features dishes of great wit and subtlety, designed to surprise and enchant the dinner guests. So you might be served "chicken bean curd soup" (*ji dou hua*), which resembles the cheap-and-cheerful "flower" bean curd eaten in eastern Sichuan but is actually made with finely puréed chicken breast; or "white cabbage in boiled water" (*kai shui bai cai*), a whole Chinese cabbage served in a bowl of perfectly clear soup. The marvel of this dish is that the cabbage is a modest, everyday vegetable, but it is served in an exquisite stock made from chicken, duck, ham, and pork bones. Platters of ornately carved vegetables arranged in forms like a "peacock spreading its tail" (*kong que kai ping*) or "panda fighting bamboo" (*xiong mao zhan zhu*) make occasional appearances on banquet tables.

Sichuanese banquets almost always supplement the exotica with expert renditions of much-loved common dishes, like the bowl-steamed dishes typical of rural feasts. Expert Sichuanese chefs have a tradition of adopting and refining rustic regional dishes, and many still make trips into the rural areas of Sichuan in order to search for fresh culinary inspiration. The higher you go on the social scale of banqueting, however, the lighter and more delicate the flavors are likely to be. Although some dishes may be a little hot and numbing in the spirit of Sichuanese homestyle cooking, these tastes won't play a major part in the meal.

In Sichuanese homes, everyone fills themselves up with steamed rice toward the end of a meal. But at banquets, rice usually isn't served at all: a symbol of the fact that feasting is not about inexpensive staple food, but about the pleasure and the luxury of eating. For this reason it is, incredibly, possible to go home after a twenty-course banquet and still feel hungry. To avoid this, restaurants usually serve each banquet guest one or two wheat- or rice-based street snacks, to offset the richness of the meal.

OTHER CULINARY TRADITIONS

Chinese Buddhist monasteries have a long-standing tradition of vegetarianism, and although most monks and nuns exist on a simple diet of beans, grains, and vegetables, the larger monasteries run special restaurants providing more elaborate vegetarian fare. The most distinctive aspect of this grand vegetarian food, known as *fo zhai cai*, is that many dishes are made to imitate meat or fish in their appearance, taste, and texture. This cuisine of artful mimicry can be found all over China, but Sichuanese monasteries have their own regional style, offering vegetarian versions of classic Sichuanese dishes such as twice-cooked pork (*hui guo rou*) and dry-fried eels (*gan bian shan si*). (For a more detailed explanation of *fo zhai cai*, see page 283.)

Chinese Muslims also cook their own versions of Sichuanese food in specialized restaurants, using beef, chicken, and sometimes lamb as substitutes for pork. Classic pork dishes are served up with a twist, creating hybrids like fish-fragrant beef slivers, chicken slices with crispy rice, and beef versions of many pork-stuffed dumplings.

EATING THE SICHUANESE WAY

If you are invited for dinner in a Sichuanese home, there will probably be a few cold dishes on the table when you arrive—perhaps some deep-fried peanuts, a plateful of preserved radish in chili sauce picked up from the market, some cold meats, or a cucumber salad. When everyone is seated at the dining table, the cook will still be in the kitchen for a while, keeping an eye on the braised meat stew, stir-frying the vegetables and mushrooms, making the simple soup that will conclude the meal. A very informal dinner will have at least one dish per person, but there's no limit to the number of dishes that you may be offered. As a guest, you will be encouraged to eat, and to eat more, and to go on eating, and attentive hosts will offer you the choicest morsels, placing them directly into your rice bowl with their chopsticks. A final soup rinses and refreshes the palate. Rice is usually offered toward the end of the meal, with a small dish of pickled vegetables to "send the rice down" (*xia fan*). Fresh fruit may be served after dinner.

More elaborate restaurant meals follow a similar pattern, but with far more dishes. Cold food is served first, and then the hot dishes emerge from the kitchen one by one until the whole table is laden with food. You may also be offered tiny individual bowls of dumplings, little fancies to be eaten on the side. A final, clear, stock-based soup is a sign that the meal is drawing to an end. This may be followed by one or two simple "send-the-rice-down" (*xia fan*) dishes, with or without the actual rice, and the inevitable Sichuanese touch, a final nibble of pickled vegetables. There's also a recent, Cantonese-influenced fashion for platters of cut fruit to be served at the end of the meal.

Among the hot dishes, there are no hard-and-fast rules about the sequence of dishes on menus, although every good cook will try to avoid repetition of ingredients, tastes, or textures. The typical Sichuanese meal starts with dry, salty, intensely flavored dishes and meanders among all manner of tastes and textures before ending with a bland, clear soup and sour pickles drizzled with chili oil. The classic Sichuanese soups are usually undersalted and often include ribbons of pickled mustard greens—another sour note. The regional style is very much in keeping with the advice of the great Qing Dynasty gourmet Yuan Mei, who made the following comments on the structuring of flavors within a meal:

> Salty dishes should come first, bland ones afterwards.
> Strong flavors should precede the weak ones.
> Dry dishes should come before soupy ones.
> There are five flavors under Heaven, so you mustn't attend only to the salty.
> If you suspect your dinner guests have eaten their fill, and their spleens are fatigued,
> You must stir them into action with spice and hotness.
> If you think your guests have drunk too much, making their digestions sluggish,
> You must enliven them with flavors sour and sweet.

To give you some idea of the variety of a Sichuanese banquet, here follows a translation of the menu of a memorable lunch at the Drifting Fragrance restaurant (*piao xiang*), held in honor of the food conference organized by Sichuan University and the Sichuan Institute of Higher Cuisine in May 2000:

Cold dishes: five-spiced "smoked" fish (*wu xiang xun gui yu*), chicken with cold rice jelly in a spicy sauce (*huang liang fen ban ji*), cucumber in mustard dressing (*jie mo qing huang gua*), "phoenix tail" lettuce stems in sesame sauce (*ma jiang feng wei*), tea-smoked pigeons (*zhang cha ru ge*), dry bean curd with peanuts (*hua ren dou fu gan*), Sichuanese cold meats (*chuan wei lu pin*), tripe in hot and garlicky sauce (*suan ni ban mao du*).

Hot dishes: braised sea cucumber (*hai shen shao shi jin*), hot-and-fragrant crab with red chiles (*hong jiao xiang la xie*), fast-fried duck tongues in fermented sauce (*jiang bao ya she*), steamed pork with rice meal (*piao xiang fen zheng rou*), braised white cabbage with Yunnan ham (*yun tui shao bai cai*), traditional bowl-steamed duck with pickled vegetables (*dong cai lao pai kou ya*), braised turtle with potatoes (*tai zi lu bao*), South Sichuan boiled beef slices in a fiery sauce (*chuan nan shui zhu niu liu*), fish with pickled vegetables (*pao cai gui hua yu*), "dragon-eye" sweet steamed pork with glutinous rice (*long yan tian shao bai*), soup of green vegetable tips with a chicken-breast coating (*ji meng kui cai tang*).

"Send-the-rice-down" dish: pickled string beans stir-fried with green chiles and minced pork (*xiao qing jiao chao lan rou jiang dou*).

Snacks: deep-fried sweet potato cakes (*zha shao bing*), boiled dumplings in spicy sauce (*hong you shui jiao*), leaf-wrapped cones of glutinous rice with Sichuan pepper (*jiao yan zong zi*).

DRINKS

Sichuan is famous not only for its food, but also for the excellence of its wines and teas. The wines are strong, vodka-like concoctions made from various grains and drunk in tiny china cups, almost like thimbles. Women scarcely touch them, so when a woman does indulge, there is a whiff of scandal and danger in the air. Men will quaff cup after cup, ritualistically, in formal toasts or casual drinking games. At formal dinners, all men present are expected to keep up a common pace of drinking—if one guest calls out "*gan bei!*" (Cheers! Bottoms up!), it's almost impossible for the others to refuse another drink.

Sichuan's most famous wine is Five Grain Wine (*wu liang ye*), an intensely fragrant clear liquor made from sorghum, rice, glutinous rice, wheat, and corn, traditionally mixed with water from the middle of the Min River. The wine, a specialty of Yibin in southern Sichuan, is 60 proof, although apparently they tone this down a bit for export. Some of the wine cellars in Yibin are thought to date back about five hundred years, to the Ming Dynasty. A more recent arrival on the Sichuan wine scene is Quan Xing, a strong white sorghum wine that has been made in Chengdu since the early nineteenth century.

At informal meals, Sichuanese people often drink beer or soft drinks, but these are very recent arrivals. More traditionally, drinks might not be offered at all, but the simple soup served at the end of the meal has a similar function, to quench thirst and rinse the palate. In the Sichuan countryside, less well-off people slake their thirst with the water left over from cooking rice—this may sound unpromising, but it's actually delicious and nourishing.

Tea is usually served before or after meals, but not while they are in progress as is the practice in Chinese restaurants in the West. One exception is a herbal tea called "red-and-white tea" (*hong bai cha*), which has cooling properties and is served all over Chengdu in the hotter months. The brewed leaves yield a liquid that is pinkish red in color—the perfect accompaniment to a typically Sichuanese meal. "Red-and-white tea" is a Daoist (Taoist) specialty and is grown on the slopes of the holy Daoist mountain, Qing Cheng Shan, which lies to the northwest of Chengdu.

THE FLAVORS OF SICHUAN

> *China is the place for food*
> *But Sichuan is the place for flavor*
> shi zai zhong guo
> wei zai si chuan

Anyone who has eaten in Sichuan will know that this common Chinese saying is no exaggeration. The Sichuanese are legendary for their ability to combine many different tastes into exquisite compound flavors (*fu he wei*). Local chefs boast of using twenty-three distinct combinations of flavor, which, applied to a wide variety of raw ingredients, create an immense diversity of tastes (they say each and every one of a hundred Sichuanese dishes will have its own unique flavor—*yi cai yi ge, bai cai bai wei*). A Sichuanese banquet can be an intriguing culinary journey, teasing the palate with a whole sequence of contrasting flavors: strong, spicy tastes, rich sweet-and-sours, gently aromatic cold meats, delicate soups . . .

Western science identifies four fundamental tastes: salty, sweet, sour, and bitter. The Chinese, however, traditionally have five, in keeping with their theories of the five elements (metal, wood, water, fire, and earth) and five directions (north, south, east, west, and center), and their liking for fives in general. The five fundamental Chinese tastes, which have been recognized since the time of Confucius, are salty (*xian*, or *han* in Sichuan dialect), sweet (*gan* or *tian*), sour (*suan*), hot or pungent (*xin* or *la*), and bitter (*ku*). The Sichuanese, who like to go their own way in so many respects, have their own localized version of these five fundamental tastes: they replace bitter with *ma*, the extraordinary numbing taste of Sichuan pepper.

Some Chinese flavoring terms defy all direct translation into English. The most important, probably, is *xian*, one of the most beautiful words in the Chinese culinary language. It expresses the indefinable, delicious taste of fresh meat, poultry, and seafood, the scrumptious flavors of a pure chicken soup, the subtle magic of freshly rendered lard. *Xian* describes the most exalted flavors of nature; it is the Chinese cook's muse, the essence of flavor itself. Much of Chinese gastronomy is concerned with bringing out the *xian* taste of fine ingredients, enhancing it here and there with chicken fat or fragrant mushrooms, teasing it out with small amounts of salt or sugar, using wine, ginger, and scallions to dispel the tastes of blood and rawness. At the giddy heights of the culinary arts, Chinese chefs lend *xian* to wonderfully textured but pale-tasting ingredients by simmering them in complex stocks made from *xian*-rich foods like pork, duck, and chicken. In more humble kitchens, people use lard or chicken fat to stir-fry vegetables, imbuing them with sumptuous *xian* flavors that don't actually recall the taste of meat. Many English writings on Chinese food translate *xian* as "fresh," "natural," or "savory," each of which captures an aspect of the word but not its whole.

Nowadays, under the influence of modern science, *xian* has become associated with foods that are naturally rich in glutamic acid and the other natural "flavor enhancers" known as nucleotides, like certain types of mushrooms and seafood. Since the beginning of this century, when a Japanese scientist discovered how to isolate glutamic acid in the laboratory in the form of monosodium glutamate, or MSG, Chinese cooks have used this fine white powder to enhance the *xian* of the dishes they prepare. In moderation, this is all very well, but unfortunately many kitchens now use MSG as a substitute for real stocks and top-quality ingredients, and at the expense of more subtle flavors. It is a bitter irony that in China of all places, where chefs have spent centuries developing the most sophisticated culinary techniques, this mass-produced white powder should have been given the name *wei jing*, "the essence of flavor."

Another concept crucial to understanding Chinese cooking is that of dispelling unpleasant odors, which are known collectively as *yi wei* ("peculiar smells") and more specifically as *xing wei* ("fishy odors"), *sao wei* ("foul odors"), and *shan wei* ("muttony odors"). To the Chinese, the smells and tastes of raw meat and fish are most unappetizing, and they use a wide variety of means to suppress or eradicate them. Raw meat destined for the stockpot or stewing pan is usually blanched first to get rid of any remaining blood and impurities. Salt, Shaoxing rice wine, Sichuan pepper, fresh ginger, and scallion are widely used in marinades, especially those involving fish or strong-tasting meats like beef or lamb. A few pieces of crushed ginger and scallion and a few husks of Sichuan pepper are invariably added to stews or stocks made from meat or poultry. (This may seem very esoteric to Western cooks, but it really does improve the flavor—just try comparing the taste and smell of pork-bone stocks made with and without a little scallion and ginger if you don't believe it.) The concern with these unpleasant raw smells in animal foods is an ancient one: they are even mentioned in the Spring and Autumn Annals, a text dating back to the Warring States period (around the third century B.C.). Some vegetables also have unpleasant tastes that must be dispelled—like the tongue-curling "astringent taste" (*se wei*) of spinach and some types of bamboo shoots.

Cantonese cooks are famously preoccupied with preserving and bringing out the natural, original *xian* tastes of their fine, fresh ingredients. They tend to add their seasonings with a light and delicate touch in order to enhance but not to overwhelm their raw materials. Sichuanese cooks, by contrast, are famous for their creation of complex *xian* tastes and strong, robust (*nong*) flavors through the audacious mixing of the five basic tastes. At the highest echelons of Sichuanese banquet cooking, tastes can be light and refined, reflecting the influence of the old imperial elite who came from outside the province.

Elsewhere, you'll find the flavors strong and hearty, lavish with chiles and Sichuan pepper, enticingly fragrant with garlic, ginger, and scallion. The strong flavors, however, are not meant to obliterate the natural tastes of the raw ingredients, and you should be able to taste their *xian* at the heart of all this spiciness (*la zhong you xian wei*).

Sichuanese cooks often refer to saltiness as the foundation, the essential background against which the colors of a complex flavor are sketched. Saltiness brings out the natural qualities of raw ingredients—there is even a saying that you cannot make a dish without it (*wu han bu cheng cai*). The most important salty flavoring is Sichuan well salt, which has been mined in the Zigong area since the Han dynasty and is lauded for its intense, pure taste. Soy sauce, fermented black beans, and chili bean paste are important secondary sources of salt. Sweetness, from white, brown, or crystal sugars, and sometimes honey, is a significant note in some compound flavors, but can also be used subtly, in tiny amounts, to tease out the natural tastes of main ingredients. Sourness comes from vinegar or pickled vegetables, and historically from salted unripe plums (*mei zi*). Bitterness, though not considered one of the five fundamental flavors, appears occasionally, in the use of tangerine peel and certain vegetables like bitter melon and bitter bamboo shoot. Chiles in various forms are the most famous source of Sichuanese hotness, but local cooks also place white pepper, fresh ginger, garlic, scallions and mustard in the same *la* (spicy-hot) flavor family. The numbing *ma* taste, of course, comes exclusively from Sichuan pepper.

These basic tastes are combined into a vast array of complex flavors and, with a typically Chinese love of numbers and of categorization, Sichuanese cooks and gourmets have precisely labeled a canon of at least twenty-three of them. Each has its own distinct characteristics, its balance of sweet and sour, its degree of spiciness, its effect on the tongue and palate. But this highly organized approach to the theory of flavor does not imply any rigidity: in fact, Sichuanese cooks are amazingly inventive, and every chef I know stresses the importance of a spirited, flexible (*ling huo*) approach to cooking. The "official" flavors are just a template, to be played with and augmented. Food writers now talk of expanding the canon to include newly popular flavors like "fruit juice flavor" (*guo zhi wei*) and "tomato sauce flavor" (*qie zhi wei*). Everyone looks forward to more exciting combinations.

For a brief description of the twenty-three "official" flavors of Sichuanese cooking, turn to page 353.

TEXTURE

One of the greatest obstacles to a profound appreciation of Chinese food among people in the West is our very limited sense of texture. For the Chinese, the texture of a dish is every bit as important as its color, taste, and smell. There is even a special word for the sensation that a piece of food creates in the mouth: *kou gan*, or, literally, "mouth-feel." The concept of *kou gan* covers not only texture in the Western sense of crispness, softness, chewiness, and so on, but also the pleasurable feeling that one gets from eating a stir-fried dish in which all the ingredients are cut harmoniously into slivers, or the satisfaction derived from eating meatballs from which every last wisp of stringy tendon has been carefully removed.

Certain types of texture are particularly prized: the crisp, rubbery bite of tripe; the slithery crunch of jellyfish and silver ear fungus; the silky tenderness of the flesh nestled in a fish's cheek. This is why Chinese people derive such immense pleasure from eating foods that many in the West find weird or even revolting. My Chinese friends positively relish using their tongues and teeth to separate bones and skin in a chicken's foot or wing, and love the contrasts in a dish of slippery bean curd scattered with deep-fried nuts and beans. Texture is one of the main attractions of Chinese exotica like shark's fin and sea cucumber, and partially explains why Chinese cooks are prepared to spend hours, or even days, making these rare and expensive ingredients palatable.

Some of the terms used to describe texture in Chinese are untranslatable because the concepts they express are simply overlooked by Western food lovers. *Cui* is the first among these—it refers to a certain quality of crispness, a texture that offers resistance to the teeth, but finally yields, cleanly, with a pleasant snappy feeling. This is a quality of kidneys, cut finely and cooked swiftly over a fierce flame; of goose intestines, scalded briefly in a Sichuan hotpot; of fresh celery and raw snow peas. *Su* refers to a different kind of crispness—the dry, fragile crispness of deep-fried dumplings or potato crisps. *Nen* expresses the delicate tenderness of young leaves and flesh and is commonly used to describe succulent foods like deftly stir-fried meat and fish. *Lao* literally means "old" and expresses the opposite of *nen*, the toughness of mature flesh and fibrous leaves, or the dryness of tender foods that have been overcooked. *Pa* describes what happens to food when it is cooked for a long time, to the point when meat falls away from bones and root vegetables become soft and pulpy.

Learning to appreciate texture in the Chinese way takes a little time and dedication, but really does add an extra dimension to gastronomic pleasure. Cold jellyfish, served in most Chinese restaurants, makes a good beginning: it is slithery, crunchy, and slightly rubbery. Cloud ear fungus, which appears in many stir-fried dishes, has an equally interesting, but not disturbing, texture. As you eat these things, try to allow your tongue, teeth, and mouth to share in the pleasure, to see the texture in itself as something to be enjoyed. Slowly, you will find the door opening wider to real enjoyment of Chinese food.

THE ART OF CUTTING

Teacher Lu prepares the ingredients for fish-fragrant pork with a smirk of discreet pleasure on his face. He eases the sharpened blade of his shiny cleaver into the meat, cutting it into even slices, and then into delicate slivers. His knife glides through a piece of translucent lettuce stem, cutting it into slender strips to complement the pork. A few wood ear mushrooms are shaken dry and finely sliced. He peels ginger and garlic and chops them into tiny grains, slices scallions, and then pummels a handful of pickled chiles to a purée. When he has finished his preparations, the seasonings are laid out on a plate like an artist's palette: the pale yellows of ginger and garlic, the light green of the scallions, and a splash of brilliant chile red.

Cutting has been fundamental to Chinese cooking since ancient times. A traditional term for the preparation of food is *ge peng*, to cut and to cook, and knife skills are still the essential starting point for any aspiring Sichuan chef. On my first day at the Sichuan cooking school, I, like every other student, was given a cleaver along with my working overalls. It was mine, to bring to class with me every day, to become familiar with, to sharpen often on the enormous whetstone in the yard, to keep clean and free from rust. Every lesson included instructions for the chopping or slicing of the raw ingredients—not an optional extra, but a fundamental part of the character of each individual dish.

There are some meat and poultry dishes, mostly steamed or stewed, where the main ingredient is left whole, but the vast majority of dishes require food that is cut into smaller pieces. This is partly because many of them are cooked quickly over a high flame, for reasons of economizing fuel as well as taste, so the pieces of food must be small and uniform in size for the heat to penetrate evenly. Uneven cutting of the ingredients for a chicken stir-fry, for example, will make the smaller pieces tough and "old" (*lao*) by the time the larger pieces are cooked through. Smaller pieces, with a high ratio of surface area to volume, also absorb the flavors of sauces and marinades more readily than large ones. Again, speed is important: most Sichuanese cooks will add the marinade ingredients to their meat just before they cook it; and sauces are frequently added to the wok just before the food is transferred to the serving dish.

Eating with chopsticks also makes its own demands: knives are never seen on the Chinese dining table, so all the cutting must be done in the kitchen. When the food is served, it should either be in small pieces or, in the case of whole fowl or steamed meats, soft enough to tear apart with chopsticks. It is acceptable in Chinese etiquette to hold a larger piece of food in your chopsticks, take a bite, and then return it to your rice bowl, but many foods are served in bite-size pieces.

The most interesting aspect of the Chinese art of cutting, however, is the aesthetic. When Chinese cooks talk about the qualities of a dish, they often refer to "color, fragrance, flavor, and form" (se xiang wei xing). A fine dish will first assail the eyes with its beauty, then the nose with its scent; the tongue is the next to be delighted, along with the inside of the mouth. The awareness of "mouth-feel," or kou gan, contributes to the diversity of Sichuanese cooking because it opens up so many permutations. A skillful cook can transform pork, the most common of meats, into countless different dishes by varying not only the flavorings and the cooking method but also the form. The meat can be sliced, ground, slivered, cut into chunks, or chopped into little cubes. Every type of slice, every thickness of sliver, every kind of chunk will produce a different sensation in the mouth and a different-looking dish, so much so that it's possible to incorporate pork in a number of dishes served at the same meal without its becoming tedious.

The cutting technique used for a particular dish is determined by the nature of the ingredient and the cooking method. Crisp vegetables like radish and kohlrabi can be sliced with a swift, clean, up-and-down motion; sinewy meat or steamed bread requires a gentle sawing movement. Poultry on the bone can be chopped into chunks, chicken breast made into cubes or slivers. Beef and lamb are almost always sliced against the grain to break up the fibers of the meat; tender chicken is cut along the grain, so the pieces don't disintegrate in the wok.

Whatever the method, there are two essential rules. One is that the cutting is as regular as possible, to ensure even cooking and a pleasant appearance and "mouth-feel." The other is that all the ingredients of a single dish are cut in harmony with one another as far as possible, again for aesthetic reasons. In Gong Bao (Kung Pao) chicken, for example, the cubed chicken meat is complemented beautifully by the small chunks of scallion; for "fish-fragrant" pork, the bamboo shoots and wood ear fungus are both cut into narrow strips to match the meat. As local cooks say, *ding pei ding, si pei si* (cubes with cubes, slivers with slivers). This aesthetic is one I find so pleasing that it has permeated much of my non-Chinese cooking and now influences the way in which I make up a salad or a stew.

There is also beauty in the process of cutting, if you choose to look for it. Watching an artful cutter at work, wielding a cleaver as delicately as though it were a scalpel, is a real joy. And although some of the techniques can be accomplished by a mandoline or a food processor, there is a certain rhythm and meditative quality to doing everything by hand that I find most soothing. My first teacher at the Sichuan cooking school, Gan Guojian, would come up and correct my posture as I hunched over the cutting board, slicing ginger with a cleaver. "Stand straight," he'd say. "Relax your shoulders and let the cutting movement involve your whole arm, not just your wrist and fingers." Cutting is not just a means to an end, it is part of the pleasure of Chinese cooking.

Sichuanese cooks use an astonishingly sophisticated vocabulary to describe the art of cutting. There are at least three basic ways of using the cleaver, known as vertical slicing (*qie*), horizontal slicing (*pian*), and chopping (*zhan* or *kan*), and when the direction of the cut and the angle of the knife are taken into account, these multiply into at least fifteen permutations, each with a different name. Another dozen or so terms refer to further knife techniques, including pounding (*chui*), scraping (*gua*), and gouging (*wan*). All in all, the latest encyclopedia of Sichuanese cooking lists thirty-three distinct cutting terms, and that's without even considering the techniques used in the more esoteric food arts like vegetable carving!

A similarly diverse collection of terms, some quite poetic, describes the shapes into which cooking ingredients can be cut: the Sichuan cooking encyclopedia describes no fewer than sixty-three. Some are specific to particular ingredients, like pickled chiles or scallions; others are very general. A basic term like "slice" (*pian*) has at least ten permutations, including "domino slices" (*gu pai pian*), "thumbnail slices" (*zhi jia pian*), "axe-blade slices" (*fu leng pian*) and "ox-tongue slices" (*niu she pian*). Strips (*tiao*) are called after chopstick handles (*kuai zi tiao*), elephant's tusks (*xiang ya tiao*), or phoenix tails (*feng wei tiao*) depending on their precise dimensions. Scallion rings are "flowers" (*cong hua*) or "fish eyes" (*yu yan cong*) according to their length, and scallions sliced at a steep angle are called "horse ears" (*ma er duo*)—just make a few and you'll see why. There are nine different ways of cutting scallions alone.

The following chapter offers a practical introduction to the essentials of the Chinese art of cutting.

basic cutting skills

Almost all the cutting in a Sichuanese kitchen is done with a cleaver. Some cooks in the West tend to see it as a crude instrument, suitable only for butchering. In fact, the cleaver is the most versatile and sensitive of knives. Its blade can be used to slice and chop all kinds of meat and vegetables; to peel ginger and even to bone a duck; the sharp back corner of the blade can be used to crack open a fish head to release its flavors; the flat of it can crush garlic, ginger, and scallions with a whack. Turn the knife upside down and the blunt back edge of the blade can be used to pummel raw meat or fish to a paste; hold it flat and use it to scoop up chopped vegetables and transfer them to the wok.

There are three essential rules for using the cleaver safely and effectively.

1 Keep the blade sharp (see instructions on page 46). A blunt knife is unwieldy, inaccurate, and frustrating to use.

2 Hold the cleaver correctly to protect your fingers (see below).

3 Concentrate on what you are doing.

TECHNIQUES

The following are the basic techniques you will need to make most of the recipes in this book. Instructions for cutting in more complicated ways are given in the few recipes that require them.

切 **Basic cutting** (*qie*): This fundamental technique is the simplest and most commonly used in the Sichuanese kitchen. Grasp the metal ring and the upper edge of the cleaver blade between the thumb and forefinger of your right hand and use the other fingers to hold the handle firmly in your palm. Use your other hand to hold the food steady on the cutting board: curve the fingers so that the middle joint presses against the knife blade, keeping it at a safe distance from the rest of your hand, and always, always keep your thumb behind the curved fingers. The knife can be moved in an up-and-down or sawing motion, or eased gently into the food, but it will always be kept in check by the middle knuckle. Move your hand backwards as you cut, gradually exposing the food to the blade. Never raise the blade higher than your knuckles.

片 **Horizontal cutting** (*pian*): This technique is particularly useful for slicing boned meat, fish, and poultry. It requires a very sharp knife. Place the food flat on the cutting board. Turn the cleaver blade onto its side, parallel to the board. Ease the blade into the side of the block of food, guiding the knife edge with the middle and index fingers of your left hand. Work slowly at first, taking care to slice off an even layer from the top of the pile. You can take the slices from the bottom of the pile instead, inserting the knife blade just above the cutting board and pressing the food down firmly with your left hand, but it's more difficult to make the slices of an even thickness if you work this way.

斬 **Chopping** (*zhan* or *kan*): To chop meat, fish, or poultry on the bone, hold the food firmly in your left hand as for basic cutting, but for safety's sake a little farther away from the place where you intend to make the cut. Raise the cleaver and bring it straight down with considerable force. If you are not absolutely confident of the accuracy of your chopping, it's best to hold the food with a fork or other implement rather than your hand—not very professional but much safer. If the bones are large and hard, you should use a heavier cleaver than that required for other cutting.

To fine-chop ingredients like garlic, coriander (cilantro), or candied fruits, you can begin by cutting them into reasonably small pieces and then simply hammer the cleaver down onto them repeatedly, keeping your wrist and arm supple and relaxed. You don't need to hold the food with your left hand if you use this technique. Some cooks use two cleavers for this kind of chopping, holding them about half an inch apart and whacking them down alternately.

 Pummeling (*chui*): Instructions for using the back of the cleaver to pummel meat to a paste are given in the recipe for chicken balls in clear soup on page 335.

SOME USEFUL SHAPES

片 **Slices** (*pian*): The most basic shape, and the first stage for making slivers, strips, and cubes, slices can be cut vertically or horizontally and vary greatly in dimensions. Different types of slice are introduced in the recipes that require them.

絲 **Slivers** (*si*): The Chinese name for food cut into fine shreds or slivers literally means "silk" or "silken thread." The pieces should be about 3 inches long and about 1/8 inch thick; the finest, which can be made only from crisp vegetable ingredients like radish and potato, are known as "silver-needle silken threads" (*yin zhen si*). To cut food into slivers, you must first cut it into slices the thickness of the desired final sliver; then pile up the slices either vertically or gradually like a flight of steps, and cut them into slivers.

條 **Strips** (*tiao*): The most basic type of strip is like a sliver, but shorter and thicker (about 2 inches long and 1/2 inch thick). It is cut in exactly the same way.

块 **Chunks** (*kuai*): This term covers all kinds of chunks of vegetables, poultry, and meats, either on or off the bone, and rectangular, lozenge-shaped, or roll-cut.

丁 **Cubes** (*ding*): Made by cutting food into slices, then strips, then cubes 1/2 inch to 3/4 inch thick.

顆 **Tiny cubes** (*ke*): The same as cubes, but less than 1/2 inch thick.

粒 **Grains** (*li*): Small, irregular pieces of chopped food, approximately the same size as rice grains, mung beans, or soybeans, depending on the recipe.

梳子背 **Roll-cut chunks** (*shu zi bei*): This technique is used for cutting long, thin root vegetables like radishes and carrots, and sometimes small potatoes and pieces of taro. It maximizes the surface area of the chunks so they can absorb flavors more readily. Hold the peeled, trimmed vegetable firmly on the cutting board and hold the cleaver blade vertically but at a steep angle to the vegetable. Cut a diagonal slice from the end of the vegetable, and then roll it away from you by 90 degrees and take another slice. Repeat.

 "Horse ears" (*ma er duo*): Used for long, thin vegetable ingredients like scallions, Chinese leeks, and pickled chiles. Trim the vegetables and then cut them at a very steep angle into slices 1 1/2 inches long. Each slice will look remarkably like a horse's ear.

cooking methods

When Westerners think of Chinese cooking, the first thing that comes to mind is usually a fast stir-fry in a smoking wok. Stir-frying and other kinds of wok cooking are certainly essential methods in the Sichuanese kitchen, but they are only part of the picture. Sichuanese chefs claim to use fifty-six distinct cooking methods. Some of these are variations on the larger themes of stir-frying (*chao*), braising (*shao*), deep-frying (*zha*), and steaming (*zheng*), distinguished from one another by subtle differences in cooking temperature or the amount of liquid used. Others, like pickling (*pao*) and oven roasting (*kao xiang kao*), are more obviously distinct. This categorization of cooking methods is a fascinating illustration of the complexities of Sichuanese cuisine, but the good thing is that you really don't have to know them all to learn to make delicious home-cooked food. For those who are interested, a description of each of the fifty-six "official" cooking methods is provided on page 358. For those who want to run straight into the kitchen, the following is a brief introduction to basic Sichuanese cooking techniques.

ORGANIZATION

The preparation of ingredients is the key to enjoyable and successful Sichuanese cooking. This is particularly true when it comes to fast, wok-cooked dishes. Try to make sure that all the ingredients are neatly laid out before you start to cook, as you would a *mise-en-place,* so the cooking process can be fluid and relaxed. Sauces can be mixed in small cups or bowls; chopped ginger, garlic, and scallions piled up separately on a little plate; marinade ingredients added to chopped meat or poultry; potato flour or cornstarch and water mixed into a thickening paste. Raw chopped vegetables can be stacked up on their final serving dish, with a little pile of spices on the side. Any other serving dishes should be near at hand.

It's always good to have a bamboo brush and paper towels nearby for rinsing and drying the wok between dishes. A heatproof container beside the stove, for the oil used for seasoning the wok, is also useful.

FOOD PREPARATION

碼味 **Marinating** (*ma wei*): Marinating ingredients are often added to raw fish, meat, and poultry to heighten flavor and to dispel any lingering raw tastes. Marinades can also improve the texture of meats and vegetables by drawing out excess water and making them more receptive to other flavorings. Salt, Shaoxing rice wine, ginger, scallions, and Sichuan pepper, all common marinade ingredients, are particularly effective in dispelling raw meaty, or fishy tastes. Soy sauce is sometimes added where color is required as well as flavor. For most stir-fried dishes (where the food is finely chopped), marinade seasonings are added to the ingredients just before cooking.

碼芡 **Coating in starch or batter** (*ma qian*): Pastes made from starch mixed with water or egg are used to keep food tender and to seal in juices and nutrients. They can be made from potato flour, cornstarch, pea flour, or wheat flour bound together with water, egg white, or whole beaten egg. These pastes are usually added after the marinade ingredients and just before cooking. The type and thickness of the paste depends on the cooking method.

過油 **Passing through the oil** (*guo you*): This refers to deep-frying as a preliminary stage in cooking. Sometimes small pieces of meat, fish, or poultry are coated in an egg white paste and deep-fried at a fairly low temperature: the purpose of this is to separate the pieces and cook them through while preserving their tenderness. Very hot oil is used to fix the shape of ingredients and to make them crisp on the outside while keeping them tender within.

 Seasoning the wok (*zhi guo*): This very simple process is an essential part of wok cooking if you use the classic Chinese wok, which doesn't have a nonstick surface. If you don't season the wok before you begin to cook, and between dishes, your food is likely to stick to its surface, which means that some pieces will dry out and even burn before the rest are cooked. If you do season the wok, you will never have this problem.

The method is as follows: heat the wok over a high flame until it is smoking. Add a few tablespoons of cooking oil and swirl it around over all the parts of the wok that will be in contact with the food. When the oil is smoking, pour it off into a heatproof container. You can then add some fresh, cool cooking oil, heat it up to the desired temperature, and begin to cook. If you are making a series of dishes, give the wok a quick rinse or scrub with a bamboo brush after each dish, and re-season the surface before you start the next one.

COOKING

 Frying-fragrant (*chao xiang*): This is a basic technique that crops up all the time in Sichuanese cooking. It involves stir-frying flavorings—usually garlic and ginger, pickled chiles, Sichuan chili bean paste, dried chiles, or Sichuan pepper—until the cooking oil has taken on their flavors and, in the case of pickled chiles or chili bean paste, their rich red color. Other ingredients are then added to the wok and tossed in the fragrant oil. The most important thing is not to burn the spices and to trust your nose to tell you when they are ready. To avoid burning them, it's best to use a medium flame and to add the spices before the oil is smoking hot—you can always heat it further if you need to make them sizzle to extract their flavors. If the oil seems to be overheating, just hold the wok away from the flame for a few seconds, stirring constantly, until it has cooled down slightly.

 Stir-frying (*chao*): Stir-frying usually begins by frying-fragrant a few spices in the cooking oil (see above). Other foods are then added in stages, depending on the time they need to cook. Sauces and seasonings are added during the cooking process. If you are stir-frying meat, fish, or poultry, you must always begin by seasoning the wok, or the food will stick. In stir-frying, the heating must be swift and even, so you must keep the food moving constantly. A wok scoop can be used to scrape the food from the base of the wok and turn it over repeatedly. Sichuanese chefs tend to use a ladle to push the food around, and they also toss the wok to dramatic effect.

Thickening sauces (*gou qian*): Chinese sauces are thickened with white starch derived from various dried beans, potatoes, or corn. The starch becomes transparent and glossy when cooked. It is this starch that gives Chinese dishes their typical luster. The starch paste is added at the end of the cooking process, and it thickens the sauce in just a few seconds. Sichuanese restaurant kitchens all have a bowlful of ready-mixed starch-and-water paste sitting by the side of the stove to be used as needed.

Always err on the side of caution when adding this paste. You can always add a little more if you need to, but you can't take it away. (Nothing ruins a Chinese dish like the gluey, gelatinous sauce that is the result of excessive starch.)

SICHUAN'S DISTINCTIVE LOCAL COOKING METHODS

Part of the character of Sichuanese cuisine lies in its widespread use of several cooking methods that are peculiar to the region. They are as follows:

 xiao chao ("small-frying"): This method involves frying marinated and starch-coated meat in hot oil until the pieces separate, then briskly placing in the secondary vegetable ingredients, adding the sauce, and just tossing once or twice more before serving. There are no initial stages of cooking—it's all done quickly in a single wok over a hot flame. Examples include "fish-fragrant" pork slivers and Gong Bao (Kung Pao) chicken with peanuts.

 gan bian ("dry-frying"): Food cut into slivers or strips is stirred constantly in a wok with very little oil, over a medium flame, until it is slightly dried out and beautifully fragrant. Seasonings are added toward the end of the cooking process, often with a little extra oil. Examples: dry-fried bitter melon, dry-fried eggplants, dry-fried beef slivers, dry-fried green beans.

 gan shao ("dry-braising"): In this method, used mainly for fish and seafood, the main ingredient is simmered with flavorings over a medium flame until the liquid has been totally absorbed or reduced to a dense sauce. Starch is never added as a thickener. Example: dry-braised fish with pork in spicy sauce.

 jia chang shao ("homestyle braising"): This method begins by stir-frying a little chili bean paste until the cooking oil is red and fragrant, and then adding stock and other ingredients. Everything is simmered gently over a low flame until the food has absorbed the rich "homestyle" flavors of the sauce. The liquid is usually thickened with starch before serving. Examples: fish braised in chili bean sauce, wild duck braised with konnyaku "bean curd."

熠 **du:** A very traditional Sichuanese cooking method used mainly for fish and bean curd dishes. It is similar to conventional braising: the food is simmered gently in a small amount of liquid until it has lost its own water content and absorbed the flavors of the sauce. Example: pock-marked Mother Chen's bean curd (*ma po dou fu*).

熗 **qiang:** A type of frying that begins by sizzling dried chiles and Sichuan pepper in a little oil until the oil is fragrant and spicy, and then tossing other ingredients, usually crisp, juicy vegetables, in the flavored oil. Example: spicy cucumber salad.

equipment

One of the most impressive things about Sichuanese cooking is the simplicity of the equipment used in most kitchens. A cleaver, a wooden cutting board, and a few bowls or plates to hold ingredients are all you need for most food preparations; and most cooking can be done with little more than a wok, a steamer, a rice cooker, a pair of chopsticks, and a ladle. A few other tools are useful—a wire strainer, a perforated spoon or ladle, a rolling pin or two—but the whole paraphernalia is much simpler and more compact than its Western equivalent. Some recipes call for the use of ordinary saucepans, frying pans, and kitchen utensils, others for less common utensils like meat hooks (these are introduced in the recipes that require them). You can make Sichuanese food without any special equipment, using ordinary kitchen knives and pots and pans, but the traditional Chinese tools are wonderful to use. Here are the utensils I find it hard to live without.

FOOD PREPARATION

CLEAVER (*cai dao*)

菜
刀
The one essential knife in a Chinese kitchen is the cleaver. Nothing matches its versatility, and once you become accustomed to it, you will find you rarely want to use anything else. It can be used for slicing, mincing, chopping, peeling, crushing, mashing, gutting fish, boning poultry, and even carrying food around. Almost all these jobs can be done with an ordinary cleaver (*cai dao*), which has a thin, light blade, but it's useful also to have a chopper (*kan dao* or *zhan dao*), a heavier cleaver with a thicker blade, for cutting poultry and spare ribs on the bone. Cleavers can be made of carbon steel or stainless steel: the former require a little looking after, but are much easier to sharpen, and I prefer them for this reason. You can buy cleavers in Chinese supermarkets and, increasingly, in Asian cooking sections of department stores and kitchenware shops. Sichuanese cooks like

to use handmade local knives, which have slightly rounded blades and wooden handles. The best are said to be those made in Dazu, a town in eastern Sichuan that is also famous for its Buddhist carvings.

Looking after your knife

It's important to keep the cleaver blade sharp. The best way is to keep a whetstone on hand and to use it regularly. Whetstones can usually be bought along with your cleaver. To sharpen the knife, wet the stone under the tap and then secure it, coarser side up, on a work surface—I usually place it on a damp kitchen towel to stop it from moving around. Hold the knife handle in your right hand and the end of the blade in your left, lay the blade facing away from you onto the whetstone at a sharp angle (about 30 degrees), and rub it backwards and forwards, moving the blade from time to time to ensure an even sharpening. Then turn the knife and repeat, but with the blade at a sharper angle, nearly parallel to the stone. When the knife is becoming sharp, you can turn the whetstone and use the finer-grained side to bring it to a keener edge. Keep moistening the stone as you go along. If you sharpen your knife regularly, the process won't take long.

Try to keep the knife in a place where it won't get banged and won't cause accidents—most Sichuanese keep theirs in a small knife rack hanging on the kitchen wall. If you have a carbon steel knife, you should make sure you rinse and dry it immediately after use and smear it with a little cooking oil to keep it from rusting.

CUTTING BOARD (*cai dun*)

 The traditional Sichuanese cutting board is a thick, round slab of tree trunk, treated with salt and vegetable oil, which lasts for many years. In restaurant kitchens these can be enormous, but for home kitchens a section of trunk 12 inches in diameter and about 4 inches high is ample. After an intense session of chopping, the cook will use a cleaver blade to scrape clean the surface of the wood before rinsing and drying it: thus the board is gradually eroded, so it's important to rotate it from time to time to keep the surface even. The best boards are made of tight-grained wood like Chinese honey locust (*zao jiao shu*), gingko (*bai guo shu*), or Chinese olive (*gan lan shu*), but birch, willow, and several other types can also be used. Ordinary cutting boards can, of course, be used instead.

Bowls and dishes

It's always useful to have a selection of little bowls, plates, and dipping dishes on hand for the mixing of sauces, the marinating of meats, and the arrangement of prepared seasonings like chopped garlic and ginger.

COOKING

WOK (*chao guo*)

炒
鍋

The wok has been used in Chinese cooking for at least two thousand years and remains an essential cooking vessel. It is ideal for stir-frying because its curved base allows for even heating and for the easy movement of food around the hot metal surface; but it is also used for deep-frying, boiling, steaming, and dry-roasting. Most Chinese woks are made from crude or cast iron, which cooks superbly but must be seasoned to prevent rusting. They vary in size from about 12 inches in diameter for an all-purpose home wok, to more than 36 inches in the kitchens of monasteries and other institutions. Some have one long handle, which makes for easy tossing, but the most common in Sichuan are those with two small handles, which must be held with a heatproof mitt but are more stable—a boon when boiling or deep-frying. You can also buy flat-bottomed woks, which work well on electric stoves but are less versatile than the traditional kind, and nonstick woks, which may be convenient but lack the wonderful patina of the seasoned iron wok. These days you can buy woks in many kitchen stores, but they are generally much less expensive (and just as good) in Chinese supermarkets.

TO SEASON A NEW WOK
Iron woks must be seasoned before use. To season a new wok, scour off any rust, give it a good scrub all over, and then heat it over a high flame. When it is hot, carefully smear it all over with a wad of paper towels soaked in cooking oil. Repeat this procedure twice more with fresh paper and oil. When the wok has cooled down, wipe it or rinse it and dry it thoroughly.

TAKING CARE OF THE WOK
After cooking, a quick rinse with water and a gentle scrub with a wok brush is usually sufficient to clean the wok. If you do have to scrub it hard and expose the surface of the metal, you must season it again exactly as described above

before you store it. If you use the wok for boiling or steaming, re-seasoning is also needed to restore the surface. Don't worry if the wok gets a little rusty—all you need to do to revive it is scour the surface and repeat the seasoning process. It is not necessary to clean the underside of the wok.

WOK LID AND WOK STAND

Wok lids are usually bought separately from the wok itself: they are not used in frying but are needed for steaming and sometimes for simmering. A wok stand is vital to stabilize the wok for steaming, boiling, and deep-frying, and it is necessary if you wish to use a wok with a curved base on an electric stove. Some modern stoves have built-in wok stands.

WOK BRUSH (*zhu shua*)

Bamboo wok brushes are used for cleaning the wok between dishes. They consist of bundles of bamboo splints and can be bought in most shops selling Asian cookware. When you have finished cooking one dish and are ready to begin another, just rinse the wok under a cold tap, using the brush to scrub away any bits of food that still adhere to it. The advantage of using a bamboo rather than a plastic brush is that it allows you to scrub the wok while it is still very hot.

WOK SCOOP OR LADLE (*guo chan, piao zi*)

Most Sichuanese chefs use a ladle rather than a wok scoop in their cooking. It is used to stir food around the wok, to ladle stock into sauces, to ladle food into serving bowls, and also to measure out ingredients and mix up last-minute sauces. Home cooks tend to use wok scoops instead—they are good for stirring ingredients and scraping the bottom of the wok, although not as versatile as the ladle.

PERFORATED LADLE (*lou piao*)

A perforated spoon or ladle is useful for lifting dumplings and noodles out of their cooking water and can also be used for lifting deep-fried foods out of the cooking oil. Many Sichuanese cooks use a large, shallow spoon (8 to 12 inches in diameter) with a short handle, which is perforated by many quite large holes, but the perforated ladles sold with other Asian cooking equipment can also be used.

A WIRE MESH STRAINER WITH A BAMBOO HANDLE (*zhao li*)

 These strainers can be purchased easily and inexpensively in Chinese supermarkets. They are used for lifting deep-fried foods out of the cooking oil and for draining them.

CHOPSTICKS (*kuai zi*)

 Plain long-handled chopsticks, easily available in Chinese cookware shops, are used to move food around the wok and to separate pieces of food while deep-frying. Ordinary chopsticks are used for tasting and for mixing.

STEAMER, TRIVET (*zheng long*)

 Steaming has been an important cooking method in China since antiquity. In contemporary Sichuan, it is widely used in country cooking and in the preparation of all kinds of dumplings and snacks.

It can also be used to cook rice or to reheat precooked foods, and it is sometimes part of a sequence of cooking methods used in more complex recipes. Chinese food can be cooked in an ordinary three-part metal steamer: you just place the food in a bowl or on a plate on the perforated part, close the lid, and steam. Alternatively, you can use the wok and one or more of those round bamboo steamers sold very inexpensively in Chinese supermarkets. If the steamer is much smaller than the wok, you may need to stand it on a trivet (which can usually be bought in the same store), but larger steamers can just sit directly in the wok. Don't forget that you can stack up several layers of the bamboo steamers if you have a lot of food to steam.

RICE COOKER (*dian fan guo*)

 If I could have only one modern gadget in my kitchen, it would have to be an electric rice cooker. These wonderful machines not only make perfect rice every time, but they also keep it warm until you plan to eat it. They can also be used to steam other foods, and some make rice porridges and stews. The great advantage of an automatic rice cooker is that it allows you to concentrate completely on the other dishes as you cook, without having to worry about the rice drying out or sticking to the bottom of the pan. The rice and water can be measured out long before the meal, and you need only push the button when you want the machine to start steaming.

OTHER BITS AND PIECES

ROLLING PINS (*gan mian zhang*)

 These are needed for some dumpling and pastry dishes. The Sichuanese use fairly thin rolling pins that taper at either end. They come in a number of sizes: thin ones for dumpling skins, medium-thickness ones for flatbreads, and thicker pins for rolling out noodle pastry. Ordinary rolling pins can be used instead.

BAMBOO BASKETS (*shao ji*)

 Most Sichuanese kitchens are equipped with an assortment of shallow bamboo baskets, round or horseshoe-shaped. They are wonderfully versatile: they can be used as colanders, storage baskets for fresh vegetables, and trays for sun-drying small amounts of herbs or spices. Dusted with flour, they can be filled with dumplings, just wrapped and ready for the stove. When they are not in use, they are simply stacked up or hung on the walls. These baskets are woven on a small scale by specialized craftsmen and then hawked around the markets, usually strung up on a wooden frame attached to a bicycle. Some of the baskets are woven with beautiful patterns. Metal or plastic colanders and ordinary trays can do the same job, but woven bamboo baskets are lovely to use and can now be bought in the Asian food sections of some cookware stores.

A NOTE ON STOVES

A gas stove is ideal for Chinese cooking because it gives you immediate control over the temperature and because the gas flames lick nicely around the base of the traditional rounded wok. If you have an electric stove, you can use a traditional wok with a wok stand, but the heating will be very inefficient, so in this case it's best to use a flat-bottomed wok. Whatever type of stove you have, an effective hood to draw away the smells of frying is extremely useful. Sichuanese urban kitchens are usually equipped with gas stoves, but in the countryside and in many old houses people rely on coal-fired stoves, great clay-built ranges with rounded holes to take the wok, which sits directly above the flaming coals. Only the most modern homes have exhaust fans, so most Sichuanese stoves are placed in a well-ventilated outer room or in balcony areas that are walled off from the main kitchen.

SERVING CHINESE FOOD

For simple meals at home, all you need are a few rice bowls and pairs of chopsticks, along with serving dishes for the food. Everyone present can use their chopsticks to help themselves from the communal dishes at the center of the table, and the final soup can be sipped directly from the bowl.

For a more formal setting, each rice bowl is placed on a little plate, which can be used to take food from the serving dishes or to hold bones and other scraps. China spoons can also be provided for soups and porridgy dishes. Chopstick stands are optional, used only in fancier restaurants. Candlelit dinners are not part of Sichuanese eating culture—partly no doubt because anything standing in the center of the table would obstruct access to the food.

SERVING DISHES

Stews and soups cooked in earthenware pots are usually brought to the table in the cooking pot, but most other dishes are turned out onto serving plates. You don't really need any special serving dishes: ordinary dinner plates can be used for most stir-fried dishes, smaller breakfast plates for cold dishes, and a random selection of serving bowls and dishes for everything else. A large, deep serving bowl is a must, however, if you want to make soups and bring them to the table Chinese-style. Sichuanese cooks would expect to use the following dishes (they can all be bought in Chinese cookware shops).

Small round plates: For cold dishes and the raw ingredients destined for the Sichuan hotpot.

Medium-sized round plates: For wok-cooked dishes where the food is cut into small pieces.

Large, deep round plates: For centerpieces like whole chickens or ducks and exotica like dried seafood.

Oval plates of various sizes: For wok-cooked dishes, deep-fried foods, and whole fish.

Large bowls of various sizes: For stews and dishes that come with lots of sauce, and for soups.

Tiny dipping dishes: For dips of spices, sauces, and relishes, and also for Sichuanese pickled vegetables.

Lacquered hors d'oeuvre box containing several small dishes: Used for little appetizers.

Wine cups: Tiny little china cups without handles that are used for quaffing strong Sichuanese liquor.

the Sichuanese pantry

The pages that follow describe almost all the dried goods and flavorings you will need to make the recipes in this book. (A few of the more unusual ingredients are described in the introductions to the recipes that use them.) Do not, however, be daunted by the length of the list. The following short list of ingredients will be enough to make most dishes.

- soy sauce (light and dark)
- Sichuan chili bean paste
- dried chiles
- whole Sichuan pepper
- fermented black beans
- Chinkiang or black Chinese vinegar
- sesame oil
- Shaoxing rice wine or medium-dry sherry
- a few spices (cassia bark and star anise will do to start with)
- potato flour or cornstarch
- fresh ginger, garlic, and scallions
- salt, pepper, and white sugar (which you are likely to have in your kitchen anyway)

Useful extras: pickled chili paste, sweet bean paste, Tianjin preserved vegetable, pickled mustard greens, dried mushrooms, dried cloud ears, brown sugar.

INGREDIENTS

Chinese speakers may notice that some of the Chinese names given below are unfamiliar: some, like the name for chiles, *hai jiao*, are Sichuanese dialect terms that I couldn't resist.

FERMENTED BLACK BEANS (*dou chi*)

These intensely tasty little beans are made by soaking dried yellow soybeans in water, steaming them, and then leaving them to ferment in a sealed container for several months. Salt, wine, and ginger are added, with perhaps a little chile and other spices. The final product is fairly dry but dark and oily, with a flavor reminiscent of top quality soy sauce. This method of fermentation has been used in China for nearly twenty-five hundred years, since the time of Confucius himself. The beans are used, in small quantities, in Sichuanese stir-fried, braised, and steamed dishes, as well as in sauces and relishes. The finest Sichuanese black beans, which are plump, glossy, and extremely tasty, come from the county of Yongchuan. Buy the dry beans rather than those preserved in brine—they are available in most Chinese supermarkets.

Chiles

DRIED CHILES (*gan hai jiao*)

Sun-dried chiles are indispensable in many Sichuanese dishes. Several varieties can be found in the region's markets. In the Sichuanese capital, Chengdu, the most common type is the "facing-heaven" chile (*chao tian jiao*), a short, plump, lustrously red chile that is moderately hot and very fragrant (the chiles grow upward, hence their name). A similar variety, the "seven-star" chile (*qi xing jiao*), is named because the chiles grow in bunches of about seven. In Chongqing and eastern Sichuan, thinner, pointier, hotter chiles from Yunnan, Henan, and Guizhou provinces are often preferred. Be cautious in substituting tiny Thai chiles (about an inch long), which can be deadly hot and quite unpalatable if used in Sichuanese quantities. Sun-dried chiles are usually snipped in half or cut into slivers before use, and as many seeds discarded as possible.

GROUND CHILES (*hai jiao mian*)

A coarse powder made from sun-dried chiles, usually the "facing-heaven" variety, with their seeds. The chiles can be directly pulverized to a powder or—for best results—first toasted gently in a wok with a touch of oil until they are crisp and fragrant. The chili powder is used both in cooking and as a dip for cooked meats and poultry. It is also the base for making chili oil, an essential ingredient in many Sichuanese cold dishes. If you can't use Sichuanese ground chiles, paprika is a possible substitute as a dip or cooking ingredient because it's not too hot. As for chili oil, any ground or flaked dried chile can be used, but the real Sichuanese chiles impart a ruby-red color that is incomparable.

CHILI OIL (*hong you*)

 The chili oil commonly sold in Chinese supermarkets usually has dried shrimps and other ingredients added and is often excessively hot. I prefer to make my own, Sichuan-style—it's quick and easy to prepare and keeps for ages in a cool, shady place. You may wish to reduce the quantities suggested in the recipes if you use store-bought chili oil.

RECIPE FOR CHILI OIL (*hong you*)

The common Sichuanese name for chili oil is *hong you*, "red oil," because at its best it is an astonishing ruby red. It is made by pouring hot oil onto coarsely ground chiles, which fizz up fragrantly before they settle into a layer of flakes at the bottom of the jar. Some cooks add a piece of crushed ginger to the oil as they heat it, and a star anise or two to the chile flakes. Chili oil is the indispensable ingredient in many famous Sichuanese cold sauces: see the recipes for chicken chunks in red-oil sauce (page 140), hot-and-numbing chicken slices (page 141), cold pork in hot and garlicky sauce (page 146). It is also offered as a condiment in many noodle and dumpling restaurants. In most homes and restaurants, chili oil is used along with its flakes, but upscale restaurants, which tend to refine the tastes and textures of hearty peasant cooking, often use the oil alone for a smoother effect. You can make chili oil with any kind of chile, but the Sichuanese particularly like to use the "facing-heaven" variety (*chao tian jiao*) because it yields a very fragrant oil that is not aggressively hot. The proportions of chiles and oil in the following recipe are classically Sichuanese, but can be varied according to taste.

It's worth using an oil thermometer for this recipe—if the oil is too hot you risk burning the chiles, and if it's too cool you won't extract their full fra-

The following recipe makes about a pint of chili oil, so be sure your glass preserving jar is big enough to take it. You can add a star anise to the chile flakes if you like. If you can only get whole chiles, you must snip them in half and then fry them with their seeds in a little oil until they are crisp and fragrant. They can then be crushed with a mortar and pestle, or in a food processor. Take great care not to burn them.

grance. If by any chance you wish to use fresh chiles, cookbooks recommend adding the oil at a slightly hotter temperature, about 300°F.

1/2 cup chile flakes or coarsely ground chiles, with seeds
2 cups peanut or corn oil

optional: a small piece of fresh ginger, with peel, crushed

1 Put the chile flakes into a glass preserving jar.

2 Heat the oil, with the ginger if used, over a high flame until smoking hot.

3 Remove from the heat, discard the ginger, and allow to cool for about 10 minutes, to 225–250°F. Pour onto the chiles, stir once or twice, and leave to cool in a shady place. The oil and chiles will fizz and swirl around at first, but the chile flakes will settle as the oil cools. You can use the oil almost immediately, but its flavor and fragrance will improve after a couple of days.

PICKLED CHILES (*pao hai jiao*)

Red chiles pickled in a solution of salt, sugar, wine, and spices are used in many Sichuanese dishes. The most important type is the long, mild, horn-shaped "two golden strips" chile (*er jin tiao*). Tiny green mountain chiles (*ye shan jiao*) are also popular. The pickled "two golden strips" chile has an intense crimson color and a subtle flavor, with a teasing hotness, and it is frequently used in a finely minced or puréed form. The hot Indonesian pickled chili paste, Sambal Oelek, is a fine substitute for this purée, as it has a beautiful color and a suitable degree of hotness. For the whole or sliced chiles, beware of substituting the pickled Thai variety sold in Chinese supermarkets, which are tiny and viciously hot—they can be used whole to add color to a Sichuanese dish, but if you cut them up they will release their full fieriness and overwhelm the other ingredients. If I can't use Sichuanese pickled chiles, I'm inclined to substitute finely sliced red bell pepper with a little pickled chile purée, which makes the dish look authentic and provides a little of that gentle pickled-chile hotness. Any suitable substitute will list water and salt rather than vinegar as the main pickling ingredients.

CHILI BEAN PASTE (*dou ban jiang*)

 A fermented paste made from fresh "two golden strips" (*er jin tiao*) chiles and fava beans that is indispensable in Sichuanese cooking. It lends its rich, delicious taste and deep red color to many hearty local dishes. The most famous version comes from the town of Pixian, just outside Chengdu, where it is available in several stages of maturity. The freshest paste is bright red and the most mature a dark purple, although it's most often used when it is a deep maroon-red. Several brands are sold under a variety of names, including chili bean sauce, chili bean paste, toban djan, and toban jhan. They tend to be fresher and more orange in color than the best Pixian paste, but still have a delicious flavor. Just read the list of ingredients to make sure they are made with the authentic fava beans rather than soybeans. The saltiness and chile-hotness varies from brand to brand, and you may have to adjust the amount of salt you add to your dishes accordingly.

CHINESE COOKING WINES (*liao jiu*)

 Mild, amber-colored cooking wines, usually known simply as "cooking wine" (liao jiu), are widely used in marinades and in stir-fried dishes to enhance the flavor of the main ingredients. Shaoxing rice wine from eastern Zhejiang province, which is 14.5 percent alcohol, is the most highly regarded, although Sichuanese cooks often use locally produced substitutes. Shaoxing has been a center of wine production since about the fifth century B.C. and is known poetically as the City of Yellow Wine (huang jiu cheng). The best Shaoxing rice wine is made from glutinous rice and should be drunk warm, like sake. A few Shaoxing wines are readily available in Chinese supermarkets, and they have been used in testing all the recipes in this book. Some Chinese recipe writers recommend using medium-dry sherry as a substitute.

Stronger vodka-like wines (*qu jiu, bai jiu*) made from various grains are occasionally, but rarely, used in cooking. A slug of Chinese vodka is, however, an indispensable ingredient of homemade pickled vegetables. The Kwangtung Mijiu (rice wine) sold in Chinese grocery stores works fine; ordinary vodka could also be used as a substitute.

CHINESE SCALLIONS (*cong*)

 Chinese scallions are very similar in appearance and flavor to Western scallions, but they never develop onion bulbs; instead they just keep growing longer. Most Chinese sources say they are native to Siberia, but they have been cultivated in China for more than three thousand years. Baby green onions (*xiao cong*) are used raw as a garnish; older onions (*da cong*) are used in marinades and all kinds of cooked dishes. The quantities given in this book assume the use of decent-sized scallions available in the West: if you do manage to find the long Asian onions, you will want to reduce the quantities accordingly.

COOKING OILS (*cai you*)

 Rapeseed oil (*cai you*), which has a deep amber color, is the traditional Sichuanese cooking oil and is still used in most homes and restaurants in the region. Expensive restaurants do, however, increasingly use more refined vegetable oils because of their lightness and lack of color (corn oil and peanut oil are well regarded). Pork lard is often used in stir-fried dishes, as well as in some sweetmeats, and beef drippings are used in the preparation of Sichuan hotpot. Chicken fat, a delicious luxury, is used occasionally. Peanut or corn oil can be used as a substitute for animal fats in most cases, though at the expense of more intriguing flavors. Coconut oil is a good substitute for the use of lard in some pastry dishes. I have used peanut oil, which is pale and neutral, and stable at high temperatures, in the testing of all the recipes in this book that don't specifically demand the use of animal fats.

CORIANDER LEAVES (*xiang cai* or *yan sui*)

 Coriander (also known as cilantro) is the only fresh herb in common use in Sichuanese cooking. Its strong fragrance and fresh taste are used to improve flavors and to cut the oiliness of heavy meat or fish dishes. The herb is also used as a colorful garnish for soups and other dishes, and its tender stems and leaves can be stir-fried or eaten as a salad. Coriander is native to the shores of the Mediterranean, but found its way into China during the Han Dynasty (around the time of Christ). It is now grown all over the country.

Dried mushrooms

WOOD EAR MUSHROOMS (*mu'er*)

木耳 Wood ear mushrooms have an intriguing texture, simultaneously slithery and crunchy, but very little flavor. They are used in many wok-cooked dishes. Avoid the fungus sold as "wood ear" in Chinese supermarkets, which tends to be thick and coarse: much better is the variety sold as "cloud ears" or "black fungus," which is similar to the type used in Sichuan. This fungus comes in small, frilly pieces, which weigh almost nothing. They must be soaked in very hot water for 15–20 minutes before use. They keep indefinitely in a cool, dry place.

FRAGRANT MUSHROOMS (*xiang gu*)

 These dried mushrooms, known in Japan as shiitake, have been cultivated in China for about a thousand years. They have an intense, delicious flavor and fragrance. There are several different varieties: the best are those with pale crisscross fissures over their brown caps. These mushrooms must be soaked in hot water for about half an hour before use, and their tasty soaking water can be added to soups and sauces. They keep indefinitely in a cool, dry place.

BAMBOO PITH FUNGUS (*zhu sun*)

 This unusual fungus, a Sichuan specialty, has a marvelous texture and a beautiful, lacy appearance. It can be used in stir-fried dishes, but is more often seen in rich chicken soups. It is available in some Chinese supermarkets, usually under the name "bamboo fungus," and must be soaked in hot water for about 15 minutes before use.

SILVER EAR FUNGUS (*yin'er*)

Also known as white wood ear fungus (*bai mu'er*) or white ear (*bai er zi*), this delicate fungus is sold dried into pale yellow, papery frills. After a good soaking, it expands into nearly transparent waves with a texture that is both crunchy and gelatinous. Wild silver ear fungus has long been considered a delicacy, prized for its intriguing texture and nutritional benefits. In Sichuanese cooking, it is mainly used in the sweet soups that round off a banquet or a feast of snacks.

FERMENTED BEAN CURD (*dou fu ru*)

 Bean curd in all its forms is often described as the Chinese equivalent of cheese. If this is so, then this intensely flavored bean curd product, with its strong, salty taste and heady fragrance, can be compared to ripe blue cheese. The two main types are "red" fermented bean curd and "white" fermented bean curd, although there are countless variations. One popular Sichuanese variety consists of chunks of bean curd packed into a jar with chili bean paste, Sichuan pepper, vegetable oil, and spices. Fermented bean curd can be eaten as a relish (it's great with steamed rice and leftover bits and pieces of food), and it's also added to some marinades.

FERMENTED GLUTINOUS RICE WINE (*lao zao*)

 Traditionally made at home, this alcoholic condiment consists of pulpy glutinous rice grains in their clear, fermented juices. It has a rich, sweet, mellow flavor. *Lao zao* is thought to dispel the raw tastes of meat and poultry, and it is commonly used in marinades. It is also the main flavoring in so-called "drunken" (*zao zui*) and "fragrant wine flavor" (*xiang zao wei*) dishes. Shaoxing rice wine can be used as a substitute because it has similar culinary functions, although its flavor is quite different.

RECIPE FOR FERMENTED GLUTINOUS RICE WINE (*lao zao*)

This sweet, boozy liquid consists of cooked glutinous rice, which is sealed into an earthenware jar with some wine yeast and left in a warm place for a few days until it ferments. The clear wine juices can be used with or without the soft, pulpy rice sediment. In the markets of Sichuan, *lao zao* is often sold in enormous, glazed clay pots, but it's also extremely easy to make at home. All you need is a jar with a tight-fitting lid and one of the wine yeast balls that are sold in some Chinese and Vietnamese food shops. When the rice has fermented, the mixture can be transferred to the refrigerator, where it will keep for months. The following recipe makes about 1 1/2 cups of *lao zao*, 1/2 cup of which is juices.

NOTE

Lao zao is a key ingredient in *lao zao ji dan*, a favorite Sichuanese breakfast dish that is traditionally offered to women who have just given birth. It's very easy to make: just mix a little glutinous rice flour with enough cold water to yield a good dough; break off marble-size pieces of dough and drop them into boiling water to cook. When they are cooked through, break in an egg for each person and let them poach gently. When the eggs are done, season the liquid with sugar to taste, stirring to dissolve (the liquid should be fairly sweet). Just before serving, add a couple of generous spoonfuls of *lao zao*, enough to give the liquid a mellow, boozy flavor. Serve each person with an egg, a few dumplings, and plenty of the sweet soup.

| 1 1/4 cup long grain glutinous rice | 1 wine yeast ball (about 1/2 ounce) |

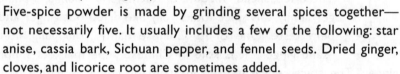

1 Rinse the rice in cold water until the water runs clear.

2 Place the rice in a steamer with 1 1/2 cups of water and steam until just cooked. Then turn it onto a large plate and spread it out to cool. Crush the wine yeast to a coarse powder with a mortar and pestle.

3 When the rice is lukewarm, scatter over the crushed yeast and mix it in. Then put the rice mixture into a jar, preferably earthenware, and close the lid tightly. Do not fill the jar completely—you must leave a gap of a couple of inches above the rice.

4 Wrap the jar in a thick cloth and leave it to ferment for 3 days in a warm place. The flavor will continue to mellow for another couple of weeks, after which you can transfer the jar to the refrigerator.

FIVE-SPICE POWDER (*wu xiang fen*)

Five-spice powder is made by grinding several spices together— not necessarily five. It usually includes a few of the following: star anise, cassia bark, Sichuan pepper, and fennel seeds. Dried ginger, cloves, and licorice root are sometimes added.

"FRAGRANT THINGS" (*xiang liao*)

"Fragrant things" is the phrase commonly used to describe a whole collection of spices that are used in the preparation of aromatic stewed meats, Sichuan hotpot, and a number of slow-cooked hot and cold dishes. The exact combination of spices used tends to vary with availability. The most essential are as follows:

CASSIA BARK (*gui pi*)

The dried bark of the Chinese cassia tree, which has a cinnamon-like flavor but is considered inferior to true cinnamon. The bark comes in long, fairly thick strips; the thin outer layer is dark brown, the inside a caramel color.

SICHUAN PEPPER (*hua jiao*)

See page 73.

STAR ANISE (*ba jiao*)

The sun-dried fruit of an evergreen tree, which, when ripe, pops open into a lovely eight-pointed star (the name means "eight horns" in Chinese). The stars are reddish-brown in color and have a deep aniseed fragrance. This spice is thought to be native to China.

AMOMUM TSAO-KUO (*cao guo*)

The olive-shaped dried fruit of a variety of "false cardamom," this spice has a cool, cardamom-like flavor. The dried fruits are dark brown and ridged and roughly nutmeg-size. They are sold in Chinese supermarkets as Tsao Kuo and are mainly used in aromatic stews.

"SAND GINGER" (*shan nai*)

The dried, sliced rhizome of *Kaempferia galanga,* a plant in the ginger family, this spice looks very like dried-out ginger and has a peppery taste. One of its Chinese names, *sha jiang,* literally means "sand ginger." It is sold in Chinese supermarkets simply as "sliced ginger." The spice, which is used in aromatic stews, is native to India, but is grown in several parts of southern China.

FENNEL SEEDS (*xiao hui xiang* or *xiao hui*)

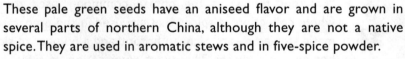

These pale green seeds have an aniseed flavor and are grown in several parts of northern China, although they are not a native spice. They are used in aromatic stews and in five-spice powder.

Other dried herbs and spices that are sometimes but less widely used in Sichuanese cooking include cloves (*ding xiang*), galangal (*gao liang jiang*), nutmeg (*rou dou kou*), other types of "false cardamom," and licorice root (*gan cao*).

GARLIC (*da suan*)

Garlic is ubiquitous as a flavoring in Sichuanese cooking, and some of its varieties are also eaten as vegetables. The type of garlic familiar to us in the West appears in countless recipes. Legend says it was brought into China by a Han Dynasty official returning from a mission to Central Asia and was given its Chinese name—*da suan* ("big garlic")—because its heads were so much larger than those of the wild native breeds. The Sichuan region is also famous for its *du suan,* or "single-headed garlic," fat, individual, purplish bulbs that are not divided into cloves. Sichuanese cooks also use a great deal of "green garlic" (*suan miao* or *qing suan*), often translated as "scallion" or "Chinese leek," but as a vegetable rather than a flavoring. Garlic sprouts (*suan tai* or *suan hao*), long, tubular, bright green garlic stems, each topped with a miniature garlic bulb, are also enjoyed as a delicious stir-fried vegetable.

GINGER (*sheng jiang*)

Fresh ginger is an essential flavoring in Sichuanese cooking and is also used to suppress raw tastes in meat, poultry, and fish. It is thought to have originated in Southeast Asia, but has been cultivated in China, and in Sichuan, since ancient times. Mature ginger is the most common and indispensable variety, but the pale, tender young stems are also used as a vegetable in stir-fried dishes and can be pickled. The fresh ginger widely available is suitable for most uses, and pickled ginger is also sold in Asian supermarkets. When whole pieces of ginger are crushed and added to a dish, the skin is left on for maximum taste and fragrance (the peel doesn't matter because the ginger is not actually eaten); when ginger is sliced, slivered, or finely chopped and used in dishes where it will actually be eaten, it should be peeled.

MONOSODIUM GLUTAMATE (*wei jing*)

Most Sichuanese cooks use monosodium glutamate (the sodium salt of glutamic acid, also known as MSG) to enhance the flavor of their dishes. On its own, this white powder is almost tasteless, but it is considered to improve the fresh, natural taste (*xian wei*) of cooking ingredients. Used in small quantities, MSG can give a certain pleasurable kick to many dishes, but most cooks use it in excessive quantities as a substitute for good ingredients and well-made stocks. Many Western people also associate it with physical discomfort and frantic thirst—the so-called "Chinese restaurant syndrome." Chinese cooks have long appreciated foods that are rich in natural glutamic acid, like certain types of mushrooms, but refined MSG is not a traditional ingredient in Chinese cooking. It has been manufactured only since the early part of the twentieth century, when a Japanese scientist discovered how to isolate glutamic acid from seaweed, and has been widely used in Sichuanese cooking for only a few decades. I regard MSG as at best unnecessary, and at worst a cheat that makes all dishes taste similar and detracts from more subtle gastronomic pleasures, so I don't use it myself and have avoided it in testing all the recipes in this book.

PEANUTS (*hua sheng mi*)

Peanuts are a popular snack in Sichuan, whether boiled with spices, encrusted with flavorings, or simply deep-fried. They are an important source of oil and are also used in some stir-fried dishes (most notably Gong Bao [Kung Pao] chicken), and as a crunchy garnish for cold dishes and snacks. Raw, red-skinned peanuts and unsalted roasted peanuts are easily available in health food stores and Asian supermarkets.

POTATO FLOUR (*qian fen*)

The Sichuanese use a mixture of water and white starch derived from peas to coat raw meat, poultry, and fish before cooking and to thicken their sauces. It has no flavor, so potato flour and cornstarch are both perfectly acceptable substitutes. I have used potato flour, which you can buy in any East Asian shop, to test the recipes in this book. The food writer Yan-kit So suggests using 50 percent more cornstarch than potato flour, which is reflected in the measurements given in the recipes.

PRESERVED FOODS

Pickled vegetables are fundamental to the spirit of Sichuanese cooking. Every household has its *pao cai tan zi*—a rough earthenware pot with a rounded belly and narrow neck, and a lip that functions as a water seal. In the darkness within, crunchy vegetables soak in a pool of brine, with a splash of rice wine and a selection of flavorings that probably include brown sugar, Sichuan pepper, and ginger, with a few pieces of cinnamon stick, cassia bark, and star anise. The vegetables come and go, replenished every day or two with fresh supplies, but the pickling brine, or mother liquor, goes on, they say, forever. With each new batch of vegetables, a little salt and wine is added, and the spices and sugar are renewed from time to time. But the rich, aromatic liquid base goes from strength to strength as the years, or even generations, pass.

Whenever we're cooking together in his Chengdu flat, my friend Zeng Bo puts his forearm into a great clay urn and plucks out handfuls of scarlet pickled chiles, pale young ginger stems, and long string beans. Some of the chiles will be sliced and stir-fried with some tender chicken meat; others will be puréed and fried in hot oil to coax out their flavors and intense red hues for a dish of fish-fragrant pork. The ginger may be stir-fried with duck, its fresh hotness a pleasing contrast to the richness of the meat, and the long string beans will be fast-fried with a scattering of ground pork, chiles, and Sichuan peppercorns.

Some vegetables are pickled for a few hours only, like the "water-shower" tidbits that are currently fashionable in Sichuan restaurants. These usually fresh, crunchy vegetables like cucumber, sweet peppers, or celery are steeped in clear water with just a splash of the rich mother liquor from the more traditional pickle jar. They taste a little salty and aromatic, but lack the deep, fermented flavors of the longer-pickled vegetables. Restaurants often display their "water-shower" vegetables in clear glass pickle jars on a countertop.

Sichuanese pickles are often used in cooking, but they are also eaten with rice porridge for breakfast and as a refreshing palate cleanser at the end of almost every other meal. During the winter, small dishes of pickled radish, pale and crunchy, are served with a scattering of white sugar and chili oil. In spring and summer, the most common pickle is the Sichuanese white cabbage, *lian hua bai*. This custom extends from the simplest home-cooked meals to extravagant restaurant dinners, and it's something the Sichuanese seem to miss most when they are away from home.

Dry-salting is another popular method of preserving vegetables. If you visit Chengdu in May, on sunny days the whole city seems to be hung with cabbage leaves—they are sun-dried and then packed into clay jars with salt and Sichuan pepper. Root vegetables like radishes and a type of swede (*da tou cai*) are processed in similar ways.

Many Sichuanese people, even in the cities, also still salt and smoke their own pork, and in the winter make their own delicious air-dried sausages.

The following is a small selection of recipes that will give you a taste of Sichuanese food preserving.

HOMEMADE BACON WITH SICHUANESE FLAVORINGS (*si chuan la rou*)

川味腊肉 Many Sichuanese households still cure their own bacon and sausages, salting them, smoking them, and hanging them under the eaves to dry in the wind. In my first Chengdu winter, many of the old wooden houses were hung with such meats in the dying days of the lunar year. Sichuanese bacon has an intensity of flavor that is rarely found in the supermarkets of the West. The dark flesh and yellowed fat are aromatic and richly smoked, and just a few slivers will enliven a simple stir-fry of cauliflower or garlic stems. The meat can also be sliced and steamed, and served on its own as an aperitif, with a little dip of coarsely ground chiles on the side.

To make the bacon, strips of pork belly or leg meat are first marinated for a week or so in a mixture of salt, sugar, wine, and spices. They are then hung up to air-dry, and finally smoked for several hours over a slow fire of wood shavings, peanut husks, rice straw, or leaves. The finished bacon is again hung in the open air, until it is needed.

There are a number of regional variations within Sichuan. In Chengdu, the meat is smoked until the fat is a dark, golden yellow and the flesh is a deep wine-red. In the mountains to the northeast, most famously Qingcheng Mountain, with its Taoist temples and scenery like a Chinese painting, the bacon is smoked until it is actually black, which makes it easy to identify on market stalls in the cities. The most celebrated bacons are always those that Westerners would call "organically produced" and that Chinese people call "rustic, earthy" (*tu*). These are made according to traditional methods from free-range pigs fed on household scraps rather than manufactured feed (*si liao*). Two types stand out in my memory as being particularly fine. One was made by the mother of a friend of mine, Peng Rui, in their family restaurant in the Wolong nature reserve. She smoked her bacon slowly, for an entire day, in the cool, lazy smoke of smoldering pinewood. The other was the bamboo leaf–smoked bacon made in the "Bamboo Sea" nature reserve in southern Sichuan, a strong, subtle, pinkish meat that was so exquisite it left us speechless with pleasure.

The following is my attempt to recreate some of these flavors in my London kitchen. The method of preparation has several stages and must be done over a period of about a week, but it isn't difficult. The resulting bacon is far tastier than most of that available in the West—it is also much saltier, so you may wish to soak it before you use it.

You will need some meat hooks to make this recipe (they can be bought in larger Chinese supermarkets). How you smoke the bacon is up to you. A smoking machine is ideal, but I've achieved satisfactory results in my wok. As for smoking materials, pine or cypress wood give the meat a lovely fragrance (I've used the remains of my Christmas tree to smoke bacon in the past), but you can of course experiment with other types of wood.

6 1/2 pounds fresh, boneless pork belly, with skin

FOR THE SALT MARINADE

3 whole cloves

a few pieces of cassia bark or cinnamon stick

3 star anise

1/2 teaspoon saltpeter

2 tablespoons Shaoxing rice wine or medium-dry sherry

2 tablespoons brown sugar

2 tablespoons whole Sichuan pepper

3/4 cup salt

SMOKING MATERIALS

If you are using a wok in a home kitchen, for every 2 pounds of meat you will need approximately:

1/2 cup all-purpose flour

1/2 cup sugar

1/4 cup pine needles or cypress shavings or peanut husks

1 Cut the pork belly into long strips about 2 inches wide. Crush the cloves, cassia bark, and star anise together with a mortar and pestle. Dissolve the saltpeter in the Shaoxing rice wine.

2 Rub all the marinade ingredients all over the pork. Then place the strips in a large pot and leave them in a refrigerator or other cold place for a week, turning them once after 3–4 days.

3 After a week, remove the strips, pierce each one with a meat hook, and hang them in a cool, well-ventilated place for several hours to air-dry (I hang mine from a cord strung up outside my north-facing kitchen window).

4 When the bacon is dry, you can begin the smoking. Line your wok with a double thickness of foil. Mix the flour and sugar together at the center of the wok. Scatter over the pine leaves, wood shavings, or peanut husks. Place a metal rack over the smoking materials—ideally about 4 inches above them, to allow for the circulation of the smoke. Place the strips of salted bacon on the rack. Place the wok over a very high flame until the smoking

materials are emitting plenty of dark smoke. Then cover with a wok lid, turn down to a medium heat, and smoke for 15–30 minutes, until the pork strips have a rich, yellowish color, turning them halfway through. The longer you smoke, the stronger the color and the flavor. Do remember that you can remove and discard the outer layer of the bacon before you serve it, if its flavor is excessively smoky.

5 The smoked bacon can be hung up or stored in the refrigerator until you want to use it.

SALT-CURED PORK WITH SWEET FERMENTED PASTE (*jiang rou*)

 This is another traditional winter treat, which many households still make in the closing weeks of the lunar year and eat as part of their New Year festivities. Strips of fat pork belly or hind leg are cured in salt and then rubbed with a selection of quintessentially Sichuanese flavorings: Sichuan pepper, *tian mian jiang* (a syrupy black paste made from fermented wheat), and fermented glutinous rice wine (*lao zao*). They are later hung out to dry. The meat is eventually steamed, sliced, and eaten cold as a first course or a nibble with wine. It has a delicate, savory taste.

The meat should be prepared when the weather is cold but not freezing. You will need 4 or 5 meat hooks to make this recipe (they can be bought in Chinese supermarkets, or perhaps from your local butcher).

2 pounds fresh, boneless pork belly, with some fat and with skin

FOR THE INITIAL SALT-CURING
1 tablespoon Shaoxing rice wine or medium-dry sherry
2 tablespoons salt
1/4 teaspoon saltpeter

FOR THE SEASONING
8 tablespoons Sichuanese

sweet wheaten paste or sweet bean sauce
3–4 tablespoons Sichuanese fermented rice wine (*lao zao*) or Shaoxing rice wine
1 tablespoon whole Sichuan pepper

TO SERVE
Sichuanese chili powder or any chili sauce

1 Cut the pork belly lengthwise into strips about 2 inches wide. Place them in a shallow container that will fit into your refrigerator. Splash the strips with about 1 tablespoon Shaoxing rice wine, and then rub them evenly with the salt and saltpeter. Place in the refrigerator for 3 days, turning the strips over after a day or two.

2 When 3 days have passed, remove the belly strips, pierce them with the meat hooks, and hang them in a cool and well-ventilated place overnight or for a few hours to air-dry (I hang mine outside my north-facing kitchen window).

3 When the meat is dry, combine the seasonings in a small bowl and rub them all over the strips. Return the strips to the refrigerator for another 2 days. Then take them out and hang them up again to air-dry.

4 To eat the meat, wash off all the paste under warm water and then steam it until it is cooked through. Allow the meat to cool thoroughly and cut into fairly thin slices to serve.

5 Serve as an appetizer with a pile of Sichuanese chili powder, or any chili sauce you prefer.

SALTY DUCK EGGS (*yan dan*)

Many Chengdu restaurants display a jar of bluish duck eggs that have been pickled in brine. These eggs have a strong salty taste, and their yolks have an intriguing, slightly granular texture. They are enjoyed as snacks and are usually quartered in their shells so the flesh can be picked out with chopsticks. Duck eggs can be cured by caking them in a paste made from salt mixed with mud or ashes (sooty ash-caked eggs are a common sight in Chinese markets and can some-times be found in Chinatowns abroad), but at home the easiest method is to use a strong salt-water solution. The eggs are at their best after 2 to 3 weeks—if you leave them in the brine for longer they can become unpleas-antly salty. You will need a 2-quart jar with a tight-fitting lid to make this recipe.

9 fresh duck eggs   **1 cup salt**

1 Give the duck eggs a good wash and a scrub with a vegetable brush to remove any dirt. Discard any cracked eggs.

2 Bring 3 1/2 cups water to a boil, add the salt, and stir to dissolve. Leave the water to cool completely.

3 Place the eggs carefully in your preserving jar. Pour over the salt solution. Place a small ceramic dish or glass at the top of the jar to keep the top eggs covered by the water. Close the lid tightly and leave in a cool place for 2–3 weeks.

4 When the eggs are ready, remove them from the brine and hard-boil them as required. Allow them to cool completely before eating.

Preserved vegetables

The traditional pickles made by Sichuanese peasant farmers to tide themselves over the winter have become a distinctive Sichuanese flavor, used in all aspects of the regional cuisine. Crisp vegetables pickled in brine, wine, sugar, and spices are eaten as a snack to cleanse and refresh the palate; salted vegetables with chile are used in some recipes and as a relish; pickled chiles (see under Chiles, page 54) have many culinary uses. The following preserved vegetables are all important flavorings in some famous local dishes.

PRESERVED MUSTARD TUBER (*zha cai*)

榨菜 This plump vegetable, often sold in cans as "Sichuan preserved vegetable," has a wonderful crisp texture and salty, sour, spicy taste. It is delicious stir-fried with pork or chopped up and scattered over bean curd. "Big-head vegetable" (*da tou cai*), made from a kind of turnip, is another famous Sichuanese pickle that has similar uses.

ya cai

芽菜 This dark, salty, aromatic pickle is made from the tender leaves of a variety of mustard green (known in Chinese as *guang gan qing cai*). The leaves are sun-dried, rubbed with salt, and then mixed with spices and sometimes sugar. They are then sealed into jars and left to mature for several months. *Ya cai* is one of Sichuan's most famous foodstuffs and is used in many local dishes and snacks. The city of Yibin is one famous producer; another prized variety is made in Nanxi. A different type of mustard green (*jian gan qing cai*) is made into "winter vegetable" (*dong cai*), a related and equally delicious pickle. The "Tianjin preserved vegetable" sold in earthenware jars in Chinese supermarkets is an acceptable substitute for these ingredients, with its similar texture and dark, salty taste.

PICKLED MUSTARD GREENS (*suan cai*)

This leafy vegetable, pickled in spiced brine, has a sour taste and is particularly favored in summer and autumn dishes. It is used in several soups and goes particularly well with fish. This pickle is readily available in Chinese shops.

PICKLED VEGETABLES (*si chuan pao cai*)

The following is a typical Sichuanese recipe for pickled root vegetables. It yields very salty pickles with a nice fermented taste, which should be eaten with rice porridge for breakfast or in small quantities at the end of a meal.

You can vary the vegetables as you please. Young ginger, cauliflower, and other crisp, crunchy vegetables work very well. More watery vegetables like cucumber and sweet peppers can be pickled, but are best left in the brine for several hours only, or overnight. White cabbage, cut into chunks, is another popular Sichuanese pickle—the cabbage is also generally used after only 24 hours. The flavor of the brine improves with time.

You will need a 1-quart pickle jar with a good sealable lid to make this recipe.

FOR THE BRINE
2 1/4 cups water
1/4 cup rock or sea salt
4 dried chiles
1/2 teaspoon whole Sichuan
  pepper
2 teaspoons strong rice wine
  or vodka
1/2 of a star anise
1 tablespoon brown sugar

a 1-inch piece of fresh ginger,
  unpeeled
a good piece of cassia bark or
  1/3 of a cinnamon stick

SUGGESTED VEGETABLES
3/4 pound red-skinned or
  white Asian radish (daikon)
1/2 pound carrots

TO SERVE
chili oil
white sugar

1 Bring the water to a boil with the salt, stirring to dissolve the salt. When it has completely dissolved, set aside and leave to cool.

2 Place the cooled water in a very clean pickle jar (I usually boil mine or pop it in the oven for a few minutes to sterilize it). Add all the other brine ingredients and give them a good stir.

3 Clean the vegetables thoroughly, removing stalks and any whiskery bits from the radishes. Allow them to dry completely. Cut the vegetables into small chunks and put them into the pickle jar. Wedge a small glass or ceramic dish or lid on top of them to make sure that the vegetables are completely immersed in the brine. Seal the lid and leave in a cool, dark place for at least 24 hours. The flavors will improve the longer you leave them. (They are very good after about a week.) You will notice a slight fizzing when you unseal the jar—this is part of the fermentation process. To serve the pickles, scoop out enough to fill a small dipping dish, drizzle with a little chili oil, and sprinkle with a few pinches of sugar if you wish.

4 As you eat the pickles, you can replenish the jar, adding more salt, sugar, and wine as you do so, to keep the brine good and salty.

ROCK SUGAR (*bing tang*)

 This pale yellow sugar has a pleasant taste and is used in many nourishing, curative recipes. It comes in large crystals and must be smashed with a hammer before use in the kitchen. Sichuanese cooks use it in sweet soups, dumpling fillings, and some meat dishes, as well as in medicinal stews and soups. It can be found in most East Asian food shops.

SALT (*chuan yan*)

 Sichuanese gourmets attach great importance to the use of the local well salt, which has been mined in the region for more than two millennia. It is very pure and strong-tasting—the sodium chloride content is almost 99 percent—with no bitter aftertaste, and many local cooks regard it as an essential ingredient in making Sichuanese dishes and in pickling vegetables. The difference between Sichuan salt and a good sea salt is, however, subtle, so it's not worth going to great lengths to use the real thing.

SESAME OIL (*xiang you*)

The Chinese name for this oil, which is made from roasted sesame seeds, means "fragrant oil," and its dark, nutty aroma is highly prized. Sesame oil figures prominently in the dressings for cold dishes, and it is also used to enhance the scent of food served straight from the stove. For the latter, because of the volatility of its fragrance, it is almost always added at the end of the cooking process, away from the fire. Toasted sesame oil is readily available in the West—but do make sure you choose a pure variety and not one blended with other oils.

SESAME PASTE (*zhi ma jiang*)

The toasted sesame paste used in Sichuanese cold dishes has a dark, nutty flavor and is mushroom-brown in color. The sesame pastes available in Chinese supermarkets in the West are very different, with a lighter, brighter taste, but they still work very well in Sichuanese recipes. Tahini, preferably dark tahini, can also be used as a substitute.

SESAME SEEDS (*zhi ma*)

The Sichuanese use both white and black sesame seeds in their cooking. Toasted white sesame seeds are mainly used as a garnish for cold meat dishes. Toasted black sesame seeds are used in sweet dishes, especially in the filling of the glutinous rice dumplings that are a traditional New Year's treat (*tang yuan*). To toast raw sesame seeds, just stir them in a dry wok over a low flame for a few minutes, until they are fragrant.

SICHUAN PEPPER (*hua jiao*)

This ancient spice, native to China, has long been associated with Sichuanese cooking and is still the region's most distinctive flavoring (see page 16 for a detailed description). At its best, Sichuan pepper consists only of the dried pepper husks of a woody shrub (*Zanthoxylum simulans*) that grows in the mountainous areas of northwestern Sichuan. The dried husks are pinkish red and knobbly on the outside, pale within. Sometimes the glossy black seeds are included too, although they have little taste. The husks are added to stocks and marinades to dispel the rankness of meat, poultry, and fish and to enhance fragrance. They are also fried in oil to flavor wok-cooked dishes, and roasted and ground to be used as a dip or scattered over all kinds of hot and cold foods. The most celebrated Sichuan pepper comes from Hanyuan county in mountainous western Sichuan. When it's relatively fresh, the scent of Hanyuan *hua jiao* is overwhelming. The quality of the Sichuan pepper sold in Chinese supermarkets is so poor by comparison that it's hardly worth using. Fortunately it is now possible to buy good-quality *hua jiao* from special suppliers (see page 377).

If you are not familiar with this spice, I recommend the following experiment: take one Sichuan pepper husk, put it into your mouth, and chew it gently ONCE OR TWICE before removing it. Wait a few seconds and a cool, tingly feeling will begin to creep over your lips and tongue. Do not chew it for half a minute, wondering why nothing is happening—if you do this, the effect will be much stronger and may seem unpleasant if you are not used to it. (You will only experience this effect if you use good-quality Sichuan pepper.)

GROUND ROASTED SICHUAN PEPPER
(*hua jiao mian*)

An essential Sichuanese condiment, this aromatic powder is found scattered on many hot dishes and mixed into dressings for a number of cold appetizers. It smells heavenly and will make your lips tingle as you eat it. The following recipe makes about 2 1/2 tablespoons of ground pepper—enough for a salt-and-pepper dip (see page 75) and a pock-marked Mother Chen's bean curd (*ma po dou fu*), with some left over for your spice rack. It's not worth making in large quantities, as the fragrance dulls with time (in many Sichuanese households the pepper is roasted and ground freshly almost every day). Do remember that you must use first-class Sichuan pepper to appreciate this flavoring.

**6 tablespoons whole
  Sichuan pepper**

1 Heat a dry wok over a low flame. Add the Sichuan pepper and stir-fry for about 5 minutes, until the pepper husks are richly fragrant—they will smoke slightly as you cook them. Take care not to burn them or they'll taste bitter. Remove from the wok and allow to cool.

2 Grind the peppercorns to a powder in a spice grinder or a mortar and

pestle—Sichuanese cooks use weighty mortars and pestles made of iron. Sift the powder to remove any remaining stalks or unground pepper husks. Use immediately or store in an airtight jar.

SOY SAUCE (*jiang you*)

醬
油

The Chinese have been fermenting soybeans, wheat, and other grains into sauces since at least the third century B.C., and these condiments have long been regarded as an essential part of people's diets. These days two types of soy sauce are in common use—thinner, saltier, light soy sauce and heavier, richer, dark soy sauce. The light soy is used mainly as a salty seasoning, the darker one for adding color to sauces and marinades. Sichuanese cooks also make their own sweet, aromatic soy sauce by simmering dark soy with brown sugar and spices—this is used in cold dishes and sauces for various snacks. The finest soy sauce is allowed to ferment naturally, but most versions rely on added yeast.

SALT-AND-PEPPER DIP (*jiao yan*)

Deep-fried dishes served with a salt-and-pepper dip are common on Chinese restaurant menus outside China, but they're usually made with black pepper rather than the Sichuan pepper used in the following recipe. The Sichuan pepper, of course, gives the condiment a distinctive and delightful aroma. I should mention that a Tibetan acquaintance of mine who once lived in Chengdu keeps a pepper grinder full of Sichuan peppercorns, which she adds to the cooking pot or serving dish much as Westerners add black pepper. You could fill a grinder with gently roasted Sichuan peppercorns for a most delicious result, but do remember that their flavor will fade if you keep them too long.

**I tablespoon ground roasted
Sichuan pepper (see above)**

3 tablespoons salt

Sichuanese cooks always fry the salt in a dry wok to get rid of any lingering moisture (a symptom of their damp and clammy climate), but I don't find this necessary with the salt available in the West. So I suggest you simply combine the condiments in a little dish and serve. Rock salt is the salt of preference if you're seeking authenticity, but sea salt or ordinary table salt will do.

SWEET, AROMATIC SOY SAUCE (*fu zhi jiang you*)

A little culinary secret that explains the intriguing flavor of "hot and garlicky" sauces and the famous Zhong dumpling dressing, it can be made in large quantities and keeps indefinitely. The spices can be varied as you please; many Sichuanese cooks would also include small amounts of licorice root (*gan cao*) and dried "sand ginger" (*shan nai*).

1/3 cup dark soy sauce
2/3 cup water
6 tablespoons brown sugar
1/3 of a cinnamon stick or a
    piece of cassia bark

1/2 teaspoon fennel seeds
1/2 of a star anise
1/2 teaspoon Sichuan pepper
a small piece of fresh ginger,
    unpeeled, crushed

Place all the ingredients in a pot and bring to a boil, stirring to dissolve the sugar. Then turn the heat right down and simmer for about 20 minutes. You can bind the spices in cheesecloth, or just put them into the liquid and strain it through a tea-strainer after simmering. Leave to cool.

SWEET WHEATEN PASTE (*tian mian jiang*)

This thick, dark paste is made from fermented wheat flour. It is used in some stir-fried dishes and in the salt-curing of winter meats, and can also be mixed with sugar and sesame oil to make a dip for meat dishes such as fragrant and crispy duck. The nearest thing available in the West is a sweet bean sauce, which has a very similar taste and works well as a substitute. Hoisin sauce can be used as an alternative dipping sauce, although it is much sweeter than the Sichuanese paste.

TANGERINE PEEL (*chen pi*)

The dried peel of mandarin oranges or tangerines is used occasionally in Sichuanese cooking. You can make it yourself by scraping the pith out from strips of fragrant orange peel and drying them in an airy place. When the strips are bone-dry, place them in an airtight jar and they will keep for ages. Dark brown dried tangerine peel can be bought in Chinese supermarkets.

Tea

Tea is one of the staples of Sichuanese and Chinese life. When you sit in a tea-house, the courtyard is alive with the sounds of clacking mahjong tiles and laughter. Songbirds peep and twitter in bell-shaped bamboo cages hanging from the trees. Their owners, retired men in dark blue Mao suits, sit nearby, chatting and drawing on their long, silver-tipped bamboo pipes. Younger men sprawl in bamboo chairs, cigarettes dangling from their mouths, poker cards splayed across their tables. Packets of peanuts, dried beef, and watermelon seeds lie open, around them a debris of skins and husks. Tea bowls, filled to varying degrees with a pale amber liquid, floating with jasmine blossoms, are dotted around. Occasionally the air is ruptured by the twang of the wandering ear cleaner, clicking his metal instruments together as he does the rounds, letting everyone know he's here. A woman hails him, haggles for a price, and then sits back as he probes and strokes, her eyes closed, an expression of quiet bliss on her face. All the while, the tea attendants bustle to and fro with copper kettles, topping up the china cups, careful not to spill a drop of water.

Teahouses are part of the fabric of Sichuanese life. In the villages and the old parts of the cities they are intimate places, clusters of bamboo chairs in a leafy courtyard or the ground floor of a timber-framed house, where older people gather to gossip or to play and sing the sounds of traditional Sichuan opera. In the Buddhist and Taoist temples, the teahouses buzz with the chatter of tourists and pilgrims, their courtyards and colonnades secluded from the bustle of the streets. In city parks, too, teahouses extend over huge areas, taking in pagodas, bamboo groves, and lakeside promontories.

From the late Qing period to the 1940s, teahouses were at the center of Sichuanese social life. Some of them were frequented by members of Sichuan's secret societies (*pao ge*), who actually used the arrangement of their teacups as an elaborate secret code. Teahouses often had an air of political subversion—many establishments of this period actually displayed signs urging their clients to avoid discussing national affairs: *wu tan guo shi*. Some teahouses specialized in theatrical performances or storytelling; others in Chinese chess or Go (*wei qi*). Certain establishments were notorious places of rendezvous for prostitutes and their clients. In recent years, many of these older tea-houses have been demolished or relocated in the course of modernization, but, after a little hunting, it is still possible to find a few of the old-style businesses, with their bamboo and copper, their masseurs and ear cleaners, and even, on occasion, a Sichuanese opera group.

According to Chinese legend, the Divine Farmer, Shen Nong, discovered the use of tea as a drink some five millennia ago, when tea leaves drifted into a pot of water he was boiling in the open air. Shen Nong is said to have enjoyed the taste and fragrance of this infusion and to have found that it had medicinal benefits. The historical origins of tea drinking are rather unclear, although many scholars believe that the wild tea plant may first have been domesticated in today's Sichuan region. One fourth-century text, Chang Qu's Treatise on the Kingdom of Huayang, mentions that tea was given in tribute to King Wen, the twelfth-century-B.C. founder of the Zhou Dynasty, by tribal heads in the region. The same text also describes the cultivation of tea in several parts of today's Sichuan, suggesting that by the time it was written, tea farming had already become common.

These days, Sichuan is one of the centers of Chinese tea production. The most famous local varieties are all green teas, and they include meng ding sweet dew tea (*meng ding gan lu*) from Mingshan county, mao feng tea from Ya'an county (*mao feng cha*), green bamboo leaf tea (*zhu ye qing*) from Emei Mountain, and snow shoot tea from Qing Cheng Mountain (*qing cheng xue ya*). The Sichuanese themselves have a particular penchant for jasmine blossom teas, which are thought to be the most refreshing and best suited to the sultry local climate. They are made by heating green tea with fresh jasmine flowers from the eastern Sichuan hills until their fragrance infuses all the leaves. Sichuanese jasmine blossom tea (known colloquially as "flower tea," *hua cha*) is far lovelier than the jasmine tea one usually finds outside China. It is wonderfully fragrant, with unfurling long, green leaves and drifting, tender blossoms.

The manner of serving tea in Sichuan also has a distinctive local flavor. The Sichuanese rarely use teapots, but brew their loose tea leaves in individual china bowls with lids and saucers (this is known as "lid-bowl tea," *gai wan cha*). The saucer catches spills and protects the drinker from the hotness of the cup; the bowl is the drinking vessel; and the lid is used to keep the tea hot and, with a gentle sweeping motion, to help the water circulate as the leaves infuse. Sichuanese tea drinkers also use the lid as a filter, fanning away any floating tea leaves as they raise the bowl to their lips. In teahouses, each new guest is given a tea bowl with a layer of dry tea leaves in the bottom. The hot water is added at the table, and the tea bowl covered as the liquid infuses. The first brewing can have a bitter taste (some connoisseurs even throw it away); the second brewing is thought to be the best. The water is topped up at regular intervals by the tea attendants with their copper kettles, some with the famous yard-long spouts that are handled with flamboyance and amazing dexterity. The same cup of tea can last as long as you want it to, although the flavor of the leaves obviously weakens with each refilling. In Sichuanese homes, tea is drunk in a similar manner, although the cups are refilled from a thermos flask rather than a kettle.

Chinese green tea has a fragrance and a clarity that is intensely pleasing. It is also thought to focus the mind, and Chinese monks have drunk it for centuries as an aid to meditation. There are many different ways of drinking tea, from the casual consumption of long-brewed infusions on trains and buses, to the eastern Chinese *gong fu cha*, with its special implements and soothing rituals. To my mind, however, sitting on a bamboo chair in a tranquil Sichuan teahouse, inhaling the scent of tea leaves and jasmine flowers, gazing at the reflection of trees on the surface of the amber liquid, is one of life's great pleasures.

VINEGAR (*cu*)

醋 Vinegar is not used as much in Sichuan as it is in north China, but it is still an essential flavoring. The finest Sichuanese variety is Baoning vinegar, made in Langzhong county from wheat bran and rice. It has a dark red-brown color and deep, mellow fragrance, with a slightly sweet aftertaste. This is the favored vinegar for use in hot dishes. Baoning vinegar is not currently available in the West, but Chinkiang vinegar is very similar in effect and makes an excellent substitute. Ordinary black Chinese vinegar can be used, although it is not as flavorful. Clear vinegar made from glutinous rice finds its way into cold dishes, especially where the darker varieties might detract from the appearance of the main ingredients. Chinese vinegars are much milder in taste than their Western counterparts. According to Chinese sources, the earliest grain vinegars in the world were made in China, and Chinese texts dating back to the middle of the first millennium B.C. refer to special vinegar-making workshops.

WHITE PEPPER (*hu jiao mian*)

Ground white pepper is used as a seasoning in many Sichuanese recipes, particularly in "white-flavored" (*bai wei*) dishes, which are pale in color and often simply seasoned with salt and pepper. It is also the spice that provides the hotness in Sichuan's famous "hot-and-sour" soups. Black pepper is rarely, if ever, used in Sichuanese cooking—its dark grains are considered unsightly.

COOKING A SICHUANESE MEAL

There are no hard-and-fast rules for deciding on the menu of a Sichuanese meal. The most important thing from the point of view of the guests is to have a variety of colors, tastes, and textures; and from the point of view of the cook to make the last-minute cooking as easy and as quick as possible. When you are planning a meal, it's best to think in terms of one dish for every person, with an extra dish or two if you have time or energy. Try to use a few different cooking methods: serving perhaps a slow-braised dish with a wok-cooked dish that involves a marinade and sauce, and a couple of simple stir-fried vegetables. Cold dishes can usually be prepared in advance and can be a delicious and intriguing part of the meal: they can also be put on the table when your guests arrive, to keep them happy while you cook the last couple of dishes. If you want to save time, you can always buy some ready-made cooked meats from a Chinese shop or restaurant—the kind you see hanging in the windows: these can be served cold or reheated in a microwave. And there's no reason why you can't supplement a Sichuanese dinner with a green salad or a few nibbles like nuts and olives—they may not be authentic but they are very much in the spirit of the Sichuanese tradition. If you want to be really Chinese about it, you should also serve a simple, stock-based soup at the end of the meal: perhaps the bean curd soup on page 337 or the fried egg and tomato soup described on page 306. And don't forget to offer your guests plenty of white rice—this can be boiled or steamed, but I find the best method is to use the infallible electric rice cooker. That way, the rice is always perfect, and you don't have to think about it as you prepare the other dishes.

Sichuanese dumplings can be eaten as snacks or as part of an informal lunch. Everyone I know loves Sichuanese boiled dumplings and wontons, and they are great fun to make with a group of friends. Make sure you stock up on plenty of wrappers and fresh filling ingredients: any leftovers can be frozen and used another time. Sichuanese cold dishes or Western-style salads make a refreshing accompaniment to a snacky dumpling meal.

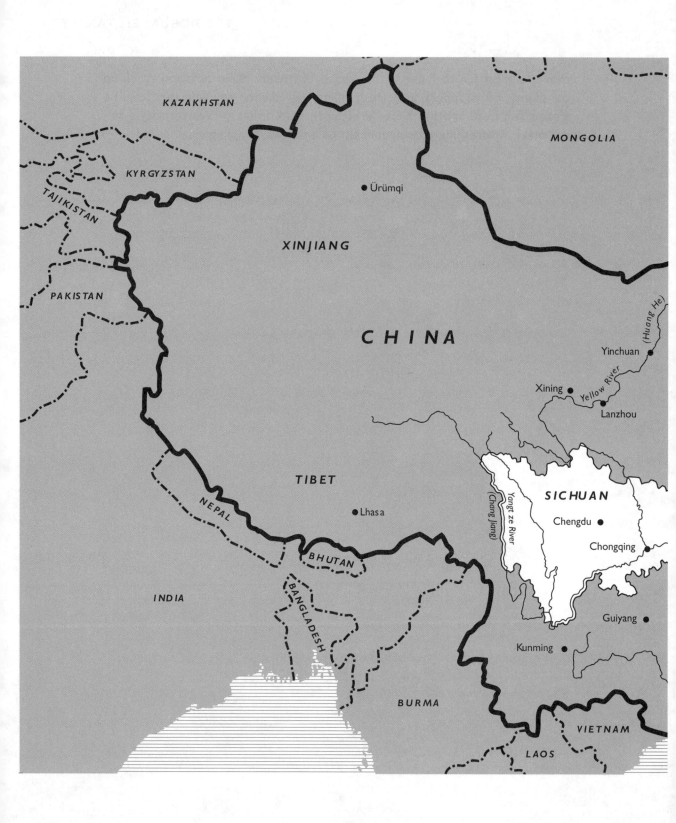

1

noodles, dumplings, and other street treats

IF YOU SIT DOWN IN ONE OF THE BUSY MARKET STREETS of old Chengdu, and close your eyes, you will gradually hear, in the midst of all the hubbub, the sounds of the itinerant street traders. The shoe cleaner passes first, knocking his wooden shoe brush against a wooden stool, beating out a gentle but insistent rhythm. Then there's the candy man, sounding his arrival with a metal clapper: *ding ding dang, ding ding dang*. Without even looking, you know that he'll be carrying a pair of woven baskets on a bamboo shoulder pole, each one filled with a pale chewy toffee that is called, unsurprisingly, ding ding candy (*ding ding tang*). Next, the sound of a man's voice calling "*Dou huar! Dou huar!*"—and you know it's the flower bean curd vendor with his red-and-black wooden barrels filled with warm curd and seasonings. And if there's a teahouse nearby, spilling its chairs and tables onto the street, you might even hear the metallic click of the ear cleaner's slender pincers as he makes his rounds, hawking for customers.

Chengdu has long been known for its bustling street life, and the city is still alive with the flower sellers and toy makers, the knife grinders and bamboo flute vendors, who gave it this vibrant reputation. Above all, however, the city is famed for its diverse and delicious street food. Chengdu boasts literally hundreds of specialized snacks, from spicy noodles to sweet dumplings and crunchy flatbreads; from steamed buns to bean curd and aromatic cold meats. Most of these tidbits, known in Chinese as *xiao chi* or "little eats," were originally made to order by street vendors who plied their trades all over the city: some of them are still sold this way. Elderly residents of Chengdu remember the early twentieth century as something of a golden era for this kind of eating; they describe how the street vendors lived or died by the quality of their food, so they were driven to create snacks of unparalleled flavor. Many sigh as they recall from their childhoods the scent of a favorite dumpling, drifting on the warm spring air. Many of today's most popular snacks date from the late imperial and early republican periods. Some of their creators have entered popular legend for the excellence of their craft, their names inextricably associated with the delicacies they invented. Many of the more successful vendors ended up opening restaurants, some of which have lasted several generations.

Some notable snacks are named after their creators, for example Zhong boiled dumplings, the specialty of a man named Zhong Xiesen, and Lai glutinous rice balls, made to perfection by one Lai Yuanxin. Others are named after their region of origin, like North Sichuan pea jelly (*chuan bei liang fen*) and Yibin "kindling" noodles. Still others take their names from the calls of their original vendors, like ding ding candy, dan dan noodles (*dan* means shoulder pole in Chinese), and the delicate steamed dumplings known as zheng zheng cakes (*zheng zheng gao*). Many of Sichuan's most famous snacks originated in Chengdu, but there are countless local specialties outside the provincial capital. Chongqing, Sichuan's hilly second city, is known for its tiny glutinous rice balls ("mountain city little rice balls," *shan cheng xiao tang yuan*), the village of Juntun for its spicy, crunchy flatbreads (*guo kuei*). Wherever you go in Sichuan you'll find unusual delicacies: at one recent lunch in Yibin in southern Sichuan I encountered several intriguing new dumplings wrapped in different fragrant leaves. There are also seasonal specialties, like the spring rolls that appear on the streets of Chengdu in the spring, and the cones of glutinous rice wrapped in bamboo leaves (*zong zi*) that are eaten around the Dragon Boat Festival on the fifth day of the fifth lunar month.

Like most aspects of Chinese culture, Sichuanese street food has been shaken up by the turbulent political events of the last century. During the Cultural Revolution, the individual economy was branded as capitalist, and individual traders were driven off the streets. Private restaurants were collectivized (although they often kept the names of their original owners), and street snacks were recycled on set menus in a new generation of impersonal, state-owned restaurants. The incentive for achieving excellence disappeared, and Sichuanese street food seems to have gone through a period of stagnation and even decline. Since the Communist Party began its economic reforms in the late 1970s, however, there has been something of a renaissance. The street vendors have reappeared with a new generation of snacks, including old favorites like flower bean curd as well as new varieties like Xinjiang potatoes and Shanghai fried chicken. Private restaurants are bringing the traditional snacks upmarket and putting pressure on the older state-owned restaurants. Foreign fast-food outlets are also beginning to invade Chengdu, with some interesting consequences. Many of the older Sichuanese snack restaurants and noodle shops are reinventing themselves as modern fast-food restaurants, with American-style backlit menus hanging over their service counters, and slick, clean dining rooms. These makeovers are clearly enabling them to compete with the foreign chain restaurants, but their food is as Sichuanese as ever.

Several specialized *xiao chi* restaurants, such as Long Chao Shou in central Chengdu, still offer sets of Sichuan's most celebrated snacks. Each person is given ten or twenty tiny individual dishes, each bearing a street-sized portion of a different delicacy. A couple of Zhong dumplings drizzled in a scrumptious spicy sauce; a dish of smoked duck; two glutinous rice balls stuffed with black sesame seeds and sugar; a steamed dumpling filled with meat and pumpkin; one pot-sticker dumpling with a toasty, golden bottom; some cold pea jelly in a hot bean sauce; a single, fragile rippled-silk fried dumpling. . . . By the time the waiters have finished dispensing their goodies, every inch of the table is covered with the sumptuous array.

A number of dishes that began as street snacks have become well established as banquet appetizers: these you will find in the next chapter, Appetizers. A few of the most famous Sichuanese snacks require special equipment or technical skills. I have not attempted to give recipes for these, but have included brief descriptions of the most interesting at the end of the chapter. The following recipes can all be made at home with a minimum of fuss.

NOODLE DISHES

TRADITIONAL DAN DAN NOODLES
dan dan mian

担
担
面

Dan dan noodles are the most famous Sichuanese street snack and have become known as the epitome of Chengdu's street food culture. They were originally sold by men who wandered the alleys of the city, carrying their stoves, noodles, and secret-recipe sauces in baskets hanging from a bamboo shoulder pole (known as *dan* in Chinese). Older people in Chengdu can remember the days when these vendors were a common sight and their calls of "*dan dan mian! dan dan mian!*" rang out in every quarter of the city. The noodles were served in small portions in tiny bowls, just enough to ease the hunger of scholars working late or mahjong players gambling into the night. They were inexpensive and nourishing and enjoyed by everyone from day laborers to the very rich, whose servants were sent to the gateways of the old courtyard houses to flag down passing noodle vendors. The name dan dan noodles didn't originally refer to a particular style of noodles, but is now firmly associated with the following recipe, which makes use of the famous Sichuanese pickled vegetable *ya cai* and an assortment of spices. Dan dan noodles have now all but disappeared from the streets of Chengdu, but the dish lives on in countless noodle shops and restaurants.

To serve the noodles Sichuanese-style, divide all the sauce ingredients into individual bowls, top each with a portion of noodles, and scatter with a little cooked meat. Otherwise, just present the noodles in one large bowl and serve them at the table.

Serves 4 as a starter or a snack, 2 for a hearty lunch

12 ounces fresh Chinese
noodles or 8 ounces dried
Chinese noodles

FOR THE SAUCE

1 tablespoon melted lard or
peanut oil

4 tablespoons Sichuanese *ya
cai* or Tianjin preserved
vegetable

3 scallions, green parts only

1 1/2 tablespoons light soy
sauce

1/2 tablespoon dark soy sauce

2–3 tablespoons chili oil to
taste

1 1/2 teaspoons Chinkiang or
black Chinese vinegar

1/2–1 teaspoon ground
roasted Sichuan pepper
(see page 74)

FOR THE PORK TOPPING

a little peanut oil

4 ounces ground pork

1 teaspoon Shaoxing rice
wine or medium-dry sherry

2 teaspoons light soy sauce

salt to taste

1   Heat 1 tablespoon of peanut oil in a wok over a high flame. Add the *ya cai* or Tianjin preserved vegetable and stir-fry for about 30 seconds, until it is fragrant. Set aside. Add another tablespoon of oil to the wok and reheat, then add the ground pork and stir-fry. As the meat separates, splash in the wine. Add the soy sauce and salt to taste, and continue to stir-fry until the meat is well cooked, but not too dry. Remove from the wok and set aside. Finely slice the scallions.

2   Put the fried vegetable and all the other sauce ingredients into a serving bowl and mix together.

3   Cook the noodles according to the instructions on the package. Then drain them and add them to the sauce in the serving bowl. Sprinkle with the meat mixture and serve immediately.

4   When the bowl is on the table, give the noodles a good stir until the sauce and meat are evenly distributed.

XIE LAOBAN'S DAN DAN NOODLES

niu rou dan dan mian

The grandfather of a friend of mine was a chef, and he came to Chengdu before the war, eager to discover the secrets of Sichuanese cooking. When he arrived he made his way to a famous restaurant that served an extraordinarily delicious fried beef. He begged the chef to teach him the recipe but was rudely turned away. Undeterred in his quest, he crept back to the restaurant after closing time and stole the bundles of rubbish lying outside. Inside the bundles he found half-eaten remains of the fabled dish, from which he was able to deduce the ingredients and cooking method and make a tasty imitation.

The following recipe is my own recreation of a legendary and unique version of dan dan noodles served in a tiny restaurant near Sichuan University. It is the fruit of repeated visits to the restaurant over a number of years, during which I begged and cajoled the unsmiling proprietor Mr. Xie for his culinary secrets. On one occasion he told me the ingredients of the delicious meaty topping; other times he let me watch as his cooks prepared the seasonings in the noodle bowls. He may have withheld a detail or two, but the following recipe has met with the wholehearted approval of several of the restaurant's most devoted and regular customers.

These noodles are not for the fainthearted—they are shamelessly spicy, but utterly delicious to those who know them well. They are generally served in individual bowls, each containing a smattering of sauce ingredients, a small portion of noodles, and a teaspoon or two of ground meat. I have, however, given instructions for one large bowlful.

In Chengdu the dish is made with fresh flour-and-water noodles, delivered every day in a pile of flour-dusted bamboo baskets. Here, simple flour-and-water noodles are only available dried, but you could use fresh egg noodles if you prefer.

Serves 4 as a starter or a snack, 2 for a hearty lunch

1 pound of fresh Chinese
noodles or 12 ounces dried
Chinese noodles

FOR THE MEAT TOPPING

1 tablespoon peanut oil

3 Sichuanese dried chiles,
snipped in half, seeds
discarded

1/2 teaspoon whole Sichuan
pepper

2 tablespoons Sichuanese *ya
cai* or Tianjin preserved
vegetable

4 ounces ground beef

2 teaspoons light soy sauce

salt to taste

FOR THE SAUCE

1/2–1 teaspoon ground
roasted Sichuan pepper
(see page 74)

1/4 teaspoon salt

4 teaspoons sesame paste

1 tablespoon light soy sauce

1 tablespoon dark soy sauce

2 tablespoons chili oil with
chile flakes (see page 55)

1 Heat 1 tablespoon of peanut oil in a wok over a moderate flame. When the oil is hot but not yet smoking, add the chiles and Sichuan pepper and stir-fry briefly until the oil is spicy and fragrant. Take care not to burn the spices. Add the *ya cai* or preserved vegetable and continue to stir-fry until hot and fragrant. Add the meat, splash in the soy sauce, and stir-fry until the meat is brown and a little crispy, but not too dry. Season with salt to taste. When the meat is cooked, remove the mixture from the wok and set aside.

2 Put the sauce ingredients into a serving bowl and mix together.

3 Cook the noodles according to the instructions on the package. Drain them and add them to the sauce in the serving bowl. Sprinkle with the meat mixture and serve immediately.

4 When the bowl is on the table, give the noodles a good stir until the sauce and meat are evenly distributed.

YIBIN "KINDLING" NOODLES

yi bin ran mian

 This noodle dish is one of the more famous culinary exports of the southern city of Yibin. Its Chinese name is hard to translate, but *ran* literally means to ignite or kindle a flame. Some say the dish is so called because the noodles, in their dry, oil-based sauce, resemble the rush wicks used in old-fashioned oil lamps; others that it's because the noodles are sometimes finished off with a drizzling of smoking-hot oil, which makes them crackle like a kindling fire. The dish is easy to make and robustly tasty—a fine vegetarian lunch.

Serves 4 as a starter or a snack, 2 for a hearty lunch

4 ounces pea shoots or baby spinach leaves

2–3 tablespoons lard or peanut oil

10 ounces dried Chinese noodles

FOR THE TOPPING

2 tablespoons walnut meats

2 tablespoons unsalted peanuts

2 tablespoons sesame seeds

1 tablespoon peanut oil

4 tablespoons Sichuanese *ya cai* or Tianjin preserved vegetable

3 scallions, green parts only

FOR THE SAUCE

3 tablespoons chili oil

2 teaspoons sesame oil

4 teaspoons dark soy sauce

4 teaspoons light soy sauce

1 Heat the oven to 250°F. When it is hot, place the walnuts and peanuts on a baking sheet and roast them for 20 minutes until they are crisp and fragrant. Turn them onto a cutting board and chop them into tiny pieces "like rice grains." Toast the sesame seeds for 3–4 minutes in a dry wok over a gentle flame until they are fragrant and delicious. Set aside.

2 Heat 1 tablespoon of peanut oil in a wok over a high flame. Add the preserved vegetable and stir-fry for about half a minute, until it is fragrant. Set aside.

3 Finely slice the scallions. Combine the sauce ingredients in a small bowl.

4 Blanch the green vegetable leaves briefly in boiling water and refresh them immediately under the cold tap. Drain well and divide up among 4 individual serving bowls. Add 1–1 1/2 teaspoons of peanut oil or lard to each bowl.

5 Cook the noodles according to the instructions on the package. Drain them well and divide them among the serving bowls. Drizzle each bowl with a quarter of the sauce mixture, and top each one with a spoonful of chopped nuts, a spoonful of sesame seeds, a spoonful of preserved vegetable, and a spoonful of scallion slices. These toppings are traditionally added in separate piles, so the dark vegetable, pale nuts and seeds, and green scallions create an attractive checkerboard effect. Serve immediately, and let your guests mix everything together at the table.

SPICY NOODLES WITH SOFT BEAN CURD
dou hua mian

About half a century ago, a man named Tan Yuxian ran a makeshift snack stall near the Temple of Peace and Happiness in Chengdu. He became famous for his way of serving tender flower bean curd, drizzled with fragrant oils and scattered with crunchy bits of nuts and pickles. The following dish was one of Mr. Tan's specialties, and it is still served in a small Chengdu noodle shop that bears his name and is run by his children and grandchildren. With its generous topping of bean curd, the snack makes a filling and nutritious vegetarian lunch. I've given instructions for making one large bowlful of noodles, but it's traditionally served in individual bowls. Divide everything into 4 portions and let your guests mix their own dishes together if you wish. This dish is usually made with flat, tagliatelle-type noodles, known in Chinese as "chive-leaf noodles" (*jiu cai ye mian tiao*).

Serves 4 as a starter or a snack, 2 for a hearty lunch

1 pound soft bean curd or flower bean curd (see page 126)	**2 tablespoons dark soy sauce** **2 teaspoons sesame oil**
10 ounces dried Chinese flat noodles	**FOR THE SCATTERING**
	1/4 cup Sichuanese preserved vegetable
FOR THE SAUCE	**3 scallions, green parts only**
3 tablespoons sesame paste	**1/4 cup deep-fried or roasted unsalted peanuts**
3 tablespoons chili oil	
2 tablespoons light soy sauce	

1 Set the bean curd to simmer very gently in a pot of lightly salted water.

2 Rinse the Sichuanese preserved vegetable and chop it finely. Finely slice the scallions. Combine all the sauce ingredients in a large serving bowl.

3 Cook the noodles according to the instructions on the package. Then drain them well and place them in the serving bowl. Drain the bean curd and place it on top. Scatter with the peanuts, preserved vegetable, and scallions. Serve immediately.

MR. XIE'S SEA-FLAVOR NOODLES

hai wei mian

Because Sichuan is an inland province ringed by mountains and cut off from the plains and oceans to the east, fresh seafood has historically been absent from the local diet. Dried seafood, however, was traditionally brought to the region by traders from the coast, who exchanged it for local goods like medicinal plants and other forest exotica. Expensive delicacies like dried abalone have long been part of Sichuanese *haute cuisine*, and they feature in the earliest regional cookbook, the eighteenth-century *xing yuan lu* by Li Huanan. But while eating exotic dried seafood is still the privilege of the wealthy, other fruits of the sea like dried shrimp and mussels do find their way into a few everyday dishes. The following noodle dish is called sea-flavor noodles because it includes a small amount of dried seafood, usually shrimp and mussels, in addition to the more ordinary pork and mushrooms. It's a well-established Chengdu snack, but this recipe is based on the peculiarly delicious seafood noodles served by Mr. Xie in his noodle shop near Sichuan University.

Serves 2–4, depending on appetite

1 ounce dried Chinese mushrooms
1 ounce dried shrimp
1/2 pound boneless pork loin, with some fat
1/4 pound fresh button mushrooms
6 ounces bamboo shoots
3 tablespoons lard, chicken fat, or peanut oil

2 tablespoons Shaoxing rice wine or medium-dry sherry
about 1 1/4 quarts everyday stock (see page 318) or chicken stock
salt and pepper to taste
12 ounces Chinese dried noodles

1 Soak the dried mushrooms and shrimp for 30 minutes in enough hot water to cover them generously.

2 Cut the pork into slices about 1/8 inch thick. Slice the fresh mushrooms and bamboo shoots to match the pork. Blanch the bamboo shoot slices in boiling water to refresh them.

3 When the dried mushrooms are soft, slice them too, reserving the soaking water.

4 Heat the fat or oil in a wok or saucepan over a high flame. When the oil is hot, add the pork and stir-fry until it whitens. Splash the Shaoxing rice wine around the edges and let it sizzle. Add the fresh mushrooms and bamboo shoots and stir-fry for another 20–30 seconds until the mushrooms are just cooked. Add the shrimp, dried mushrooms, soaking water, and stock. Bring to a boil, season with salt to taste, and leave to simmer over a low flame for about an hour, until the pork is very tender.

5 When the meat stew is nearly ready, season it with salt and pepper to taste. Fill a separate saucepan with water and bring it to a boil—this will be for cooking the noodles.

6 When the water is boiling, add the noodles. Cook them for a few minutes until they are just done, then drain them in a colander. Divide the noodles into four bowls, spoon over each a shade of the meat mixture, and then fill up with the soupy stock.

SPICY COLD NOODLES WITH CHICKEN SLIVERS

ji si liang mian

This is an extremely easy, delicious dish that is distinctively Sichuanese. Cold, moist noodles are served with blanched bean sprouts and cooked chicken meat in a sauce that incorporates many different flavors. Sichuanese cooks generally use noodles made with wheat flour and water, but egg noodles can be used as a substitute. You can either serve these noodles in a large bowl or street-style in 4 small, individual bowls.

Serves 4 as a snack, 2–3 as a main lunch dish

about 1/2 pound fresh
Chinese noodles, Shanghai-
style, a little thicker than
spaghetti
1 1/2 tablespoons peanut or
salad oil
3 ounces bean sprouts
1 small cooked chicken breast
or some leftover chicken
meat
4 scallions, white and green
parts, thinly sliced
SEASONINGS
2 tablespoons sesame paste,
thinned with 1 tablespoon
water

1 1/2 tablespoons dark soy
sauce
1/2 tablespoon light soy sauce
1 1/2 tablespoons Chinkiang
or black Chinese vinegar
1 tablespoon white sugar
2–3 cloves of garlic, crushed
1/2 teaspoon ground roasted
Sichuan pepper (see page
74)
2–3 tablespoons chili oil with
chile flakes (see page 55)
1 tablespoon sesame oil

1 Cook the noodles in plenty of boiling water until they are just *al dente*—take care not to overcook them. Rinse them with hot water from the kettle, shake them in a colander and quickly spread them out to dry. Sprinkle over the peanut oil and mix it in with chopsticks to prevent the noodles from sticking together.

2 Blanch the bean sprouts for a few seconds in boiling water, then refresh in cold water. Drain them well. Squash the chicken breast slightly or whack it with a rolling pin to loosen the fibers, and tear or cut it into slivers about 1/4 inch thick.

3 When the noodles and bean sprouts are completely cold, lay the bean sprouts in the bottom of your serving bowl or bowls. Add the noodles.

4 To serve, either combine all the seasonings in a bowl and pour the mixture over the noodles, or just scatter them over one by one. Top the dish with a small pile of chicken slivers and a scattering of scallions. Allow your guests to toss everything together at the table.

VARIATIONS

Vegetarians can omit the chicken and enjoy the nutty sauce.

A scattering of toasted sesame seeds is a nice addition.

DUMPLINGS

MR. LAI'S GLUTINOUS RICE BALLS WITH SESAME STUFFING

lai tang yuan

In 1894, a young man named Lai Yuanxin traveled from his native town to Chengdu, where he took up a place as an apprentice in a restaurant. Sadly, it wasn't long before he fell out with his boss and lost his job. Stuck with no means to support himself, he borrowed money from a cousin, bought a bamboo shoulder pole and a few cooking utensils, and started selling glutinous rice dumplings on the streets. After making a living this way for many years, he was able to open a shop on Zongfu Street in the center of Chengdu. Mr. Lai's unusually good *tang yuan* are now celebrated all over China. The descendant of his original dumpling shop, which now serves a whole selection of Sichuanese snacks, has so far survived nationalization under the communists and ruthless competition with a new generation of restaurants (including Kentucky Fried Chicken, which has opened a branch on the floor directly above).

Tang yuan are a traditional snack all over China and are eaten in great quantities as part of the Lunar New Year festivities. Like many festive foods, their name is treated as a luck-giving pun, in this case because it sounds like *tuan yuan*, which means "reunion"—a fitting symbol for the annual family get-together. In rural Sichuan, many households still make their dumplings according to the time-honored traditional method, which involves soaking glutinous and long-grained rices for several days (changing the water at regular intervals), then stone-grinding them to a paste and squeezing this in a piece of cheesecloth to make the dough. This "damp flour" is regarded as far superior to the dried flour used as a convenience in the cities.

97

Before the communists came to power and clamped down on "capitalist" street vendors, *tang yuan* sellers were a common sight in Chengdu. They carried their stoves, ingredients, and serving bowls around the city on bamboo shoulder poles and set up flickering oil lamps to light their work as the nights drew in.

Makes 30–40 glutinous rice balls, enough for about 6

FOR THE STUFFING
2 tablespoons black sesame seeds
2 tablespoons superfine sugar
2 tablespoons fresh pork lard or coconut oil

FOR THE PASTE
1 1/2 cups glutinous rice flour

3 tablespoons ordinary white rice flour
1 cup tepid water

FOR THE DIP
4 tablespoons sesame paste
4 teaspoons superfine sugar
sesame oil

THE STUFFING

Note that the stuffing is much easier to handle if it is made a few hours in advance (in Sichuan it is usually made in large batches and used as needed—it will keep in a refrigerator for months). Black sesame seeds are commonly available in Chinese supermarkets.

1 Toast the sesame seeds in a dry wok or frying pan over a gentle flame for 5–10 minutes, stirring constantly, until they smell and taste delicious. Because they are black, you won't notice a change in color, so do take care not to burn them—they will taste bitter if overdone. Trust your nose and tongue to tell you when they're ready—the roasted aroma and taste are unmistakable.

2 When the seeds are done, use a mortar and pestle to grind them coarsely (this can be done in a food processor, but take care not to reduce the seeds to a powder—they taste better with a little crunch). Add the sugar to the crushed seeds and mix well.

3 Heat the lard or coconut oil over a gentle flame until melted, and then stir

into the seed mixture. Press the stuffing firmly into a baking sheet making a layer about 3/4 inch thick, and refrigerate until set. When you are ready to stuff the *tang yuan*, use a table knife to cut the stuffing into 3/4-inch cubes.

MAKING THE *tang yuan*

1 Mix the two flours together. Add the water and stir to make a soft, squishy dough (you can add a little more glutinous rice flour or water if you need to adjust the consistency).

2 Divide the dough into 2 or 3 parts. Working on a surface dusted with rice flour or glutinous rice flour, roll each part into a sausage about 1 1/2 inches thick and break off pieces the size of small walnuts.

3 Take one piece of dough, flatten it slightly and use your thumb to make an indentation in its center. Place a cube of stuffing in this indentation and then draw the sides of the dough up around it to enclose it completely. Roll it gently between your palms to make a round ball. (Make sure there is no stuffing peeking out or the dumpling will disintegrate when you cook it.) Lay the finished *tang yuan* on a tray or bamboo platter dusted with flour until you are ready to cook them (they can be made in advance and frozen or refrigerated).

MAKING THE DIP

Combine the sesame paste and sugar in a tiny serving bowl, adding enough toasted sesame oil or oil from the sesame paste jar to give a good dipping consistency if you like. (In snack restaurants each helping of 2–4 dumplings is served in a small rice bowl with an accompanying tiny saucer of sesame paste and sugar.)

COOKING THE *tang yuan*

1 Fill a large pot with water and bring it to a boil. Add the *tang yuan*, one at a time, and simmer them for about 15 minutes. Do not allow the water to bubble vigorously or it will rupture the dumplings—keep an eye on the pot and throw in half a coffee-cupful of cold water as necessary to calm the water down.

2 Serve the *tang yuan* in small bowls filled with some of the hot cooking water to keep them warm. Your guests should lift them out of the water with chopsticks and dip them in the sesame paste to eat.

VARIATIONS

Several *tang yuan* fillings are used in Sichuan, most based on a simple mixture of white sugar and lard. For rose-flavored stuffing, add to the sugar-lard base a small amount of candied rose petals; for tangerine stuffing, add finely minced candied tangerine and crushed rock sugar; for cherry stuffing use glacé cherries; for three-nut stuffing add walnuts, melon seeds, and peanuts that you have roasted and crushed to a coarse meal.

Mr. Lai used to make *tang yuan* stuffings out of sweet-scented osmanthus blossoms and jujube (Chinese date) paste, and then serve one of each of four different types of *tang yuan* in the same bowl (this is known as *si wei tang yuan*, four-flavor *tang yuan*). Four-flavor *tang yuan* can be given an extra flourish by molding each type of dumpling into a slightly different shape, so there are egg-shaped and pointed *tang yuan* as well as the ordinary round ones.

"ZHONG" CRESCENT DUMPLINGS

zhong shui jiao

Boiled crescent dumplings (*jiao zi*) is the traditional New Year dish in northern China. Whole families gather to knead the dough, roll out the circular skins, and wrap the dumplings, which are often made in such huge quantities that they cover every plate, tray, and flat surface in the kitchen and dining room. The dumplings are devoured piping hot, with dips of soy sauce, vinegar, and perhaps a little sesame or chili oil. The favorite northern filling for the dumplings is a mixture of ground pork and Chinese cabbage, but there are countless variations. Chinese Muslims, for example, make their *jiao zi* with lamb instead of pork, while country people in some areas of Gansu province make unusually large *jiao zi*, each about 4 inches long.

The Sichuanese have, with their customary ingenuity, developed their own distinctively Sichuanese way of preparing and serving *jiao zi*. The dumplings are wrapped small and dainty, with a very plain ground pork filling, and are served with a heavenly sauce of chili oil, aromatic soy sauce, and garlic.

According to scholars, Chinese people have been eating this type of dumpling for at least fourteen hundred years. The style was popular during the Tang Dynasty (618–907 A.D.), when it spread all over the region—apparently archaeologists found a wooden bowl filled with *jiao zi* in a Tang Dynasty tomb they excavated in remote Turpan! Zhong dumplings have a rather more recent history—legend has it that this Sichuanese variation was invented by a peddler named Zhong Xiesen in 1893. He later opened a shop in Lychee Lane (*li zhi gai*), the descendant of which is still trading in a side street not far from the Mao statue in central Chengdu.

If you want to be really traditional, you must serve each guest with about four tiny dumplings in a little bowl, with 1 or 2 teaspoons of dipping sauce. This has echoes of the origins of the dish as a street snack sold in tiny, inexpensive portions. But if you find these too much fuss, just make them as I've suggested below with larger dumpling skins (which you can make yourself or buy in Chinese supermarkets), and serve them in hearty bowlfuls with a generous slosh of the spicy sauce.

If you use store-bought dumpling wrappers, *jiao zi* are extremely quick and easy to prepare. Making your own wrappers takes a little more time and trouble, but it's great fun to enlist friends and family to help you make a collective dumpling lunch. If I'm having a dumpling party, I always find it worthwhile to buy more dumpling wrappers and fresh ground pork than I think I will possibly need—any excess can be frozen and used another time. And if you have any wrapped dumplings left over, they can be frozen raw and then boiled straight from the freezer for a quick and delicious snack.

Do remember that if any of your guests don't like eating chiles, they can dip their dumplings into a northern-style mixture of soy sauce and black vinegar.

Serves 4

60–80 circular flour-and-water dumpling wrappers (about four 7-ounce packages) (instructions for making your own dumpling wrappers are given after this recipe)

FOR THE FILLING

a 4-inch piece of fresh ginger, unpeeled

1 egg

1 tablespoon Shaoxing rice wine or medium-dry sherry

3/4 teaspoon salt

6–8 turns of a black pepper mill

1 pound ground pork

FOR THE DIP

3 tablespoons sweet, aromatic soy sauce (see page 76) or 3 tablespoons light soy sauce and 2 teaspoons sugar

1 1/2 tablespoons chili oil

1 teaspoon sesame oil

2 cloves garlic, crushed and mixed with 1–2 teaspoons cold water

1 Smash the ginger with the flat side of a cleaver blade or a heavy object and leave to soak for a few minutes in about 1 cup of cold water.

2 Mix the egg, wine, and salt and pepper into the pork, and then gradually add the ginger-water (discarding the crushed pieces), so it is absorbed by the meat to form a fragrant, floppy paste. Mix the dipping ingredients in a little bowl—always add the garlic at the last minute to make the most of its strong, fresh fragrance.

3 Place a dumpling skin flat on your hand and add a generous teaspoon of filling. Fold one side of the skin over the meat, make one or two tucks in it, and then press it tightly to meet the other side and make a little, half-moon-shaped dumpling. You can seal the dumpling with a series of little pinches if you wish. Make sure you pinch the skins together tightly so the filling can't ooze out. Lay the dumplings, separately, on a lightly floured tray, plate, or work surface.

4 Heat a generous pot of water to a vigorous boil over a high flame. Stir the water briskly, and place in a couple of handfuls of dumplings. Stir once to prevent them from sticking to the bottom of the pot. When the water has returned to a boil, throw in a coffee-cupful of cold water. Allow the water to

return to a boil again, and add another coffee-cupful of cold water. When the water has returned to a boil for the third time, the dumpling skins will be glossy and puckered and the meat should have cooked through—cut one dumpling in half to make sure. Remove from the pot with a slotted spoon, drain well, and serve steaming hot with the spicy, aromatic dip. (Take note: the cold water is added to prevent the water from boiling too vigorously and tearing the dumplings apart.) Continue cooking the dumplings in batches until your guests are incapable of eating any more.

TO MAKE YOUR OWN DUMPLING WRAPPERS

This recipe makes enough dough to wrap the stuffing in the recipe above.

I pound all-purpose flour
(about 2 1/2 cups)

3/4 teaspoon salt
about 2/3 pint cold water

I Put the flour and salt onto a pastry board, make a well in the center, and add enough cold water to make a stiff but pliable dough. Mix well, and knead for several minutes until the dough is smooth and elastic—the more thoroughly you knead, the better the dough. Cover with a damp kitchen towel and leave to rest for about 20 minutes.

2 Rolling out the dough: to make the traditional, tiny Sichuanese dumplings, roll the dough into long sausages about as thick as your thumb, and break off small pieces the size of cherries. Flatten these with the palm of your hand on a lightly floured surface, and roll with a rolling pin to form discs about 2 inches in diameter. Pile them up as you work, adding small sprinklings of flour as necessary to prevent them from sticking together. If you wish to save time and make the larger, northern-style dumplings, break off slightly larger pieces of dough and roll them into discs 2 1/2–3 inches in diameter. Remember that the tiny Sichuanese dumplings will take less time to cook through than the northern ones (you will probably need to add only one coffee-cupful of cold water before they are done).

"LONG" WONTON DUMPLINGS

long chao shou

龍
抄
手
Wontons are probably China's most ancient type of dumpling. According to Chinese scholars, they have been eaten in the Middle Kingdom since the Western Han Dynasty (206 B.C.–A.D. 24), which makes them even older than the northern-style *jiao zi*. By about the fifth century A.D., they were a common snack, and over the next couple of hundred years were reaching great levels of sophistication—one Tang Dynasty source mentions twenty-four styles with different forms and different fillings.

These days wonton dumplings are eaten all over China, prized for their wonderful silky, slippery "mouth-feel" (*kou gan*). They are called by different names in different regions: the Sichuanese dialect name is *chao shou*. Sichuanese *chao shou* are filled with a simple pork stuffing seasoned with ginger and sesame oil. The meat is extremely finely ground, almost to a purée—local chefs achieve this by pounding lean pork with the back of a cleaver blade. Because the back of the blade is blunt, the wispy white tendons are not broken but can be plucked out with the fingers, leaving unbelievably tender mince.

The recipe given below is for wontons in a savory stock (*long chao shou*), Sichuan's most famous wonton dish. They are the star attraction at the wonderful Long Chao Shou restaurant in central Chengdu, which was established in 1941. I have also offered several classic variations—the wontons in chili oil sauce is one of my personal favorites. If you happen to have a generous pot of stock and a few seasonings on hand, it is easy to serve several of these at one meal, to the inevitable delight of your guests.

If you are buying wonton wrappers, always make sure you select the thinnest available. Wontons wrapped in thicker skins are still tasty, but they lack the exquisite "mouth-feel" of finer versions, which ruffle up and cling to the ball of stuffing, their edges fluttering free like frilly goldfish tails. You can of course make your own wonton wrappers (instructions are given below), but making them sufficiently thin and strong is quite an art, and I don't recommend it for the casual cook. Wontons can be frozen raw and boiled directly from the freezer.

Serves 4–6, depending on greed

about 80 wonton wrappers (two to four 7-ounce packages, depending on thickness of wrappers)

FOR THE FILLING

a 4-inch piece of fresh ginger, unpeeled

1 pound finely ground pork

1 egg, beaten

2 teaspoons Shaoxing rice wine or medium-dry sherry

2 teaspoons sesame oil

3/4 teaspoon salt

6–8 turns of a black pepper mill

1/2 cup cold everyday stock (page 318) or chicken stock

TO SERVE IN SAVORY STOCK

2 1/2 cups piping hot everyday stock (see page 318) or chicken stock

1/4 cup fresh pork lard or peanut oil

freshly ground black pepper

salt

1 Crush the ginger with the flat side of a cleaver or a heavy object and leave it to soak for a few minutes in about 1/2 cup of cold water.

2 Place the ground pork in a bowl and add the beaten egg, wine, ginger-soaking water (pieces discarded), sesame oil, salt, and pepper. Mix well, using your hand to stir the stuffing briskly in one direction, then add the stock in several stages, making sure each batch has been fully absorbed by the meat before you continue.

3 There are several ways of stuffing the wontons. Here are three, starting with the easiest:

    i   Lay the wonton skin flat on your hand. Place a teaspoon of filling in the center, and then flip the skin in half diagonally, pressing the two sides lightly together. This is the speedy method used by the dumpling-makers at the Long Chao Shou restaurant, who wrap thousands of wontons every day.

    ii   Lay the wonton skin flat on your hand. Place slightly less than a teaspoon of filling in the center, and then bring the sides up to make a little gathered bag. Squeeze the neck gently to keep the bundle in place.

iii The third one is called "water caltrop shape" after the strange horned nuts enjoyed in eastern China.

4 Lay the wrapped wontons out, separately, on lightly floured plates, trays, or work surfaces.

5 Bring a generous pot of water to a boil over a high flame, and set the stock to simmer gently in another pot. When the water is boiling vigorously, place in each of 4 serving bowls the following seasonings: a 1/4 cup of piping hot stock, 1 1/2 teaspoons of lard or peanut oil, 5 turns of the pepper mill, and salt to taste.

6 To cook the dumplings, give the boiling water a good stir, drop in 10 dumplings, and stir once to prevent sticking. When the water has returned to a boil, throw in one coffee-cupful of cold water. Allow the water to return to a boil once more, and the dumplings should be cooked through (test one to make sure). Remove from the water with a slotted spoon, place in one of the prepared bowls, and serve. Repeat to fill the other bowls. When your guests are ready for more dumplings, just cook another few batches and top up their serving bowls, adding more salt and pepper if necessary.

VARIATIONS

Wontons in clear stock—*qing tang chao shou*: place in each serving bowl the following seasonings: 2 teaspoons Sichuanese *ya cai* or Tianjin preserved vegetable, 2 teaspoons finely sliced scallion greens, 1 teaspoon sesame oil, 1/2 teaspoon light soy sauce, 1/3 cup piping hot clear stock, 4 turns of the pepper mill, and salt to taste. The soup is light and refreshing, with an enticing flash of sourness from the preserved vegetables.

Wontons in chili oil sauce—*hong you chao shou*: place in each serving bowl the following seasonings: 2 teaspoons chili oil, with or without the chile flakes (see page 55); 2 teaspoons light soy sauce, 1 1/2 teaspoons white sugar; and 2 teaspoons stock. You can add a little crushed garlic, too, if you feel like it. This is a perfect winter dish, hot and spicy with a lingering sweet aftertaste.

Wontons in hot-and-sour soup—*suan la chao shou*: place in each serving bowl the following seasonings: 1/2 teaspoon of soy sauce, 1 1/2 teaspoons Chinkiang or black Chinese vinegar, 1/2 teaspoon lard or peanut oil, 1/2 teaspoon sesame oil, 2 teaspoons chopped scallion greens, 1/4 cup piping hot stock, lots of freshly ground black pepper or white pepper (10–20 turns of the pepper mill to taste), and salt to taste. This variation is considered to be a pleasant summer dish.

TO MAKE YOUR OWN WONTON WRAPPERS

1 Place 1 pound of all-purpose flour (about 2 1/2 cups) on a large pastry board and make a well in the center. Add one beaten egg and about 1 cup cold water. Mix the egg and water with your fingertips, then draw in the flour and mix to a stiff dough (you can add a little more flour or water if necessary to get the right consistency). Knead vigorously for several minutes, then cover with a damp kitchen towel and set aside for about 30 minutes.

2 Roll the dough out on a surface dusted with potato or all-purpose flour, until it is thin and slightly translucent. Cut the paste into strips about 2 1/2 inches wide (about the width of your four fingers), and then cut these into squares.

LEAF-WRAPPED GLUTINOUS RICE DUMPLINGS

ye'er ba

Sometimes you can still catch, fleetingly on a Chengdu street corner, a vendor of these glistening, greenish dumplings. He'll have a huge, round steamer balanced on the back of his tricycle, steaming away over a portable stove. The steamer will be packed with sausage-shaped dumplings, each half-wrapped in a piece of fragrant leaf, sold for a few *jiao* apiece. Some are sweet, stuffed with sesame seeds, candied fruits, or blossoms; some are filled with a salty mix of pork and pickled vegetables. They are eaten there and then, nibbled from the leaf, the moist filling oozing out from the succulent rice paste.

These days they are also served in specialized restaurants, at banquets of traditional snacks. Each guest is served with a pair of *ye'er ba* in a tiny dish, one sweet and one savory, the sweet one distinguished by a single spot of pink food coloring. The dumplings are traditionally made from a fresh paste of soaked rice grains milled with water; using flour is a modern convenience, but the results are still delectable. The dough is mixed with vegetable juices to stain it a pale green color, "like jade." Frozen banana leaves can be bought in Asian food shops. *Ye'er ba* can be frozen raw and steamed directly from the freezer.

Makes about 12 large or 20 little dumplings

1 package frozen banana leaves
peanut oil
optional: pink food coloring
FOR THE DOUGH
  optional: 1/4 cup packed
    spinach leaves
  1 cup glutinous rice flour
  1/2 cup white rice flour
  1 tablespoon melted lard or
    peanut oil
FOR THE SAVORY STUFFING
  2–3 tablespoons lard or
    peanut oil
  1/3 pound ground pork
  1 1/2 teaspoons Shaoxing rice
    wine or medium-dry sherry
  1/2 teaspoon light soy sauce
  1/2 teaspoon dark soy sauce

1/2 teaspoon salt
2 tablespoons Sichuanese *ya cai* or Tianjin preserved vegetable
2 scallions, white parts only
1/2 teaspoon sesame oil
a few turns of a black pepper mill
FOR THE SWEET STUFFING
4 tablespoons toasted sesame seeds or 2–3 ounces candied cherries or other candied fruits or flowers
1/2 cup white sugar
2 tablespoons all-purpose flour
4–5 tablespoons softened lard or peanut oil

1 *Make the savory stuffing:* Heat the lard or oil in a wok over a high flame. Add the pork and stir-fry. When the meat has separated, add the Shaoxing rice wine, soy sauces, and salt. Add the preserved vegetable and stir-fry for a few seconds more until it is fragrant and the meat is cooked through. Place everything into a bowl and stir in the scallions, sesame oil, and black pepper to taste.

2 *Make the sweet stuffing:* If you are using sesame seeds, crush them in a mortar and pestle to split the individual grains. If you are using candied fruits, chop them very finely. Combine the sugar and flour in a bowl. Add the lard and mix well. Finally, stir in the sesame seeds or candies.

3 *Blanch the leaves:* Blanch the banana leaves briefly in boiling water with a splash of oil. Cut the leaves into 4-inch squares if you want to make larger dumplings, 2 1/2-inch squares for dainty banquet snacks.

4 (Optional) *Make the spinach dye:* Put the spinach leaves into a food processor with 3 tablespoons of water and whizz to a bright green paste. Strain the paste through a sieve lined with a double layer of cheesecloth. Add 1/2 cup of water to the strained liquid.

5 *Make the dough:* Combine the two flours in a mixing bowl. Add the green spinach liquid and just enough extra water to make a fairly stiff but putty-like dough. (If you are not using spinach, just add enough water to make the dough.) Mix in the lard or oil.

6 *Make the dumplings:* Lightly oil the upper side of all the leafy squares. Break off small pieces of dough, 2–3 tablespoons for larger dumplings, 1 1/2 tablespoons for dainty snacks. Roll each piece into a ball and flatten it slightly in the palm of your hand, making a gentle indentation in the center with your other thumb. Place about a teaspoon of stuffing in the indentation and gently ease up the sides of the circle to close the dumpling. Gently roll the dumpling between your hands to make a short croquette shape. Place it on one of the oiled leaves, wrapping the leaf up the sides but leaving the top open, and place it in a steamer. Arrange all the dumplings in the steamer in neat, closely packed rows, keeping the sweet and savory ones separate. If you wish, put a spot of pink food coloring on each of the sweet dumplings.

7 *Cook the dumplings:* Steam the ye'er ba for 15 minutes over water kept at a good rolling boil. Serve them in their leaves and eat piping hot.

STEAMED PORK AND PUMPKIN DUMPLINGS

nan gua zheng jiao

The Sichuanese wrap these steamed dumplings in a pastry made by adding flour to a wokful of boiling water (*san sheng mian*). After cooking, it has a soft, glutinous texture that goes nicely with the salt-savory, succulent stuffing in this recipe. The stuffing is usually made with an orange-fleshed variety of pumpkin (*nan gua*), but zucchini works very well too. The raw dumplings can be frozen and steamed directly from the freezer.

Makes 25–30 dumplings

FOR THE PASTRY WRAPPERS
- 1 cup water
- 1 1/2 teaspoons lard or peanut oil
- 1 1/4 cups all-purpose flour

FOR THE STUFFING
- 1/3 pound pumpkin or zucchini flesh
- lard or peanut oil for frying
- 2 teaspoons finely chopped fresh ginger

- 1/2 pound ground pork
- 1 teaspoon light soy sauce
- 1 teaspoon dark soy sauce
- 1/2 teaspoon salt
- 6–8 turns of a black pepper mill or a few pinches of white pepper
- 4 teaspoons finely chopped scallion, white and green parts
- 1 teaspoon sesame oil

1 Peel and finely chop the pumpkin or zucchini. Blanch the pieces briefly in boiling water and drain them well.

2 Season the wok, then heat 3 tablespoons of lard or peanut oil over a high flame. Add the ginger and stir-fry for a few seconds until you can smell its fragrance. Add the pork and stir-fry for a minute or two until it has separated out. Then add the pumpkin or zucchini and stir-fry briefly. Allow to cool and then add the soy sauces, salt, pepper, scallion, and sesame oil. Mix well.

3 *Make the pastry:* Bring the water and 1 1/2 teaspoons of lard or peanut oil to a boil in a wok. When the water is boiling, gradually add in the flour, stirring. When everything is mixed together and piping hot, transfer it onto a work surface. As soon as it is cool enough to handle, knead to make a smooth dough. Working on a lightly floured surface, break the dough into about three pieces and roll these out into sausages about 1 inch thick. Break the sausages into walnut-sized pieces. Flatten each with the palm of your hand and then use a rolling pin to make round dumpling skins about 2 1/2 inches in diameter. (Unless you are working very quickly, it's a good idea to cover the remaining dough with a damp kitchen towel to prevent it from drying out.)

4 Place about a teaspoon of stuffing into the center of each dumpling skin. Fold the skin gently in half and, starting at one end, join the two sides together with a series of pinches. Place the finished dumpling on your work surface, pushing it slightly to give it a flat base. You should end up with a shape variously described as a crescent moon (*yue ya*) or a bean pod (*dou jia*).

5 Place the finished dumplings in a lightly oiled steamer, making sure they don't touch one another. When you are ready to eat them, steam them for about 6 minutes over a high flame until piping hot.

STEAMED PORK AND CABBAGE DUMPLINGS
xiao long zheng jiao

Four of these dumplings are usually served together in a small steamer (*xiao long*). Make the pastry and wrap the dumplings as described in the previous recipe, but substitute the following stuffing.

Makes 25–30 dumplings

1/4 pound tender leaves of
   Chinese cabbage or baby
   bok choy
3 tablespoons lard or peanut oil
1/2 pound ground pork
2 teaspoons Shaoxing rice
   wine or medium-dry sherry

1 teaspoon light soy sauce
1 teaspoon dark soy sauce
1/2 teaspoon salt
1 teaspoon sesame oil
6–8 turns of a black pepper
   mill or a few pinches of
   white pepper

1 Blanch the vegetable leaves briefly in boiling water, and then refresh immediately under a cold tap. Chop finely and squeeze to get rid of any excess water.

2 Season the wok, then heat 3 tablespoons of lard or oil over a high flame. Add the pork and stir-fry for a minute or two until it has separated out, adding the wine, soy sauces, and salt as you go. Tip the pork into a bowl, add the chopped leaves, sesame oil, and pepper, and mix well.

POT-STICKER DUMPLINGS
WITH CHICKEN STOCK
ji zhi guo tie

These dumplings are a Sichuanese version of a kind more usually associated with eastern China. They are made by a cooking method that part steams, part pan-fries them, so they end up moist and tender with golden, toasty bottoms. In Sichuan they are served with a bowl of simple chicken soup (*dun ji tang*). They also taste delicious with a dip of vinegar, soy sauce, and chili oil, mixed according to taste. In Sichuan, the dumplings are made with a hot water dough (*tang mian*) that gives them a slightly glutinous texture. You can also wrap them in store-bought round dumpling wrappers (which are made with cold-water dough) and cook them according to the following recipe. These wrappers will give you dumplings like the "pot-sticker" dumplings served in Chinese restaurants in the West.

Makes 25–30 dumplings

lard or peanut oil

FOR THE PASTRY

1 1/4 cups all-purpose flour

1/4 teaspoon salt

1/2 cup water

FOR THE STUFFING

a 1-inch piece of fresh ginger, unpeeled

1 scallion, white part only

1/3 pound ground pork

1/4 cup chicken stock (stock should not be hot)

1 1/2 teaspoons Shaoxing rice wine or medium-dry sherry

3/4 teaspoon salt

1/2 teaspoon white sugar

6–8 twists of a black pepper mill or a couple of pinches of white pepper

1 1/2 teaspoons sesame oil

1 Crush the ginger and scallion with the flat side of a cleaver blade or a heavy object and leave to soak for 5–10 minutes in 1/4 cup of cold water.

2 *Make the stuffing:* Place the pork in a bowl. Add the fragrant soaking water from the ginger and scallion, discarding the pieces, and mix well until it has been absorbed. Gradually pour in the chicken stock, mixing well to allow the pork to absorb it. You should end up with a loose, moist stuffing. Add all the seasonings and mix well.

3 *Make the pastry:* Combine the flour and salt in a large mixing bowl and make a well in the center. Bring the water to a boil, remove it from the heat to let it stop bubbling, and then pour it onto the flour. Mix in quickly with the handle of a wooden spoon. When the mixture is cool enough to handle, transfer it to a work surface and knead to a smooth dough.

4 *Make the wrappers:* Working on a lightly floured surface, break the dough into two or three pieces. Roll each one out into a sausage about 1 inch thick. Break off teaspoon-sized pieces and flatten them with the palm of your hand. Roll the flattened pieces into circles about 2 1/2 inches in diameter. (Unless you are working very quickly, it's a good idea to cover the remaining dough with a damp kitchen towel to prevent it from drying out.)

5 Place about a teaspoon of stuffing into the center of each dumpling skin. Fold the skin gently in half and, starting at one end, join the two sides

together with a series of pinches. Place the finished dumpling on your work surface, pushing it slightly to give it a flat base.

6 *Cook the dumplings:* Heat a heavy, flat-bottomed frying pan or skillet over a medium flame. Pour in enough lard or peanut oil to coat the surface generously. When the oil is hot, arrange all the dumplings in the pan in neat rows. Drizzle them with warm water—2–3 tablespoons for every 5 dumplings. Cover the pan with a lid and steam over a medium heat for 4–5 minutes. Then remove the lid to allow the steam to escape, drizzle the dumplings with a little oil (about 1/2 tablespoon for every 5 dumplings), replace the lid, and fry for 2–3 minutes more, until their bottoms are toasty and golden brown. As the dumplings cook, move the pan around the hot plate to brown them evenly. To serve, remove them with a spatula and turn them upside down onto a serving plate, so you can see their golden bottoms. Serve immediately.

"GLASSY" STEAMED DUMPLINGS
bo li shao mai

The day our pastry teacher offered us samples of these dumplings at the Sichuan cooking school, there was a near-riot as all the students pounced. The dumplings are shaped like old-fashioned moneybags with gathered necks, stuffing peeping out enticingly from their tops. The oil or fat in the stuffing mixture makes them moist and delicious: it also seeps into their skins, making them semi-translucent, which is why they are called "glassy" dumplings.

Shao mai dumplings are found all over China: the best-known version is the Cantonese *siu mai*, which are tightly packed with pork and traditionally topped with a little bright orange crab coral. In Sichuan, "glassy" *shao mai* are the most common, but you can also find sweet *shao mai* filled with glutinous rice, nuts, and candied fruits, and banquet *shao mai* with green pasta skins and a scattering of pink chopped ham.

Sichuanese cooks traditionally make "glassy" *shao mai* with a mixture of raw lean pork and cooked fatty pork, both finely chopped. In the following recipe, I have used a slightly different method that is equally delicious but requires only the slightly streaky ground pork that is easily available in butcher shops and supermarkets. At the suggestion of head chef Fan Shixian at the Long Chao Shou restaurant, I have added a little extra vegetable oil to provide the slick "mouth-feel" that is an essential part of this dish. In the unlikely event that you have any of the uncooked dumplings left over, they can be frozen and steamed directly from the freezer.

Makes 30–40 dumplings

FOR THE WRAPPERS
1 1/4 cups all-purpose flour
about 1/2 cup cold water (or
    just use about 40 store-
    bought round dumpling
    wrappers made from flour-
    and-water, about 2 1/2
    inches in diameter)
potato flour or cornstarch for
    dusting the work surface

FOR THE STUFFING
8 ounces tender leaves of
    baby bok choy or another
    leafy green vegetable such
    as baby spinach or Swiss
    chard
14 ounces ground pork
2 tablespoons Shaoxing rice
    wine or medium-dry sherry
salt and pepper
1/2 cup peanut oil
2 teaspoons sesame oil

1 *To make the stuffing:* Blanch the vegetable leaves briefly in hot water, and immediately refresh under the cold tap. Drain well, squeeze out excess water, and then chop finely.

2 Place about a quarter of the pork in a bowl and add 1 tablespoon of wine, 1 1/2 teaspoons of salt, and several turns of the pepper mill. Mix well and set aside.

3 Season the wok, then add the peanut oil and heat over a high flame. Add the remaining ground pork and stir-fry until it has separated out and is just cooked, splashing in 1 tablespoon wine and 1/2 teaspoon salt as you go. When the pork is done, add it to the raw pork with the peanut and sesame oils. Add the chopped leaves and mix everything together with a pair of chopsticks.

4 *To make the dough:* Put the flour into a mixing bowl and make a well in the center. Add just enough cold water to make a fairly stiff dough. Transfer the dough to a lightly floured work surface and knead vigorously for about 10 minutes, until it is smooth and elastic. Cover with a damp kitchen towel and let rest for 30 minutes.

5 *To make the wrappers:* Dust the work surface with potato flour or cornstarch. Break the dough into 3 or 4 pieces and roll each one into a sausage about 1 inch thick. Break or cut each sausage into 1-inch pieces. Flatten each piece with the palm of your hand and roll out into a circle about 2 1/2 inches in diameter. Pile up the circles with a dusting of potato flour or cornstarch between each layer.

6 Take a pile of about 10 circles and put it at the edge of the work surface. Use the handle of a wooden spoon to whack the edges of each pile, turning the pile so you can whack all the way round a couple of times. This process makes the outer part of each circle thinner than the center and gives the circle a slightly frilly appearance "like a lotus leaf." When you have finished, the circles should be 3 1/2–4 inches in diameter. (If you are using store-bought dumpling skins, you can whack them in the same manner to make them larger and their edges thinner.)

7 *To wrap the dumplings:* Place a dumpling wrapper in the palm of one hand. Place a generous teaspoon of filling in the center and use the fingers of the other hand to draw the edges up into a little bundle. Gently squeeze the neck of the bundle and then push its base onto the work surface so that it stands up straight. The filling should peep out of the top. (The Sichuanese call this shape "white cabbage shape" because the frilly tops and firm bases are reminiscent of Chinese leaf cabbages.) Place as many dumplings as will fit comfortably into a lightly oiled steamer tray.

8 *To steam the dumplings:* Steam the dumplings over a high flame for 3 minutes, then remove the lid and sprinkle them with a little cold water, taking care to wash away any remnants of the dusting flour. Replace the lid and steam for another 3 minutes. Serve piping hot.

"THREE CANNONSHOTS"
san da pao

One cool spring morning I went with some friends to the hills of Long Chuan Yi, just east of Chengdu, to celebrate the opening of the peach blossoms. This annual festival attracts crowds of visitors, and the whole area had been mobilized to cater for them. Makeshift teahouses and snack shops had been erected on the edges of the hilly orchards, artisans milled around selling traditional children's toys made from paper and bamboo. Down below in the town, a temporary food market sold Sichuanese snacks and other local produce. Although there wasn't a single peach blossom to be seen, anywhere, because of a recent run of cold weather, we did have a splendid day sampling various unusual snacks and dumplings, which I suppose was really the point in the first place. Many Chinese excursions appear, in the end, to be clever excuses for eating in unusual places and situations.

It was at Long Chuan Yi that I first encountered "three cannonshots," warm blobs of glutinous rice rolled in golden soybean flour and draped in a dark sugar syrup. They are traditionally made in flamboyant style by food craftsmen who pound the warm rice to a rough paste with wooden cudgels and then shape it into little balls. The individual balls are tossed with some force onto a wooden board, where they bounce into a potful of soybean flour. The flour-dusted balls are served in threes on little plates, with a generous drizzling of syrup. As you might guess, they get their name from the thudding sound that the rice balls make as they hit the wooden board.

Serves 4 for dessert

1/2 cup glutinous rice
2 tablespoons soybean flour

3 tablespoons dark brown sugar

1 Soak the rice overnight in plenty of water.

2 Dry-roast the soybean flour in a heavy-bottomed pan over a gentle heat until it is evenly cooked and a light golden brown, stirring constantly (this will take 4–5 minutes). Set aside.

3 Drain and then cook the rice: you can either steam it for 10–15 minutes in a steamer lined with a double layer of cheesecloth or boil it. To boil the rice, place it in a saucepan with an equal amount of water. Bring to a boil and simmer very gently until it is completely cooked.

4 Place the sugar in a small pan with about 1 tablespoon of water and melt over a gentle heat. Keep warm.

5 Pound the rice with a wooden spoon or fork to make a squishy paste, adding a little boiling water if necessary. You should aim for a consistency that allows you to shape the paste into balls—moist but not too runny. It isn't necessary to break up all the rice grains.

6 When the paste is just cool enough to handle, shape it into walnut-sized pieces and roll them in the prepared soybean flour. Place on a serving dish and serve, still warm, with a drizzling of syrup.

SWEET POTATO CAKES
hong shao bing

These sweet potato cakes are a delicious snack that has recently become a fashionable side order in some of Chengdu's pseudo-rustic restaurants. They are crunchy and golden outside, buttery and smooth within. You can eat them just as they come, or with a dip of white sugar or honey. Some people fill them or dress them up with a rose-petal sauce, which is used to distract from what is seen as the natural muddiness of the sweet potatoes. The sauce recipe below is my own adaptation: I've used honey and rose water instead of the sugar syrup and candied rose petals that most recipe books suggest. Sometimes these cakes are filled with lotus seed or red bean paste, flattened slightly, and then dipped in beaten egg and breadcrumbs before frying (these sweet pastes can be bought ready-made in Chinese supermarkets). Anyone who enjoys eating the caramel bananas served in Chinese restaurants in the West will love this snack in all its varieties.

Most recipes specify that you should use the type of sweet potatoes with yellow skins and orange flesh. It's typically Chinese to use what we in the West would consider strictly dessert flavorings with vegetables—they don't share our tendency to separate "sweet" and "savory" foods.

Makes about 25 small potato cakes

I large or 2 small sweet potatoes (about 1 1/2 pounds)
1/2 cup glutinous rice flour
optional: sugar

potato flour or cornstarch for dusting
oil for deep-frying

OPTIONAL ROSE PETAL SAUCE
4 tablespoons honey
1 teaspoon rose water

1 Peel the sweet potatoes and steam them over a high flame for about 30 minutes, until they are completely mushy. Leave them to cool.

2 Mash the potatoes with the glutinous rice flour. You can add a little sugar at this stage if you wish to make them sweeter.

3 Break off small plum-sized pieces of the potato paste and roll them into croquette shapes. Dust them with a little potato flour or cornstarch.

4 Heat the deep-frying oil to about 325°F. Add the potato cakes and fry, stirring gently, until golden brown—this will take about 8 minutes. Keep an eye on the oil temperature, which shouldn't shoot up too much above 325°F: the oil should just bubble gently around the potato cakes.

5 While the potato cakes are frying, gently heat the honey in a saucepan. Add the rose water and mix well. When the cakes are ready, drain them and serve immediately, drizzled with the rose water honey.

PEARLY RICE BALLS

zhen zhu yuan zi

These steamed dumplings take their name from the outer layer of whole glutinous rice grains that gives them a pearly appearance. They can be sweet or savory, but are most commonly stuffed with pastes made from fruits or nuts and sugar. Several of these pastes, such as red bean paste and lotus seed paste, can be bought canned in Chinese supermarkets.

Makes 20–25 rice balls

3/4 cup glutinous rice
2/3 cup red bean paste or
  lotus seed paste
1 1/4 cups glutinous rice flour
2 tablespoons ordinary white
  rice flour

1 cup tepid water
potato flour or cornstarch for
  dusting
a little peanut oil
15 candied or maraschino
  cherries

1 Leave the rice to soak overnight or for several hours in plenty of cold water.

2 Cut or break the stuffing paste into small, marble-sized pieces (canned stuffings can be cut into 1/2-inch slices and then into cubes).

3 When you are ready to make the dumplings, mix the flours together. Add the tepid water and stir to make a soft, squishy dough (you can add a little more glutinous rice flour or water if you need to adjust the consistency).

4 Divide the dough into 2 or 3 parts. Working on a surface dusted with potato flour or cornstarch, roll each part into a sausage about 1 inch thick. Then break off pieces of dough the size of small walnuts.

5 Take one piece of dough, flatten it slightly, and use your thumb to make an indentation in its center. Place a piece of stuffing in this indentation, and then draw the sides of the dough up around it to enclose it completely.

Roll it gently between your palms to make a round ball. (The method is the same as for Mr. Lai's glutinous rice balls on page 97.)

6 Drain the rice and scatter it onto a small plate. Roll each dough ball in the rice to give it a "pearly" coating, and arrange all the finished rice balls on a lightly oiled steamer tray. Make sure the balls are not too close together in the steamer—they will spread out slightly during the cooking.

7 When all the balls are ready, cut the glacé cherries in half and put them into the spaces among the dumplings. Steam at high heat for 20 minutes.

8 When the dumplings are ready, top each with a piece of cherry and serve immediately. (The cherries are steamed separately so they don't stain the white dumplings during the cooking.)

STEAMED BREADS

Wheat has traditionally been the staple food of the northern Chinese. In rural areas of the northern provinces, it still forms the bulk of almost every meal, whether in the form of noodles (*mian tiao*), steamed bread (*man tou*), or deep-fried twists of dough (*ma hua*). The southern Chinese, by contrast, exist mainly on rice, and wheat is seen very much as a supplementary staple. The Sichuanese may eat wheat noodles for lunch or nibble steamed bread with their breakfast of rice porridge, but most people find it hard to envisage a main meal without rice. Most Sichuanese people complain that wheat grown locally is of a poor quality because of the dampness of the Sichuan climate.

The most ordinary kind of steamed bread is known as *man tou*, and consists merely of buns of steamed dough. The term *man tou* has a fascinating history. According to one ancient text, it dates back to the time of the great statesman and strategist Zhu Ge Liang, who lived in the third century A.D. and is commemorated in the Wu Hou Temple in Chengdu. An ancient southern Chinese custom dictated that military chiefs should make sacrifices to the gods using the heads of the barbarians they encountered. The original *man tou* actually meant "barbarian head"—the character *man* was an ancient name for the southern barbarians (or the "minority nationalities of the south" as more politically correct modern sources put it). The story goes that Zhu Ge Liang ended this unsavory sacrificial practice by instructing his troops to use dough balls stuffed with meat as a substitute for human heads. As time went by, the term *man tou* entered the everyday Chinese vocabulary and the sacrificial bun became a daily staple, although the specific character *man* was eventually replaced by a more innocuous *man* with no such racist meaning. The character for head, *tou*, remains as a legacy of its gory history. These days, *man tou* tends to refer only to plain steamed buns; filled steamed buns are known as *bao zi*, which literally means "wrapped-up thing."

STEAMED FLOWER ROLLS

hua juan

When bread is served with Sichuanese meals, it often takes the form of "flower rolls," which are pieces of risen dough twisted into interesting shapes and then steamed. There are all kinds of ways of twisting them, some quite elaborate, and they can also be colored or flavored, perhaps with sugar and candied rose petals, or with chopped scallions and vegetable oil. The following recipe includes instructions for making a *hua juan* dough and for shaping two of the simpler forms. Sichuanese pastry chefs usually raise the dough by adding a bit of the previous day's batch: I have given instructions using dry yeast. If you wish to play around, you can knead sugar and lard into the dough after it has risen and sprinkle the rolled out dough with candied fruit or petals, or a mixture of vegetable oil and finely sliced scallions, or a mixture of salt and Sichuan pepper. Roll up the dough and cut it according to the instructions in the recipe.

Makes 20–25 pieces of bread

1 tablespoon sugar	**3 cups all-purpose flour**
1 tablespoon dried yeast	**a little lard or peanut oil**

1 Add the sugar and yeast to 1 cup of lukewarm water and leave in a warm place for about 15 minutes, until the liquid has grown a good head of froth.

Place the flour in a mixing bowl, make a well in the center, and pour in the yeast mixture. Mix well, adding about 1/4 cup more lukewarm water—enough to make a dough.

2 Turn the dough onto a lightly floured surface and knead vigorously for 5–10 minutes until it is smooth and elastic. Place in an oiled bowl, cover with a damp kitchen towel, and leave in a warm, draft-free place until it has doubled in size—1–2 hours, depending on temperature.

3 When the dough has doubled, punch it to knock it back to its original size and leave for another 15–30 minutes, until it has risen again.

4 Turn the risen dough onto a lightly floured work surface and knead for another few minutes.

5 There are countless ways of shaping the dough—the following two are very simple and attractive:

i Roll the dough out into a long strip about 8 inches wide and 1/4 inch thick. Use a pastry brush to oil the surface with melted lard or peanut oil. Lift the long side nearest to you and roll it away, rolling the dough up tightly like a jelly roll. Gently press the end into the roll to seal it, and then slice the roll into 1-inch sections. These can be laid spiral side up in the steamer; after cooking they will puff up into pretty spiral flowers. (If you want to be more elaborate, lay the spiral slices down on the work surface and use a pair of chopsticks to push two opposite sides of the circle together to make a figure-eight shape. Leave them like that, or push the other sides together in the same manner to make a four-petaled flower shape.)

ii Roll the dough out into a strip as described above, but roll it up from both sides so you get something like a double jelly roll. Roll this into a cylinder again, and then cut 1-inch sections to make double-spiral slices.

6 Brush a steamer tray lightly with oil. Lay the shaped pieces of dough on it, making sure there is plenty of space between them. Then steam over a high heat for 8–10 minutes, until they have puffed up. Serve hot or cold.

VARIATION

Lotus-leaf buns—*he ye bing*: These are sometimes served with Sichuanese tea-smoked duck (see page 180). Break the dough into 4 pieces. Roll each piece out into a sausage about 1 1/2 inches thick. Break or cut each sausage into 5 or 6 pieces. Take each piece, roll it into a ball, and flatten it with the palm of your hand into a circle about 1/4 inch thick. Brush the surface with melted lard or oil and fold the circle in half, pressing the two sides gently together. Use the teeth of a comb to make a crisscross pattern on the dough, and its back to make 2 evenly spaced indentations on the rounded outside edge. The bun should vaguely resemble a folded lotus leaf.

STEAMED BUNS WITH SPICY BEAN SPROUT STUFFING

dou ya bao zi

豆芽包子

Round steamed buns with moist, meaty stuffings (*bao zi*) are eaten all over China, but food experts say they have only been popular in Sichuan since the 1930s, when people from the coastal areas took refuge there during the Japanese invasion. Sichuan's most famous maker of these buns was one Liao Yongtong, who began his career by selling them on the streets of Chengdu in the 1930s. He blended traditional Sichuanese methods with the bun-making skills of eastern China and devised the acclaimed "dragon-eye" *bao zi*, so called because its stuffing peeps up through a small round hole at the top of the bun, like a beady eye. Mr. Liao's fame spread far and wide, and there is still a small restaurant selling his specialty pork-stuffed *bao zi* in central Chengdu. The restaurant, *zhi hu zi long yan bao zi*, is named after Mr. Liao's distinguishing facial characteristic, a large mole with a few long, sprouting hairs (*zhi hu zi*).

Another famous Sichuanese steamed bun is the Han *bao zi*, devised by a man named Han Yingdou in the 1920s. Mr. Han filled his buns with a mixture of pork, fresh shrimp, and spices, and they are still sold in a number of Chengdu outlets that bear his name.

The following type of *bao zi* is the most distinctively Sichuanese of all the local specialties, which is why I have chosen to include it. Nowhere else in

China do you find a *bao zi* stuffing flavored with Sichuanese chili bean paste or made with bean sprouts. The stuffing is gently spicy, a nice contrast to the bland steamed bread. Sichuanese cooks would make it with soybean sprouts, bean husks and whiskers discarded, but the more easily obtained mung bean sprouts are a perfectly acceptable substitute.

Note: The stuffing can be made while the dough is rising.

Makes about 20 large buns or 40 small ones

a bit more than a pound of risen dough (the dough should be made with 3 cups all-purpose flour exactly as in the recipe for steamed flower rolls on page 122: just add 3 tablespoons melted lard or peanut oil at the mixing stage)

FOR THE STUFFING
8 ounces bean sprouts
peanut oil

14 ounces ground pork
2 tablespoons Sichuanese chili bean paste
2 teaspoons light soy sauce
1 teaspoon dark soy sauce
1 teaspoon salt to taste
1 tablespoon Shaoxing rice wine or medium-dry sherry
8–10 turns of a black pepper mill or a couple of pinches of white pepper

1 Chop the bean sprouts into 1/2-inch sections (remove and discard the bean husks and whiskery bits if possible).

2 Season the wok, then add 4 tablespoons of oil and heat over a high flame. Add the pork and stir-fry briskly until it has separated out. Add the chili bean paste and stir-fry until it has stained the oil a reddish color. Add all the seasonings (remember that the stuffing must be quite salty to pep up the unsalted bread wrapping) and mix well. Finally, add the bean sprouts and stir-fry briefly until they are just cooked. Tip the stuffing into a bowl.

3 When the dough is ready, break it into about 4 pieces on a lightly floured work surface. To make snack-sized buns, roll each piece into a 1-inch sausage and break or cut the sausage into 1-ounce pieces. To make larger

buns, roll slightly thicker sausages and break them into 2-ounce pieces. Flatten each piece with the palm of your hand, make an indentation in the center, and then fill the indentation with a teaspoon of stuffing. Pinch around the edge of the circle to draw it up into a round dumpling with a small hole in the top.

4 Lightly oil a steamer tray. Place the finished buns in the steamer, making sure they are well spaced out. Steam over a high flame for 8–10 minutes (for small buns) or 12–15 minutes (for large buns). Serve piping hot.

FLOWER BEAN CURD
dou hua

豆花

It's a sleepy, sunny afternoon in one of Chengdu's teahouses, tucked away down a back alley near Sichuan University. In the main courtyard, a few students are sitting back in their creaking bamboo chairs, reading books or newspapers. Four people sit in a side room smoking cigarettes and shuffling mahjong tiles. The owner of the teahouse wanders around among the tables with her copper kettle, refilling the lidded tea bowls, stopping here and there for a chat with the regulars. Then a call goes up in the street outside, slowly approaching: "*Dou huar! Dou huar!*" A few minutes later, the bean curd vendor walks into the courtyard and sets down the pair of red-and-black barrels hung from his bamboo shoulder pole. For a small sum, he scoops some of his homemade flower bean curd into a bowl, drizzles it with chili and sesame oils and soy sauce, and then scatters over finely chopped pickled vegetables, scallions, and crunchy yellow soybeans, with a sprinkling of ground roasted Sichuan pepper. The bean curd is still warm, and meltingly tender, the dressing piquant and richly satisfying.

Flower bean curd is one of the few traditional Sichuanese snacks that is still commonly sold on the streets of the city. The bean curd vendors, with their trademark red-and-black barrels, set up shop wherever they can—in teahouses, in markets, outside the main department store in the center of town.

This type of bean curd, at its best, is as tender and silky as crème caramel. It's enjoyed all over China, although the Sichuanese often make theirs a little stiffer than the southern Chinese, just stiff enough to be eaten with chopsticks instead of a spoon. "Flower bean curd" is also a Chengdu dialect term: elsewhere in China this snack is known as "bean curd brain" (*dou fu nao*) because of its consistency. In the south, people like to eat it sweet, with almond essence, fruit, and syrup. In Sichuan, predictably, they think a little spice is nice. The Chengdu street vendors serve it with chili oil and Sichuan pepper; in the mountains near Chongqing they serve it plain with intensely flavored dips of chili paste, garlic, ginger, and scallions. Gourmets say that the most important aspect of flower bean curd is the quality of the water used to make it, so some areas of Sichuan with notably pure and delicious water sources are celebrated for their *dou hua*.

If you can remember to set the soybeans to soak the night before you wish to use them, flower bean curd is amazingly easy to make, and I highly recommend the homemade version. The only special equipment you need is a blender and a clean piece of cheesecloth to strain the milk. The coagulant, gypsum, can be found in Asian supermarkets. If you don't wish to make your *dou hua* from scratch, you can use the plain "tofu mix" made by Japanese manufacturers and sold in Asian grocery stores ("tofu" is one transliteration of the Chinese characters for bean curd). All you have to do is follow the instructions on the package, but use only three-quarters of the coagulant they provide (the full package leads to firm, ordinary bean curd). The texture of this kind of *dou hua* is very pleasing, but its taste isn't nearly as good as the fresh version. Otherwise, you can use the soft "silken tofu" sold in cartons in health food stores and supermarkets. It's not quite soft enough, but still tastes good.

Flower bean curd is often eaten as a between-meals nibble, but you can also serve it as part of a Chinese meal, perhaps as an accompaniment to a feast of Zhong dumplings or Long wontons, with a simple cold vegetable dish or a salad on the side.

The seasonings given in the following recipe are those used by the bean curd vendor described above, who has been in the trade for many years.

Serves 4 as a snack or part of a light, informal lunch

3/4 cup dried soybeans and
  2 1/4 teaspoons gypsum, or
  one 2-ounce package of
  tofu mix (makes about 1
  1/2 pounds *dou hua*), or two
  10-ounce packages of soft
  silken tofu

SEASONING
  4 teaspoons light soy sauce
  2–4 teaspoons chili oil with
    chile flakes (see page 55)
  1 teaspoon sesame oil

1/2–1 teaspoon ground
  roasted Sichuan pepper
  (see page 74)
2 tablespoons crunchy deep-
  fried soybeans or Indian
  deep-fried lentils or
  unsalted peanuts
2 tablespoons finely chopped
  preserved mustard tuber
4 scallions, green parts only,
  sliced into tiny rings

1 To make your own bean curd: Leave the soybeans to soak overnight in plenty of cold water, changing the water a few times if possible. The following day, rinse the beans very well under the tap, and then put them into the blender with 1 quart of water (do them in 2 batches if necessary). Whizz them up for a few minutes until you can no longer see any bits of bean and there is a good head of froth on the liquid. Line a sieve or colander with a double layer of cheesecloth and strain the soybean liquid into a saucepan. Squeeze the cheesecloth very tightly to extract as much soybean milk as possible.

    Dissolve the gypsum in 1 cup of hot water. Bring the strained soybean milk to a boil over a high flame. Skim off the surface foam with a slotted spoon and discard it. Pour the boiling milk into a bowl. Give the gypsum mixture another stir and scatter it over the soybean milk. Give it a quick stir and then leave to set for 20 minutes. As it sets, gently press the surface of the curd with a slotted spoon to firm up the mixture and allow any excess water to escape.

    Bring about 2 1/2 cups of water to a boil in a wok or saucepan. When the curd has set, use a large spoon to transfer it, chunk by chunk, into the hot water, and let it simmer over an extremely low flame for about 20 minutes, or until you are ready to eat it.

2 If you are using tofu mix, follow the instructions on the package to make the bean curd, remembering to add only three-quarters of the coagulant. If you are using store-bought soft bean curd, warm it up in a pot of gently simmering, lightly salted water.

1. Ingredients (left to right, row by row from top): Sesame paste, p. 73; Thai pickled chiles, p. 56; Fresh coriander (cilantro), p. 58; Sichuan chili bean paste, p. 57; "Horse ear" scallion slices, pp. 39, 57–58; Whole Sichuan pepper, pp. 73–74; Chopped ginger, p. 63; Fermented black beans, p. 54; Chopped garlic, p. 63; Homemade chili oil, pp. 55–56; Scallion "flowers," pp. 57–58; "Fragrant things" (star anise, fennel seeds, dried "sand ginger," cloves, *cao guo*, cassia bark), pp. 61–62; "Facing-heaven" chiles, p. 54; Sichuanese *ya cai* (preserved mustard greens), pp. 70–71; Homemade fermented glutinous rice wine, pp. 60–61; Shaoxing rice wine, p. 57

2. Appetizers (from back to front): Man-and-wife meat slices, p. 178; Soybeans in their pods, p. 186; Preserved eggs with green peppers, p. 153; Deep-fried crispy peanuts, p. 191

3. A Sichuanese hors d'oeuvre box (*cuan he*) containing (clockwise, from top): Five-spiced "smoked" fish, p. 169; Spicy cucumber salad, p. 185; Tea-smoked duck, p. 180; haricots verts in ginger sauce, p. 150; Spicy beef slices with tangerine peel, p. 165; Sweet-and-sour red peppers, p. 154; and Strange-flavor chicken (center), p. 144

4. Fish-fragrant pork slivers, p. 196

5. Chili bean paste, p. 57

6. "Facing-heaven" chiles, p. 54

7. Boiled beef slices in a fiery sauce, p. 226

8. Vegetable dishes (clockwise from top left): Stir-fried amaranth, p. 294; Stir-fried mixed mushrooms, p. 292; Dry-fried bitter melon, p. 296; Stir-fried water spinach, p. 295

9. Gong Bao (Kung Pao) chicken with peanuts, p. 237

10. Sweet-and-sour crispy fish (before cooking), p. 264

3 While the bean curd is still warm, drain it and divide it up among four bowls. Drizzle over the liquid seasonings, sprinkle lightly with Sichuan pepper, and scatter over the other ingredients. Serve immediately, and let your guests mix the seasonings into the bean curd themselves.

VARIATIONS

Hot-and-sour flower bean curd—*suan la dou hua*: this is one of the snacks served at "Mr. Tan's" famous flower bean curd shop, which I used to pass every day on my way to classes at the Sichuan cooking school. It's especially popular in the summer months. The method is exactly the same as the one described above, but the seasonings should be as follows: 4 teaspoons light soy sauce; 4 teaspoons Chinkiang or black Chinese vinegar; 2–4 teaspoons chili oil with chile flakes (see page 55), 1/2–1 teaspoon ground roasted Sichuan pepper (see page 74); 2 tablespoons finely chopped preserved mustard tuber; 4 teaspoons deep-fried soybeans and 4 teaspoons deep-fried unsalted peanuts, or 2 1/2 tablespoons of roasted or deep-fried peanuts; and 4 scallions, green parts only, sliced into tiny rings. The sour note adds a delicious extra dimension.

At the Long Chao Shou restaurant, they make a version that plays with sesame flavorings and Sichuan pepper (*shuang ma dou hua*). Quantities are as follows: 4 teaspoons light soy sauce; 4 teaspoons sesame paste mixed with 1–2 teaspoons sesame oil; 1/2–1 teaspoon ground roasted Sichuan pepper (see page 74); 2 tablespoons finely chopped preserved mustard tuber; 4 teaspoons crushed deep-fried noodles and 4 teaspoons deep-fried unsalted peanuts or 2 1/2 tablespoons roasted or deep-fried unsalted peanuts; and 4 scallions, green parts only, sliced into tiny rings.

Flower bean curd can also be served plain, with a separate dip made from chili bean paste. To make the dip, stir-fry a couple of tablespoons of chili bean paste in a little oil, over a medium flame, until the oil is red and fragrant. Off the heat, stir in finely chopped garlic and scallions to taste.

EIGHT-TREASURE BLACK RICE PORRIDGE
ba bao hei mi zhou

Every morning a woman used to set up her portable stove in the courtyard outside my apartment in Chengdu. She would heat up a big pot of black rice porridge and sell it by the bowl to local residents. It was a wonderful, nutritious breakfast, a warm mess of rice scattered with the colors of tiny mung beans, red Chinese dates, wolfberries, and peanuts, and stained purple by the grains of black glutinous rice. I would eat it with a little sugar or some shavings from a miraculous block of wild Yunnan honey that I found by chance one day in my local market.

The following recipe is based on the one taught to me by my Chinese teacher Yu Weiqin, who used to feed me such comfort foods whenever she thought I was sad or homesick. The "eight treasures" are highly flexible—no one is actually counting—just try to make sure you have a few contrasting colors to liven up the snack. All the ingredients in the following recipe have Chinese medicinal functions, so the dish is nutritious as well as colorful (they can all be bought in good Chinese supermarkets). For a more simple, everyday breakfast, you can use ordinary rice with a handful of mung or azuki beans, and perhaps accompany the porridge with stuffed steamed buns and pickled vegetables. In the summer, the Sichuanese like to add whole fresh lotus leaves to a simmering pot of plain rice porridge. The leaves tinge the porridge with green and lend it a subtle fragrance; they are also thought to relieve the physical discomforts of heat and humidity. Rice porridge is always cooked for at least a couple of hours, until the individual rice grains rupture and spill out their flesh—the Chinese call this *kai hua*, "bursting into flower."

You might find this porridge served at snack restaurants or, in tiny bowls, as a banquet side dish. I have also eaten it at friends' houses as a final filler-up after dinner—not so strange when you consider Chinese people habitually serve rice at the end of the meal, after the meat and vegetable dishes.

Serves 6–8 for breakfast

1 tablespoon lotus seeds

1 tablespoon lily buds (*bai he*)

1 tablespoon raw peanuts in their pink skins

1 tablespoon walnut meats

2 teaspoons mung beans

2 teaspoons azuki beans

1 1/2 tablespoons dried Chinese dates (jujube)

2 teaspoons Chinese wolfberries (*Lycium chinense*)

(other possible additions are 2 teaspoons raw barley and 2 teaspoons dried foxnuts, which are occasionally found in Chinese groceries)

1/4 cup black glutinous rice

1/4 cup white glutinous rice

1/4 cup ordinary long-grain rice

sugar or honey to serve

1 Soak the lotus seeds and lily buds in water overnight.

2 Give all the ingredients except for the wolfberries a good rinse, then place them in a large saucepan (this includes the drained lotus seeds and lily buds). Add 3 quarts of water.

3 Bring the liquid to a boil, skim off any scum, then simmer on a very gentle heat for about 2 hours, stirring occasionally to prevent sticking and adding more water if necessary. You should end up with a loose, soupy porridge. Shortly before the porridge is ready, add the wolfberries and let them simmer for a minute or two. Serve warm, with sugar or honey to taste.

OTHER SPECIALTY SNACKS

ZHENG ZHENG CAKES (*zheng zheng gao*)

These marvelously delicate concoctions of steamed rice, with sweet fillings made from lotus seeds or pine kernels, were traditionally sold by street vendors who used to call out the name of their wares to attract the attention of passersby (this explains why their name, *zheng zheng gao*, has such a delightful ring when said in Chinese—it simply means "steamed cake"). Food scholars trace their origins back at least three centuries. Sadly, the street vendors have disappeared, but their snack lives on in one or two restaurants like Long Chao Shou. To make the authentic *zheng zheng gao*, you need specially made equipment: individual wooden dumpling molds which fit onto steam pipes on a portable stove, channeling the steam directly through each hexagonal dumpling. The finished dumplings have a consistency somewhere between sponge cake and cooked rice—moist, crumbly, and delicious, with a nugget of sweet paste inside. They are usually sprinkled with candied fruits, roasted peanuts, or white sugar.

RIPPLED-SILK FRIED DUMPLINGS (*bo si you gao*)

Rippled-silk dumplings are made from a special oily dough that flowers out into great diaphanous waves when they are deep-fried. They have a most delectable texture: a crisp, delicate outer coating that melts in the mouth, and sweet, heavy centers. Making and cooking *bo si you gao* requires immense skill, so they are found only in restaurants that specialize in them. The dumpling was invented by one of the great Sichuanese cooks of the twentieth century, Kong Daosheng, who, in a throwback to the old teaching tradition, passed the recipe on to a handful of apprentices. His students included my pastry teacher at the Sichuan cooking school, Li Daiquan, and the head chef of Long Chao Shou, Fan Shixian. According to Mr. Fan, Master Kong told his students that the snack originated in a happy accident in a small Sichuanese restaurant. The restaurant's owner was playing around with a small blob of leftover pastry, and he repeatedly smeared his hands with oil to stop it sticking. After a while he grew bored and tossed the blob into the deep-frying pan to get rid of it, where to his amazement it puffed up like a flower. Master Kong heard about the discovery, added a stuffing to the oily dough, and created *bo si you gao*.

STUFFED EGGY PANCAKES (*dan hong gao*)

Dan hong gao are small, fluffy pancakes made in miniature copper frying pans with convex bases. A spoonful of batter, made from flour, eggs, and yeast, is poured into the pans, which are then covered with matching copper lids. When the pancake is nearly cooked, a spoonful of stuffing is added, and the pancake folded in half. It is served like that, folded into a semicircle, crisp and golden on the outside, soft within, and filled with a sweet or savory stuffing. Sweet stuffings are often made with sugar and crushed unsalted peanuts or sesame seeds; savory stuffings with minced fried pork and salty pickled vegetables.

CARAMELIZED GLUTINOUS RICE BALLS (*tang you guo zi*)

Children love eating these glutinous spheres, glazed with caramel and studded with sesame seeds. The rice balls are deep-fried in a wok that contains both oil and molten, caramelized sugar, and then are rolled in a bamboo tray filled with seeds. The finished balls are often impaled on thin bamboo skewers, so they can be nibbled without making one's fingers too sticky.

SICHUANESE FLATBREADS (*guo kuei*)

Guo kuei is a general term for a kind of flatbread that is a popular Sichuanese snack. There are many different varieties. The most delicious of these are *jun tun guo kuei*, named after Jun Tun, the village near Chengdu where they are said to have originated. *Jun tun guo kuei* are crisp, golden pinwheels of dough, filled with a scattering of ground meat and spices. I used to buy them for breakfast, hot from the stove, from a stall near one of the back entrances to Sichuan University. Watching the vendor rolling the dough is always a spectacle: he uses the heel of his thumb to smear a small ball of dough into a long, tongue-like strip, then spreads this sparingly with lard and a paste made from ground pork seasoned with ginger, scallions, five-spice powder, and Sichuan pepper. Then he rolls each strip into a cylinder, stands it on its end, and squashes it into a flat round, before finally using a rolling pin to make it into a 4- to 5-inch disc. The rolled flatbreads are cooked on a portable burner that serves both as hot plate and oven. The vendor begins by frying them in plenty of oil, until they are golden, then he removes his frying pan from the stove and stacks the *guo kuei* underneath, on a special shelf just above the flaming charcoal, where they are baked until crisp. The finished *guo kuei* are scrumptious: perfect for breakfast or as a snack at any time of the day.

Another Sichuan specialty is plain white *guo kuei*, toasted on a griddle until they curl, then baked, and finally split open and served with one of a variety of fillings. They can be stuffed with thin slices of stewed meat and a drizzling of aromatic gravy, or chili oil sauce, or perhaps with some salted pickled vegetables. Sweet *guo kuei* are made by adding brown sugar to the dough and scattering the flatbreads with sesame seeds.

GLUTINOUS RICE CONES WRAPPED IN BAMBOO LEAVES (*jiao yan zong zi*)

Zong zi are bundles of glutinous rice shaped into cones, wrapped cleverly in long bamboo leaves, and tied up tightly with string. They are eaten around the Dragon Boat Festival (*duan wu jie*) on the fifth day of the fifth lunar month, a tradition that goes back at least sixteen centuries. The origins of this practice are uncertain. Some people suggest that *zong zi* were eaten as part of ceremonies held in honor of gods or ancestors, but the folk explanation, which has been around only since the sixth century, long after the practice began, is that they are eaten to commemorate the death of the poet Qu Yuan. Qu Yuan, who lived in the third century B.C., is remembered as a loyal and sagacious adviser to the Duke of Chu. The poet committed suicide by throwing himself into the Miluo River after the Duke's failure to heed his advice led to political disaster. Grieving local people are said to have thrown packets of rice into the river in the hope that the fish would eat them and leave the poet's body untouched. (Commemorating the deaths of past political figures renowned for their honesty has often been used by the Chinese as a way of expressing anger at political corruption—this is how the Tiananmen demonstrations began in 1989.) *Zong zi* are eaten all over China to mark the Dragon Boat Festival—the Sichuanese like to mix their rice with red beans, salt, and Sichuan pepper, and sometimes little bits of pork.

STARCH JELLIES (*liang fen*)

Sichuanese people adore eating jellies made from starchy foods like peas, fava beans, rice, and buckwheat. The jellies are cut into cubes, ribbons, or chunky strips and served with all kinds of delicious spicy dressings. They can also be mixed with cold chicken or eaten hot with carp and other foods. They are usually sold in the markets alongside the bean curd and bean curd products. One stall owner, a Mrs. Luo, was kind enough to take me to her village near Chengdu to show me how the jellies were made. In the small rural workshop, a man heated water in an enormous earthenware jar about three feet high. It was heated by steam that bubbled out from a pipe connected to a roaring furnace nearby. When the water was boiling, the man mixed pea starch with water and a coagulant in a separate bucket and poured the mixture into the pot. He then used all his strength to stir the starch into the water, working furiously. After the mixing, the liquid was left to bubble away, again heated only by the steam pipe. After about 20 minutes, when it had become viscous and semitranslucent, he scooped it up into bowls and left it to set. The finished jelly was a silvery, translucent white, with a cool, pudding-like texture. Jellies made with other ingredients have different appearances and textures—rice jelly (*mi liang fen*), for example, is yellowish and opaque. The most famous style of *liang fen* is North Sichuan pea jelly (*chuan bei liang fen*), which is dressed in a rich sauce made from fermented black beans, pickled mustard greens, rock sugar, ginger, Sichuan pepper, and chili oil.

GOLDEN-THREAD NOODLES (*jin si mian*)

These noodles are made with a paste of whole egg and flour, which is rolled out by hand until it is as thin as strudel pastry. It is then cut into extremely thin noodles, like "threads of silk." The noodles are briefly boiled and are often served simply with seasoned stock and sesame oil. Because of the skill involved in making them, these noodles are considered a banquet snack and are sometimes served with toppings made from expensive banquet ingredients, such as seafood. A variation is pale "silver-thread noodles," which are made from a dough bound with egg white alone.

2
appetizers

A SICHUANESE FEAST ALWAYS BEGINS WITH A TEASING
spread of little dishes, served cold or at room temperature, to arouse the senses, open the stomach (*kai wei*), and set the mood for the meal to come. Often a ravishing selection of delicacies arranged with an eye to variety in color, taste, and texture, they might include sliced cold poultry dressed in spicy sauces; chewy beef with numbing Sichuan pepper; cool, colorful vegetables; and seasonal salads. In fancy restaurants, it is customary to start the meal with a selection of appetizers served in a round, black-lacquered hors d'oeuvre box (*cuan he*) richly embellished with dragon and phoenix designs. The box is presented whole, with its decorated lid, and then the small dishes it contains are lifted out and spread around the table. The simplest *cuan he*, which has four small dishes arranged around a larger central one, is called a "five-color" box; larger "seven-color" and "nine-color" boxes are also offered. At its best, a nine-color box will amaze with its unexpected and delicious variations. The presentation of the *cuan he* signifies the start of the banquet, and as the guests eat these dishes with their chopsticks, the hot dishes will start to arrive, slowly but surely, from the kitchen.

The precise hors d'oeuvre menu is a matter of the cook's discretion, local flora and fauna, and the shifting seasons. One "seven-colored" *cuan he* served to my family at the Shufeng restaurant in Chengdu included rabbit with Sichuan pepper; chicken gizzards with pickled mountain chiles; rabbit's kidneys in chili oil sauce; a type of beef innard with shreds of lettuce stem and carrot in a mustard-oil sauce; celery in a garlicky dressing, served with bean curd skin; bitter melon with sesame oil; and red peppers in a sweet-and-sour sauce.

These kinds of dishes are also served at home, in a less flamboyant style. A dish of cold meats or a cold-dressed vegetable is not only a pleasant contrast to stir-fried, braised, or soupy hot dishes, but a great convenience to the cook, because it can be prepared in advance. Many Sichuanese hosts will also buy a few ready-to-eat delicacies from specialized street vendors—perhaps some tea-smoked duck, stewed meats, or pickled vegetables draped in spicy sauces—and serve them as part of an otherwise home-cooked meal. At home, these dishes will be on the table at the start of the meal, to be augmented by hot dishes as they emerge from the kitchen.

There's also a recent fashion for eating these appetizers with drinks as part of a casual, snacky restaurant meal. This Sichuanese version of *tapas* is known as *leng dan bei*, a term that doesn't translate well but means something like "a few cold dishes and a glass of beer." The food is displayed on great platters in restaurants open to the streets and is served on small round plates. Whole evenings will slip away in conversation over the beer and assorted nibbles. The food served is simple and hearty—various cold meats and stir-fries, salted eggs, and aromatic peanuts. Cycling through the back streets of Chengdu, it's sometimes difficult to concentrate on the road as one passes these tables of plenty, laid out under the eaves of the wood-framed houses.

This chapter includes recipes for many of Sichuan's most popular appetizers. They are recipes that I have returned to again and again, not least because they blend so well with other, everyday types of cooking. A plateful of Sichuanese chili-oil chicken livens up any kind of buffet lunch; hot-and-numbing beef goes deliciously with a cool aperitif; and many of these dishes can be served as Western-style appetizers.

APPETIZERS WITH DRESSINGS (*liang ban cai*)

One of the easiest ways to get to the heart of Sichuanese cooking is to try a few of its delicious sauces on cold meats and vegetables. The main ingredients can be cooked, simply, in advance, the sauce rustled up quickly at the last minute. Most of the following recipes are extremely simple to prepare, but are intriguing, different, and wonderfully tasty. The hot, spicy ones are typical of Sichuanese cooking in their bold combinations of several intense flavors in a single dish, and in their liberal use of the two favorite local flavorings, chile and Sichuan pepper. The exact amounts of these two spices used in each sauce are very much a matter of personal taste. I have chosen to offer the level of spiciness you might find in a typical Chengdu restaurant or a Chengdu home. Some Sichuanese, in particular the people of Chongqing, who are notorious even among other Sichuanese for their chile-guzzling tastes, would probably double my suggested quantities of both chili oil and Sichuan pepper; fancy restaurants catering to visitors from other parts of China might halve them. So feel free to tone down the flavors if you need to, but be adventurous—my friends and family, most of them originally unaccustomed to this kind of spicing, have raved about these dishes.

It should be remembered that if, in a Western kitchen, you asked someone to make a salad dressing, they wouldn't follow a recipe, but would play around with oils, vinegars, salt, pepper, mustard, and honey perhaps, and make up something that tasted good that day. In Sichuan, it's the same with dressings for cold meats and vegetables, except that the basic pantry ingredients are a little different. Sichuanese home cooks will play around with soy sauce (light and dark), vinegar, chili and sesame oils, sugar, salt, minced garlic, and Sichuan pepper. They will blur the boundaries between the classic sauces, each time creating something that's a little different. The following recipes will give you an overview of the standard types of flavoring described in cookbooks and taught in cooking schools. But once you have a feel for them, it's fun to play around with different combinations.

COOKED CHICKEN FOR SICHUANESE APPETIZERS

The Chinese are very particular about how they eat their chicken. Old hens (*mu ji*, "mother chickens") may be simmered for hours to create a rich soup base, but young, meaty birds must never be overcooked, for fear of ruining their delicate white flesh. Serious gourmets and Cantonese chefs will plunge their chickens into a measured amount of boiling stock, bring it back to a boil, and then turn off the heat. The pot is covered with a lid and the chicken left to poach gently as the boiling stock cools down. When the liquid reaches room temperature, the flesh should be just cooked, but still firm, juicy, and subtly flavored, with a little raw pinkness in the bones. I have to admit that I'm slightly wary of cooking chickens this way because of the health risks if they're not cooked properly. I have quite happily eaten just-cooked chicken in many good Chinese restaurants with no ill effects, but at home I tend to poach it according to the following method. I should add that this is how several Sichuanese friends, both restaurant chefs and home cooks, prepare their chickens.

Don't forget that although the chickens in Sichuanese cold dishes are always cooked in water, the following sauces also make delightful dressings for the remains of a braised or roasted bird. And do cook the chicken the day before you wish to entertain guests if you want to lighten the last-minute cooking load.

| a 1 1/2-inch piece of fresh | 1 chicken, about 3 pounds |
| ginger, unpeeled | 2 scallions, white parts only |

1   Choose a pot large enough to hold the chicken snugly, fill it with water to cover, and bring to a vigorous boil. Crush the ginger slightly with the side of a cleaver blade or a heavy object.

2   Plunge the chicken into the water, return it quickly to a boil, and skim the surface. Add the ginger and scallions, close the lid, and then turn the heat down to a very gentle simmer. Poach at this temperature for about 30 minutes, depending on the size of the chicken. Test it by poking a skewer deep into the thigh joint. If it's not yet cooked, pink juices will ooze out of the hole. These will run clear when the bird is ready.

3   When the chicken is just cooked (and take care not to overdo it), remove it from the pot and rinse in cold running water. You can then leave it in a potful of cold water for an hour or two until you wish to use it, or just leave it to cool and then place in the refrigerator. The chicken flesh should be moist, silky, and not disintegrating.

FOUR WAYS OF DRESSING COLD CHICKEN MEAT
The following sauces are a simple yet dramatic introduction to Sichuanese cooking. Make one to serve with half a leftover chicken—otherwise cook a whole bird and surprise your guests with a choice of three or four different sauces, served in little bowls around a central dish of piled-up chicken meat. In keeping with the spirit of the Sichuan kitchen, you should cut the chicken into chunks *or* slices *or* slivers—mixing different shapes in the same dish is seen as messy and unbalanced. You can dilute the chili oil with salad oil if you want something less spicy—but do make sure that the dish retains its deep red color.

All these recipes will serve 4 as a starter or 2 as a main dish, but you can make them go further by serving them with a few other appetizers or dishes.

1. CHICKEN CHUNKS IN RED-OIL SAUCE
hong you ji kuai

Red-oil sauce, which combines chile hotness with salty soy and sweet undercurrents of sugar, is typically used for cold chicken and rabbit meat. The chicken in this recipe is generally served in chunks (with chunks of scallion), or in slices 1 1/2 inches long (with diagonally cut "horse ear" slices of scallion).

For about 1 pound cooked chicken meat (about 1/2 a chicken), cooled

3–4 scallions, white and green parts
3 tablespoons light soy sauce
2 teaspoons white sugar

3–6 tablespoons chili oil with chile flakes (see page 55)
1 teaspoon sesame oil
salt to taste

1 Cut the chicken into bite-sized chunks.

2 Cut the scallions into bite-sized lengths.

3 Mix the chicken and scallions in a serving dish and sprinkle with a little salt.

4 Combine the soy sauce and sugar in a small bowl and stir to dissolve the sugar. Add the chili and sesame oils, stir well, and then pour over the chicken and scallion pieces. Mix well.

VARIATION

This dressing is also used for an unusual vegetable, *ze'er gen* (*Houttuynia cordata*), which grows in the southern Yangtze River area. The tender leaves and stems of this purplish vegetable, which has a sour taste and a texture a little like watercress, are eaten raw as a great delicacy in the spring and early summer. The leaves are sometimes tossed like a salad with slivers of lettuce stem or fresh fava beans.

2. HOT-AND-NUMBING CHICKEN SLICES
ma la ji pian

Like the chili-oil sauce above, this dressing combines the salty richness of soy sauce with fiery chili oil and a hint of sugar sweetness, but with an extra zing from ground roasted Sichuan pepper. Its Chinese name comes from the two characters that are the epitome of Sichuanese cooking for people in other parts of China: *ma*, the strange, tingling, numbing taste sensations of Sichuan pepper; and *la*, which means hotness, usually the hotness of chiles, but also that of ginger and black pepper. Restaurants tend to serve the chicken on a bed of scallions, but most home cooks just pour the sauce over the meat and scallions in a serving bowl and toss it like a salad.

For about 1 pound cooked chicken meat (about 1/2 a chicken), cooled

salt to taste
4–6 scallions, white parts only
4 teaspoons white sugar
3 tablespoons light soy sauce
3–6 tablespoons chili oil with
   chile flakes (see page 55)

2 teaspoons sesame oil
1/2–1 teaspoon ground
   roasted Sichuan pepper
   (see page 74)

1 Cut the chicken as evenly as possible into slices and sprinkle with a little salt.

2 Thinly slice the scallions diagonally, 1 1/2 inches long, to form "horse ear" slices.

3 Stir the sugar into the soy sauce to dissolve it, and then add the oils.

4 Place the scallion slices on a serving dish, and then add the chicken.

5 Sprinkle with the ground pepper and drizzle with the sauce. The dish can be gently mixed with chopsticks when your guests are at the table.

3. FISH-FRAGRANT CHICKEN SLIVERS

yu xiang ji si

So-called fish-fragrant sauces are most commonly used in hot dishes, but the combination of flavors works equally well with cold food, as this recipe shows. It's a lovely, intensely flavored sauce, dense with fresh ginger, garlic, scallion, and the famous Sichuan pickled chiles. The chiles and chili oil give it a gentle kick, which never overwhelms the sweet-sour and salty notes, and the red, green, and pale yellow colors are beautiful together. It's fun to serve this and a couple of other, contrasting sauces with a whole cold chicken, but you can also use it as a starter on its own, draping it over a small pile of chicken or rabbit slivers or perhaps some freshly steamed scallops. The same sauce is also sometimes used as a dressing for deep-fried fresh peas.

For about 1 pound cooked chicken meat, cooled

2 or 3 scallions, green parts only
1 tablespoon very finely chopped fresh ginger
1 tablespoon very finely chopped garlic
3 tablespoons light soy sauce

1 tablespoon Chinkiang or black Chinese vinegar
1 tablespoon white sugar
2 tablespoons chili oil
2 teaspoons sesame oil
1–2 tablespoons pickled chili paste

1 Cut the chicken into slivers and lay them on a serving dish. Finely slice the green parts of the scallions.

2 Make sure the ginger and garlic are very finely and evenly chopped.

3 Combine the soy sauce, vinegar, and sugar in a small bowl and stir to dissolve the sugar. Add the oils, and then the ginger, garlic, chili paste, and scallions. Mix well.

4 Pour the sauce over the chicken and serve. You may wish to mix the dish with chopsticks when your guests are at the table.

4. CHICKEN SLICES IN SICHUAN PEPPER AND SESAME OIL SAUCE
jiao ma ji pian

This summery sauce is most commonly used with chicken. The Sichuan pepper is used raw, with a potency that is usually mellowed by roasting, so it should be used with great caution by newcomers to Sichuanese food. You can serve the chicken on a base of some crunchy vegetable like cucumber or celery if you wish—if so, it's best to sprinkle the cut vegetables with salt and let them sit for 20–30 minutes to draw out excess water.

For about 1 pound cooked chicken meat, cooled

1/2–1 teaspoon whole Sichuan pepper	3 tablespoons chicken stock
5 scallions, green parts only	2 tablespoons light soy sauce
1/4 teaspoon salt	1 1/2 tablespoons sesame oil

1 Set the Sichuan pepper aside to soak for a few minutes in very hot water. Slice the chicken. Remove and discard the outer leaves of the scallions, and finely slice the remainder.

2 If you have a small food processor, whizz the scallions to a green paste with the Sichuan pepper and salt. Otherwise, follow the traditional Sichuanese method: lay the scallion slices on a cutting board, scatter with the Sichuan pepper and salt and use a cleaver to reduce them to a fine paste. You can start by using a spice grinder (a coffee grinder used only for spices) to finely grind the Sichuan pepper, which makes the chopping easier. For best results sift the peppercorn powder to remove any remaining husky bits.

3 Combine the stock, soy sauce, and scallion paste in a small bowl, adding more salt to taste if you wish. Add the sesame oil. Drizzle the sauce over the chicken slices and serve.

STRANGE-FLAVOR CHICKEN
guai wei ji si
(OTHERWISE KNOWN AS BANG BANG CHICKEN
—bang bang ji si)

This tempting dish is one of the few Sichuanese dishes to have become internationally popular while keeping something of its original identity. The name "bang bang chicken" originates from a town near Leshan, to the south of Chengdu. This place, Hanyang Ba, has long been famed for the quality of its chickens, which are what we in the West would call free-range birds, fed on scraps of grain, insects, and leftovers from the local peanut crop. Early in the twentieth century, many Hanyang street vendors sold chunks of cooked chicken meat, draped in a spicy sauce, as a snack. This became known as "bang bang chicken" because of the wooden cudgels (*bang*) they used to hammer the backs of the cleaver blades to help them through the meat. The dish began to be featured on Chengdu menus from about the 1920s, but by this time the wooden cudgel was used to loosen the fibers of the chicken meat so that it could be torn into slivers by hand. The sauces for bang bang chicken and strange-flavor chicken use more or less the same ingredients, but in slightly different proportions—local chefs say there should be a slightly heavier emphasis on the hot-and-numbing tastes in bang bang chicken.

The curious name "strange-flavor" derives from a bizarre but deeply satisfying combination of salty, sweet, sour, nutty, hot, and numbing flavors. The taste of sesame, enlivened by hints of salt-sweet-sour, hits you first, quickly followed by the warm and tingling tastes of chili oil and roasted Sichuan pepper. Any heaviness in the sauce is beautifully lightened by the freshness of the scallions. I have found this recipe one of the most difficult to commit to paper, because I have enjoyed so many different versions of it.

Sichuanese cooks use a dark, toasty sesame paste to make the sauce, but it's equally delicious made with *tahini* or the honey-colored sesame paste commonly found in Chinese supermarkets. You can finish the dish with a sprinkling of crushed, roasted peanuts if you like. Cucumber can be used instead of scallions—it's best to sprinkle the pieces lightly with salt at least 30 minutes before you need them, to let some of their water drain away. The cucumber should be cut into thin strips to complement the chicken slivers.

For about 1 pound cooked chicken meat, cooled

6–8 scallions, white parts only
1 tablespoon white sugar
salt to taste
1 tablespoon light soy sauce
1 tablespoon Chinkiang or
  black Chinese vinegar
3 tablespoons well-blended
  Chinese sesame paste

1 tablespoon sesame oil
2 tablespoons chili oil with
  chile flakes (see page 55)
1/2–1 teaspoon ground
  roasted Sichuan pepper
  (see page 74)
3 teaspoons toasted sesame
  seeds

1 Cut the chicken, with any remaining skin, into slivers about 1/2 inch wide. (If you want to be really authentic, hit it a few times with a rolling pin to loosen the fibers and then tear the flesh into shreds by hand.)

2 Cut the scallions into sections and then slice these lengthwise into fine slivers. Put them into a bowl of cold water to refresh.

3 Stir the sugar and salt in the soy sauce and vinegar until dissolved. Gradually stir in the sesame paste to make a smooth sauce. Add the other ingredients except the sesame seeds and mix well.

4 Shortly before serving, drain the scallions and pile them neatly in the cen-

ter of your serving dish. Lay the chicken slivers on top of them. Pour over the prepared sauce.

5 At the last minute, sprinkle with the sesame seeds.

VARIATION

The same sauce can be used to dress cold rabbit meat.

COLD PORK IN HOT AND GARLICKY SAUCE

suan ni bai rou

The dark dressing for this dish is made with a specially prepared soy sauce that has undertones of sweetness and a delicate, spicy aroma (although I have added below an instant version of the recipe that requires only the soy sauce in your pantry). It's a favorite spring and summer sauce for cold pork, but is also commonly used for fresh cucumber or boiled, tender young fava beans in season.

Sichuanese people would choose a piece of pork butt that is half fat and half lean, with the skin still attached, to enjoy the variety of textures and tastes. The cooked meat is then cut so that each slice is also half fat and half lean, with a thin edge of tender skin. You can of course use an entirely lean piece of meat if you'd rather, or even the leftovers from a pork roast, but the fatty Sichuanese version is most delicious.

The pork can be prepared a day in advance and refrigerated until you wish to use it. The sauce ingredients can also be mixed in advance—except for the garlic purée, which must be added at the last minute to keep it fresh and fragrant. The bean sprouts are optional—the meat is often served alone with the sauce, but I like to have something fresh to counterbalance its richness.

Serves 4 as a starter with one other dish

1 generous pound of boneless
   pork tenderloin, in one
   piece
a 1 1/2-inch piece of fresh
   ginger
2 scallions, white parts only
1/2 pound bean sprouts

FOR THE SAUCE
4 tablespoons sweet aromatic
   soy sauce (see page 76)
2–4 tablespoons chili oil
2–3 teaspoons crushed garlic
2 teaspoons sesame oil

FOR THE GARNISH
the green parts of a scallion,
   or fresh coriander (cilantro)

1 Heat enough water to cover the pork in a pot or wok. Crush the ginger slightly with the side of a cleaver blade or a heavy object.

2 When the water is boiling furiously, add the meat and skim the surface after a few seconds. Throw in the ginger and scallions, bring back to a boil and then turn the heat down. Simmer until the meat is just cooked, 30–60 minutes, depending on its thickness. You can see whether it's ready by poking a skewer into the thickest part—if no pink juices ooze out, it's properly cooked.

3 When the pork is ready, place it skin side down in a bowl, cover it with some of the cooking liquid, and allow it to cool. Place it in the refrigerator until you wish to use it—this will help to firm up the texture so it doesn't disintegrate as you slice it. (Keep the remaining cooking liquid to use as stock if you wish.)

4 Shortly before serving, blanch the bean sprouts for about 20 seconds in plenty of boiling water. Rinse in cold water and then drain well.

5 Cut the pork as thinly and evenly as possible into large slices (traditionally about 2 inches by 4 inches), preferably each with a mixture of fat and lean meat.

6 Combine the sauce ingredients in a small bowl.

7 Arrange the blanched bean sprouts on a serving dish. Pile the pork slices on top, and then drizzle with the spicy sauce. Garnish with sliced scallions (green parts) or chopped fresh coriander (cilantro).

VARIATION

Instant hot garlicky sauce

The following quick version can be used if you don't wish to prepare the special soy sauce required for the recipe above.

4 tablespoons light soy sauce   2 teaspoons crushed garlic

2 tablespoons white sugar   2 teaspoons sesame oil

2–4 tablespoons chili oil

Stir the sugar into the soy sauce to dissolve it. Add all the other ingredients.

RABBIT WITH PEANUTS
IN HOT BEAN SAUCE

hua ren ban tu ding

花
仁
拌
兔
丁

This splendid autumn dish is typical of Sichuanese home cooking, but it also works very well with bread and a couple of salads as part of a Western-style lunch. The tender rabbit flesh contrasts nicely with the crisp peanuts and crunchy scallions; the sauce is a glossy dark red and robustly spicy. The following recipe is closely related to the famous "second sister rabbit cubes" (*er jie tu ding*) invented by a skillful Chengdu woman called Chen Yonghui. Her dish was so delicious that it even became the subject of a poem written by a member of the local literati. Mrs. Chen's special extra touch, we're told, was to add a final sprinkling of ground roasted Sichuan pepper, crushed peanuts, and toasted sesame seeds.

Serves 4 as a starter or as part of a light salady lunch

a 2-inch piece of fresh ginger,
unpeeled
2 scallions, white and green
parts
about a pound of cooked
rabbit meat
4 scallions, white parts only
2/3 cup roasted or deep-fried
unsalted peanuts

FOR THE SAUCE
1 tablespoon fermented black
beans
3 tablespoons peanut oil
2 1/2 tablespoons Sichuan
chili bean paste
2 teaspoons light soy sauce
1/4 teaspoon white sugar
1 teaspoon sesame oil
optional: 1–2 tablespoons chili
oil

1 Optional first step: blanch the rabbit in plenty of boiling water for 5–10 seconds to remove any bloodiness.

2 Bring a separate pot of water to a boil. Crush the ginger and whole scallions slightly with the side of a cleaver blade or a heavy object.

3 When the water is boiling, add the rabbit, return to a boil, and skim. Add the ginger and scallions and simmer over a gentle heat until the meat is just cooked. When it is done, remove and drain, discarding the ginger and scallions. When the rabbit has cooled, chop it into 1- to 1 1/2-inch cubes, on or off the bone.

4 Mash the fermented black beans, either with your fingertips or using a mortar and pestle. Heat the peanut oil in a wok over a moderate flame until hot but not smoking. Add the chili bean paste and mashed black beans, and stir-fry for about 30 seconds until the oil is a glossy red and richly fragrant, taking care not to let the flavorings burn. Tip into a small mixing bowl, add the soy sauce, sugar, sesame oil, and chili oil if desired, and mix well.

5 Chop the white parts of the scallions into 1/2-inch sections.

6 Just before serving, combine the rabbit cubes, scallions, and peanuts in a bowl. Pour over the sauce and toss like a salad, making sure everything is evenly coated.

VARIATIONS

Chicken meat can be used as a substitute for rabbit, although I've never seen it prepared this way by Sichuanese cooks.

For a vegetarian version (dry bean curd with peanuts—*hua ren dou fu gan*), use cubes of firm bean curd instead of the rabbit.

HARICOTS VERTS IN GINGER SAUCE

jiang zhi jiang dou

In Sichuan, this dish is usually made with "yard-long beans," those fine, string-like beans that are sold by the bunch in Asian supermarkets. Haricots verts (fine French beans) or green beans are perfectly acceptable substitutes. The same dressing can also be used as a sauce for blanched Chinese spinach or other leafy green vegetables, blanched snow peas, and cold chicken. The delicacy of the sauce means you must use the best ingredients—if the ginger isn't fresh, tender, and fragrant, the sauce is not worth making. Do make sure the ginger is very finely and evenly chopped, for the sake both of appearance and of texture. You could use water as a substitute for the chicken stock, but obviously at the expense of subtler flavors.

Serves 4 as a starter with one other dish

salt
a generous pound of haricots
   verts or green beans
FOR THE SAUCE
4 teaspoons very finely
   chopped fresh ginger

3 tablespoons chicken stock
2 teaspoons Chinkiang or
   black Chinese vinegar
salt to taste
4 teaspoons sesame oil

1 Trim the beans and cut them into 2-inch sections.

2 Bring a large pot of water to a boil. Salt generously, then add the beans.

Return quickly to a boil and cook for 2–3 minutes, until just crisp-tender. Rinse immediately in cold running water and shake dry in a colander. Arrange the beans neatly on a serving dish.

3 Combine the ginger with the stock and vinegar in a small bowl. Season with salt to taste, then add the sesame oil. (The vinegar should lend the sauce a light "tea color" and gentle sourness.) Pour the sauce over the beans.

LAMP-SHADOW SWEET POTATO CHIPS

deng ying shao pian

Sweet potatoes are traditionally considered to be poor man's food, a substitute for rice in the mountains of western Sichuan where the cultivation of rice is impossible and local farmers have to use crops like this, one which clings more readily to the arid land. In times of famine during the twentieth century, the communist government sent relief supplies of sweet potato chips to rural areas where there was nothing else to eat. But this dish is a fancy banquet appetizer, an extravagance cooked up out of this most basic of staples, perhaps a symbol of better times. The crude, muddy potatoes are transformed into translucent wisps of crispiness, piled delicately on the serving dish, and dressed in a piquant red sauce. In China they are served at high-level banquets. In the West, they go deliciously with a glass of wine or a martini as an aperitif, a welcome variation on the tortilla chip theme.

Makes a generous bowlful of sweet potato chips

about a pound of sweet
  potatoes
peanut oil for deep-frying
FOR THE SAUCE
  3 tablespoons chili oil

1 tablespoon sesame oil
3/4 teaspoon salt
2 teaspoons white sugar

1 Wash and peel the sweet potatoes. Cut them into the thinnest possible slices, preferably using a mandoline or a food processor. Banquet chefs in Chengdu will trim their potatoes so that the slices are perfectly rectangular, but I usually take them as they come. Soak the slices in cold, salted water to remove excess starch and crisp them up.

2 Mix the sauce ingredients together.

3 Heat oil in a wok for deep-frying to about 250°F. Thoroughly pat the potato slices dry and add them a batch at a time to the wok, dropping them in separately and stirring with long chopsticks to make sure they don't stick together. Fry until they are golden, crisp, and translucent, taking great care not to let the oil overheat (add a little cool oil if necessary to calm it down). When each batch is cooked, remove from the pan with a slotted spoon and drain well on paper towels. If you are not intending to eat them immediately, put them into an airtight jar as soon as they have cooled.

4 To serve, toss the chips gently in the sauce to coat them evenly and pile them up elegantly on a serving dish. Serve immediately.

VARIATIONS

Omit the sugar from the sauce and use a little ground roasted Sichuan pepper (see page 74) or oil infused with Sichuan pepper instead for a "hot-and-numbing" (*ma la*) flavor.

Cut the sweet potatoes into very fine slivers and soak and fry them as above, but omit the sauce and sprinkle this "sweet potato floss" (*hong shao song*) with a little white sugar.

Large, red-skinned radishes or daikons can also be slivered, soaked, and fried in the same manner, but they are usually served with a sprinkling of brown sugar.

PRESERVED EGGS
WITH GREEN PEPPERS

qing jiao pi dan

First encounters with the delicacy known in the West as "thousand-year-old eggs" can be disconcerting for Westerners—I have to admit I was revolted by their gray-black color the first time I came across them in Hong Kong. But now I adore them, and most people who actually try them find them delicious—something like an exaggerated egg with their rich, creamy yolks. The secret I have discovered through experimenting on my friends is to close your eyes for the first bite, so that you taste them without prejudice.

The preserved duck eggs sold in Chinese markets in the West are the more mature, darker ones favored by the Cantonese. They have gray yolks, creamily liquid in places, and their whites are a dark but translucent jelly. The milder preserved eggs eaten by the Sichuanese are less daunting for foreigners, although their taste is similar. Their yolks are usually still yellow, but tinged with gray or green, and their whites are an amber-colored jelly. Sometimes the whites are threaded with fern-like, crystalline patterns reminiscent of fossils. Duck eggs are generally used, although quail eggs are also popular in Sichuan.

The raw eggs are caked in a paste made from soda, quicklime, salt, and ash, often with the addition of tea leaves or grain husks, and then left in storage for about three months. This method is thought to have been used in China for about seven centuries.

Until about 1998 in Britain these eggs were imported and sold individually with their thick encrustation of ash and lime still intact, piled up in waist-high ceramic pots encircled by sculpted dragons. But sadly some bureaucratic decision had them banned in favor of preserved eggs produced in the U.K., which are sold washed clean and packaged mundanely in plastic egg-boxes. Their flavors are less subtle, but they are still an interesting treat. If you do manage to find the encrusted eggs, just work off the paste with your fingers, wash the shells in cold water, and pick them open like hard-boiled eggs.

The following simple recipe is one of my favorite Sichuanese starters.

Serves 4 as a starter with one or two other dishes

<table>
<tr><td>1 green bell pepper</td><td>3 preserved duck eggs</td></tr>
<tr><td>1 teaspoon peanut oil for
  cooking</td><td>light soy sauce
chili oil (optional)</td></tr>
<tr><td>salt to taste</td><td></td></tr>
</table>

1 Cut the pepper in half and remove stem and seeds. Flatten slightly by whacking with the side of a cleaver blade or a heavy object.

2 Heat 1 tablespoon of peanut oil in a wok over a medium flame. Add the green pepper pieces and fry for several minutes, until tender. Keep turning the peppers and pressing them into the base of the wok. Add salt to taste when they are nearly done.

3 Turn the pepper pieces out onto a cutting board and, when they have cooled down, chop them finely.

4 Shell the preserved eggs and cut each into 8 sections. Pile up the chopped peppers in the middle of a shallow serving plate and surround with slices of egg arranged like the petals of a flower. Pour 2–3 tablespoons of soy sauce over the peppers and drizzle with chili oil to taste. Some of my Sichuanese friends add a pinch of sugar, too.

SWEET-AND-SOUR RED PEPPERS

tang cu tian jiao

Sweet peppers are also known in Chinese as lantern peppers (*deng long jiao*) because they look a bit like China's traditional festive red lanterns. In Sichuanese cooking, they are often stir-fried with pork or beef, but they also feature in a number of cold banquet dishes. The following mellow, gentle starter, which I enjoyed at the Shufeng restaurant in Chengdu, is easy to prepare. It needs to be served with one or two other dishes with contrasting tastes and textures—perhaps some smoked duck or other cold meat and a crisp green vegetable (olives might be a nice accompaniment, too, although they're not Sichuanese). The same sauce can be used as a dressing for other cold vegetable dishes.

Serves 4 as a starter with one or two other dishes

2 red bell peppers	**salt to taste**
3 teaspoons white sugar	**2 teaspoons sesame oil**
3 teaspoons clear rice vinegar	

1 Cut the peppers in half and remove the stems and seeds. Steam or boil for a few minutes until just cooked.

2 Rinse in cold water, and then peel away the skins (this step can be omitted, but it gives a more sensuous result). Cut the peppers into strips and put into a mixing bowl.

3 Dissolve the sugar in the vinegar. Add 1 or 2 pinches of salt to taste.

4 Pour this sauce over the peppers and toss together. Then add the sesame oil and toss once again.

5 Arrange prettily on a serving plate.

STEAMED EGGPLANTS WITH CHILE SAUCE

hong you qie zi

Eggplants are most commonly cooked in oil, which makes them rich and buttery in taste and texture. The following recipe is interesting because it shows an entirely different side to this delicious vegetable, a pale, soft juiciness and delicate flavor. This dish is a very homey starter, which you won't find in fancy restaurants. The sauce is based on one made by my friend Xu Jun for a festive dinner in her rooms at Sichuan University.

Serves 4 as a starter with two or three other dishes

2 large eggplants or an equivalent amount of slender Asian eggplants (6–8, depending on size) salt	**1 1/2 teaspoons Chinkiang or black Chinese vinegar**
	2 teaspoons sugar
	2 tablespoons chili oil with chile flakes (see page 55)
3 tablespoons light soy sauce	**1 teaspoon sesame oil**

1 If you are using large eggplants, trim them, cut them in half, and sprinkle the cut sides lightly with salt. Leave for at least half an hour to draw out the bitter juices. Asian eggplants do not need this treatment and can be left whole.

2 Steam the eggplants over a high flame for 5–10 minutes, until tender. Peel them if desired. Leave to cool and then cut into chunks (tiny Asian eggplants can simply be split in half lengthwise).

3 Combine the soy sauce, vinegar, and sugar in a small bowl, stirring to dissolve the sugar. Add the oils.

4 Serve the eggplants with the sauce as a dip.

BITTER MELON WITH SESAME OIL
xiang you ku gua

Bitter melon isn't to everyone's taste, and Chinese chefs rarely list it on their English-language menus because they are convinced Westerners won't like it. However, those who enjoy the taste of chicory and dark chocolate may find they love its limpid green bitterness. In this recipe a quick blanching in salted water lightens the taste, and the sesame oil, as always, is delicious. The dish doesn't work well on its own, but should be served with a couple of other appetizers, perhaps a plate of cold meat with a small pile of ground dried chiles for dipping (they are used dry, like a salt-and-Sichuan-pepper dip) and something soothing like sweet-and-sour red peppers.

Serves 4 as a starter with two or three other dishes

3/4 pound bitter melon   salt to taste
   (about 1/2 a large one, or 1   2 teaspoons sesame oil
   or 2 smaller melons)   3–4 tablespoons chicken stock

1 Cut the melon in half lengthwise and scoop out the seeds and pithy part. Chop each half into sections about 2 inches long, and then cut these into long, thin slices.

2 Bring a pot of water to a boil and throw in a little salt. Add the bitter melon slices, return to a boil, and blanch them briefly to "break the rawness"—the slices should remain *al dente*. Drain and refresh immediately under cold running water.

3 In a bowl, smear the bitter melon with salt and sesame oil, then pour over the stock. Pile the slices neatly on a small round plate to serve.

VARIATIONS

Green peas with sesame oil (*xiang you qing yuan*), red peppers with sesame oil (*xiang you tian jiao*), broccoli florets with sesame oil (*xiang you xi nan hua*), cauliflower with sesame oil (*xiang you hua cai*), and so on: blanch fresh, tender vegetables in boiling water and then refresh them in cold water. Cut larger vegetables evenly into bite-size pieces. Smear with a little salt and sesame oil. Just before serving, sprinkle them with more salt and dress with chicken stock and sesame oil to taste.

DAIKON SLIVERS IN A SPICY DRESSING

liang ban luo bu si

 Raw dishes are traditionally rare in Chinese cooking. In ancient times, China (*zhong guo*, which literally means "middle kingdom") was thought by the Chinese to be the fount of all civilization; those who lived beyond the reach of its culture were barbarians. The Chinese divided their barbarians into the "raw" (*sheng*) and the "cooked" (*shu*) according to the food they ate: those who lived on raw food were seen as the most uncivilized. These days the stigma seems to have disappeared, although you still won't find many raw dishes on the Sichuanese table. The following is one of the handful of raw dishes I've encountered. It is extremely easy to prepare, and the sauce is typically Sichuanese. This particular recipe comes from the Converging Rivers Fish Restaurant in Chengdu.

Asian radishes are much larger than those found in the West and have a milder flavor.

Serves 4–6 as a starter with two or three other dishes

a generous pound of daikon
1 teaspoon salt
FOR THE SAUCE
4 teaspoons white sugar
4 teaspoons Chinkiang or
　black Chinese vinegar
1 tablespoon pickled chili paste

1–2 teaspoons crushed garlic
3–4 tablespoons chili oil to
　taste
2 scallions, green parts only,
　very finely sliced
a handful of fresh coriander
　(cilantro)

1 Wash and trim the daikons. Use a cleaver, mandoline, or food processor to cut them into very fine slivers, about 1/8 inch thick. Sprinkle with the salt, mix well, and then spread out in a colander or bamboo basket and leave for about 30 minutes, to let some of their water drain away.

2 Just before serving, combine the sugar and vinegar in a small bowl and stir to dissolve the sugar. Add the pickled chili paste and garlic and mix well.

Pour in the chili oil (you can dilute it with salad oil if you don't want the dish to be too spicy). Add the sliced scallions, and then finely chop the coriander and stir it in.

3 Shake the daikon slivers dry and drizzle them with the dressing. Allow your guests to mix the dressing in at the table.

VARIATIONS

An alternative sauce can be made with the following ingredients:

1/2 teaspoon white sugar	4 tablespoons chili oil
2 teaspoons light soy sauce	2 teaspoons sesame oil
1/2 teaspoon Chinkiang or black Chinese vinegar	1 teaspoon Sichuan pepper oil, if available

Simply stir the sugar into the soy sauce and vinegar, and then add the oils.

Either of these dressings can also be used for slivers of carrot or other raw vegetables.

LETTUCE IN SESAME SAUCE

ma jiang xian cai

The Sichuanese use this nutty sauce to dress various types of variety meats, as well as the leafy stems of a delicious local lettuce, which are cut into frilly "phoenix tail" pieces. The lettuce is sometimes blanched in boiling water before use (and refreshed immediately in cold water). In the following recipe I've suggested using lettuce hearts or crisp lettuce leaves, but you can vary the vegetable as you please. Cucumber is a pleasant substitute.

Serves 2 as a starter, 4 with two or three other dishes

3/4 pound crisp lettuce leaves

FOR THE SAUCE

5 tablespoons Chinese sesame
   paste or dark tahini

2 teaspoons sesame oil

a pinch of sugar

salt to taste

optional garnish: 1/2 teaspoon
   toasted sesame seeds

1 Clean the lettuce. If using lettuce hearts, quarter them lengthwise; small, crisp leaves can be used whole. Arrange the lettuce pieces neatly on a serving plate.

2 Combine the sesame paste and oil in a small bowl and season with the sugar and salt to taste. (The sauce should have a luxurious pouring consistency: it can be thinned if necessary with a little groundnut or salad oil.) Pour over the lettuce leaves. Sprinkle with the sesame seeds, if using, and serve.

FRESH FAVA BEANS
IN A SIMPLE STOCK SAUCE

yan shui hu dou

The fava bean is native to West Asia and North Africa, but has been cultivated in China since ancient times. It is thought to have reached China during the Han Dynasty, at around the time of Christ, and its Sichuanese dialect name is still *hu dou* ("foreign bean"), a sign that it belongs to a family of Han Dynasty imports like black pepper and cucumber, which share the same prefix. (The character *hu*, which originally referred to the non-Chinese peoples living to the north and west of China, also appears in all kinds of phrases meaning to talk nonsense, to rave like a madman, or to really mess things up—which gives you some idea of what the ancient Chinese thought of foreigners.) The fava bean's more common Chinese name is *can dou* ("silkworm bean"), because its pod is thought to resemble the adult silkworm.

Sichuan is China's center of fava bean cultivation, and the fresh beans often crop up on local seasonal menus. Sometimes they are stir-fried, other times eaten in cold dishes like this one. The dried beans are also, most famously, one of the key ingredients of chili bean paste.

Serves 4 as a starter with two or three other dishes

3/4 pound shelled, skinned fava beans (about 2 pounds in their pods)

1/2 teaspoon salt

1/2 teaspoon sesame oil

3 or 4 Sichuan pickled red chiles or 1/2 a red bell pepper

FOR THE SAUCE

4 tablespoons chicken stock

1/2 teaspoon sesame oil

1/2 teaspoon salt

1 Blanch the fava beans in boiling water for a minute or two until they are just cooked. Refresh immediately in cold water, drain, and smear with 1/2 teaspoon of salt and 1/2 teaspoon of sesame oil. Leave to cool.

2 Cut the pickled chiles, if using, in half lengthwise and then diagonally into small lozenge shapes. If using red pepper, blanch briefly in boiling water, refresh in cold water, and then cut into small squares or lozenge shapes. Combine the sauce ingredients in a small bowl. Mix everything together to serve.

VARIATIONS

Fresh soybeans in a simple stock sauce (*yan shui qing dou*).

Fresh fava beans with shrimp (*jin gou hu dou*): omit the pickled chiles or red pepper and substitute 1/2 ounce of dried shrimp. (Bring water to a boil and leave the shrimp in it to soak for about 30 minutes, until soft.)

Fresh fava beans in hot and garlicky sauce (*suan ni hu dou*): use the sauce given in the recipe for cold pork on page 146.

ZHA SHOU DISHES AND OTHER DELICIOUS SNACKS

In the street markets of Sichuan, there's usually a stall or two specializing in snacks and cold foods made by a method—known as *zha shou*—that leaves pieces of meat and fish chewy, glossy, and sumptuously moist with all manner of aromatic oils and spices. When I went to the town of Pixian in search of the home of the famous Pixian chili bean paste, I was distracted for an hour or more by one such stall. Ten or twelve great platters were piled high with the most mouthwatering snacks—little wisps of intensely sweet "shrimp's whisker" beef, sesame seed–scattered pork slivers, translucent slices of "lamp-shadow" beef, and sweet-and-sour spare ribs. I nibbled, sniffed, made comparisons, and chatted to the stall vendor as the bean paste factory seemed less and less compelling (I did make it there in the end).

Because their cooking methods involve several stages, zha shou dishes are not often cooked at home, but are bought in the markets or enjoyed in restaurants. The basic methods are not difficult, however, and the results are worth the labor, particularly if you want to make them in large quantities for a party. The sweet-and-sour spare ribs have almost universal appeal, and those with a taste for hot food will adore the more unusual flavors of the rabbit with Sichuan pepper or the hot-and-numbing dried beef.

Zha shou literally means "deep-fry and draw in," a description of the cooking method, which involves deep-frying pieces of marinated meat or fish until they are crisp and golden and then simmering them in a mixture of stock and flavorings. As the water in the stock evaporates, the flavors are "drawn in" by the meat. The dish is finished with a dressing of spicy oils and sometimes a scattering of ground spices or sesame seeds.

A related dish, and one of Sichuan's most famous snacks, is "lamp-shadow" beef—paper thin, translucent slices of beef all juicy with chili oil and "hot-and-numbing" spices. In his wonderful introduction to famous Sichuan dishes (see page 382), Zhang Furu describes the origins of one of its most celebrated versions, the "lamp-shadow" beef made in the town of Daxian. According to local legend, it was discovered by a ninth-century Tang Dynasty poet, Yuan Zhen, who was given an official posting in the town that is now called Daxian. During his tenure, a drought caused famine among the local population. Yuan Zhen, they say, "loved the people like his own son," and out of concern for their suffering he sometimes dressed in humble clothes and mingled in the villages and markets. One day, as he was on his way home at dusk, he felt so weary and hungry that he stumbled into a wine shop to rest. The owner took pity on him and plied him with wine and morsels of dried beef. The large slices of beef were so paper thin that the golden light shone through when he held them up to the lamp. Their hot-and-numbing flavors, with a long, dreamy aftertaste, were so exquisite that they left him speechless. He asked the name of the dish, but the owner just laughed and told him to give it a name himself. That evening, he took the recipe for "lamp-shadow" beef back to the cook at his official residence and served it to his friends until its fame spread all over the region.

The cooking method for this delicacy is extremely complicated. Thin slices of lean beef are rubbed with salt, rolled up, and left to dry out in a well-ventilated place. They are then spread out on a rack and baked gently over a fire of dying embers, and later steamed. Next they are deep-fried until translucent, and finally they are dressed in a mixture of chili, five-spice, and Sichuan pepper powders, with sesame oil and sugar. The laborious method and advanced cutting skills required for this dish mean that it is made by producers specialized in this skill and sold either in market stalls or in small plastic packages for munching on long bus or railway journeys. I hope that the following recipes, which are of a similar character but less daunting for the home cook, will offer you a taste of the marvelous family of snacks to which "lamp-shadow" beef belongs.

HOT-AND-NUMBING DRIED BEEF

ma la niu rou gan

These dark, chewy strips of beef are delicious, bursting with the flavors of Sichuan. They can be served as a banquet starter or eaten as a very casual snack, perhaps with drinks. For me they bring back memories of difficult but spectacular journeys into the mountains of western Sichuan, when my friends and I used to buy them in packages and munch them with peanuts whenever the bus broke down.

Makes 1 bowlful of dried beef—enough for 4 people as a starter with a couple of other dishes or as a nibble with drinks

about a pound of lean beef
(flank steak is good)
peanut oil for deep-frying
FOR THE BOILING
I star anise
I small piece of cassia bark or
1/2 a cinnamon stick
optional: I *cao guo* (see page
62)
FOR THE MARINADE
a I 1/2-inch piece of fresh
ginger, unpeeled
4 scallions, white parts only
1/2 teaspoon salt
2 teaspoons Shaoxing rice
wine or medium-dry sherry
FOR THE SIMMERING
2 tablespoons peanut oil

a I 1/2-inch piece of fresh
ginger, unpeeled
2 scallions, white parts only
I 1/2 tablespoons white sugar
1/2 teaspoon salt
I tablespoon dark soy sauce
THE DRESSING
1–2 tablespoons chili oil, to
taste
1/2–I teaspoon ground
roasted Sichuan pepper
(see page 74)
1–2 teaspoons ground
Sichuan chiles to taste
2 teaspoons sesame oil
2 teaspoons toasted white
sesame seeds

1 *Optional first step:* blanch the beef for a few seconds in boiling water and then rinse it under the tap to remove some of the bloody juices.

2 Bring the beef to a boil in a pot of fresh water with the star anise, cassia, and *cao guo,* and then turn the heat down and simmer until it is cooked through. When the beef is done, remove it to a cutting board, reserving the stock.

3 Cut the beef with the grain into 1/2-inch slices, and then cut against the grain into 1/2-inch strips. Chop the strips in half if they are very long, and place them all in a bowl. Slightly crush the ginger and scallions for the marinade with the side of a cleaver blade or a heavy object and then chop them into a few pieces. Add them to the beef with 1/2 teaspoon of salt and the Shaoxing rice wine, mixing well. Set aside to marinate for about 30 minutes.

4 Heat oil for deep-frying to 300–325°F. Add the beef and deep-fry for about 4 minutes until red-brown and crispy. Remove with a slotted spoon and drain. (The scallion and ginger from the marinade can be discarded.) Pour the oil into a heatproof dish.

5 Heat another 2 tablespoons of oil in a wok until it begins to smoke. Add the second batch of ginger and scallions, also crushed, and fry for 30–60 seconds until the oil has taken on their fragrances. Add 2 cups of the reserved stock, the sugar, salt, and the dark soy sauce. Add the beef, bring to a boil, and then simmer over a gentle flame for 20–30 minutes until the water has entirely evaporated, leaving the beef in just a little glossy, delicious oil. Remove the wok from the stove and stir in the dressing oils and spices. Mix well.

6 Just before serving, sprinkle with the toasted sesame seeds.

SPICY BEEF SLICES WITH TANGERINE PEEL

chen pi niu rou

陳
皮
牛
肉

The peel of mandarin oranges or tangerines is rarely thrown away in Sichuan. Many people keep the peelings from the fruit and string them up in the open air to dry. It's a habit I've fallen into myself, whenever I eat fragrant, thin-skinned tangerines. I just take off the peel in one or two long pieces, drape them over a piece of string in a sunny window, and leave them for a few days until they are bone dry. If they are then stored in an airtight jar, they keep amazingly well—even after a year you have only to open the lid to be overwhelmed by their sumptuous, fruity fragrance. You can buy dark brown dried tangerine peel in Chinese supermarkets, though its fragrance is rarely as wonderful as the best homemade kind.

Tangerine peel is not often used in Sichuan cooking, but it is particularly associated with this intriguingly flavored little dish, which frequently crops up on banquet menus. It is seasoned with the hallmark Sichuanese spices, dried chiles and Sichuan pepper, but also has a lingering tangerine taste and fragrance and just a hint of sweetness. If you use pale homemade peel, it is also beautiful to look at as you cook, the dark, simmering beef surrounded by the orange-colored peel and dark red chiles. This dish keeps well and can be made a day or two in advance of a dinner party. Do remember when eating that you don't have to eat the fried spices or tangerine peel—just lift out the pieces of meat with your chopsticks.

Makes a generous bowlful, enough for 4–6 people as a nibble with drinks or as part of a starter course

about a pound of lean beef (flank steak is good)
peanut oil for deep-frying
FOR THE MARINADE
a 1 1/2-inch piece of fresh ginger, unpeeled
1 scallion, white and green parts
1/2 teaspoon salt
2 teaspoons Shaoxing rice wine or medium-dry sherry
FOR THE SAUCE
dried tangerine peel

a generous handful of dried Sichuanese chiles (1/2–1 ounce)
2 teaspoons whole Sichuan pepper
1 cup everyday stock (see page 318) or chicken stock
1/2 teaspoon salt
3 teaspoons sugar
1 teaspoon dark soy sauce
1 tablespoon Sichuanese fermented rice wine or Shaoxing rice wine
AND FINALLY
1 teaspoon sesame oil

1 Soak the tangerine peel in enough cold water to cover for at least an hour.

2 Cut the beef across the grain into 2 1/2-inch-square slices, about 1/8 inch thick, discarding any fat or gristly bits. Place in a bowl. Slightly crush the ginger and scallions with the side of a cleaver blade or a heavy object and roughly chop them. Add them to the beef with the other marinade ingredients. Let sit for 30 minutes.

3 Wearing rubber gloves, snip the chiles in half or into 1 1/2-inch sections with a pair of scissors and discard the seeds. Snip the tangerine peel into 1 1/2-inch strips, reserving the fragrant soaking liquid.

4 Heat peanut oil for deep-frying to 325–375°F. Add 2 teaspoons of peanut oil to the beef to help keep the slices separate, stir well, and drop them into the hot oil. Deep-fry for a minute or two until they are cooked, and then remove and drain. Reheat the oil to 350–375°F, return the beef to the wok, and deep-fry for a second time until the slices are crisp and deep brown in color (this should take another minute or two). Remove and drain. (The scallion and ginger from the marinade can be discarded.)

5 Return the wok to a medium flame with about 1/3 cup of the cooking oil. When it is hot, but not smoking-hot, add the chiles and Sichuan pepper and stir-fry for 10–20 seconds until they are fragrant, taking great care not to burn them (add a little cool oil if they are overheating). Then add the tangerine peel and stir-fry for a few seconds more until you can smell its fragrance, too. Add the stock, the beef, the tangerine soaking water, and all the other sauce ingredients. Bring to a boil and simmer gently for 20–30 minutes, stirring from time to time until the stock has evaporated, leaving only a rich, oily sauce. Turn onto a serving dish and drizzle with the sesame oil. Serve at room temperature.

VARIATIONS

The same flavors and cooking technique can be used to cook rabbit or chicken. Because these meats are very pale, you may wish to add a little dark soy sauce to the marinade to give them a richer color.

For vegetarians: I have also tried this recipe successfully with small cubes of crispy, deep-fried bean curd—just omit the marinade stage. (You may wish to add a little extra salt to the simmering sauce.)

BEEF SLIVERS WITH SESAME SEEDS

zhi ma niu rou si

The Sichuanese provincial capital, Chengdu, has a population of several tens of thousands of Muslims. Most belong to the Hui ethnic group, who look Chinese and speak the Chinese language; but some are ethnic Uighur migrants, who speak a Turkic language and come to Chengdu from their native Xinjiang region to sell kebabs or trade in sultanas (yellow raisins) and other local products. The center of the city's Muslim community was for centuries the few narrow streets around the Imperial City mosque, a sprawling, peaceful building with tiled roofs and leafy courtyards. There had been a mosque on the same site for more than four hundred years, but like many of China's historic buildings it was demolished in 1998 in the name of modernization, along with all the surrounding streets. The demolition also claimed most of the Muslim restaurants that had traded in the area. Some were simple noodle shops, others more formal eateries that served special Muslim versions of many of Sichuan's most famous dishes. Naturally, they banished pork from their menus, substituting for it beef or lamb.

The following dish is most commonly made with pork, but I've used beef for the sake of offering a dish typical of Muslim adaptations of Sichuanese cuisine. This version obviously has a stronger flavor and texture than the usual pork dish, but I think it's equally delicious. If you'd rather use pork, just go ahead. The strips of beef have a wonderful chewy consistency and a mellow, aromatic taste. They are particularly good as a nibble with wine, but can also be eaten with other dishes as part of a cold starter course. They keep well and can be made in large batches a day or two in advance of a dinner party.

Makes a generous bowlful of beef pieces, enough for 4–6 as a nibble with drinks or as part of a starter course

about a pound of lean beef
   (flank steak is good)
peanut oil for deep-frying
FOR THE MARINADE
a 2-inch piece of fresh ginger,
   unpeeled
I scallion, white and green
   parts
1/2 teaspoon salt
2 teaspoons Shaoxing rice
   wine or medium-dry sherry
FOR THE SAUCE
I cup of everyday stock (see
   page 318) or chicken stock

I teaspoon dark soy sauce
I teaspoon Shaoxing rice
   wine or medium-dry sherry
1/4 teaspoon salt
2 1/2 teaspoons white sugar
I star anise
a few pieces of cassia bark or
   1/3 of a cinnamon stick
FOR THE GARNISH
1/2 teaspoon sesame oil
optional: I tablespoon chili oil
I tablespoon toasted sesame
   seeds

I Cut the beef against the grain into strips about a 1/4 to 1/2 inch wide and 4 inches long, removing any gristly bits. Place in a bowl. Slightly crush the ginger and scallion with the side of a cleaver blade or a heavy object and roughly chop them. Add to the beef with the other marinade ingredients. Mix well, and leave for 20 minutes or so.

2 Heat the peanut oil for deep-frying over a high flame to 325–375°F. Discard the ginger and scallion from the marinade, and then mix 2 teaspoons of oil into the beef to help the strips separate. Drop the strips into the hot oil and deep-fry for 1–2 minutes, stirring occasionally to separate, until they are cooked. Remove and drain. Allow the oil temperature to return to 350–375°F, then return the beef to the wok and continue to deep-fry for another couple of minutes until the strips are crisp and a rich dark brown. Remove and drain.

3 Bring the stock to the boil in a clean wok. Add the beef strips and the other sauce ingredients and simmer over a gentle heat for 10–15 minutes, stirring from time to time, until the liquid has reduced by half; then add 1 tablespoon of peanut oil and stir it in. When the liquid has all but evaporated, remove from the heat and stir in the sesame and chili oils. When the beef has cooled, stir in the sesame seeds and serve at your leisure.

VARIATIONS

Use pork (butt or shoulder), as in the original dish, or lamb (shoulder) or chicken (thigh). If you are using lamb, make sure to cut the strips against the grain.

Vegetarians can use strips of firm bean curd to make a similar dish. Just omit the marinade stage and deep-fry once only.

FIVE-SPICED "SMOKED" FISH
wu xiang xun yu

Smoked fish is a traditional Chinese food, but this modern variation rarely passes through a smoking stage, despite its name. It's a sensational dish, with crisp chunks of tender fish draped lavishly in a rich, dense, aromatic sauce. It is usually made with small, flavorful crucian carp, served three to the plate, but since they are unavailable in the West, I've written the recipe using chunks of a larger fish. Grass carp would be the choice of the Sichuanese cook, but sea bass or ocean perch works just as well. Some cooks use five-spice powder, but I prefer the superior flavor of a couple of whole spices (you can add to these if you wish).

Serves 4 as a starter or as part of a light lunch, 6–8 as part of a Chinese starter course

2 pounds sea bass or ocean perch fillets	**3/4 cup everyday stock (see page 318) or chicken stock**
peanut oil for deep-frying	**2 teaspoons Shaoxing rice wine or medium-dry sherry**
FOR THE MARINADE	**1 teaspoon dark soy sauce**
a 2-inch piece of fresh ginger, unpeeled	**1/2 teaspoon white sugar**
1 scallion, white and green parts	**1 star anise**
2 teaspoons Shaoxing rice wine or medium-dry sherry	**1/4 teaspoon whole Sichuan pepper**
1/2 teaspoon salt	**a couple of bits of cassia bark or 1/3 of a cinnamon stick**
FOR THE SAUCE	**1/2 teaspoon salt**
2 scallions, white and green parts	**a couple of pinches of ground white pepper or 6–8 turns of a black pepper mill**
3 tablespoons peanut oil	FOR THE GARNISH
2 teaspoons finely chopped garlic	**1 teaspoon sesame oil**
2 teaspoons finely chopped fresh ginger	

1 Leaving the skin on, cut each fish fillet into slices 1 1/2 inches wide, cutting across the fish. Put the fish pieces into a bowl. Slightly crush the ginger and scallion for the marinade with the side of a cleaver blade or a heavy object and roughly chop them. Add to the fish with the other marinade ingredients. Leave for 15–20 minutes.

2 Finely slice the 2 scallions for the sauce, separating the green and white parts.

3 When the fish is ready, discard the ginger and scallion pieces from the marinade and pat the pieces dry with paper towels or a dry kitchen towel. Heat the oil for deep-frying to 325–350°F. Add the fish pieces and deep-fry for 3–4 minutes until they are crisp and golden (you may wish to fry them in more than one batch). Remove and drain well.

4 Heat 3 tablespoons of oil in a clean wok over a high flame. When it is hot, add the garlic, ginger, and the scallion whites and stir-fry until they are fragrant. Then add the stock and the other sauce ingredients, stir well, and gently add the fish pieces to the liquid. Return to a boil, then turn the heat down and simmer gently, basting the fish and stirring gently from time to time. After 10–15 minutes, when the stock has almost completely evaporated, turn off the heat and transfer the fish pieces to a serving plate with a slotted spoon. Drizzle them with the sesame oil, scatter with the scallion greens, and then pour over the remains of the sauce from the wok. You can eat it immediately, but it's usually served at room temperature.

VARIATION

Vegetarians can use the same seasonings and cooking method to prepare chunks of crispy deep-fried bean curd. Just omit the marinade stage.

SWEET-AND-SOUR SPARE RIBS

tang cu pai gu

This recipe is not unique to Sichuan, but it's a tasty and popular starter that I have enjoyed on many occasions in the restaurants of Chengdu. The ribs should be succulent and tasty, glistening in a dark, syrupy sauce.

Serves 4 as a starter, with one or two other dishes

a 2-inch piece of fresh ginger,
  unpeeled
4 scallions, white parts only
about a pound of meaty spare
  ribs, chopped into 1-inch
  lengths
salt
1 tablespoon Shaoxing rice
  wine or medium-dry sherry

peanut oil for deep frying
1 teaspoon dark soy sauce
4 tablespoons white sugar
1 tablespoon Chinkiang or
  black Chinese vinegar
1 teaspoon sesame oil
2 tablespoons toasted sesame
  seeds (optional)

1 Slightly crush the ginger and scallions with the side of a cleaver blade or a heavy object and roughly chop them. Bring a large pot of water to a boil. Add the spare ribs, return to a boil, and skim after a few seconds. Then add about a quarter of the ginger and scallions and simmer until the meat is cooked—about 5 minutes. Transfer the meat to a bowl, reserving the stock. While the ribs are still steaming hot, add a marinade of 1/4–1/2 teaspoon of salt, 1 tablespoon of Shaoxing rice wine, and two-thirds of the remaining scallions and ginger. Let sit for about 30 minutes.

2 Heat plenty of oil for deep-frying until it is smoking hot. Add the spare ribs and fry until crisp and golden brown—this will take 4 or 5 minutes. Remove from the oil and drain.

3 Drain all but 2 tablespoons of oil from the wok. Return the wok to a hot flame, add the remaining ginger and scallions, and stir-fry until fragrant. Add the ribs and about 1/2 cup of the pork stock. Add the dark soy sauce to give the sauce a rich caramel color, and season with salt (about 1/4 teaspoon). When the liquid has come to a boil, add the sugar and lower to a gentle flame.

4 Simmer for 10–15 minutes, stirring often, until the water has evaporated and the sauce is of a lazy, syrupy consistency. Add the vinegar and stir in. Simmer for a very short time, until the sauce is syrupy again, and remove from the heat. Stir in the sesame oil.

5 Allow to cool before serving, removing the pieces of ginger and scallion. Sprinkle with sesame seeds if desired.

RABBIT WITH SICHUAN PEPPER

hua jiao tu ding

花
椒
兔
丁

This wonderful dish will make your lips tingle and warm your heart. The chunks of rabbit are glazed in a lustrous sauce filled with the fragrance of chiles and Sichuan pepper. Spice fans will adore it. Do remember when eating that you don't have to eat the fried spices—just pluck out the pieces of rabbit meat with your chopsticks.

Serves 4 as a starter, with one or two other dishes

1 1/4 pounds rabbit meat, on or off the bone (about 1/2 a rabbit)
peanut oil for deep-frying

FOR THE MARINADE

3 scallions, white parts only
a piece of fresh ginger, unpeeled
1 tablespoon Shaoxing rice wine or medium-dry sherry
1/2 teaspoon salt

FOR THE SAUCE

a generous handful of dried Sichuanese chiles
2 tablespoons whole Sichuan pepper
3/4 cup everyday stock (see page 318) or chicken stock
1/2 teaspoon sugar
1 teaspoon dark soy sauce
salt

AND FINALLY

1 teaspoon sesame oil

1 Chop the rabbit, on or off the bone, into 1-inch chunks. Slightly crush the scallion and ginger with the side of a cleaver blade or a heavy object and roughly chop them. Add them and the other marinade ingredients to the rabbit and leave in a cool place for 30 minutes or more. Snip the chiles in half or into 1/2-inch sections, discarding the seeds.

2 Heat plenty of oil for deep-frying until beginning to smoke. Add the rabbit chunks and fry over a high flame for about 5 minutes, until golden brown but not dried out. Remove and drain.

3 Heat 3 tablespoons of oil in a wok over medium heat. Add the chiles and

Sichuan pepper and stir-fry until the oil is richly fragrant. Do not do this over too high a flame or the spices will burn. Add the cooked rabbit chunks and stir into the fragrant oil. Add the stock and bring to a boil. Turn down the heat and add the sugar and soy sauce, which should give the liquid a rich caramel color. Season with salt to taste.

4 Simmer for about 15 minutes, until the liquid has all but evaporated. Remove from the heat, stir in the sesame oil, and leave to cool. Serve at room temperature.

RABBIT WITH ROCK SUGAR
bing tang tu ding

Rock or crystal sugar is known as "ice sugar" (*bing tang*) in Chinese, for obvious reasons. The large transparent crystals are sold by weight in Sichuanese markets and must be smashed with a hammer or other heavy implement before they are used in the kitchen. Rock sugar is valued for the purity of its sweetness and has several uses in Chinese medicine. It is also used in many Sichuanese dishes that are prepared specifically for their medicinal or nutritional value. The following dish is a delicious luxury, and I suspect it will be enjoyed by anyone who has eaten sweet-and-sour spare ribs with pleasure. The rabbit chunks are embraced by a sweet, lustrous, chestnut-red sauce and scattered with a few white sesame seeds.

Serves 4 as a starter, with one or two other dishes

about a pound rabbit meat, on or off the bone (about 1/2 a rabbit)
peanut oil for deep-frying
FOR THE MARINADE
3 scallions, white parts only

a 2-inch piece of fresh ginger, unpeeled
1 tablespoon Shaoxing rice wine or medium-dry sherry
1/2 teaspoon salt

OTHER INGREDIENTS
  1/2 cup rock sugar
  1/3 cup hot water
  salt

1 teaspoon sesame oil
2 teaspoons toasted white
  sesame seeds

1 Chop the rabbit, on or off the bone, into 1-inch chunks. Slightly crush the scallion and ginger with the side of a cleaver blade or a heavy object and roughly chop them. Add them and the other marinade ingredients to the rabbit and leave in a cool place for 30 minutes or more.

2 Heat plenty of oil for deep-frying until beginning to smoke. Add the rabbit chunks and fry over a high flame for about 5 minutes, until golden brown but not dried out. Remove and drain.

3 Crush the rock sugar—you can do this by wrapping it in a plastic bag and a kitchen towel, laying it on a cutting board or other hard surface not susceptible to damage, and then whacking it with a hammer or a rolling pin.

4 Put 4 tablespoons of oil into a wok. Add the crushed rock sugar and warm over a gentle heat. Stir constantly as the sugar melts and changes color. When the liquid is a rich red-brown, quickly add the hot water, standing well back to avoid the steam, and stir well. Add the deep-fried rabbit chunks and season with salt to taste.

5 Simmer gently for about 15 minutes, until the sauce is heavy and syrupy.

6 Turn out onto a serving dish, drizzle with the remaining sauce and then sprinkle with the sesame oil. When cold, scatter the sesame seeds over and serve.

STEWED AROMATIC MEATS (lu rou)

All over the city of Chengdu there are street stalls specializing in stewed, aromatic meats and poultry. Caramel-colored ducks and bronzed chickens hang overhead; below them are trays of chicken wings, pig's tails and ears, poultry innards, and all kinds of other delicious tidbits. All have been cooked until tender in a rich broth seasoned with salt, sugar, wine, and spices, and then left to cool. They are eaten at room temperature, with perhaps a splash of the cooking liquid and a dash of sesame oil, or a dish of ground roasted chiles.

The broth (*lu shui*) is usually based on pork bones, but also absorbs the flavors of whatever meats are cooked in it. Most professional vendors have a virtually everlasting broth—it is simply replenished with stock, salt, sugar, wine, and spices as needed, and boiled up and skimmed regularly to keep it clean. (Western cooks might like to strain and freeze the broth and use it again another time.) Beef and lamb tend to be cooked in a separate broth from pork and poultry, because of their stronger flavors. Firm bean curd (*dou fu gan*) can also be stewed in this way, but its cooking liquid should be thrown away after only one use.

Don't feel obliged to use exactly the spices suggested below—they can be varied according to your mood and their availability. Most Sichuanese cooks try to include about ten different spices, which may also include cardamom (*cao dou kou*), a type of dried ginger (*shan nai* or *sha jiang*), *Fructus amoni* (*sha ren tou*), and sometimes dried chiles. The spices can be bought individually from large sacks in the open markets, or in little bags of mixed spices that are specifically sold for making *lu shui*. Some Sichuanese recipes suggest making the broth much saltier than the recipe below.

It should be remembered by those who live within reach of any China-town that many restaurants sell stewed meats for take-out. These already cooked meats are delicious and reasonably priced and make a convenient addition to a home-cooked Chinese meal. Many of my Sichuanese friends buy some tea-smoked duck or stewed chicken wings when they invite friends for dinner—this takes the stress off the cook by reducing the number of dishes that have to be prepared at the last minute. If you are using cooked meats bought in Chinatown, you can give them a Sichuanese touch by serving them with a dish of ground chiles.

AROMATIC BROTH
lu shui

The following recipe makes enough broth to cook a whole chicken or duck, but you can use it to stew meats of your choice. Chicken drumsticks and wings, duck wings, bean curd, and hard-boiled eggs (bashed slightly to crack them all over and then stewed in their shells) are all particularly good. Rabbit, lamb, and beef can also be cooked this way. Meats are best prepared by blanching them first in boiling water and rinsing under the tap before adding to the broth. This removes most of the bloody juices and keeps the broth clean. Some cooks also marinate beef or lamb in ginger, scallion, salt, and wine before blanching.

a 3-inch piece of fresh ginger, unpeeled

5 scallions, white and green parts

2 tablespoons peanut oil or corn oil

1 1/4 cup rock sugar

5 quarts everyday stock (see page 318) or chicken stock

3/4 cup salt

1/3 cup Shaoxing rice wine or medium-dry sherry

optional: a double layer of cheesecloth to wrap the spices

THE SPICES

2 tablespoons whole Sichuan pepper

1 1/2 tablespoons cassia bark or cinnamon stick bits

1 1/2 tablespoons licorice root (optional)

2 tablespoons star anise

3 tablespoons fennel seeds

1 tablespoon whole cloves

4 cao guo (see page 62) (optional)

TO SERVE

sesame oil

ground Sichuanese chiles, paprika, or cayenne pepper to taste

optional: ground roasted Sichuan pepper (see page 74)

salt

1 Place all the spices onto the pieces of cheesecloth and tie securely with string. (The spices can be used loose, but are then harder to remove from the cooked meats.) Crush the ginger and scallions slightly with the side of a cleaver blade or a heavy object and cut each scallion into 2 or 3 sections.

2 Bring a pot of water to a boil. In a wok, heat the peanut oil with 1/2 cup of rock sugar over a very low flame. Stir constantly as the sugar melts (if the rock sugar is in very large pieces you may wish to crush them first). Then turn the heat up to medium and continue to stir until the liquid is a rich caramel brown. Quickly splash in about 1 cup of the boiling water from the kettle—make sure you stand back, as the wok will release a lot of heat and steam. Stir well.

3 Put the stock, caramel liquid, and all the other broth ingredients, including the rest of the rock sugar, into a very large saucepan and bring them to a boil. Give them a good stir and then simmer over low heat for at least an hour until flavorful.

4 Add the meats, poultry pieces, eggs, or bean curd and cook until they are tender and aromatic. Add enough fresh stock to cover if necessary.

5 To serve, thinly slice any large chunks of meat; cut poultry or rabbit into strips. Serve hot or cold, with a drizzling of the cooking broth and some sesame oil, and small piles of ground chiles, Sichuan pepper, and salt.

MAN-AND-WIFE MEAT SLICES
fu qi fei pian

夫
妻
肺
片

"Man-and-wife meat slices" is a popular cold meat dish that is based on the stewing method described above in the recipe for aromatic broth (page 179). This dish began as a street snack, but it is now a famous appetizer in Sichuanese restaurants. It is named after a man called Guo Chaohua, who invented it with his wife in the 1930s and sold it on the streets of Chengdu. The name fei pian literally means "lung slices," and the dish is traditionally made with a mixture of lean beef and innards (including ox hearts, tongues, and stomachs), all stewed in a delicious aromatic broth. It's equally good made simply with lean or marbled meat, as in the following recipe. The meat is subtly spiced and tender, the sauce hot and zingy, and the celery and toasted nuts offer an interesting crunch. Chinese celery, which has stems more slender than its Western counterpart, can sometimes be found in Chinese supermarkets.

Serves 4 as a starter

about a pound of lean beef
(flank steak), in one piece

TO COOK THE BEEF

a 2-inch piece of fresh ginger,
unpeeled

1 tablespoon peanut oil

2 tablespoons rock sugar, crushed

1 quart everyday stock (see
page 318) or chicken stock

1 1/2 tablespoons salt

2 scallions, white and green
parts, cut into thirds

1 teaspoon whole Sichuan pepper

a few bits of cassia bark or 1/2 a
cinnamon stick

1 teaspoon fennel seeds

2 star anise

4 whole cloves, their powdery

heads pinched off and
discarded

TO SERVE

3–4 stalks of celery or an
equivalent amount of thin
Chinese celery

1 tablespoon dark soy sauce

1–2 tablespoons chili oil with
chile flakes (see page 55) to
taste

1/2 teaspoon ground roasted
Sichuan pepper (see page 74)

2 teaspoons toasted sesame
seeds

2 tablespoons roasted unsalted
peanuts, crushed

coriander (cilantro) leaves to
garnish

1 Slightly crush the ginger with the side of a cleaver blade or a heavy object.

2 Bring a pot of water to a boil. Add the beef and blanch for 10–20 seconds. Throw away the water and rinse the beef under the tap.

3 Heat the peanut oil with half the rock sugar in a wok over a gentle heat. When the sugar has melted, raise the temperature and boil until the liquid is a rich, caramel brown. Quickly throw in a small coffee-cupful of cold water, standing well back to avoid the rush of steam, and stir briskly to incorporate. Transfer the liquid to a saucepan.

4 Add the stock, the rest of the sugar, the salt, ginger and scallions, and all the spices, tied in a double layer of cheesecloth if you wish. Bring the liquid to a vigorous boil and add the blanched beef. Return to a boil, cover, and simmer gently for about an hour and a half, until the beef is beautifully tender.

5 Remove the beef from the cooking liquid, cover, and set aside to cool completely. Keep the cooking liquid.

6 To serve, remove the fibrous outer edge of the celery stalks and slice them thinly. You can chop up the leaves too if they are tasty. (If you are using Chinese celery, just chop it into 2-inch lengths.) Lay the celery on a serving plate. Thinly slice the cold beef, against the grain of the meat. Lay it attractively on top of the celery. Combine 4 tablespoons of the cold cooking liquid with the soy sauce and pour over the meat. Drizzle with the chili oil and sprinkle with the Sichuan pepper, sesame seeds, peanuts, and coriander (cilantro).

TEA-SMOKED DUCK

zhang cha ya zi

Smoked duck is one of Sichuan's most lauded delicacies. At its best it is juicy, rich, and infused with the delicate aromas of jasmine-scented tea and fragrant wood shavings. In Chengdu, it will forever be associated with one particular alley that was famous in the early days of republican China for its lively teahouses and wine shops. Because of its narrow, inconspicuous entrance and capacious interior, this place was nicknamed "The Mousehole." In 1928, one Zhang Guoliang set up a duck stall at the entrance to the Mousehole, which soon became known for its exquisite smoked duck. The rest is culinary history. There's still a restaurant in Chengdu called Mr. Zhang's Mousehole Duck (*hao zi dong zhang ya zi*) in Zhang Guoliang's honor, which specializes in smoked duck and other traditional Sichuanese dishes. The duck produced here, which can be eaten in or taken out, is exceptionally fine.

Tea-smoked duck is not a dish that is normally attempted in the home kitchen, as the recipe is somewhat complicated, involving a long marinade, air-drying, smoking, steaming, and deep-frying. Most people simply buy it from specialized manufacturers who have the right equipment and often years of experience. I have found it hard to recreate in my simple wok the depth of flavor I've enjoyed in the real Sichuanese duck, which is smoked over a wood fire to exquisite effect. However, it is possible to make a pretty tasty imitation if you are so inclined. The following recipe has been worked out from local sources, with some tips from Yan-kit So's *Classic Food of China* on how to smoke a duck in a Western kitchen.

The Sichuanese duck is traditionally smoked over a mixture of jasmine tea, cypress or pine twigs, and sawdust. Since these types of wood are a little hard to track down, I've suggested using a more easily arranged mixture of jasmine tea, flour, and sugar. If you do manage to lay your hands on untreated sawdust, or twigs of cypress, just go ahead and use them instead of the flour and sugar. Don't oversmoke the bird—it should be subtly, not overpoweringly, smoky in taste.

Most Sichuanese cookbooks give the name of this dish as "camphor and tea-smoked duck" (*zhang cha ya zi*) and suggest using camphor (*zhang*) leaves and twigs as smoking materials. But according to China's leading authority on Sichuanese food, Professor Xiong Sizhi, this is based on a confusion over Chinese characters. He says the dish is called *zhang cha ya zi* not because of any connection with camphor, but because it was originally smoked over a special kind of tea leaves from Zhangzhou, in Fujian province. The cooking method, he says, was invented by a man called Huang Jinlin, one-time manager of the Dowager Empress Cixi's kitchens in Beijing, who brought the dish to Sichuan when he opened a restaurant in Chengdu.

To make this dish you will need aluminum foil, a smoking rack that fits into your wok (see below), and a steamer that is big enough to accommodate the whole duck in a deep bowl.

Serves 4–8 as part of a cold lunch or a starter course

1 duck, weighing about 5 pounds

FOR THE MARINADE
2 tablespoons salt
2 teaspoons whole Sichuan pepper
1/2 teaspoon ground black or white pepper
1 1/2 teaspoons saltpeter
6 tablespoons Shaoxing rice wine (or medium-dry sherry) and 4 tablespoons Sichuanese fermented rice wine, or 8 tablespoons Shaoxing rice wine (or medium-dry sherry)

SMOKING MATERIALS
3/4 cup all-purpose flour
3/4 cup white sugar
1/2 cup jasmine blossom tea

FOR THE STEAMING
a 2 1/2-inch piece of fresh ginger, unpeeled
4 scallions, white parts only

FOR THE DEEP-FRYING
plenty of peanut oil—at least enough to half immerse the duck

FINALLY
1 teaspoon sesame oil

1 *Marinating*: Mix the salt, Sichuan pepper, ground pepper, and saltpeter in a mortar, mixing well and crushing the Sichuan pepper. Combine the Shaoxing rice wine and fermented rice wine in a small bowl. Rub the duck all over, inside and out, with the salt and spices and then with the wine mixture. Let it sit breast-down in a cool place for 12 hours or overnight. Afterward, place the duck in a colander and scald it by pouring a pot of boiling water over it—this will improve the final texture of the skin. Wipe the duck dry, inside and out, with a clean kitchen towel or paper towels and hang it in a well-ventilated place to air-dry for 6 hours or more.

2 *Smoking*: Line a wok with two layers of aluminum foil. Mix together the flour and sugar and lay them all over the base of the wok, scattering the tea leaves over the top. Arrange some sort of rack to hold the duck a good couple of inches above the smoking materials—I use a small metal trivet with a round metal rack laid on top (I bought both in a Chinese supermarket). Place the wok over a very high flame. When the tea leaves are beginning to smoke merrily, place the duck, breast-down, on the rack, cover the wok with a lid and leave for 30 minutes, turning the bird after 15 minutes. You can turn the heat down to medium when the tea leaves are smoldering, but make sure the smoke is still emerging. After 30 minutes the bird should be a light golden yellow.

3 *Steaming*: When the smoking is finished, lay the bird breast-up in a large bowl or deep dish in your steamer. Slightly crush the ginger and scallions with the side of a cleaver blade or a heavy object and place them in the bowl with the duck. A few pieces can also be put inside the duck. Bring the water in the steamer to a fast boil, cover, and steam the duck for an hour or so, until it is tender and cooked. You can test it by inserting a skewer in the fattest part behind the leg, but take care to cause minimal damage to the skin, or it may rupture during the final deep-frying. When the duck is cooked, remove it gently from the bowl and leave it to cool. Gently tilt the duck and pour out as much of the juices as possible from the cavity, but make sure to keep the bird intact. (The juices left in the steaming bowl make a fantastic base for a noodle soup or stew.)

4 *Deep-frying*: Heat enough oil in a wok or deep-fat fryer to generously immerse at least half the duck. If you are using a wok, make absolutely sure it is anchored securely in a wok stand, for safety reasons. When the oil

reaches a temperature of about 350°F, gently lower in the duck using a Chinese wire-mesh spoon or a couple of perforated spoons. The temperature will drop initially if the duck is cold—bring it quickly back to 325°F and fry at this temperature for about 4 minutes. Then gently turn the duck and fry the other side for the same amount of time, until the skin is crisp and a rich, caramel brown in color. Remove it from the pan and set it aside to cool down. While the duck is still warm, brush the skin very sparingly with the sesame oil to enhance its gloss and fragrance.

5 *Serving:* To serve, you can just slice the duck as you please or cut it into 2-inch by 3/4-inch sections on the bone, Chinese style, and reassemble in an approximate duck shape on your serving platter. At high-class banquets this dish is sometimes accompanied by lotus-leaf buns (see page 124), but it is more commonly eaten on its own, alongside other cold dishes.

VARIATION

The same method can be used to smoke quails or geese, adjusting the quantities and cooking times accordingly.

COLD CHICKEN WITH FRAGRANT RICE WINE

xiang zao ji tiao

In this dish, steaming is used to infuse chicken meat with the sweet, mellow fragrance of fermented glutinous rice. It is usually served cold, although you can eat it straight from the steamer.

Serves 4 as a starter with one or two other dishes

3/4 pound cooked chicken meat

1/2 cup fermented glutinous rice wine (see page 60)

a good pinch of ground white pepper

1/2 teaspoon salt

2–3 teaspoons sesame oil

1 Cut the chicken into strips 1/2–1 inch wide and about 2 1/2 inches long. Lay the strips neatly in a bowl that will fit into your steamer (make sure you lay the tidiest strips of chicken at the base of the bowl, as they are the ones that will be seen when the dish is turned onto a plate for serving). Mix together the wine and seasonings and then pour them over the chicken.

2 Place the bowl in a steamer and steam for 10 minutes over a high flame.

3 Allow the chicken to cool, and then turn it on to a plate. Drizzle with a little sesame oil before serving.

STIR-FRIED DISHES

With a few exceptions, stir-fried dishes are generally intended to be eaten hot, with rice, as part of a main meal. Many, however, taste delicious at room temperature and are eaten that way for more informal meals. Home cooks often serve up leftovers from the previous night, either reheated or simply served cold, and cold stir-fried dishes are often a major feature of *leng dan bei*, the casual, tapas-style eating enjoyed in the back streets of Chengdu on sultry summer evenings. One *leng dan bei* restaurant whose menu I jotted down was serving a number of stir-fried dishes cooled to room temperature, including green beans with chiles and ginger, lotus root cubes with chiles and green bell peppers, water spinach, bitter melon with green peppers, pickled string beans with minced pork, "tiger-skin" peppers, salty sweet corn, and eggplants with green bell peppers. They were accompanied by platters of soybeans in their pods, preserved duck eggs, dry bean curd in chili oil, boiled and roasted peanuts, deep-fried crayfish, snails in chile sauce, and all kinds of cold meats.

Recipes for stir-fried dishes like these are given in the vegetable section of this book, because they are mostly eaten hot. I have indicated which of them can be enjoyed equally well cold. As a general rule, any stir-fry that doesn't involve animal fats or starch-thickened sauces can be cooled without spoiling.

The following dish, which is one of my favorites, is unusual in that it is stir-fried with spices (*qiang*), but invariably eaten at room temperature or chilled.

SPICY CUCUMBER SALAD

qiang huang gua

This salad is wonderfully simple to prepare—the only secret is to keep the cooking *brief*—and it has the advantage that it can be made hours in advance of the meal. Don't let the simplicity of its ingredients deceive you into thinking this is a dull dish—it is not. The slippery cucumber is permeated with the intriguing rumor of spice and sesame, and it looks lovely, too, with its scattering of red chiles and Sichuan pepper. In Sichuan you might find it served at a banquet as part of a mixed hors d'oeuvre, perhaps with a selection of cold meats and peanuts, or accompanied by several different types of dumpling. I usually serve it as part of a Chinese meal or a simple salady lunch.

Serves 4–6 as part of a Chinese meal or as a vegetable side dish

2 average-size cucumbers	2 teaspoons whole Sichuan
3 teaspoons salt	pepper
2 tablespoons peanut oil	3 teaspoons sesame oil
8 long dried chiles or 16 small	
Sichuanese chiles snipped	
into 1 1/2-inch sections	

1 Cut the cucumber into 2 1/2-inch sections. Quarter these lengthwise, remove the seeds and pulp, and then cut evenly into batons the size of french-fried potatoes. Sprinkle with the salt, mix well, and set aside for at least 30 minutes, preferably 2 hours or more, to draw out some of the juices. Then drain well and press gently to get rid of as much water as possible. Pat the cucumber pieces dry with paper towels or a clean kitchen towel.

2 Heat a wok over a high heat until smoke rises. Add the peanut oil and swirl around to cover the base of the wok. Turn the heat down to a medium flame and then add the chiles and Sichuan pepper. Stir these swiftly for a few seconds until they smell deliciously spicy and the chiles are turning a darker red. Take great care not to burn the spices.

3 Add the cucumber pieces and stir and toss for about 10 seconds to coat them in the flavored oil. Remove from the heat, add the sesame oil, and stir thoroughly before tipping the cucumber onto a serving dish. The cucumber should not be cooked through, just swiftly heated so that it absorbs the flavor of the spices. Allow to cool before serving.

OTHER DELICIOUS TIDBITS

SOYBEANS IN THEIR PODS
mao dou

 On sticky summer evenings in Chengdu, my friends and I used to gather on the banks of the Brocade River for drinks and a lazy supper. Small tables and chairs would have been set up at dusk on the edge of the river and the sidewalk nearby, as a row of little restaurants spilled their trade into the open air. Candles burned in empty beer bottles, and the occasional lantern hung from the trees. We would order little platefuls of exquisite smoked pig's liver, preserved eggs with hot green peppers, stir-fried sweet corn kernels, glossy peanuts sprinkled with Sichuan pepper, and salty duck eggs cut into sections on the shell. One of my favorite snacks, however, was the fresh soybeans served in their pods. These we would nibble idly, squeezing the tender, juicy beans from their rough shells. If you can't find fresh soybeans, you can buy them frozen in some Asian supermarkets (the Japanese call them *edamame*). If you do find them fresh, they must be boiled until they are really tender.

Serves 4–6 as a starter, with drinks

about 1 pound frozen, precooked soybeans in their pods	**1 teaspoon whole Sichuan pepper**
1/2 teaspoon salt	**a walnut-size piece of unpeeled fresh ginger, crushed**

1 Put the frozen beans in a pan and cover generously with boiling water. Bring the water back to a boil, add the seasonings, and then simmer for 5–6 minutes.

2 Drain and then refresh in cold running water.

3 Serve at room temperature. Eat them with your fingers, discarding the shells.

CORAL-LIKE SNOW LOTUS

shan hu xue lian

The lotus, or water lily, is a traditional symbol of spiritual enlightenment for Buddhists because its roots lie in mud and filth but its stems reach skywards to blossom in pure, exquisite beauty. The plant also has many culinary uses. Its seeds are made into sweetmeats and its leaves are used in various dishes. The following recipe makes use of the underground segmented stem of the lotus, which bulges into great fat bulbs of crystalline white flesh. Inside, it is threaded with hollow tubes, so a cross section reveals a beautiful pattern. This method of preparing the rhizome brings out its beauty, translucent whiteness, and wonderfully crisp texture—qualities that explain the name of the dish.

Serves 4–6 as a starter

about 1 pound lotus root (this is the amount typically packaged for sale in Chinese markets)
a 1-inch piece of unpeeled fresh ginger, slightly crushed or roughly sliced

3/4 cup white sugar
salt
4 teaspoons clear rice vinegar
optional garnish: 1/2 a red bell pepper

1 Scrape the lotus root clean with a sharp knife and slice it thinly (at about 1 1/2-inch intervals). Rinse the slices and place immediately into a bowlful of lightly salted water with the crushed ginger to prevent discoloration. Leave for an hour or two.

2 Drain the lotus slices and plunge them into a big panful of boiling water. Return to a boil, and after another 5 or 10 seconds remove the slices and rinse them in cold water until cool. Drain well and set aside.

3 Dissolve the sugar and a generous pinch of salt in about 1 cup of water over a gentle heat. Allow to cool.

4 Add the vinegar, and then pour this sweet-and-sour sauce over the lotus slices. Leave to soak for at least an hour, preferably several.

5 If using the red bell pepper garnish, slice the pepper thinly, blanch the slices briefly, and refresh in cold water. Arrange on a plate with the drained lotus slices to serve.

THREE WAYS WITH PEANUTS

In the West, peanuts are almost invariably eaten simply dry-roasted or roasted and tossed in salt—the only exception I can think of is the raw peanuts that are eaten with raisins as a healthy snack. But in China, where this New World crop has been an important source of food for about four centuries, they are treated in a number of different ways. Dry-roasted peanuts are a vital ingredient in the famous Gong Bao (Kung Pao) chicken and all its variations. They are also the basis of many snacks, like the starch-encrusted peanuts that have found their way into Western cocktail parties and the "strange-flavor" peanuts featured below. As most Sichuanese restaurants and homes lack ovens, the nuts are usually salt-roasted in a wok. The peanuts are mixed with large quantities of salt—enough almost to cover them—and stirred over a gentle heat. The salt acts as a conductor and guarantees an even roasting. It is later sifted away from the peanuts and set aside for the next batch of roasting. The peanut skins are rubbed away with the fingertips and gently blown out of a nearby door or window.

The following recipes will show you something of the diverse uses of peanuts in Sichuanese cooking.

BOILED AROMATIC PEANUTS

lu hua sheng

Where peanuts are eaten on their own as a nibble, they are often deep-fried, which gives them a delicious fragrance and an attractive gloss. But the method Westerners find most surprising is boiling them in an aromatic broth, which makes the peanuts swollen and delicately flavored, moist and crunchy, not crisp as they are when fried or roasted. They are usually served with a selection of cold dishes, or just as a nibble with drinks. I suspect they would also work rather well as a crunchy element in a salad or coleslaw. The spices can be varied according to taste and availability.

Serve as a nibble or a side dish

about 1 pint water
8 ounces raw peanuts, in their
   husks, or just their pink
   skins
2 teaspoons salt
1 teaspoon whole Sichuan
   pepper
a few bits of cassia bark
   (about 1 teaspoon) or a
   cinnamon stick

1 star anise
2 whole cloves, powdery tips
   nipped out and discarded
1/2 teaspoon fennel seeds
1–2 slices dried ginger
   (optional)
1 *cao guo* (see page 62)
   (optional)

Bring the water to a boil. Add the peanuts, salt, and all the spices (the latter wrapped in a double layer of of cheesecloth if you have one) and return to a boil. Then turn the heat down, cover, and simmer for 40 minutes. When they are cooked, drain the peanuts and leave them to cool and dry out a little, discarding the spices.

STRANGE-FLAVOR PEANUTS

guai wei hua ren

Like strange-flavor chicken, this concoction is named for its weird combination of several different flavors, although the two dishes bear no actual resemblance. The crisp peanuts are encrusted in a delicious fudgy paste that is unexpectedly spiced with chili powder and Sichuan pepper. They are eaten as part of a cold course at a banquet, but are also sold on the streets with other snack foods. The recipe is a sort of Sichuanese version of the caramelized peanuts occasionally encountered on city streets in Europe. If you'd like something even "stranger," you could add a small amount of very finely minced ginger, garlic, and scallion along with the other flavorings. And those who don't fancy the idea of chile-hot sweetmeats could omit the spices and use a few toasted sesame seeds instead. Deep-fried or toasted walnuts or cashews can also be prepared in this manner.

Serve as a nibble or a side dish

1/2 teaspoon salt	**3/4 cup white sugar**
1/2 teaspoon chili powder	**1 teaspoon clear rice vinegar**
1/2 teaspoon ground roasted Sichuan pepper (see page 74)	**8 ounces roasted unsalted peanuts, skins rubbed off and discarded**

1 Combine the salt, chili powder, and Sichuan pepper in a small dish.

2 Put the sugar and 1/3 cup of water into a wok and heat gently, stirring to dissolve the sugar. When the sugar has disappeared, turn up the heat and boil almost to the hardball stage—about 250°F (the syrupy bubbles that keep rising to the surface are known as "fish-eye bubbles"—you will be able to see exactly why!). When the syrup is suitably hot, turn off the heat, allow to cool down a little, and add the spices and the vinegar. Stir well to combine, and lastly add the peanuts. Stir vigorously to coat the nuts in syrup. Keep mixing as the syrup cools down and solidifies, taking care to keep the nuts from sticking together in large blobs.

3 Set aside to cool.

DEEP-FRIED CRISPY PEANUTS

you su hua ren

油酥花仁

I have enjoyed this nibble so many times: with drinks on the Chengdu riverside on balmy summer's evenings, as a side dish in homes and restaurants, even with a hasty breakfast of rice porridge and pickled vegetables on my way to classes at the Sichuan cooking school. The peanuts are dark red and glossy, crisp and fragrant. They should be served on a small plate, topped with salt and ground roasted Sichuan pepper, which are mixed in with chopsticks at the table. Do resist the temptation to be impatient and deep-fry at too high a temperature—the nuts can easily be burned and develop a bitter taste. And remember that fried peanuts keep cooking when they are taken off the heat, so spread them out quickly to let them cool down. You could also scatter Sichuan pepper on precooked and salted peanuts for an exciting change of taste.

Serve as a nibble or a side dish

8 ounces red peanuts in their
  skins
oil for deep-frying

TO SERVE
1/2 teaspoon salt
1/2 teaspoon ground roasted
  Sichuan pepper (see page 74)

1 Heat the oil over a gentle flame to 200–250°F and add the peanuts as it starts to warm up. Fry the nuts for about 20 minutes, stirring often and taking great care not to let the oil overheat. When they are crisp and fragrant, remove them with a slotted spoon or strainer, drain well, and spread out on paper towels to cool down completely.

2 To serve, pile the nuts onto a small plate and top with about 1/2 teaspoon of salt and 1/2 teaspoon of ground roasted Sichuan pepper to taste. Let your guests mix in the seasonings at the table.

NOTE
Some cooks start by blanching the peanuts for a couple of minutes in boiling water—this is supposed to improve the texture, but I don't find the difference great enough to merit the extra effort.

3
meat dishes

WHEN SICHUANESE PEOPLE SAY "MEAT" THEY USUALLY
just mean pork. Pork is the meat of daily life, so ubiquitous that most local
butchers' stalls sell nothing else. It can be stir-fried, braised, steamed, deep-
fried, stewed, roasted, boiled, salted, or smoked. It can be cooked on its own,
tossed in a wok with plenty of vegetables, or made into stocks. Its sweet, delicate lard can add magic to meat or vegetable dishes; its fat can be cooked to
slow, tender perfection. For if pork is ordinary, it is by no means inferior, and
it is highly prized for its tenderness, its sweet, fresh taste, and its lip-smacking
juiciness. In one of his poems, "Eating Pork" (*shi zhu rou*), the great Sung
Dynasty poet Su Dongpo ridiculed those who looked down on this most
humble of meats:

> The good pork of Huangzhou,
> It's as cheap as dirt,
> The rich won't eat it,
> The poor don't know how to cook it,
> With a slow flame, and just a little water,
> When it's done it's scrumptious.
> Eat a bowlful every day
> And you'll feel as if you haven't a care in the world.

Archaeological evidence from northern China suggests that the Chinese
were rearing pigs around the fifth or sixth millennium before Christ; by the

third century B.C., pigs had become one of the main kinds of livestock and were also used in sacrifices. Written sources from that period refer to various ways of cooking pork, including roasting, boiling, and steaming, and making it into thick soupy stews (*geng*). Nowadays, pork accounts for nearly 90 percent of meat consumption in China, and it's the only meat you're likely to encounter on the dinner table in Sichuanese people's homes. The Sichuanese have a use for almost every part of the pig, from the ears to the trotters, from the soft tenderloin meat to the innards and the bones.

In Chinese antiquity, oxen appear to have been a similarly important source of meat—they were also used in ritual sacrifices. According to the *Chinese Classic of Food* (*zhong guo shi jing*), published in Shanghai in 1999, there are many references to beef-eating in ancient texts, including the Book of Rites (*li ji*). With the development of agriculture, however, the ox came to be seen primarily as a farm animal, a tool to help plough the fields and carry heavy loads, and many imperial governments passed decrees banning its slaughter for food. From the Han Dynasty onward, beef was rarely mentioned in texts discussing food, and it seldom won the praise of poets or gourmets. Some of the herding peoples on the fringes of China, like the Tibetans, continued to regard beef as an important foodstuff; elsewhere, its consumption was limited to the meat of working beasts that died off in the cold winter months. These days beef is still far less common than pork and has to be searched for in Sichuanese markets. Sichuan does, however, have a handful of famous and most delicious beef dishes, which are represented in this chapter.

Lamb is a rarity on Sichuanese menus. It's more often associated with cooking in the northern provinces, where the culinary legacy of China's conquest by lamb-eating Mongols in the thirteenth century is more keenly felt. You do, however, occasionally find lamb in the cooking of Sichuan's Muslim communities, where it stands in for pork.

This chapter includes a selection of Sichuan's most famous and most delicious meat dishes.

TWICE-COOKED PORK

hui guo rou

Hui guo rou, which literally means "back-in-the-pot meat," is the most famous and profoundly loved of all the dishes of Sichuan. This quirky combination of intensely flavored, fragrant pork and fresh green vegetables is a source of great nostalgia for Sichuanese people living abroad, and it often seems to be tied up with elderly people's childhood memories. One Chengdu roast duck vendor, Mr. Liu, told me that in the preindustrial days, when pork came from free-range, naturally fed pigs, a whole neighborhood would know immediately if someone was eating *hui guo rou*, so captivating was its smell. According to one of my written sources, the dish was eaten with ritual-istic regularity at meetings of Sichuan's notorious secret societies—before the communists wiped them out. It is still nicknamed "secret society meat" (*pao ge rou*) in some parts of western Sichuan.

Hui guo rou derives its name from the fact that the pork is first boiled, then fried in a wok, with plenty of hot, beany flavorings, until it is sizzlingly delicious. Sichuanese cooks traditionally use a cut of pork thigh that is split evenly between fat and lean, with a layer of skin over the top. The cooking method makes it extraordinarily tasty, and if you eat it with plain steamed rice, it makes a wonderful meal. The old Chengdu word for the curved shape of the pork pieces in the final dish is *deng zhan wo xing*, "lamp-dish slices," because they look like the tiny dishes that were filled with oil and used as lamps in pre-revolutionary China.

Sichuanese cooks traditionally use a vegetable known as green garlic or Chinese leeks (*suan miao*) in this dish. Baby leeks are a very acceptable substi-tute. Ordinary leeks can be substituted if they are green and leafy, but since they are less tender they must be prefried (just toss them in a wok over a high flame, with a little peanut oil, for less than a minute to "break their raw-ness," and set them aside. The fried leeks can be added to the wok at the same time as the baby leeks in the recipe). The cut of pork favored in Sichuan is hard to come by, so I've suggested using pork belly, which is of a similar character and available in Chinese as well as Italian and Hispanic markets.

Please note that the pork is best cooked at least a couple of hours in advance of the main wok-frying (it can be cooked the day before).

Serves 2 as a main dish served with plain rice, 4 with two or three other dishes as part of a Chinese meal

3/4 pound fresh, boneless pork belly, with skin still attached	**1 1/2 teaspoons Sichuanese sweet wheaten paste or sweet bean paste**
6 baby leeks or 6 tender, leafy leeks	**2 teaspoons fermented black beans**
2 tablespoons peanut oil or lard	**1 teaspoon dark soy sauce**
1 1/2 tablespoons chili bean paste	**1 teaspoon white sugar**
	salt

1 Bring a large pot of water to a boil. Add the pork, return to a boil, and then simmer at a gentler heat until just cooked—this should take 20–25 minutes, depending on the thickness of the pork. Remove the pork from the water and allow to cool (don't forget that you can reserve the cooking water and add it to the stockpot). Place the meat in the refrigerator for a couple of hours or more to firm up the flesh—this makes it possible to slice it thinly without the fat and lean parts separating.

2 When the meat is completely cold, slice it thinly. (In Sichuan, each piece would be about 2 inches by 1 inch and half fat and half lean meat, with a strip of skin at the top.)

3 Chop the leeks diagonally at a steep angle into thin, 1 1/2-inch-long "horse ear" slices.

4 Season the wok, then add another 2 tablespoons of oil or lard over a medium-hot flame, add the pork pieces, and stir-fry until their fat has melted out and they are toasty and slightly curved. Push the pork to one side of the wok and tip the chili bean paste into the space you have created. Stir-fry it for 20–30 seconds until the oil is richly red, then add the sweet bean paste and black beans and stir-fry for another few seconds until they too smell delicious. Mix everything in the wok together and add the soy sauce and sugar, seasoning with a little salt if necessary.

5 Finally, add the leeks and stir and toss until they are just cooked. Turn onto a serving dish and eat immediately.

VARIATIONS

The core of this legendary dish is the fat-lean pork, first boiled and then fried, but there are infinite variations. Some cooks use red or green bell peppers instead of leeks; others add deliciously crunchy pieces of deep-fried flatbread (*guo kuei*) in the final stages of cooking to make what's called *guo kuei hui guo rou* (deep-fried pita bread can be used instead). Long, green Chinese scallions can also be used instead of leeks.

FISH-FRAGRANT PORK SLIVERS

yu xiang rou si

The so-called fish-fragrant flavor is one of Sichuan's most famous culinary creations, and it epitomizes the Sichuanese love for audacious combinations of flavors. It is salty, sweet, sour, and spicy and infused with the heady tastes of garlic, ginger, and scallions. The hot taste comes from pickled chiles, which also stain the cooking oil a brilliant orange-red. The most classic fish-fragrant dishes are based on pickled chiles chopped to a purée with the blade of a cleaver, although some versions use Sichuan chili bean paste instead, which is made with pickled fava beans as well as chiles.

This delicious combination of flavors is thought to have originated in traditional Sichuanese fish cooking, which would explain why other ingredients prepared in the same way would have instantly recalled the taste of fish to those who ate them, hence the name. Some food experts, like the famous chef Xiao Jianming of the Piaoxiang Restaurant in Chengdu, say the flavors conjure up the actual taste of tiny crucian carp (*ji yu*), which are widely eaten in Sichuan—another explanation for the title. The term may also be connected with the fact that whole crucian carp, which are particularly delicious, are sometimes actually added to vats of pickling chiles to improve their taste. Everyone agrees that the fish-fragrant style grew out of home cooking and was only later adopted by professional chefs.

Fish-fragrant dishes have been one of Sichuan's most successful culinary exports, but the strangeness of the term has led to a great variety of translations on English-language menus: "mock-fish," "sea-spice" (a great misnomer in inland Sichuan) and "fish-flavored" among them. The two Chinese characters literally mean "fish" and "fragrant," which is why I prefer my translation.

Fish-fragrant pork slivers is the most famous of all Sichuan's "fish-fragrant" dishes. Sichuanese chefs tend to use fine strips of lettuce stem (*wo sun*) as a crunchy element in this dish, but I've written the recipe using the more easily available bamboo shoots or celery. This dish should be cooked very quickly, to preserve the tenderness of the pork.

Serves 2 as a main course with one vegetable dish and rice, 4 with three other dishes

a small handful of dried cloud
    ear mushrooms
10 ounces boneless pork loin
    (the meat from about 2
    pork chops), preferably
    with a little fat
2/3 cup fresh or canned bamboo
    shoots or 2 celery stalks
salt
peanut oil
2 tablespoons pickled chili
    paste
1 1/2 teaspoons finely
    chopped garlic
2 teaspoons finely chopped
    fresh ginger
2 scallions, green parts only,
    very thinly sliced

FOR THE MARINADE
1/4 teaspoon salt
1 teaspoon light soy sauce
1 tablespoon potato flour or
    1 1/2 tablespoons cornstarch
1 tablespoon cold water
1 teaspoon Shaoxing rice
    wine or medium-dry sherry

FOR THE SAUCE
1 1/2 teaspoons white sugar
1 1/2 teaspoons Chinkiang or
    black Chinese vinegar
3/4 teaspoon light soy sauce
1/2 teaspoon salt
3/4 teaspoon potato flour or
    1 1/8 teaspoons cornstarch
3 tablespoons chicken stock
    or water

1 Cover the cloud ear mushrooms in very hot water and soak for 30 minutes.

2 Cut the pork into thin slices (ideally about 1/8 of an inch thick), and then cut these into long, fine slivers. Place in a bowl, add the marinade ingredients, and stir in one direction to combine.

3 Blanch the bamboo shoots in boiling salted water for a minute or two. Rinse in cold water, then slice thinly and cut the slices into very fine strips to match the pork. (If you are using celery, cut them into thin strips. Sprinkle with a few pinches of salt and let them sit for 15 minutes or so to drain out some of their water content.) Thinly slice the cloud ear mushrooms, discarding any knobbly bits. Combine the sauce ingredients in a small bowl.

4 Season the wok, then add a 1/4 cup of cool oil to the wok and reheat over a high flame.

5 When the oil is beginning to smoke, add the pork and stir-fry briskly. As soon as the strips have separated, push them to one side of the wok, tip the wok toward the other side, and tip the chili paste into the space you have created. Stir-fry very briefly until the oil is red and fragrant, and then add the garlic and ginger and mix everything together, tilting the wok back to normal. Stir-fry for another 30 seconds or so until you can smell the aromas of garlic and ginger. Tip in the bamboo shoots and mushrooms and stir-fry briefly, until just hot.

6 Stir the sauce in its bowl, and then add to the wok. Stir quickly to incorporate, throw in the scallions, toss briefly, and turn onto a serving dish.

PORK IN LYCHEE SAUCE
WITH CRISPY RICE
guo ba rou pian

This dish is quite a party piece. A steaming hot bowl of soupy sauce is taken to the table along with a deep platter piled with pieces of crispy rice. As the guests sit back in their seats, the sauce is poured over the rice to explosive effect—not for nothing is the dish known in some places as "a sudden clap of thunder" (*ping di yi sheng lei*). It's not just dramatic, however, but also a delightful mixture of tastes and textures. The pieces of rice crust soak up the sauce in a nice, half-juicy, half-crunchy way. As you will notice, there is not a lychee to be seen—the name just refers to a type of sauce known in Sichuan as "lychee flavor." It is a sort of sweet-and-sour in which the sour notes stand out a little more than the sweet, rather like the fruit. The crispy rice (*guo ba*) is made from the crusty, toasted layer that sticks to the bottom of the pan when rice is cooked over a fire. Sprinkled with salt and spices, this *guo ba* is a favorite children's snack and can be bought in packages like potato chips. Children love this dish, with its element of surprise and mild flavors. (You could easily substitute slivers of red bell pepper for the chiles if you want to eradicate every hint of hotness.)

Serves 4 with three other dishes

1/4 pound boneless pork loin (the meat from a pork chop)

FOR THE MARINADE
1 teaspoon Shaoxing rice wine or medium-dry sherry
1 teaspoon light soy sauce
2 generous pinches of salt

FOR THE RICE CRUST
3 cups cooked, white, long grain rice (about 1 cup raw)

OTHER INGREDIENTS
4 dried Chinese mushrooms
2/3 cup bamboo shoots, fresh or canned
2 scallions, white parts only
2 Sichuanese pickled chiles or 6 tiny Thai pickled chiles
5–6 leaves of a leafy green vegetable such as baby bok choy or napa cabbage

peanut oil for deep-frying
2 large garlic cloves, thinly sliced, and an equivalent amount of fresh ginger, peeled and thinly sliced
2 cups chicken stock

SEASONINGS
2 tablespoons sugar
1 1/2 teaspoons light soy sauce
salt to taste (about 1/4 teaspoon)
2 1/2 tablespoons potato flour mixed with 4 teaspoons cold water, or 3 3/4 tablespoons cornstarch mixed with 6 teaspoons cold water
2 1/2 tablespoons Chinkiang or black Chinese vinegar
1 teaspoon sesame oil

1 Soak the dried mushrooms in very hot water for 30 minutes.

2 Preheat the oven to 300°F.

3 Make the rice crust: spread the cooked rice onto a lightly greased baking sheet in a layer about 1/2 inch thick. Bake in the oven for 30–40 minutes, until it is crisp but still white. Remove from the baking sheet and set aside to cool. When it is cold, break the rice crust into quite large chunks. (This step can be done in advance.)

4 Slice the pork thinly. Put the slices into a bowl, add the marinade ingredients, and mix well.

5 If using canned bamboo shoots, blanch them for 2 minutes in boiling water, rinse in cold water, and then slice thinly. Slice the scallions and chiles thinly, at a steep angle, into slices 1 1/2 inches long ("horse ears"). Slice the reconstituted dried mushrooms and add their soaking water to the stockpot. Tear the green leaves into pieces the same size as the meat slices.

6 Start heating some oil for deep-frying in a pan on a back burner as you prepare the sauce.

7 As the deep-frying oil warms up, season the wok, then add 3 tablespoons of oil and heat over a high flame. When it is beginning to smoke, add the pork and stir-fry until it whitens and the slices separate. Then add the garlic, ginger, scallions, and chiles and stir-fry for 30–60 seconds until they are fragrant. Slide in the mushrooms, bamboo shoots, and leafy greens and toss in the fragrant oil for a few moments before pouring in all the stock.

8 Mix the soupy sauce well, add the sugar and soy sauce, and season with salt to taste. Add the potato flour or cornstarch mixture and stir as the sauce thickens. Finally, remove from the heat, stir in the vinegar and sesame oil, and pour into a deep bowl. Cover with a plate to keep it piping hot.

9 Lastly, deep-fry the rice crust: adjust the oil temperature to about 375°F, add the rice crust pieces, and deep-fry for about 2 minutes, until they are crisp but still pale in color. Remove with a slotted spoon, drain, and transfer immediately to a deep serving dish. Take the bowl containing the sauce and the rice crust to the table, tell your guests to sit well back, and then pour the sauce over the rice crust.

VARIATIONS

For a grander dish, some restaurants use squid instead of pork; chicken is also a fine substitute, and vegetarians will enjoy using a selection of fresh mushrooms instead of any kind of meat.

The garlic, ginger, and scallions are essential flavorings, but you can vary the vegetable ingredients at will—just try to have an attractive variety of colors. I've used yellow bamboo shoots, dark brown mushrooms, green cabbage, and pickled chiles for a splash of scarlet—some cooks I know use slices of large tomatoes and soaked cloud ear mushrooms.

PORK STEAMED IN LOTUS LEAVES

he ye zheng rou

荷葉蒸肉

Mr. Li leaned toward me in the Taoist temple where we were enjoying a rest from our Qi Gong lesson. Incense smoke drifted up from the feet of two looming gods. Outside, the bamboo and Chinese parasol trees hung gently in the damp autumn air. He whispered in a conspiratorial tone: "You won't find this dish in restaurants. Never the meat as tender and beautiful as the meat I am about to describe." His eyes widened as he talked me through this recipe for steamed Sichuanese pork, and mimed for me, with the perfectly balanced gestures of a Qi Gong master, how to dress the little parcels and wrap them up in the lotus leaves.

Lotus plants are grown widely in Sichuan. As you drive through the lush farmland to the south of Chengdu, their wide, round leaves extend over many ponds and reservoirs. Virtually every part of the lotus plant is used in Sichuanese cooking. The seeds, *lian zi*, a symbol of fertility because their Chinese name sounds like "successive sons," are made into a sweet, sugary stuffing for glutinous rice dumplings or simmered with rice for a health-giving porridge. The underwater rhizome is used as a vegetable or a sweetmeat, and the leaves are used to wrap steamed foods, to which they impart their subtle, herby fragrance.

The following recipe is a hearty country dish, and absolutely scrumptious. It's not at all difficult to make, and your guests will enjoy unwrapping the little packets to find the meat topped with green peas, yellow ginger, and a tiny splash of brilliant red pickled chile. If by any chance you are using fresh lotus leaves, you should begin by blanching them briefly in boiling water.

(There is a cheater's tip that I should mention: I have found that this dish works very nicely with couscous instead of the homemade rice meal—the effect is very similar to that of the rice coating, and it cuts down considerably on the preparation time. For best results, stir in 1/4 teaspoon of five-spice powder before you add the couscous to the meat.)

Serves 4 with two or three other dishes

1–1 1/4 pounds fresh, boneless pork belly, with or without skin

4 dried lotus leaves

3–4 Sichuanese pickled chiles (optional)

a 1 1/2-inch piece of fresh ginger, peeled

2/3 cup fresh or frozen peas, soybeans, or fava beans, shelled

FOR THE RICE MEAL

3/4 cup white long-grain rice

1/2 teaspoon Sichuan peppercorns

1/4 of a star anise

a small piece of cassia bark or cinnamon stick

FOR THE MARINADE

1 tablespoon light soy sauce

1 tablespoon dark soy sauce

1 tablespoon Sichuanese fermented rice wine (optional)

2 tablespoons Shaoxing rice wine or medium-dry sherry

1 tablespoon Sichuanese sweet wheaten paste or sweet bean paste

1 tablespoon red fermented bean curd with its juices

1 tablespoon brown sugar

2 scallions, green parts only, finely sliced

2 teaspoons very finely minced fresh ginger

1 Prepare the aromatic rice meal: place the rice and spices in a dry wok and stir over a moderate flame for 10–15 minutes, until the rice grains are brittle, yellowish, and slightly fragrant. Remove from the wok and leave to cool. Discard the whole spices. When the rice has cooled completely, grind it in a food processor until it is of a coarse consistency, like couscous, not powder-fine.

2 Cut the pork into slices about 2 inches long and 1/8 inch thick. Add all the marinade ingredients, mix well, and leave to stand for about 15 minutes.

3 While the pork is marinating, soak the lotus leaves in hot water for 5–10 minutes until they are soft and pliable. Cut the pickled chiles diagonally into small sections, and cut the ginger into fine slivers.

4 Cut the lotus leaves as best you can into roughly equilateral triangles, with sides about 5 inches long. It doesn't matter if these are irregular, as long as they don't have holes that will let the filling escape. You can use a few ragged bits of lotus leaf to line the steamer if you like—discard the rest. You should end up with about 20 triangles.

5 Add the rice meal and 3–4 tablespoons water to the marinated pork and mix it in, making sure every piece of pork is nicely encrusted with rice.

6 Lay a triangle of lotus leaf on your work surface with its base facing toward you. Place on it two or three slices of pork, making sure they include a good mix of fat and lean meat. Press a few peas or beans (6 or 7) into the meat, and top with a couple of slivers of ginger and a piece of pickled chile. Fold the two base corners of the triangle into the center of the leaf, and then roll away from you to make a small rectangle. Lay the packets, folded side down, in the base of your steamer. Repeat with the rest of the meat. If you only have a single, smallish steamer, you may have to lay the packets two layers thick.

7 To cook, steam the lotus packets over water at a good rolling boil for about 2 hours. Allow your guests to unwrap the packets with their chopsticks and eat directly out of the lotus leaves.

STEAMED PORK KNUCKLE
IN GINGER SAUCE

jiang zhi zhou zi

姜
汁
肘
子

In my early days in Sichuan, a friend and I visited the fishing village of Huang Long Xi (Yellow Dragon Stream). We wandered along the banks of the river, passing thatched cottages and paddy fields, to visit a Buddhist temple. All around was red earth and lush bamboo, the drip and flow of water, the misty, moist, intense greenness of rural Sichuan. Later, we drank tea in a teahouse overlooking the wharf and explored the narrow, winding streets with their creaking wooden houses. As the evening drew in, we stopped at a riverside restaurant and asked the staff to serve us with whatever were the local specialties. We ended up with a splendid platter of the famous local yellow catfish (*huang la ding*) braised in a spicy bean sauce, and a dish of this magnificent steamed pork knuckle with ginger sauce. The pork was produced from one of the enormous bamboo steamers bubbling away by the entrance, where it had been cooking gently for a couple of hours, and was swiftly dressed with the ginger sauce. The pork alone was extremely tasty; with the sauce it was sublime.

The following is just one of many methods used in Sichuan for cooking pork knuckle, which is a favorite treat at rural banquets. Sometimes the joint is braised in chili bean sauce, sometimes stewed with snow-white butter beans (*xue dou*). The famous Song Dynasty poet, calligrapher, and gourmet Su Dongpo, who came from the Meishan area of Sichuan, left written descriptions of some methods of cooking pork knuckle. I've chosen to include the following recipe not just because it is a personal favorite, but also because the flavors used are a pleasing contrast to the rich ruddiness more famously associated with Sichuanese cooking.

Serves 4 with two or three other dishes

1 fresh pork knuckle, with
    skin (about 2 pounds)
3 pieces of fresh ginger, about
    2 inches each, unpeeled
2 scallions, white and green
    parts
1/2–3/4 teaspoon salt
1/2 teaspoon whole Sichuan
    pepper

2 tablespoons Shaoxing rice
    wine or medium-dry sherry

FOR THE SAUCE
a 2-inch piece of fresh ginger
2 tablespoons Chinkiang or
    black Chinese vinegar
1 tablespoon light soy sauce
1 tablespoon sesame oil

1 Use a gas stove flame or a blowtorch to scorch the skin of the pork knuckle until the outer layer is crusty and blackened. Place it in a bowl of hot water, soak for a few minutes, then use a knife to scrape away the burn layer, leaving a gently browned skin.

2 Place the knuckle in a pot of boiling water with 1 piece of ginger, crushed with its skin (use the flat side of a cleaver or a heavy object), and 1 scallion. Return to a boil and simmer for about 30 minutes, until just cooked. Discard the cooking water, the ginger, and scallion, and allow the knuckle to cool slightly.

3 When the knuckle is cool enough to handle, use a sharp knife to cut the meat away from the bone. Work carefully so the meat remains in one piece. Lay the boned knuckle skin side down on a cutting board. Make parallel slashes into the meat, but not all the way through the skin, at 1-inch intervals. Then make similar cuts at right angles to these, leaving a chunky crisscross pattern.

4 Place the scored meat skin side down in a bowl that will fit into your steamer. Roughly slice the remaining pieces of ginger and scallion and scatter them over the pork. Sprinkle with the salt, Sichuan pepper, and Shaoxing rice wine. Place in a steamer and steam until absolutely tender—this will take 1 1/2–2 hours.

5 When the pork knuckle is nearly ready, peel and finely chop the ginger for the sauce. Mix it with just enough cold water to cover it. Add the vinegar, soy sauce, and sesame oil.

6 Remove the pork knuckle from the steamer and turn it skin side up onto a serving dish. Pour over the sauce and serve. (The cooking juices can be poured over, too, or used as the base for a delicious soup.)

BOWL-STEAMED PORK BELLY WITH PICKLED VEGETABLES

han shao bai

Most Westerners think of pork fat with distaste: it's the horrid bits you leave at the side of a steak, or a dangerous substance best bred out of farm animals. The Chinese, however, have long regarded pork fat as a delicious luxury, and when you try eating it the Chinese way you will probably understand why. In the following recipe, the initial blanching and browning of a piece of fresh, boneless pork belly is followed by a long steaming that transforms the heavy raw fat into something melting and voluptuous. The salty pickled vegetables provide a sharp note that complements the meat beautifully. It is, as the Chinese say, richly fat without being greasy (*fei er bu ni*). And if you eat it as the Sichuanese might do, with one or two simple stir-fried vegetables and plain white rice, you won't find it overwhelming.

Han shao bai is one of the steamed dishes traditionally served at feasts in rural Sichuan. Steamed dishes tend to feature prominently on the menus of these "field feasts" (*tian xi*) because they can easily be made in advance and left to steam gently while the other dinner preparations are made, unlike last-minute stir-fried dishes—a great boon when catering for hordes of people. One of the folk names for such celebration dinners is actually "three steamed dishes and nine steamed bowls" (*san zheng jiu kou*). At one wedding lunch I attended, a makeshift stove had been built in a courtyard from bricks and clay, and a special team of helpers spent two days preparing the food. By the time the guests arrived to greet the bride and groom, the dozen or so round tables were already laden with cold dishes and deep-fried tidbits, and later the kitchen team unloaded bowl after bowl of piping hot steamed meats from a towering stack of bamboo steamers simmering away on the stove.

To make this dish you will need a ceramic bowl about 2 inches deep and 8 inches in diameter and a steamer that will accommodate it—the bamboo steamers sold very reasonably in Chinese supermarkets are ideal.

Serves 4 with three other dishes and plenty of rice

1 pound fresh, boneless pork belly, in one piece, with skin still attached
about 2 teaspoons dark soy sauce
1/2 cup peanut oil for frying

optional: 3–4 Sichuanese pickled chiles
1 tablespoon fermented black soybeans
1 cup Sichuanese *ya cai* or Tianjin preserved vegetable

1 Bring a pot of water to a boil, add the pork, and blanch for about 5 minutes. Remove, then rinse in cold water. While the meat is still hot, pat it dry with paper towels or a clean kitchen towel and smear it all over (especially the skin) with 1/2–1 teaspoon of dark soy sauce.

2 Heat the peanut oil in a wok to about 325°F, add the pork, skin side down, and sear it for about 3 minutes until the skin is slightly crispy and a dark red-brown. Remove the meat from the wok and return it to the hot cooking water, where it should soak for 5–10 minutes until the skin is supple again. Then remove it from the liquid and set it aside to cool completely.

3 When the pork is cool, cut it into 1/4-inch slices, each with a strip of skin along the top. If the slices are very wide, cut them in half across the direction of the skin (ideally the pieces should be about 3 inches by 2 inches). Cut each of the pickled chiles into 2 or 3 sections.

4 Lay the pork slices in one or two tidy rows across the whole base of your bowl. Each slice should overlap the last, and the most important thing is that the strip of skin on each piece should be in contact with the surface of the bowl (the Chinese say this arrangement is "like the pages of a book," *yi feng shu*). Lay any fragments or broken slices on top, and then sprinkle a scant teaspoon of dark soy sauce all over the meat. Add the fermented beans and pickled chiles, and then fill the bowl with the preserved vegetable, pressing down gently with your hand.

5 Place the bowl in your steamer, cover with the lid, and steam over energetically boiling water for about 2 hours. Do make sure you replenish the water from a boiling kettle whenever necessary.

6 To serve, turn the contents of the bowl out onto a serving dish and let your guests help themselves. The dark strips of skin should make an attractive pattern.

VARIATIONS

Some cooks will elaborate on the basic recipe above to make "dragon-eye" steamed pork with pickled vegetables (*long yan han shao bai*). They stuff a single fermented black bean into a section of pickled red chile, and then wrap each slice of pork around a chile. These tubes are then stacked up in the bowl, with a surrounding wall of chopped pickles to keep them in place. When the bowl is turned out onto the serving dish, the tops of the stuffed chiles stare up like a dozen beady red dragon's eyes.

There is also a sweet version of this dish that is very popular in Sichuan (*tian shao bai*). The pork belly is first boiled and then sliced. The slices are laid in the steaming bowl with some sweet bean paste, and the bowl is then topped up with cooked glutinous rice that has been mixed with lard and sugar. The dish is steamed for 2 hours, just like the salty version, and is then turned out onto a plate and sprinkled with white sugar.

RED-BRAISED PORK
hong shao rou

This dish is made with fresh pork belly, known poetically in Chinese as "five-flower" pork (*wu hua rou*) because of its five or six layers of fat and lean meat. The meat and fat are braised to slow, tender perfection in a sauce that finally reduces to a dark, syrupy glaze, delicately flavored with star anise. It's extremely easy to make and tastes sensational. My Sichuanese friends all eat it with stir-fried vegetables, rice, and soup as part of a Chinese meal, but it's equally delicious served with a pile of plain mashed potatoes and a crisp salad or a simple dish of vegetables. Bear in mind that the meat is very rich, so you won't want to eat it with anything too oily. Red-braised pork is usually made in a flat-bottomed Dutch oven or other braising pot, leaving the wok free to make the other, faster dishes at the last minute. For best results, use a pot big enough to cook the pork in a single layer.

Serves 4 with two or three other dishes as part of a Chinese meal

1–1 1/4 pound fresh, boneless pork belly, preferably with skin

a 2-inch piece of fresh ginger, unpeeled

2 scallions, white and green parts

3 tablespoons peanut oil

2 cups everyday stock (see page 318) or chicken stock

1 tablespoon dark soy sauce

2 tablespoons Shaoxing rice wine or medium-dry sherry

3/4 teaspoon salt

3 tablespoons brown sugar

1/2 of a star anise (4 segments)

1 Blanch the pork for a couple of minutes in boiling water, then remove and rinse in clean water (this step can be omitted if you are in a hurry). Cut the pork into 2- to 3-inch chunks, leaving each piece with a layer of skin and a mixture of lean meat and fat. Crush the ginger slightly with the flat side of a cleaver or a heavy object, and cut the scallions into 3 or 4 sections.

2 Heat the oil in the pot until it is just beginning to smoke. Add the pork chunks and stir-fry for a couple of minutes. Then add the stock and all the other ingredients and stir well.

3 Bring the liquid to a boil, then simmer, half-covered or uncovered, over a very low flame for about 2 hours, stirring from time to time, until the liquid is much reduced and the meat is fork tender.

VARIATIONS

You can use exactly the same method to cook spare ribs, chicken, rabbit meat, or beef, although beef is more commonly "red-braised" by an alternative method that involves Sichuanese chili bean paste and root vegetables (see page 232).

SWEET-AND-SOUR PORK

tang cu li ji

糖醋里脊

In the smoky kitchen of the Bamboo Bar, one of my favorite Chengdu restaurants, a desperate pandemonium reigns. The place is always filled with guests demanding long lists of complicated dishes, but most of the cooking is done in a single wok. The head chef stands over the coal-fired stove stirring and tossing, flinging spices and sauces into the wok with wild abandon. His three assistants rush around the tiny kitchen, mincing garlic and ginger, chopping meat into slices, dices, and slivers, and washing dishes. The kitchen seems precariously balanced on the brink of chaos. Bamboo baskets overflowing with scallions, celery, and Chinese cabbage stand on every shelf and surface in riotous disorder. Huge tubs of soaking squid and dried mushrooms obstruct the floor. But, miraculously, out of this mad mess comes some of the best Sichuanese food in the district. Authentically spiced, nicely cooked, served with a complete lack of pretension. This is not a place for fancy vegetable carving or elaborate garnishes, but is great for a delicious everyday feast.

One of the dishes that the Bamboo Bar does best is sweet-and-sour pork. Deep-fried strips of tender pork are dressed in a dark, tangy sauce that is light-years away from the synthetic-looking orange confections served under the same name in the West.

Serves 2 as a main dish with one vegetable, 4 with three other dishes

3/4 pound boneless pork loin (the meat from 2 or 3 pork chops)
peanut oil for deep-frying
FOR THE BATTER
2 eggs

1/4 cup potato flour or 3/8 cup cornstarch
FOR THE MARINADE
1/2 teaspoon salt
2 teaspoons Shaoxing rice wine or medium-dry sherry

FOR THE SAUCE
1/4 teaspoon salt
3 tablespoons white sugar
2 tablespoons Chinkiang or
   black Chinese vinegar
1 teaspoon light soy sauce
2 1/2 teaspoons potato flour
   or 3 3/4 teaspoons
   cornstarch

3 scallions, green parts only
3 tablespoons peanut oil
2 teaspoons finely chopped
   garlic
2 teaspoons finely chopped
   fresh ginger
3/4 cup everyday stock (see
   page 318) or chicken stock
1 teaspoon sesame oil

1 Trim any fat from the meat. Cut it into slices 1/2 inch thick, and then cut these into 1/2-inch strips. Place in a bowl. Add the marinade ingredients, mix well, and let sit for 30 minutes.

2 Combine the salt, sugar, vinegar, soy sauce, and potato flour or cornstarch for the sauce in a small bowl. Finely slice the scallion greens.

3 Heat oil for deep-frying to 300°F. Beat the eggs together. In a bowl, mix the potato flour with enough beaten egg (about 1 1/2 eggs) to make a thick batter. When the oil is hot, mix the batter with the pork strips. Drop some of the battered strips into the oil, adding them individually to prevent sticking, and stir with long chopsticks to separate. Fry the strips at about 300°F for 3 minutes or so, until they are just cooked through. Remove and drain. Repeat with more pork strips until you have cooked all of them.

4 Reheat the deep-frying oil to 375°F. Add the pork strips in one or two batches and deep-fry them until they are crisp and golden. Remove, drain, and place on your serving dish. Keep them warm while you prepare the sauce.

5 Heat the 3 tablespoons of oil in a clean wok over a medium flame. Add the garlic and ginger and stir-fry for about 30 seconds, until they are fragrant. Add all the stock, bring the liquid to a boil, and then add the prepared sauce ingredients from the small bowl. Stir briskly as the liquid thickens, then add the scallions and sesame oil, stir once or twice, and pour the sauce over the waiting pork strips. Serve immediately.

VARIATION

Deep-fried pork with salt and Sichuan pepper(*jiao yan li ji*): omit the sauce, and serve the deep-fried pork strips piping hot, with a dry dip of salt and ground roasted Sichuan pepper (see page 74).

SALT-FRIED PORK

yan jian rou

   This dish, like the more famous twice-cooked pork, is "homestyle flavor," that is, salty and beany and a little bit hot. The main difference between the two dishes is that the pork is added raw, so it has a very different texture in the end. Salt-fried pork is just the kind of dish you might find on a family dinner table in Sichuan, with a few stir-fried vegetables, a simple soup, and plenty of rice. Leeks are the most standard vegetable ingredient in the dish, but long green Chinese scallions, green bell peppers, young ginger, celery, and even strips of dry bean curd can be used instead.

Serves 2 as a main dish with rice and one vegetable, 4 with three other dishes

1/2 pound fresh, boneless
   pork belly
2–3 baby leeks or 5 scallions,
   white and green parts
peanut oil
salt to taste

I 1/2 tablespoons Sichuanese
   chili bean paste
I 1/2 tablespoons fermented
   black beans
I teaspoon light soy sauce
1/2 teaspoon sugar

I Cut the pork into very thin slices, about 3 inches by 2 inches. Cut the leeks thinly, at a steep angle, into slices I 1/2 inches long.

2 Season the wok. Add 3 tablespoons of fresh oil and heat until hot but not yet smoking. Add the pork slices and stir-fry briskly for 3–4 minutes, until the oil has cleared and the pork has lost most of its water content. Add 1/8 teaspoon of salt about halfway through the cooking.

3 When the oil has cleared and begun to sizzle, push the pork slices up to one side of the wok and tilt the wok so the oil runs into the space you have created. Drop the chili bean paste and fermented black beans into the oil and stir-fry them for about 30 seconds, until the oil is red and fragrant. Then mix in the pork slices, add the soy sauce and sugar, and throw in all the leeks. Continue to stir-fry until the leeks are just cooked, seasoning with salt to taste. Serve.

PORK SLIVERS WITH PRESERVED MUSTARD TUBER

zha cai rou si

This simple, homestyle dish is most delicious, a gentle entwining of pale pork slivers, salty pickled vegetable and fresh scallion. It's also quick and easy to prepare. The preserved vegetable, *zha cai*, whose name literally means "pressed vegetable," is made from the stem of a type of mustard green. It was originally eaten fresh or pickled in spicy brine, and it was only in the late nineteenth century that an enterprising farmer from Fuling tried dry-salting it as a way of preserving an unusually abundant harvest. The result was so good that, with the encouragement of his brother, the farmer went into business, and within a few decades he and his imitators were producing *zha cai* all over the province. The method of preparation is as follows: the mustard stems are first semidried on wooden frames in the gentle winds of the Yangtze River valley; then they are salted, pressed to extract some of their water content, mixed with ground chiles, Sichuan pepper, and a selection of other spices, and sealed into an earthenware jar to ferment.

The final product is soft, crunchy, salty, and subtly flavored. Pickled mustard tuber is often eaten as a relish or chopped up and scattered over noodle or bean curd dishes, but it's particularly delicious in the following stir-fry. It is easily available canned in Chinese supermarkets.

Serves 4 with three other dishes

1/2 pound boneless pork loin (the meat from about 2 pork chops)
2/3 cup Sichuanese preserved mustard tuber
4 scallions, white and green parts
peanut oil

FOR THE MARINADE
a pinch of salt
1 teaspoon potato flour or 1 1/2 teaspoons cornstarch
2 teaspoons cold water
1 teaspoon Shaoxing rice wine or medium-dry sherry

FOR THE SAUCE
1/2 teaspoon light soy sauce
3/4 teaspoon potato flour or 1 1/8 teaspoons cornstarch
3 tablespoons chicken stock

1 Cut the pork into very thin slices and cut these evenly into thin strips, ideally 1/8 inch thick. Place the strips in a bowl, add the marinade ingredients, and stir in one direction to combine. Set aside while you prepare the other ingredients.

2 Rinse the chile sediment from the preserved vegetable and cut it first into slices and then into very thin strips to match the pork. Wash and trim the scallions, chop them into 3 sections, and then slice these pieces lengthwise into thin strips. Combine the sauce ingredients in a small bowl.

3 Season the wok, then add 3 tablespoons of oil and heat over a high flame until smoke starts rising. Add 2 teaspoons of oil to the pork, mix well, then slide it into the wok and stir-fry briskly. As soon as the pork strips have separated and are starting to turn white, add the preserved vegetable and stir-fry for 30–60 seconds, until the vegetable is hot and fragrant. Give the sauce a stir, pour it into the wok, and stir quickly. Immediately add the scallions, stir and toss for another 10–15 seconds, and then transfer to a serving dish.

STIR-FRIED PORK SLIVERS WITH SWEET FERMENTED PASTE

jing jiang rou si

Jing jiang rou si is a popular everyday meat dish in the homes and restaurants of Sichuan. The dark, glossy mound of pork slivers is topped with a pile of crisp, white scallions, a nice contrast to the richness of the meat. Serve it, perhaps, with a spicy dish like fish-fragrant eggplants and a couple of simple stir-fried vegetables. For best results, the pork slivers should be very finely and evenly cut—this way they will be quickly and simultaneously cooked and can be served while still very tender. As with all stir-fried meat dishes, make sure you season the wok before you begin to cook to prevent sticking.

Serves 2 as a main dish with one simple vegetable, 4 with three other dishes

3/4 pound boneless pork loin (the meat from 2 or 3 pork chops) with some fat

4 scallions, white parts only

about 5 teaspoons Sichuanese sweet bean paste

1/3 cup peanut oil

FOR THE MARINADE

1/2 teaspoon salt

2 teaspoons potato flour or 3 teaspoons cornstarch

2 teaspoons cold water

1 teaspoon Shaoxing rice wine or medium-dry sherry

FOR THE SAUCE

1/2 teaspoon light soy sauce

1/2 teaspoon white sugar

2 tablespoons chicken stock

1 Cut the pork into thin slices and then into long, thin slivers, ideally about 1/8 inch thick. Place in a small bowl, add the marinade ingredients, and stir in one direction to combine. Leave for about 15 minutes. Cut the scallions into 4-inch sections and then lengthwise into fine slivers. Leave in a bowl of cold water to refresh. Dilute the sweet paste with 1 tablespoon of water, to give a runny consistency. Combine the sauce ingredients in a small bowl.

2 When you are ready to cook, drain the scallion slivers and set aside.

3 Season the wok, then add the oil and heat over a high flame until it begins to smoke. Add the pork slivers and stir-fry briskly. After a minute or two, when they have separated and are becoming pale, push the slivers to one side of the wok, tilt the wok, and let the oil run to the other side. Place the sweet paste into the space you have created and stir-fry for 10–20 seconds until it is fragrant. Then tilt the wok back to normal, mix the paste and pork slivers together, and add the prepared sauce. Mix well, check that the pork slivers are cooked through, and then turn onto a serving plate.

4 Top with the scallion slivers to serve.

PORK SLIVERS WITH YELLOW CHIVES

jiu huang rou si

Yellowed chives (*jiu huang*), which can be found in some Chinese food stores, are ordinary Chinese chives that have been grown in hothouses and deprived of sunlight. The darkness steals their greenness, leaving their leaves a pale, shy, delicate yellow. These chives have a powerful aroma that will fill your shopping bag and your kitchen. When cooked, they are silky and succulent, a real treat. Chinese chives have flat leaves and are much larger than common European chives. They are native to China, where they are thought to have been cultivated for some three thousand years. There are several varieties, most notably the leaf chives used in this recipe and the flowering chives you will find described on page 291. The technique of yellowing leaf chives in hothouses has been known since the Han Dynasty. These days it is a Sichuanese specialty, although not exclusive to the region.

The following recipe is a common home-cooked dish. It's one of a whole series of recipes for pork slivers fried with one vegetable or another (see variations below).

Serves 4 with three other dishes

1/2 pound boneless pork loin
(the meat from about 2
pork chops)
1/3 pound Chinese yellowed
chives
4 tablespoons peanut oil

FOR THE MARINADE
just over a 1/4 teaspoon salt
1 teaspoon Shaoxing rice
wine or medium-dry sherry
1 1/2 teaspoons potato flour

or 2 1/4 teaspoons
cornstarch
2 teaspoons water

FOR THE SAUCE
1/2 teaspoon light soy sauce
3/4 teaspoon Chinkiang or
black Chinese vinegar
1/4 teaspoon salt
1/2 teaspoon potato flour or
3/4 teaspoon cornstarch
2 tablespoons chicken stock

1 Cut the pork as evenly as possible into very fine strips, discarding any fatty
   or gristly bits. Ideally, the strips will all be about 2 inches long. Place them
   in a bowl, add the marinade ingredients, and stir in one direction to mix.
   Leave to stand for about 15 minutes.

2 Wash and trim the chives, and then cut them into 2-inch lengths. Combine
   the sauce ingredients in a small bowl.

3 Season the wok, then add 4 tablespoons of oil and heat over a high flame.
   When the oil is really hot, add the pork slivers and stir briskly to separate
   them. Stir-fry for a minute or so until the meat is just about cooked, then toss
   in the chives. Continue to stir-fry until the chives are tender, and then give
   the sauce a stir and add it to the wok. Cook for a few seconds more until the
   sauce has thickened, and then turn onto a serving plate. Serve immediately.

VARIATIONS

Similar stir-fried dishes can be made with celery, red or green bell peppers,
and several other vegetables. If you're using celery, the texture is much
improved if you sprinkle the strips with a little salt and leave them for
15–30 minutes to drain out excess water. Fleshy vegetables are best stir-
fried in advance for a minute or two over a moderate heat, to "break their
rawness": they can then be added to the meat at the last minute. (If you
don't pre-fry them, the pork may be overdone by the time the vegetables
are ready.) You can substitute chicken or beef for the pork in the above
recipe if you like.

PORK SLICES WITH BLACK CLOUD EAR FUNGUS

mu'er rou pian

This simple but colorful stir-fry often appears on Sichuan dinner menus at home or in restaurants. The pale pork slices are tossed in the wok with bright red pickled chiles, slithery black fungus, and slices of crisp green lettuce stem. The sauce is called "white-flavored" (*bai wei*) because it is seasoned only with salt and white pepper, rather than deeply colored flavorings like soy sauce and Chinese vinegar. Do use pork that is a little fatty if you can—the texture of the fat much improves the dish. I've suggested using celery as a substitute for lettuce stem, but thin slices of cucumber could also be used.

Serves 2 as a main dish with rice, 4 with three other dishes

a small handful of cloud ear
    mushrooms
1/2 pound boneless pork (the
    meat from about 2 pork
    chops), preferably with
    some fat
3 celery stalks
salt
1 scallion, white and green
    parts
2–3 Sichuanese pickled chiles
    or a 1/4 of a red bell pepper
1 large clove of garlic and an
    equivalent amount of fresh
    ginger

peanut oil
FOR THE MARINADE
1/2 teaspoon salt
1 teaspoon Shaoxing rice
    wine or medium-dry sherry
4 teaspoons potato flour or 6
    teaspoons cornstarch
2 tablespoons water
FOR THE SAUCE
1/4 teaspoon salt
1/8 teaspoon ground pepper
3/4 teaspoon potato flour or
    1 1/8 teaspoons cornstarch
1/4 cup chicken stock

1 Soak the cloud ears in hot water for about 15 minutes until soft.

2 Slice the pork as thinly as possible (ideally into pieces about 2 inches by 2 inches). Place in a small bowl, add the marinade ingredients, and mix well.

3 Cut the cloud ears into slices of a similar size to the pork, discarding any knobbly bits. With a knife, remove the tough outer strings from the celery stalks and cut each stalk at a steep angle into thin slices (you may wish to cut the thick ends of the stalks in half lengthwise to make the slices uniform). Sprinkle with 2 or 3 pinches of salt and mix well. Cut the scallion and pickled chiles or red bell pepper at a steep angle into very thin slices. Peel and thinly slice the garlic and ginger. Mix the sauce ingredients together in a small bowl.

4 Season the wok, then add 1/3 cup of oil and heat over a high flame until it just begins to smoke. Stir 1 tablespoon of oil into the pork, mix well, and then tip the meat into the wok and stir-fry briskly. When the pieces have separated and are turning white, pour off any excess oil, leaving 2–3 tablespoons in the wok, and add the ginger, garlic, and pickled chiles or red bell pepper. Stir-fry for about 20 seconds until the ginger and garlic are fragrant. Then add the celery, cloud ears, and scallions, and continue to stir-fry for 30–60 seconds until the celery is just cooked. Finally, give the sauce a stir and add it to the wok. Stir a few times until the sauce has thickened, and then turn out onto a serving plate. Serve immediately.

ANTS CLIMBING A TREE (BEAN THREAD NOODLES WITH MINCED MEAT)

ma yi shang shu

If you dangle a few strands of these noodles from your chopsticks, tiny morsels of meat will cling to them "like ants climbing a tree." This is an economical and hearty dish, typical of Sichuanese home cooking and modest restaurants, but it's tasty and attractive—a great interlaced mound of glassy noodles dotted with ground meat, flakes of scarlet chile, and tiny rings of green scallion. Some cooks deep-fry the dried noodles instead of soaking them, to delicious effect. The noodles do, however, tend to disintegrate with that method. These noodles, which are made from pea or mung bean starch, are readily available in Asian food stores.

Serves 4 with two other dishes

1/4 pound bean thread noodles
1 teaspoon Shaoxing rice wine or medium-dry sherry
salt
1/4 pound ground pork or beef
peanut oil
3 teaspoons light soy sauce

1 1/2 tablespoons chili bean paste
1 2/3 cups everyday stock (see page 318) or chicken stock
1/2 teaspoon dark soy sauce
3 scallions, green parts only, finely sliced

1 Soak the noodles in hot water for at least 15 minutes before you begin (drain them just before cooking). Add the Shaoxing rice wine and a couple of generous pinches of salt to the ground meat and mix well.

2 Season the wok, then add 2 tablespoons of oil and heat over a high flame. Add the ground meat and stir-fry until lightly browned and crispy, with a teaspoon or so of light soy sauce. Add the chili bean paste and stir-fry until the oil is red and fragrant, taking care not to burn it (remove the wok from the heat for a few moments if it becomes too hot). Add the stock and the drained noodles and stir well. Tip in the dark soy sauce for color, and season with light soy sauce and salt to taste.

3 When the stock has come to a boil, simmer over a medium flame for about 10 minutes, until the liquid has mostly evaporated and been absorbed. Finally, add the scallions, mix well, and transfer to a serving dish.

FIRE-EXPLODED KIDNEY FLOWERS

huo bao yao hua

The first time I ever visited Chengdu, my friend Zhou Yu offered me this dish in a restaurant and, as I savored it, challenged me to guess what I was eating. I looked at the pinkish, frilly morsels tossed with lettuce root and pickled chiles in a honey-colored sauce and had no idea at all. *Huo bao yao hua* is kidneys as you have never seen or tasted them before—crisp, dainty, and quite delicious. The dish is for me a perfect example of the ability of Sichuanese cooks to transform the most clumsy offal into unexpected delicacies. It is also an illustration of the old truism that Chinese cooking is all in the preparation—the kidneys must be cut carefully in a special manner, the vegetables chopped and laid out neatly on a plate, the sauce ingredients blended in a bowl. The actual cooking takes no time at all. *Huo bao*, which literally means "fire-exploded," is the name of a cooking method that involves stir-frying briefly at a very high temperature. It is a method that is superb for preserving the crispness and freshness of certain ingredients that, like kidney and liver, become "old" (*lao*) if overcooked. The *hua* in the name of the dish means "flower," a term often used to describe meat that is cut in such a way as to make it unfold like a blossom during cooking.

Don't be put off by the tricky cutting method, which is similar to that used for preparing fresh squid in Chinese recipes—if you have a sharp knife, it's not as complicated as it sounds. As far as the cooking is concerned, the most important thing to remember is to use a high flame and to keep the time as short as possible. The dish as cooked in Sichuan is usually made with strips of lettuce stem and pickled red chiles, but it's still delicious if you substitute the more readily available celery and red bell pepper.

Serves 2 as a main dish with rice, 4 with two or three other dishes

3 pig's kidneys (about 3/4–1
    pound)
1 or 2 celery sticks
salt
2 scallions, white parts only
2 Sichuanese pickled red
    chiles or a 1/4 of a red bell
    pepper
2 cloves of garlic and an
    equivalent amount of fresh
    ginger
10 tablespoons peanut oil

FOR THE MARINADE

1 1/2 Shaoxing rice wine or
    medium-dry sherry

1/4 teaspoon salt
1/2 teaspoon potato flour or
    3/4 teaspoon cornstarch

FOR THE SAUCE

1/4 teaspoon salt
3/4 teaspoon potato flour or
    1 1/8 teaspoons cornstarch
a couple of pinches of ground
    white pepper or 6–8 turns
    of a black pepper mill
1 teaspoon light soy sauce
1 teaspoon Shaoxing rice
    wine or medium-dry sherry
2 tablespoons chicken or beef
    stock

1 Lay the kidneys flat on a cutting board and use a cleaver or sharp knife to cut them in half, parallel to the board. Lay each half skin-side-down on the board. Then use the knife, again held parallel to the board, to slice away the core of each kidney, leaving only the pale pink-brown kidney flesh. You may need to make several delicate cuts to do this. Now hold the knife at about a 30-degree angle to the board and make little cuts across the entire inner surface of each kidney, about 1/8 inch apart, taking care not to cut all the way through to the board. Then, with the knife held at a right angle to the board, make similar cuts perpendicular to the original cuts, again taking care not to cut right through the kidneys. The entire inner surface of each kidney should now be cross-hatched with little lines. Finally, cut each kidney into rectangular or diamond-shaped pieces about the size of a couple of small postage stamps. Don't worry if these are a bit uneven—they will all curl up during the cooking anyway. (For more elaborate ways of cutting, see below.) Put the kidney pieces into a bowl, add the marinade ingredients, and stir well. Set aside while you prepare the other ingredients.

2 De-string the celery sticks and cut them into 2-inch strips about the thickness of chopstick handles. Sprinkle with 2 pinches of salt and mix well. Cut the scallions and Sichuanese chiles at a steep angle into "horse ear" slices.

If you are using red bell pepper, cut it into thin slices about 2 inches long. Peel and thinly slice the garlic and ginger. Combine the sauce ingredients in a small bowl.

3 Heat the oil in a wok until it is smoking (about 350°F). Add the kidneys and stir-fry for 10–15 seconds until they have separated and are just beginning to turn pale. Then pour off all but about 2 tablespoons of the oil into a heatproof container, return to a high flame, and toss in the ginger, garlic, and scallions (and the Sichuanese chiles, if you are using them). Stir just once or twice and then add the celery (and red bell pepper, if using). Continue to stir-fry for about a minute until the kidneys are just cooked. Then pour in the sauce and stir for a few seconds more until it has thickened slightly. Turn onto a plate and serve immediately.

VARIATIONS

If you are enjoying the cutting and want to try something even fancier, you might have some fun with the following two variations on the method described above:

"Eyebrows" (*mei mao yao hua*): Make the 30-degree cuts in the kidney flesh as described above. Then make the perpendicular cuts in the same manner, but cut all the way through to the board on every third cut. Trim any very long pieces to make them about 3 inches in length. You will end up with frilly strips of kidney that do look a little like very hairy eyebrows when cooked.

"Phoenix tails" (*feng wei yao hua*): Prepare as for "eyebrows," except cut right through to the board for part of each perpendicular cut, and then sever the piece completely for every third cut. This way, one end of each piece will have three fronds branching out like the tail of the mythical bird.

STIR-FRIED PIG'S LIVER
bai you gan pian

Liver, like kidneys, is best cooked swiftly, which makes it particularly well suited to the Chinese stir-fry. The following dish is everyday fare, but it has a delicacy that is rare in European liver dishes. For best results, use a very sharp knife and take care to make the liver slices as thin and even as possible.

One of my sources for this recipe is a 1980s cookbook that, amazingly, was once treated as classified information. On its back cover it bears the tell-tale phrase *nei bu fa xing*, "for internal circulation only," which is most commonly associated with political documents. The book appears to be a simple collection of recipes, and so far I've been unable to find any atomic formulae or underground maps hidden among its lists of ingredients for twice-cooked pork and dry-fried eels. Did someone think that the United States might use China's culinary secrets to subvert its political system? Or are "pork" and "bamboo shoots" part of some complex food-related cipher? The mind boggles.

Serves 2 as a main dish with rice and one vegetable dish, 4 with two or three dishes as part of a Chinese meal

a small handful of dried cloud
    ear mushrooms
a small handful of tender baby
    bok choy leaves or 2 celery
    sticks
salt
2 scallions, white parts only
3 Sichuanese pickled chiles or
    1/2 of a red bell pepper
2 cloves of garlic and an
    equivalent amount of fresh
    ginger
9 ounces pig's liver
about 10 tablespoons peanut
    oil

FOR THE MARINADE
1/4 teaspoon salt
2 teaspoons potato flour or
    1 1/8 teaspoons cornstarch
a couple of pinches of ground
    white pepper or 6–8 turns
    of a black pepper mill
1 teaspoon Shaoxing rice
    wine or medium-dry sherry
1 teaspoon light soy sauce
2 tablespoons everyday stock
    (see page 318)
1 teaspoon sesame oil

1 Soak the cloud ears in very hot water for about 30 minutes.

2 If you are using baby bok choy, use only the very tender leaves. If using celery, de-string the sticks and cut them into 2-inch strips about the thickness of chopstick handles. Sprinkle with 2 pinches of salt. Remove any hard bits from the cloud ears and cut them into chunky strips. Cut the scallions and Sichuanese chiles at a steep angle into "horse ear" slices. If you are using red bell pepper, cut it into thin strips about 2 inches long. Peel and thinly slice the garlic and ginger. Combine the sauce ingredients in a small bowl.

3 Remove the outer membrane from the liver. If the main part of the liver is still in one piece, cut it in half lengthwise. Then cut each piece of liver as evenly as possible into thin slices—the thinner the better. Discard any gristly bits. Put the slices into a small bowel, add the marinade ingredients, and mix well.

4 Heat 1 tablespoon of oil in a wok until very hot. Add the cloud ear slices and 2 pinches of salt and stir-fry for 20–30 seconds over a high flame. Tip into a bowl and set aside.

5 Heat 10 tablespoons of peanut oil in the wok until it is just beginning to smoke. Add the liver and cook for 10–15 seconds until the slices separate and start turning pale. Immediately pour off all but about 2 tablespoons of oil, add the garlic, ginger, and scallions (and the pickled chiles, if using), and return the wok to a high flame. Stir once or twice, then add the cloud ears and bok choy or celery (and the red bell pepper, if using) and continue to stir-fry for about a minute until the liver is barely cooked. Give the sauce a stir and add it to the wok. Stir-fry for a few seconds more until the sauce has thickened slightly. Turn onto a plate and serve immediately.

BOILED BEEF SLICES IN A FIERY SAUCE

shui zhu niu rou

Sichuanese people joke that outsiders, wary of the fiery local flavors, order this dish in restaurants in the hope of eating something mild and soothing—its name in Chinese just means "beef boiled in water." In fact it's sensationally hot, a dish based on lashings of chili bean sauce and finished off with a sizzling pile of ground chiles and lip-tingling Sichuan pepper. It's said to have originated in Zigong, the city poetically known as Sichuan's "salt capital" (*yan du*) because it was the center of the region's historic salt-mining industry. Oxen used to drive the machinery that drew up the salty liquid buried deep in the earth; the brine was then evaporated over a fire to leave an unusually pure and intensely flavored salt. The oxen, poor things, ended up in dishes like this one, which did at least nourish the salt workers as they carried out their punishing outdoor labor. It's not for the fainthearted, but if you have a taste for spicy food, it's fabulous, and perfect for a cold winter's day when you need firing up with energy and warmth. As they say in Sichuan, it'll make you pour with sweat, even on the coldest days of the year. Serve it with plenty of plain white rice. You will need a large, deep serving bowl for this dish.

Serves 2 as a main dish, 4 with rice and two or three other dishes

I head of celery (about I pound)
4 scallions, white and green parts
a small handful of dried chiles (8–10 chiles)
about I pound lean beef (flank steak is good)
salt
I tablespoon Shaoxing rice wine or medium-dry sherry

about 1/3 cup peanut oil
2 teaspoons Sichuan pepper
3 tablespoons chili bean paste
3 cups everyday stock (see page 318) or chicken stock
2 teaspoons dark soy sauce
4 tablespoons potato flour mixed with 4 tablespoons cold water, or 6 tablespoons cornstarch mixed with 6 tablespoons cold water

1 Clean and remove the fibrous outer edge of the celery stalks. Chop each stalk into 3 or 4 sections, then slice these lengthwise into 1/2-inch sticks. Gently crush the scallions and chop them into 3 sections to match the celery. Wearing rubber gloves, snip the chiles in half, discarding as many seeds as possible. Remove any fat from the beef and cut it, against the grain, into thin slices about 1 inch by 2 inches (you should have about 3/4 pound of beef after trimming). Add a 1/4 teaspoon of salt and the Shaoxing rice wine, mix well, and leave to marinate while you prepare everything else.

2 Heat 3 tablespoons of oil in a wok until hot but not yet smoking. Add the chiles and Sichuan pepper and stir-fry until they are fragrant and the chiles are just beginning to brown (take care not to burn them). Then immediately slide the spices out into a bowl, leaving the oil in the wok. When they have cooled down a little, move them onto a cutting board and chop them finely with a gentle rocking motion, using a cleaver taken in both hands or a two-handled chopper. Set them aside to use later.

3 Return the oily wok to the stove and heat over a high flame. When it is smoking, add the vegetables and stir-fry for a minute or two, adding 1/4–1/2 teaspoon of salt to taste, until they are hot and just-cooked but still crunchy. Then pour them into the serving bowl.

4 Heat another 3 tablespoons of oil in the wok over a high flame, until just beginning to smoke. Turn the heat down to medium, add in the chili bean paste, and stir-fry for about 30 seconds, until the oil is red and fragrant. Add the stock and the dark soy sauce, season to taste with salt, and return to a boil over a high flame. Then add the potato flour or cornstarch mixture to the beef and stir well in one direction to coat all the pieces. When the sauce is boiling vigorously, drop in the beef slices. Wait for the sauce to return to a boil and then use a pair of chopsticks to gently separate the slices. Simmer for a minute or so, until the beef is just cooked, and then spoon it onto the waiting vegetables. Pour over the sauce.

5 Swiftly rinse out the wok and dry it well. Heat another 3–4 tablespoons of oil in the wok until smoking. Sprinkle the chopped chiles and Sichuan pepper over the beef dish and then pour over the smoking oil, which will sizzle dramatically. If you move quickly, the dish will still be fizzing when you bring it to the table.

VARIATIONS

Exactly the same method can be used to cook slices of pork or fish, as well as eels and exotic seafood. If you are using eels or whole fish, you won't need the potato flour or cornstarch coating that keeps the slices slippery-soft in the recipe above.

The vegetable part of the dish can be varied at will: in Sichuan they often use Chinese leeks, lettuce stems, or bean sprouts, whether on their own, mixed together, or with celery. The important thing is to have something fresh and crunchy to contrast with the soft, rich meat.

DRY-FRIED BEEF SLIVERS
gan bian niu rou si

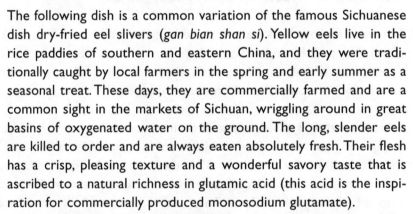

The following dish is a common variation of the famous Sichuanese dish dry-fried eel slivers (*gan bian shan si*). Yellow eels live in the rice paddies of southern and eastern China, and they were traditionally caught by local farmers in the spring and early summer as a seasonal treat. These days, they are commercially farmed and are a common sight in the markets of Sichuan, wriggling around in great basins of oxygenated water on the ground. The long, slender eels are killed to order and are always eaten absolutely fresh. Their flesh has a crisp, pleasing texture and a wonderful savory taste that is ascribed to a natural richness in glutamic acid (this acid is the inspiration for commercially produced monosodium glutamate).

The dry-frying method is a Sichuanese invention. It uses neither marinade nor sauces, but relies on the gradual drying out of the main ingredient over a moderate heat and the subsequent addition of spices and flavorings. The principal ingredient, which is usually cut into strips or fine slivers, ends up slightly crisp and chewy, but succulent within, with a delicious toasty fragrance and a dry, spicy taste. Eels, beef, pork, and dried squid can all be dry-fried, as well as some vegetable ingredients, such as green beans, eggplant, and bitter melon.

Fresh yellow eels (*shan yu* or *huang shan*) are the Sichuanese ingredient of choice, but I have written the recipe using beef, which is a variation often used by Sichuanese cooks.

Serves 2–3 as a main dish with rice and one vegetable dish, 4 with three other dishes as part of a Chinese meal

**1 pound lean beef (flank steak
   is good)**
4 celery stalks
salt to taste
**a 1 1/2-inch piece of fresh
   ginger**
2 scallions, white parts only
1/3 cup peanut oil
**1 tablespoon Shaoxing rice
   wine or medium-dry sherry**

**2–3 tablespoons Sichuanese
   chili bean paste**
1 teaspoon light soy sauce
1/2 teaspoon sesame oil
chili oil to finish (optional)
**1/2 teaspoon ground roasted
   Sichuan pepper (see page
   74)**

1 Cut the beef evenly into thin slices and then against the grain into fine slivers (less than a 1/4 inch thick). Discard any fat or gristly bits. Using a knife, scrape off the tough outer strings of the celery stalks, chop them into 3-inch sections, and then cut these lengthwise into thin strips to match the beef. Sprinkle the celery with a little salt to draw out some of the water (about 1/4 teaspoon will do). Peel the ginger, slice it, and cut it into fine slivers. Cut the scallion whites into fine slivers to match the ginger.

2 Season your wok, then add 1/3 cup of fresh peanut oil. Heat over a high flame until smoking, and then add the beef and mix well. The liquid will become cloudy initially as the beef releases its juices. Stir-fry constantly until the liquid has cleared and the beef has lost most of its water content and is beginning to crisp up—this will take about 10 minutes, depending on the beef you use (you will notice that the beef starts sizzling as the water disappears). As the meat dries out, splash the Shaoxing rice wine around the edges of the wok and let it sizzle.

3 When the oil is clear, turn the heat down to medium, push the beef up to one side of the wok, and tilt the wok so the oil runs into the space you have created. Drop the chili bean paste into the oil and stir-fry for about 30 seconds, until the oil is red and fragrant. Add the ginger and scallions, mix everything together, and continue to stir-fry for another 10 seconds or so until you can smell the ginger. Finally, add the celery strips, soy sauce, and

salt to taste, and continue to stir-fry until the celery is just cooked. Remove the wok from the heat, stir in the sesame oil, and tip onto a serving plate.

4 Drizzle with a little chili oil, if desired, and sprinkle with a few generous pinches of Sichuan pepper.

SPICY STEAMED BEEF WITH RICE MEAL

fen zheng niu rou

In the narrow back streets of the old Manchu district of Chengdu, the tiny snack shops and restaurants are open to the street. Often, under the eaves of the wood-framed buildings, a few clay pots of spare ribs or chicken are simmering gently to tempt passersby. Nearby, a huge wokful of water bubbles away under towers of tiny bamboo steamers. If you lift their lids you will be assailed by the scent of rich, aromatic chunks of beef that have been steamed to melting tenderness, languidly embraced by a soft, comforting layer of rice meal. The beef is served in the steamer, drizzled with sesame oil, and scattered with ground spices and the fresh sharpness of garlic, scallions, and coriander (cilantro). The marinade ingredients vary from place to place—some people add a spoonful or two of the liquid from jars of Sichuan preserved bean curd, and some add fermented rice wine. The following recipe is based on one described to me by a vendor who specializes in steamed dishes at a market near the Chengdu riverside. You can make it with lamb or fatty pork if you'd rather.

See the recipe for pork steamed in lotus leaves on page 201 for a cheater's substitute for homemade rice meal.

Serves 4 with three other dishes

about a pound of flank steak

2/3 cup long grain white rice

FOR THE MARINADE

2 tablespoons Sichuanese
  chili bean paste

1 tablespoon dark soy sauce

1 tablespoon light soy sauce

3 teaspoons finely chopped
  fresh ginger

4 tablespoons everyday stock
  (see page 318) or chicken
  stock

2 tablespoons Sichuanese
  fermented rice wine or
  Shaoxing rice wine or
  medium-dry sherry

3 tablespoons peanut or
  vegetable oil

TO SERVE

1/2 teaspoon ground
  Sichuanese chiles

1/2 teaspoon ground roasted
  Sichuan pepper (see page
  74)

2 teaspoons sesame oil

2 cloves of garlic, puréed and
  mixed with a little cold
  water

2–3 scallions, white and green
  parts, sliced into thin rings

a small handful of fresh
  coriander (cilantro) leaves,
  torn or roughly chopped

1 Cut the beef against the grain into 2-inch by 2-inch slices about 1/4 inch thick. Put the slices into a bowl, add all the marinade ingredients, mixing well, and let sit in a cool place for 30 minutes.

2 While the beef is marinating, stir-fry the rice in a dry wok over a moderate flame, until the grains are brittle, yellowish, and slightly fragrant. This will take 10–15 minutes. (Some cooks fry the rice with a star anise and a few bits of cassia bark to enhance its fragrance.) Remove from the wok and leave to cool. When the rice is cold, grind it in a food processor until it is of a coarse consistency, a bit finer than couscous but not powder-fine.

3 Add the rice meal to the beef, with about 1/4 cup of cold water. Mix well to encrust the beef with rice grains. Put the beef into an earthenware bowl, place this in a steamer, and steam over boiling water for about 2 hours, replenishing the water as needed. When you are ready to eat, remove the bowl from the steamer; scatter the beef with the ground spices, sesame oil, garlic-water, scallions, and coriander; and serve.

VARIATION

If you are using pork, it's best to use spare ribs or fresh pork belly, with the skin left on if you want to be really Chinese—the fat will become deliciously soft during the long steaming. Add a teaspoon or so of Sichuan pepper and a couple of finely sliced scallion greens to the marinade, and omit the garnishes, except for the garlic and coriander (cilantro). Most cooks will also place a few fresh peas or chunks of yam or potato, with a sprinkling of salt, on top of the pork in the steaming bowl. The soft blandness of the vegetables is a nice contrast to the rich meat.

RED-BRAISED BEEF
WITH WHITE RADISH
hong shao niu rou

Red-braising is a cooking method used all over China that generally involves slow cooking with plenty of soy sauce. In Sichuan, however, the main flavoring used to red-braise beef is not soy sauce but chili bean paste, which gives the gravy a glorious chestnut color and a deep chile kick. The radish, which is added toward the end of the cooking time, remains clear and crisp, in delightful contrast to the rich and tender beef. In Sichuanese restaurants, stews like this are often put into tall, glazed pots and left to simmer by the entrance in the hope of luring potential customers. If you want to serve this dish Sichuan-style, with rice and a few stir-fried dishes, it has the advantage that you can make it in advance and just reheat it when you want to eat. The dish also works very well as a stew, served perhaps simply with mashed potato. Lamb can be used instead of beef to delicious effect. (I have actually used Sichuanese chili bean paste in the same way to create new and exciting versions of traditional Western-style stews involving lamb and root vegetables. The chile taste makes them even more warm and comforting.)

Serves 4 as a main dish with rice, 6 with three or four other dishes

2 1/2–3 pounds short ribs or
 other rich stewing beef
a 1- to 2-inch piece of fresh
 ginger, unpeeled
2 scallions, white and green
 parts
3 tablespoons peanut oil
6 tablespoons Sichuanese chili
 bean paste
1 quart beef stock
4 tablespoons Shaoxing rice
 wine or medium-dry sherry

2 teaspoons dark soy sauce
1 teaspoon whole Sichuan
 pepper
1 star anise
1 *cao guo* (see page 62)
1 1/3 pounds Asian white
 radish (daikon) or kohlrabi
salt
fresh coriander (cilantro) to
 garnish

1 Blanch the beef in boiling water for a minute or two until scum has risen to the surface, then remove the meat and rinse it under the tap. (This step is intended to remove the bloody juices and improve the flavor.) Cut the beef into 1- to 2-inch chunks. Crush the ginger slightly using the side of a cleaver blade or a heavy object. Cut the scallions into 2 or 3 sections.

2 Heat the oil in a flat-bottomed pot over a medium heat. When it is hot, add the chili bean paste and stir-fry for about 30 seconds until the oil is red and richly fragrant. Add the stock, beef, wine, ginger, scallions, soy sauce, spices, and salt to taste. Bring the liquid to a boil, skim if necessary, and then turn the heat down and simmer gently until the beef is beautifully tender—2 hours is ideal.

3 When the beef is nearly ready, trim the radishes or kohlrabi and chop them into chunks to match the beef. If you are using radishes, blanch the pieces in boiling water to remove any sharpness. Add the vegetables to the beef, replenishing with stock or boiling water if necessary. Continue to simmer until just tender, turning up the heat to reduce the sauce if you wish. Season with salt if necessary. Serve garnished with fresh coriander (cilantro).

SHREDDED BEEF WITH SWEET PEPPERS

tian jiao niu rou si

 This colorful stir-fry is a common dish in everyday Sichuanese restaurants. The beef is cooked quickly to keep it tender, and the sweet bean paste adds an extra intensity of flavor. You can use pork instead of beef, but in that case it's best to omit the sweet bean paste.

Serves 2 as a main dish with rice, 4 with three other dishes

1/2 pound lean beef (flank
   steak is good)
1/2 a red bell pepper and 1/2
   a green bell pepper
1/4 teaspoon salt
2 teaspoons Sichuanese sweet
   bean paste mixed with 2
   teaspoons water
peanut oil

FOR THE MARINADE
  1/2 teaspoon salt
  2 teaspoons Shaoxing rice
    wine or medium-dry sherry

2 teaspoons potato flour or
  3 teaspoons cornstarch
2 teaspoons water

FOR THE SAUCE
  1 1/2 teaspoons light soy
    sauce
  1/4 teaspoon salt
  1/2 teaspoon potato flour or
    3/4 teaspoon cornstarch
  3 tablespoons everyday stock
    (see page 318) or chicken
    stock

1 Cut the beef against the grain into very fine slivers and place it in a bowl. Add the marinade ingredients and mix well. Cut the peppers into long, thin strips to match the beef. Combine the sauce ingredients in a small bowl.

2 Heat 1 tablespoon of oil in a wok over a medium flame. Add the bell peppers and 1/4 teaspoon of salt and stir-fry for about a minute, until they are just cooked. Remove and set aside. Rinse out the wok.

3 Add 2 teaspoons of oil to the beef and mix well.

4 Season the wok, then add 3 tablespoons of oil and heat over a high flame. When it is just beginning to smoke, add the beef and stir-fry briskly. When the meat strips have separated out, add the sweet bean paste and stir-fry for about 10 seconds until the sauce is hot and fragrant. Add the peppers and mix well. Immediately give the sauce a stir and add it to the wok. Stir for a few seconds more until the sauce has thickened and then turn everything out onto a serving plate.

4
poultry

THE CHICKEN HAS A PLACE AT THE HEART OF CHINESE gastronomy. Not only is its meat enjoyed in countless dishes, but its natural juices, extracted by gentle stewing, are thought to possess the very essence of flavor. For rich, dense chicken stock is the embodiment of *xian*, that elusive, delicious, savory taste that is in many ways the inspiration for the Chinese culinary arts (for a more detailed description of *xian*, see page 28). This is why chicken, and chicken stock, are vital ingredients in so many of China's most celebrated dishes, particularly those made with "treasures from the mountains and the seas" (*shan zhen hai wei*). It is also why you'll find chicken added to dishes made with other meats, like the oxtail soup on page 326, where the chicken is invisible in the final dish, but its juices enhance and refine the coarser natural flavors of the beef.

The Chinese, like many other ethnic groups, also regard chicken soup as a tonic and a particularly important source of nourishment. The finest chicken soups—the most *xian*, the most nutritious—are made from mature female chickens that are what we would refer to as "organically raised" and what the Chinese call "rustic, earthy, farmyard chickens" (*tu ji*). Younger, male chickens usually provide the tender meat for stir-fried dishes. There are several notable breeds of chicken in China—the Sichuanese specialty is the "black-boned chicken" (*wu gu ji*), a black-skinned fowl with a froth of fluffy white feathers. The ancestors of the Chinese were among the earliest people to domesticate chickens, and they have been bred in the Sichuan region since about the third century B.C.

The chicken's poetic alter ego is the phoenix, a gorgeously plumed mythical bird that was a symbol of the empress in imperial China. The phoenix, along with the emperor's symbol, the dragon, is a common decorative motif, and you still see images of the two creatures on the lacquered hors d'oeuvre dishes that are offered up at banquets in Sichuan. The phoenix lends its name to some chicken dishes—so you know what to expect when you find "phoenix claws" on a Chinese restaurant menu.

The duck is the other main cooking fowl in Sichuan, although it is not used as widely as the chicken. Its flavor is not thought to be as *xian*, but its meat has a special fragrance (*xiang*) that is highly prized. In Sichuanese cooking, the duck is often used whole, its fragrance coaxed out by roasting or deep-frying. Perhaps because some of Sichuan's most famous duck recipes demand extravagant amounts of cooking oil or the use of an oven (an extreme rarity in home kitchens), cooking duck is often left to the professionals. The finished dishes, however, such as tea-smoked and roasted duck, are bought in shops and served in people's homes.

Geese, pigeons, and quails are occasionally used in Sichuanese cooking—the latter most commonly for their eggs.

CHICKEN RECIPES

GONG BAO (KUNG PAO) CHICKEN WITH PEANUTS
gong bao ji ding

This dish, also known as Kung Pao chicken, has the curious distinction of having been labeled as politically incorrect during the Cultural Revolution. It is named after a late Qing Dynasty (late nineteenth century) governor of Sichuan, Ding Baozhen, who is said to have particularly enjoyed eating it—*gong bao* was his official title. No one can quite agree on the details of its origins: some say it was a dish Ding Baozhen brought with him from his home province of Guizhou; others that he ate it in a modest restaurant when he went out in humble dress to observe the real lives of his subjects; still others, rather implausibly, that his chef invented the finely chopped chicken dish because Ding Baozhen had bad teeth. Whatever the truth of its origins, its association with an imperial bureaucrat was enough to provoke the wrath of the Cultural Revolution radicals, and it was renamed "fast-fried chicken cubes" (*hong bao ji ding*) or "chicken cubes with seared chiles" (*hu la ji ding*) until its political rehabilitation in the 1980s.

Gong Bao chicken is beautiful to look at: a glorious medley of chicken flesh, golden peanuts and bright red chiles. The sauce is based on a light sweet-and-sour, pepped up with a deep chile spiciness and a trace of Sichuan pepper that will make your lips tingle pleasantly. The ingredients are all cut in harmony, the chicken in small cubes and the scallion in short pieces to complement the peanuts. The chicken should be just cooked and wonderfully succulent; the nuts are added at the very last minute so they keep their crispness.

Serves 2 as a main dish with a simple stir-fried vegetable and rice, 4 as part of a Chinese meal with three other dishes

2 boneless chicken breasts, with or without skin (about 2/3 pound total)

3 cloves of garlic and an equivalent amount of fresh ginger

5 scallions, white parts only

2 tablespoons peanut oil

a generous handful of dried red chiles (at least 10), preferably Sichuanese

1 teaspoon whole Sichuan pepper

2/3 cup roasted unsalted peanuts

FOR THE MARINADE

1/2 teaspoon salt

2 teaspoons light soy sauce

1 teaspoon Shaoxing rice wine or medium-dry sherry

1 1/2 teaspoons potato flour or 2 1/4 teaspoons cornstarch

1 tablespoon water

FOR THE SAUCE

3 teaspoons sugar

3/4 teaspoon potato flour or 1 1/8 teaspoons cornstarch

1 teaspoon dark soy sauce

1 teaspoon light soy sauce

3 teaspoons Chinkiang or black Chinese vinegar

1 teaspoon sesame oil

1 tablespoon chicken stock or water

1 Cut the chicken as evenly as possible into 1/2-inch strips and then cut these into small cubes. Place in a small bowl and mix in the marinade ingredients.

2 Peel and thinly slice the garlic and ginger, and chop the scallions into chunks as long as their diameter (to match the chicken cubes). Snip the chiles in half or into 2-inch sections. Wearing rubber gloves, discard as many seeds as possible.

3 Combine the sauce ingredients in a small bowl—if you dip your finger in, you can taste the sweet-sour base of the *gong bao* flavor.

4 Season the wok, then add 2 tablespoons of oil and heat over a high flame. When the oil is hot but not yet smoking, add the chiles and Sichuan pepper and stir-fry briefly until they are crisp and the oil is spicy and fragrant. Take care not to burn the spices (you can remove the wok from the heat if necessary to prevent overheating).

5 Quickly add the chicken and fry over a high flame, stirring constantly. As soon as the chicken cubes have separated, add the ginger, garlic, and scallions and continue to stir-fry for a few minutes until they are fragrant and the meat is cooked through (test one of the larger pieces to make sure).

6 Give the sauce a stir and add it to the wok, continuing to stir and toss. As soon as the sauce has become thick and shiny, add the peanuts, stir them in, and serve.

VARIATIONS

The same dish can be made with cubes of pork, shrimp, or prawns.

Cashew nuts can be used instead of peanuts for a grander version of this dish, although peanuts are more traditional.

CHICKEN WITH CHILES

la zi ji

The first time you encounter this dish, it appears terrifyingly spicy, the cubes of chicken surrounded by improbable quantities of blood-red chiles. But in fact, it's not particularly hot. The chiles that make the dish look so dramatic are used to give fragrance and a gentle spiciness to the cooking oil and are not usually eaten. Guests just pick out the delicious pieces of chicken with their chopsticks, leaving the chiles and Sichuan peppercorns on the serving plate. The dish is a Chongqing specialty. Sichuanese cooks tend to use chicken on the bone, which is more intensely flavored than breast meat, but it can be frustrating to find so little actual flesh on a dish piled high with meat and chiles. The most important thing to remember in this recipe is not to burn the chiles, which must keep their glorious red color.

Serves 4 with two or three other dishes as part of a Chinese meal

2 boneless, skinless chicken breasts (about 2/3 pound total)

FOR THE MARINADE

2 teaspoons Shaoxing rice wine or medium-dry sherry

1 teaspoon light soy sauce

1 teaspoon dark soy sauce

1/4 teaspoon salt

OTHER INGREDIENTS

1 small rice bowl filled generously with dried red chiles, preferably Sichuanese (about 2 ounces)

peanut oil for deep-frying

2 cloves of garlic, sliced, and an equivalent amount of fresh peeled ginger, sliced

1 tablespoon whole Sichuan pepper

2 scallions, white parts only, each cut into about 3 sections

salt to taste

a generous pinch of sugar

2 teaspoons sesame oil

1 Cut the chicken into 1-inch cubes and put them into a small bowl. Add the marinade ingredients and mix well. Set aside for 30 minutes if possible.

2 Wearing rubber gloves, snip the chiles in half with a pair of scissors and remove and discard as many seeds as possible.

3 Heat the oil for deep-frying to a very high temperature. Add the chicken and fry for 4–5 minutes until the pieces are cooked through, golden-brown, and a little crispy on the outside. Drain well and set aside.

4 Heat 3 tablespoons of oil in a wok over a moderate flame. Add the garlic and ginger and stir-fry until they are fragrant and just taking color. Then add all the chiles and the Sichuan peppercorns and stir-fry for 10–20 seconds until the oil is spicy and fragrant, taking great care not to burn the chiles (remove the wok from the stove for a few seconds if the oil seems too hot). Add the chicken and scallions and stir in. Season with salt to taste and a generous pinch of sugar. Stir well so that the chicken is coated with the fragrant oil. Finally, remove from the heat, stir in the sesame oil, and serve.

CHICKEN WITH VINEGAR
cu liu ji

The chicken in this dish is beautifully white and tender, lolling in a pool of red oil. Its succulent flesh is complemented by the fresh crunchiness of the celery. The sauce is gently vinegar-sour, with a deep, lingering spiciness from the pickled chiles. In Sichuan the chicken is usually accompanied by bamboo shoots or tender lettuce stems: I find celery a fine substitute, with its similar crunchy freshness and subtle herby flavor. The initial frying of the chicken in a protective coating of egg white batter, and in fairly cool oil, keeps it soft and delicate, ready to receive the delicious draping of the sauce. The most important thing in this dish is not to overcook the chicken—do, however, check one of the larger pieces to make sure there is no rawness left inside before you tip it onto the serving dish. This recipe is based on one I saw demonstrated by chef Gong Xingde of the catering department at the Sichuan Provincial Business and Services School.

Incidentally, many of my Chinese friends associate vinegar with betrayal in love: "eating vinegar" (*chi cu*) is a common phrase that means to be cheated on or to be jealous in love.

Serves 4 with two or three other dishes

2 boneless, skinless chicken
  breasts (about 2/3 pound)
FOR THE MARINADE
  1 1/2 teaspoons Shaoxing rice
    wine or medium-dry sherry
  1/2 teaspoon salt
FOR THE BATTER
  2 tablespoons egg white
  2 tablespoons potato flour or
    3 tablespoons cornstarch
FOR THE SAUCE
  1 1/2 teaspoons white sugar
  2 teaspoons Chinkiang or
    black Chinese vinegar
  1/4 teaspoon salt
  1 teaspoon Shaoxing rice
    wine or medium-dry sherry

1 teaspoon potato flour or
  1 1/2 teaspoons cornstarch
3 tablespoons chicken stock
OTHER INGREDIENTS
3 celery stalks
plenty of peanut oil for
  cooking
2 tablespoons pickled chili
  paste
3 teaspoons finely chopped
  fresh ginger
3 teaspoons finely chopped
  garlic
2 scallions, white and green
  parts, sliced into tiny rings

1 Cut the chicken breasts as evenly as possible into 1/2-inch strips and then diagonally into small lozenge shapes. Place in a small bowl and add the marinade ingredients. Set aside while you prepare the other ingredients.

2 Using a knife, remove the fibrous outer edge of the celery stalks, slice them in half lengthwise, and then chop into small lozenge shapes to match the chicken pieces.

3 Mix the sauce ingredients together in a small bowl.

4 Add the batter ingredients to the chicken and mix well, stirring in one direction.

5 Heat 1 1/2 cups of peanut oil over a medium flame to about 200°F. Add the chicken, followed closely by the celery, and prod gently with a chopstick to separate the pieces. Keeping an eye on the oil temperature, which shouldn't rise above about 175°F after the chicken is added, stir very gently until the pieces of chicken have separated and are just turning white. Remove immediately from the wok with a slotted spoon and drain off excess oil. The chicken will still be half raw—resist the temptation to cook it through at this stage or you'll find the finished dish less than succulent.

6 Drain off most of the oil in the wok, leaving behind a scant 2 tablespoons. Heat this over a medium flame until hot but not smoking. Add the chili paste and stir-fry for about 20–30 seconds until the oil is a rich, deep red. Add the ginger and garlic and continue to stir-fry for another 30 seconds or so until they are cooked and fragrant. Return the chicken and celery to the wok and stir in quickly. Still working swiftly, give the sauce a stir and add to the wok. Add the scallions, stir or toss a few more times until everything is well mixed and the sauce has thickened, and then turn onto a serving dish. The chicken should be just cooked and very tender—test the largest piece to make sure it's cooked through.

DRY-FRIED CHICKEN

gan bian ji

The Sichuanese apply the local dry-frying method to many different ingredients. In this recipe, small chunks of chicken become delightfully toasty and flavorful; fresh vegetables provide a nice, crisp contrast to the meat. The dish has a deep, gentle chile hotness and looks very appetizing with its chile-reddened oil. You can vary the vegetables as you please—I've seen Sichuanese cooks use leeks on their own, or plenty of chopped green bell peppers (the latter are best fried separately until tender, with a little oil and salt, and then added to the chicken at the end).

Serves 2 with one other dish and rice, 4 with two or three other dishes

2 celery stalks
about 1 pound chicken meat,
   preferably on the bone
   (about 2 chicken breasts or
   3–4 thighs)
3 whole scallions
1/4 cup peanut oil
6–8 dried chiles (about 1/8
   ounce)

1 teaspoon whole Sichuan
   pepper
1 1/2 tablespoons Sichuan
   chili bean paste
1 tablespoon Shaoxing rice
   wine or medium-dry sherry
1 teaspoon dark soy sauce
salt
2 teaspoons sesame oil

1 Using a knife, remove the fibrous outer bits from the celery stalks and cut them at a steep angle into 1/2-inch slices. Sprinkle with a few pinches of salt and set aside while you prepare the other ingredients.

2 Cut the chicken as evenly as possible into 1-inch chunks. Cut the scallions at a steep angle into slices to match the celery.

3 Season the wok, then add 1/4 cup of oil and reheat until smoking hot. Add the chicken and stir-fry over a high flame for 4–5 minutes, until it has lost much of its water content. (You can achieve this by deep-frying—rather quicker but more extravagant with the oil.) Turn the heat down to medium, add the chiles and Sichuan pepper, and stir-fry until they smell wonderfully spicy. Add the chili bean paste and stir as it releases its fragrance and stains the oil a red-orange color. Splash in the Shaoxing rice wine and stir in the dark soy sauce and 1/4–1/2 teaspoon of salt to taste. Keep stirring over a medium heat for 10–15 minutes, until the chicken is dry, toasty, and fragrant. Then add the vegetables and stir-fry for another minute or two until they are just tender, adding a little more salt to taste. Remove from the heat, stir in the sesame oil, and serve.

TAI BAI CHICKEN
tai bai ji

This dish is named in honor of the great Tang Dynasty poet Li Bai, who lived in the eighth century A.D. and was nicknamed Great Purity (*tai bai*—also the name given to the star Westerners call Venus). He was born in northern China, but moved to Sichuan in his childhood. Later he led a wandering life, spurned by the decadent political circles he tried to enter, taking refuge in wine and poetry. In one of his most famous works, Li Bai wrote of the perils of traveling to Sichuan, that green, fertile basin ringed by forbidding mountains. He described a path flanked by towering peaks, plunging chasms, and thundering river torrents, with the strange cries of wild birds emanating from the trees and the constant threat of snakes and tigers. He finished with a warning:

> *The City of Brocade [Chengdu] may be a pleasant place,*
> *But it is best to seek your home.*
> *For it is easier to climb to Heaven*
> *Than to take the Sichuan road.*
> *I gaze into the west, and sigh.*

Li Bai, "The Sichuan Road," from Zong Shi, ed., *Selected Poems from the Tang Dynasty* (Beijing: Chinese Literature Press, 1999)

These days, in the City of Brocade, you will often find the following soothing, warming dish, Li Bai's namesake. The golden chicken pieces, mixed with the green parts of scallions and red pickled chiles, loll in a fragrant, spicy, orange oil. Tai bai chicken is not difficult to make—you just have to take care not to burn the spices. The flavors are much gentler if you use Sichuanese pickled chiles instead of Thai ones.

Serves 2 as a main dish with one vegetable and rice, 4 with three other dishes

about 1 pound chicken leg or thigh meat, on or off the bone
1/2 cup peanut oil
a small handful of dried red chiles, preferably Sichuanese, snipped in half (seeds discarded)
4 Sichuanese pickled chiles, cut into 2 1/2-inch sections, or 6 Thai pickled chiles with 1 teaspoon pickled chili paste
5 scallions, cut into 2 1/2-inch sections, white and green parts separated

1 cup everyday stock (see page 318) or chicken stock
1 tablespoon Shaoxing rice wine or medium-dry sherry
1 1/2 teaspoons dark soy sauce
1 teaspoon whole Sichuan pepper
1 1/4 teaspoons sugar
3/4 teaspoon salt
2 pinches of ground white pepper to taste
1–2 teaspoons sesame oil

1 Chop the chicken into 1 1/2-inch chunks (2-inch chunks if you are cutting it on the bone). Season the wok, then add 1/2 cup of oil and heat over a high flame until just smoking. Add half the chicken and stir-fry for one minute, until it is white but not crisp or cooked through. Remove and set aside. Repeat with the rest of the chicken.

2 Drain off all but about 3 tablespoons of oil. Return the wok to medium heat, and when the oil is hot but not smoking, add the dried chiles and stir-fry until you can smell their fragrance, taking great care not to let them burn. Then add the pickled chiles and pickled chili paste (if using) and stir-fry until the oil is reddish and they smell good, too. Add the scallion whites and stir-fry for another 10–20 seconds until you can smell their fragrance. (All this frying should be done over medium heat so the spices don't burn.)

3 Add the stock and the chicken and season with the Shaoxing rice wine, dark soy sauce, Sichuan pepper, sugar, salt, and white pepper. Bring to a boil and then simmer over gentle heat for about 20 minutes, stirring from time to time. As the stock dries out, remove the dried chiles and scallions with a pair of chopsticks and discard them.

4 When the stock has almost all evaporated, leaving just the spicy oil, add the scallion greens and stir-fry for another 30 seconds or so, until they are just cooked. Remove the wok from the heat, stir in the sesame oil, and spoon onto a serving dish.

BRAISED CHICKEN WITH CHESTNUTS
ban li shao ji

 As the Sichuanese summer fades and the damp winter nights draw in, roasted chestnuts begin to appear on the streets. Itinerant vendors roast them in their shells in enormous wokfuls of charcoal. They wrap the roasted chestnuts in cloths and tuck them snugly into baskets to keep them warm. The hot nuts are the perfect thing to palliate your hunger in a streetside teahouse where you stop for an hour before lunch. Chestnuts have been cultivated in China since antiquity: the character for chestnut (*li*) appears on the Shang Dynasty oracle bones, the earliest examples of the Chinese script, and they are also mentioned in the ancient Book of Songs. The great Qing Dynasty gourmet Yuan Mei left behind notes for his own recipe for chicken stewed with chestnuts; the following dish is a contemporary Sichuanese version that is widely enjoyed in the chestnut season. Sichuanese people eat it with rice and a few stir-fried dishes, but it can also be eaten Western-style, with potatoes and a simple vegetable side dish. The dish can be made in advance and reheated.

Serves 4 as a main course, with one or two other dishes

1–1 1/2 pounds chestnuts
1 whole chicken (about 4 pounds)
a 2-inch piece of fresh ginger, unpeeled
2 scallions, white and green parts
peanut oil

4 tablespoons Shaoxing rice wine or medium-dry sherry
2 2/3 cups everyday stock (see page 318) or chicken stock
4 teaspoons brown sugar
4 teaspoons dark soy sauce
salt to taste

1 Slice off the base of the chestnuts and blanch them in plenty of boiling water for about 2 minutes. Drain them well, and when they are cool enough to handle, remove the shells and skins as far as possible (some will slip off like gloves, others will defy all gentle coaxings).

2 Using a cleaver, chop up the chicken, bones and all, into small chunks. Crush the ginger and scallions slightly with the side of a cleaver blade or a heavy object.

3 Season the wok, then add 3 tablespoons of oil and heat over a high flame. When the oil is hot, add the chestnuts and stir-fry them for about 5 minutes, until they are golden. Remove with a slotted spoon and set aside. Add the chicken pieces to the wok and fry over a high heat until they are browned. Drain off some of the excess oil at this stage if you wish. Splash in the Shaoxing rice wine and stir well. Add the ginger and scallions and fry for about 30 seconds, until they are fragrant. Then slowly add all the stock.

4 Bring the stock back to a boil and add the sugar and dark soy sauce, with salt to taste. Then turn the heat down and simmer for 30 minutes, stirring from time to time.

5 Add the chestnuts, mix well, and continue to simmer until they are moist and pasty and the liquid is much reduced. Adjust the seasoning, if necessary, and serve.

STIR-FRIED CHICKEN HOTCHPOTCH

chao ji za

 My Sichuanese chef friends might be surprised to see me include the following recipe in this book—it's not a fancy dish and I've never seen it on a restaurant menu. But the circumstances in which I learned to make it are for me a perfect illustration of the resourcefulness of Sichuanese cooks, and it tastes delicious too.

My friend Feng Rui had invited me to spend a day cooking (and eating) with two of his friends, both former chefs of two of Chengdu's best hotels. In the morning we went to the local street market to buy our raw ingredients. The chickens, of course, were still clucking around in their pen. Feng Rui chose a fowl with a scarcely developed thumb, a sign that it was young and tender. The vendor slaughtered, plucked, and dressed it, and we took it home. The astonishing thing was that almost nothing of that bird was wasted. We ate the meat cold with a chili oil dressing (see page 55), the bones made the stock base of our winter melon soup, and all the innards went into the following dish, including intestines, heart, and blood. It was an enticing mix of strong flavors and different textures, all set off by the crunchy celery and a delicate assortment of spices.

The following is a recreation of the dish that uses only the readily available chicken livers.

Serves 4 with two or three other dishes (we enjoyed it with twice-cooked pork, chili-oil chicken, and a very simple steamed fish, as well as a soup to finish)

1 head of celery (about 10 stalks)
salt
1/3 pound chicken livers
3 Sichuanese pickled chiles or 6 Thai pickled chiles
about 1 tablespoon pickled young ginger, sliced or shredded
peanut oil
FOR THE MARINADE
1/2 teaspoon salt
1 teaspoon Shaoxing rice wine or medium-dry sherry

2 teaspoons potato flour or 3 teaspoons cornstarch
1 teaspoon water
FOR THE SAUCE
1/2 teaspoon salt
1/2 teaspoon sugar
a pinch of ground white or black pepper
3/4 teaspoon potato flour or 1 1/8 teaspoons cornstarch
3 tablespoons chicken stock or water

1 Wash and remove the fibrous outer layer of the celery, cut it into 3-inch sections, and then slice these lengthwise into 1/2-inch sticks. Sprinkle the

sticks with a few pinches of salt, mix well, and set aside. Cut the chicken livers into 1/2-inch slices and place them in a small bowl. Add the marinade ingredients and stir in one direction to combine. Mix the sauce ingredients together in another small bowl.

2 Shake the celery dry just before you start cooking.

3 Season the wok, then add 4 tablespoons of oil and heat over a high flame until smoking. Add the chicken livers and stir-fry. When the pieces have separated, add the chiles and ginger and continue to stir-fry until they are fragrant and the chicken livers are nearly cooked. Add the celery and stir and toss for a couple of minutes until it is hot but still crunchy (this is called "breaking the rawness," *duan sheng*). Then add the sauce and continue to stir for another few seconds until it has thickened. Spoon everything into a large bowl and serve.

DUCK RECIPES

Sometimes ducks are mercifully still sold with their giblets, even in supermarkets. Do not throw these away. They can be brought to a boil and simmered gently with a piece of crushed ginger and perhaps a scallion or two, to make a delicious soup base or aromatic broth (*lu shui*—see page 179). The liver and heart are also Chinese delicacies, and I always lift mine out of the stockpot as soon as they're cooked. When they've cooled, they are delicious just dipped in a mixture of salt and Sichuanese ground chiles. Of course, Sichuanese cooks make use of just about every part of the duck's body, as witnessed by the menu of a restaurant called the Mousehole (*hao zi dong*) that specializes in duck. The Mousehole offers dishes made from whole ducks, duck gizzards, duck intestines, duck blood, and duck tongues, to name but a few examples.

SICHUANESE ROAST DUCK

si chuan kao ya

四川烤鴨 Everyone has heard of Peking duck, but few will have encountered the following Sichuanese version, which has been sold on the streets of Chengdu for about a century. Liu Xuezhi of the Sichuan Institute of Higher Cuisine says the dish was developed, like its more illustrious Peking relative, from the techniques used to roast suckling pigs in the emperor's kitchens. The Sichuanese roasting method is similar to that used in Beijing, but the flavorings in the stuffing are pure Sichuan, and the serving method, too, is quite distinctive. While Peking duck is sliced and rolled up in pancakes with fresh, crisp vegetables and a sweet fermented sauce, Sichuan duck is chopped up on the bone and served in a deep bowl, dressed in a rich, aromatic stock made from pork bones and the duck's roasting juices. The chunks of duck are pulled out with chopsticks, dripping with gravy—the leftover juices can then be mopped up with a chunk of steamed bread or recycled as the base for a nourishing noodle soup.

One day as I was walking in the old Manchu quarter of Chengdu, exploring the tiny alleys flanked by sprawling courtyard houses, I came across a crowd of people in a bustling market street. They were lining up around a tiny stall to buy roast duck, fresh from the oven and piping hot. A row of steaming, gleaming red-brown ducks hung from the eaves of the open shop-front, and the shopkeeper lifted them down one by one. He chopped them neatly on a slab of tree trunk and put the pieces into the customers' bowls. He then spooned over some gravy from a simmering pot and sprinkled over a little salt, pepper, and sesame oil. Later that afternoon, we fell into conversation, and Mr. Liu talked me through the entire second roasting.

Mr. Liu stuffs his ducks with salty preserved vegetables, pickled chiles, ginger, scallions, fermented black beans, and Shaoxing rice wine, with perhaps a few spices selected according to his mood. They are then scalded in boiling water to tighten their skins, smeared with a malt sugar syrup, and hung up in the open air to dry for a few hours. The ducks are roasted in a special clay oven, where they hang over the smoldering embers of Asian white oak logs (*qing gang shu*). As they roast, their fragrant juices drip into earthenware pots arranged beneath them.

The aromatic broth is based on pork bone stock, augmented by the delicious duck-roasting juices and great handfuls of dried spices. It is strained and boiled up every day to keep it clean. Fresh spices are added as required, and the flavor just gets better and better as time goes by.

The duck stuffing also acts as a marinade, so the flavor of the meat improves with time. The best way to make this recipe is to stuff the duck the day before you eat it, leave it to marinate in the refrigerator overnight, and then scald, glaze, and air-dry it the following day. You can then roast it in time for dinner.

If you want to take a shortcut, just leave it to marinate for a couple of hours. You will need a couple of meat hooks to air-dry the duck.

Serves 4 with two or three other dishes and rice

1 duck (4–5 pounds), with giblets
sesame oil

FOR THE STUFFING
a 2-inch piece of fresh ginger, unpeeled
2 scallions, white and green parts
1 tablespoon fermented black beans
3 tablespoons Sichuanese *ya cai* (page 70) or Tianjin preserved vegetable
3 tablespoons Sichuanese pickled chili paste or chili bean paste
1 tablespoon Shaoxing rice wine or medium-dry sherry
2 teaspoons whole Sichuan pepper
1/2–1 teaspoon salt

FOR THE GLAZE
3 tablespoons honey

3 tablespoons Chinkiang or black Chinese vinegar
2 tablespoons water

FOR THE AROMATIC GRAVY
a 1 1/2-inch piece of fresh ginger, unpeeled
1 scallion, white and green parts
1/2–3/4 teaspoon dark soy sauce
1 teaspoon whole Sichuan pepper

AND SOME OR ALL OF THE
FOLLOWING SPICES
1 star anise
1 piece of cassia bark or a cinnamon stick
1 *cao guo* (see page 62), optional
1 teaspoon fennel seeds
2 cloves, their powdery heads pinched off and discarded
1 slice of dried ginger, optional

1 Remove the giblets from the duck and set aside. Make the stuffing: crush the ginger and scallions slightly with the side of a cleaver blade or a heavy object. Mash the black beans with your fingers or a spoon. Add all the other stuffing ingredients. Push the stuffing into the duck's inner cavity, fold over the flap of skin at the neck end, and fix it with one or two metal or bamboo skewers. Close the other end of the duck with another skewer. Let the duck marinate in the refrigerator for a couple of hours or overnight.

2 Make the gravy: crush the ginger and scallion slightly with the side of a cleaver blade or a heavy object. Place the giblets in a saucepan with about a quart of water. Bring to a boil, skim off any scum, and then add the ginger, scallion, soy sauce, and spices. Return to a boil, then turn the heat down and simmer gently for at least 2 hours. Replenish the liquid with boiling water if necessary. When the gravy is rich-tasting, set it aside to reheat when required.

3 When the duck has been marinated, bring a large pot of water to a boil. Place the duck in a sieve and pour over all the boiling water—you will see the skin contract as you do this. For best results, repeat with another pot of boiling water. Then dry the duck's skin with paper towels.

4 Heat the glaze ingredients in a pan until the honey has liquefied. Then use a pastry brush to brush it generously all over the duck. Stick a meat hook or two into the neck end of the duck and hang it up in a cool place to air-dry (I hang mine outside a north-facing window). When the first coating of glaze has dried, you can add subsequent layers for an even glossier finish. Allow the duck to dry for at least 6 hours, until the skin feels papery.

5 Preheat an oven to 350°F. Fill a roasting pan with about 1/2 inch of water. Place the duck breast side down on a roasting rack set in the pan. Place in the oven and roast for about an hour, turning it halfway through. Finally, turn the heat up to 400°F and roast for another 15 minutes or so, until the skin is beautifully brown and crisp. Remove from the oven and let sit for 10 minutes.

6 Skim as much fat as possible from the roasting juices in the bottom of the pan, and then add the juices to the gravy. Unpin one end of the duck and add the remains of the stuffing and any more juices to the gravy pan. Reheat the gravy, seasoning with salt and pepper to taste.

7 To serve the duck, either chop it into pieces on the bone with a cleaver, Chinese-style, and serve it in a deep dish with a tiny splash of sesame oil and the strained gravy poured over, or carve it into slices and serve with the gravy served separately.

FRAGRANT AND CRISPY DUCK

xiang su quan ya

Sichuanese crispy duck has become *de rigueur* in Chinese restaurants abroad. The duck flesh is tender and succulent, the skin marvelously crisp and golden. Most Chinese restaurants in the West serve it like Peking duck, with Mandarin pancakes, hoisin sauce, and strips of crunchy vegetables like leek and cucumber, but in Sichuan it is usually served on its own. The recipe has several stages, but it's not difficult to follow. If you do wish to serve it in restaurant style, you can buy frozen Mandarin pancakes and hoisin sauce in most Chinese food shops.

Serves 4

1 duck (4–5 pounds)

FOR THE MARINADE

3 teaspoons salt

1 teaspoon whole Sichuan pepper

1 piece of cassia bark or a cinnamon stick

1 star anise

2 cloves, their powdery heads pinched off and discarded

1/2 teaspoon fennel seeds

1/2 of a *cao guo* (see page 62)

1–2 slices dried "sand ginger" (see page 62)

3 tablespoons Shaoxing rice wine or medium-dry sherry

a 1 1/2-inch piece of fresh ginger, unpeeled

2 scallions, white and green parts

OTHER INGREDIENTS

plenty of peanut oil for deep-frying

1 tablespoon sesame oil

1 Roughly crush the spices with a mortar and pestle. Rub the duck all over, inside and out, with the salt, spices, and wine. Put it into a large bowl that will fit into your steamer. Roughly slice the ginger and tear the scallions into a few sections. Put some of the ginger and scallions into the cavity of the duck and place the rest around it in the bowl. Leave to marinate in a cool place for at least 1 hour, preferably several or overnight.

2 Put the duck into a steamer and steam over a high flame for about 1 hour and 30 minutes, until it is completely tender. Remove from the heat and let cool and dry out slightly.

3 Remove the ginger and scallions from the cavity and pat the duck dry, inside and out, with paper towels.

4 Heat oil for deep-frying to 325–350°F. You will need enough oil to at least half-submerge the duck. If you are using a wok, make sure it sits absolutely stable on the burner of your stove.

5 Carefully lower the duck into the deep-frying oil and fry until the skin is crisp and golden brown—about 10 minutes for each side. When it is ready, remove it from the oil, drain it well, and then brush it sparingly all over with the sesame oil. If you wish, you can cut the duck into small pieces and pile them up, breast pieces on top, in something resembling the original shape of the duck. Otherwise, set the whole duck on a big serving platter and let your guests serve themselves from it with their chopsticks. The duck should be served piping hot.

WILD DUCK BRAISED WITH KONNYAKU "BEAN CURD"

mo yu shao ya

魔芋燒鴨

Konnyaku yam, known as *mo yu* in Chinese, is a Sichuanese specialty. This pale root vegetable is dried and ground to a fine flour before being boiled up with water and set into a kind of jelly (this method, and its jelly-like texture, is why it is sometimes referred to as konnyaku "bean curd"). Konnyaku jelly is sold in all the markets of Chengdu, alongside the bean curd and other jellies made from rice and dried beans. It has a strong odor, which is why it is usually blanched before cooking.

In the following dish, long strips of konnyaku jelly are added to a rich, spicy duck stew. It's one of the most famous Sichuanese dishes, and it is thought to be of value in treating many diseases, including cancer. Sichuanese cooks use ordinary ducks. I've used mallard because it is flavorsome and seems to me in keeping with the exotic konnyaku, although Sichuanese people would not appreciate the gamey flavor of a hung bird. The konnyaku isn't easy to find, but it is sold in packages in some Japanese food shops.

Serves 2 as a main dish, 4 with three other dishes

I wild mallard or small duck (about 1 1/3–1 1/2 pounds)
1 1/2 cup konnyaku yam jelly
1/2 cup peanut oil
3–4 tablespoons Sichuanese chili bean paste
1/8 teaspoon whole Sichuan pepper
3 cups everyday stock (see page 318) or chicken stock
1 tablespoon pickled or fresh ginger, peeled and sliced

1 tablespoon Shaoxing rice wine or medium-dry sherry
1 teaspoon dark soy sauce
1 teaspoon light soy sauce
2–3 baby leeks or tender, leafy leeks
salt and pepper to taste
4 teaspoons potato flour mixed with 2–3 tablespoons cold water, or 6 teaspoons of cornstarch mixed with 3–4 tablespoons cold water

11. Sichuanese-style steamed fish (before cooking), p. 267

12. Dry-fried green beans, p. 289

13. Pock-marked Mother Chen's bean curd, p. 313

14. Noodle dishes (clockwise from top left): Spicy cold noodles with chicken slivers, p. 95; Yibin "kindling" noodles, p. 91; Mr. Xie's sea-flavor noodles, p. 93; Xie Laoban's *dan dan* noodles, p. 89

15. Dumplings (left to right, row by row from top):
"Long" wonton dumplings, p. 104; Leaf-wrapped glutinous rice dumplings, p. 107; "Glassy" steamed dumplings,
p. 114; Pot-sticker dumplings with chicken stock, p. 112;
"Zhong" crescent dumplings, p. 100; Mr. Lai's glutinous
rice balls with sesame stuffing, p. 97

16. *Tu cha*, a Yunnanese tea popular in Chongqing (left), and Chengdu jasmine blossom tea (right), pp. 77–79

17. Hotpot dipping ingredients (left to right, row by row from top): Air-dried sausage, Winter melon, Lotus root, Soybean sprouts, Smoked bean curd, Smoked bacon, Oyster mushrooms, Scallions, Enoki mushrooms, pp. 350–51

18. Spicy hotpot broth, p. 348

1 Cut the duck, on the bone, into chunks about 2 inches by 1 inch. Cut the konnyaku jelly into strips of a similar size.

2 Bring a pot of lightly salted water to a boil and blanch the konnyaku pieces for 1 minute. Place them into a bowlful of hot, lightly salted water and set aside.

3 Season the wok, then add 1/4 cup of oil and heat over a high flame until smoking. Add all the duck and stir-fry over a high flame for 4–5 minutes, until the pieces have begun to brown and smell delicious. Remove from the wok and set aside. Rinse and dry the wok.

4 Return the wok to the stove and heat another 1/4 cup of oil over a medium flame. When the oil is hot, add the chili bean paste and the Sichuan pepper and stir-fry for 20–30 seconds, until the oil is red and richly fragrant. Pour in the stock and bring to a fast boil. Skim the liquid if necessary and remove the solid pieces of chile and Sichuan pepper with a perforated spoon (they have lent their flavors to the oil and stock and can now be discarded). Add the duck, ginger, Shaoxing rice wine, and soy sauces. Return to a boil and then turn the heat down and simmer, covered, until the duck is tender. Most Sichuanese cooks would let it cook for 30–40 minutes, but you can leave it longer if you wish—just make sure enough stock remains to nearly cover the duck. You can top up the liquid with stock or water if necessary.

5 When the duck is ready, add the soaked konnyaku strips, bring to a boil, and then simmer gently for another 5–10 minutes until the konnyaku has absorbed some of the flavors of the sauce. Do simmer it very gently—the konnyaku can become rubbery and "old" (*lao*) if overcooked. While the konnyaku is simmering, cut the baby leeks into 2-inch sections.

6 Add the leeks to the sauce and simmer for another minute or so until they are just tender. Season with salt or pepper if necessary. Finally, add just enough potato flour or cornstarch mixture to give the sauce a nice gravy-like consistency—add it in a couple of stages, stirring briskly as the liquid thickens, so you don't add more than you need. Serve.

5

fish

BECAUSE SICHUAN IS A LANDLOCKED PROVINCE, FAR FROM
the Chinese coast, saltwater fish scarcely feature in its traditional cooking. The
only exceptions are dried seafood, like mussels, and the more exotic squid
and sea cucumber. Freshwater fish, however, are an important part of the local
cuisine, as the region is threaded by rivers and streams. The Yangtze River
thunders down from the Tibetan plateau, circles Chongqing, and then courses
on toward the wetlands of the east coast and Shanghai. The Brocade River (*jin
jiang*), named because Sichuan's famous woven silks were once washed in its
crystalline waters, flows through Chengdu. The Min River swirls around the
feet of the giant stone Buddha at Leshan.

Over the centuries, the Sichuan region has developed a reputation for the
excellence of its fish. The poet Zuo Si, in his third-century ode to the ancient
Shu capital (the ancestor of today's Chengdu), recalled "tasting precious fish"
in the city; centuries later, the Tang poet Du Fu said the local fish were "a
pleasure to be seized." There are several notable local breeds, most famously
the rock carp (*yan li*), the *ya yu* carp, the *jiang tuan* catfish, the *shi pa yu* catfish,
and the Yangtze sturgeon (*chang jiang xun*). Sichuanese cooks also use more
common fish like carp (*li yu*), grass carp (*cao yu*), the Chinese perch (*gui yu*),
catfish (*nian yu*), and crucian carp (*ji yu*), as well as eels (*huang shan*) and
loaches (*ni qiu*). The crucian carp has a particularly delicious (*xian mei*) flavor
and is often used to make milky-white soups and stocks. (See the Glossary
for the Latin names of these fish.)

The finest flavors obviously come from wild river fish: those bred in lakes
or rice paddy fields are darker in color, their flavors tainted by the muddy, still

waters in which they live. Chengdu residents remember the not-so-distant days when people bathed in the Brocade River and the clear waters were alive with fish and other wildlife. When I was a student in Chengdu, I did once see a cormorant fisher drifting by with his punt full of great black birds. His long-necked cormorants were fitted with tight collars so they couldn't swallow the fish they caught, but would give them up to the fisherman in exchange for tiny fishes from his own supply. But this man was a rarity: pollution has wiped out most of the wildlife in the Brocade River, and those in search of unfarmed fish have to head west to the edges of the Tibetan plateau. Even there, stocks are low, and several breeds of fish are now officially protected species.

In Sichuan, fish are still leaping, living things when you buy them in the market, and they are always eaten fresh. Many restaurants will bring a wriggling fish to the table before they cook it as a guarantee of freshness. Sichuanese fish cooking makes much use of pickled chiles, garlic, scallions, and ginger: this is the origin of the famous "fish-fragrant" style of flavoring. But some Sichuanese fish dishes are mild and delicate, and there's also a Sichuanese version of that universal Chinese treat, sweet-and-sour crispy fish. I have suggested using carp or sea bass for most of these dishes, but the same cooking methods can be used for many other fresh- and saltwater fish. Fancy restaurants in Sichuan are increasingly using traditional cooking methods to prepare seafood air-freighted in from the coast.

FISH BRAISED IN CHILI BEAN SAUCE

dou ban xian yu

This recipe is one of my personal favorites and is typical of Sichuanese home cooking. The fish is clothed in a rich, ruddy sauce scattered with scallion greens and little flecks of garlic and ginger. The flavor is dominated by the intensity of the chili bean paste, but the addition of a little vinegar at the end lifts it and makes it sing.

Chili bean paste is one of the indispensable seasonings in Sichuanese cuisine and is the specialty of Pixian county, near Chengdu. Legend has it that the secret of this delicious flavoring was, like so many other wonderful recipes, discovered through a happy accident. According to the famous Pixian Chili Bean Paste

Factory, the story goes that in the seventeenth century an immigrant named Mr. Chen was making his way to Sichuan with a small supply of fava beans to eat on the road. When a spate of wet weather mildewed his beans, he couldn't bear to throw them away, so he let them dry out a bit and then ate them with a few fresh chiles. The beans were unexpectedly tasty, so when he settled down he continued to ferment his beans and eat them in a similar way. In 1804, one of Mr. Chen's descendants set up a workshop in Pixian to produce paste according to what had by then become the family recipe, but on a larger scale. This, they say, was the origin of today's Pixian Chili Bean Paste Factory.

These days, the beans are left to ferment in a vat of salty water for several months. They are then mixed with salted red chiles and left in vats in a courtyard for anything from six months to three years to continue their fermentation. On sunny days, the staff lifts the lids of the vats to let the paste bake in the sun, and on clear nights they expose it to the dew. The paste is stirred regularly for an even exposure to the elements, and as time goes by it darkens and becomes soft and fragrant.

In the Pixian Chili Bean Paste Factory some of the paste is mass-produced, but one part of the factory courtyard is still devoted to making the paste according to the traditional method. Here, twelve hundred large earthenware pots, each with its own conical bamboo hat, are neatly lined up. The paste in these pots, the factory's finest, is turned by hand and tended carefully for at least two years, until it is a deep, purplish brown. Through this special process, they say, the paste absorbs the essences of the universe and breathes in the spirit of the Sichuan earth.

Serves 2 as a main course, 4 with three other dishes

1 carp, trout, or sea bass weighing about 1 1/2 pounds, cleaned, with head and tail still attached
peanut oil
FOR THE MARINADE
3/4 teaspoon salt
1–2 tablespoons Shaoxing rice wine or medium-dry sherry

FOR THE SAUCE
4 tablespoons Sichuanese chili bean paste
1 tablespoon finely chopped fresh ginger
1 tablespoon finely chopped garlic
1 1/3 cup everyday stock (see page 318) or chicken stock

1 teaspoon white sugar	1/2 teaspoon Chinkiang or
1–2 teaspoons light soy sauce	black Chinese vinegar
1 1/4 teaspoon cornstarch	3 scallions, green parts only,
dissolved in 1 tablespoon	finely sliced
cold water	

1 Use a cleaver or sharp knife to make 4 or 5 shallow diagonal cuts into each side of the fish, and to pierce its head (this releases more flavorsome juices). Rub the fish inside and out with the salt and Shaoxing rice wine and leave to marinate while you assemble the other ingredients.

2 Season the wok, then heat 1/3 cup of oil over a high flame until smoking. Dry the fish with paper towels and fry it briefly on each side, just long enough to crisp up the skin. (The fish can be briefly deep-fried instead if you have the oil handy.) Remove and set aside. Rinse and dry the wok.

3 Return the wok to a medium flame with 4 tablespoons of fresh oil. When it is hot, add the chili bean paste and stir-fry for 20–30 seconds until the oil is red and smells delicious. Add the ginger and garlic and stir-fry for another 20 seconds or so until you can smell their fragrance. Then pour in all the stock, turn up the heat, and bring the liquid to a boil. Season to taste with the sugar and soy sauce.

4 Gently place the fish into the wok and spoon some sauce over it. Turn the heat down, cover, and simmer for 8–10 minutes until the fish is cooked and has absorbed some of the flavors of the sauce. Turn the fish once during the cooking time, spooning over some more sauce.

5 When the fish is done, gently transfer it to a serving dish. Add the cornstarch mixture to the sauce and stir briefly until it thickens. Add the vinegar and scallions, stir a couple of times, and then pour the sauce over the waiting fish.

NOTE

A common Sichuanese practice is to return any leftover sauce to the wok after the fish is eaten, add some bean curd, and continue the meal. To do this, cut a cake of bean curd into thick slices or cubes, simmer it very gently in lightly salted water for 5 minutes or so, and add to the reheated sauce. Simmer for a few minutes until the bean curd has absorbed some of the flavors, and serve.

FISH SOUP WITH PICKLED GREENS

suan cai yu

Suan cai yu is a new Sichuanese dish with a traditional flavor. It is supposedly a 1980s innovation that became all the rage in urban Chongqing, and later in Chengdu, in the 1990s. Some say the dish was created by a modest restaurant in the Chongqing countryside; others, more romantically, that it was invented by the wife of an elderly fisherman who accidentally dropped her husband's catch into a simmering soup of pickled greens. Whichever, it's a wonderful, hearty dish and terribly easy to make.

Grass carp is the favored fish, although sea bass works beautifully, too. The mustard greens, which the Sichuanese pull out of their earthenware pickling jars in whole long green leaves, give the soup a delicately sour and salty flavor. They look lovely too, floating in the soup with the pale fish flesh, the few pieces of red chile adding a spot of vibrant color. The ginger, garlic, and chile give the soup a peppery zing, but local people often enhance this by adding a final scattering of spices and hot oil, which can make the soup so hot it will blow your head off. Instructions for this optional final cooking stage are given at the end of the recipe. The Sichuanese often serve a huge fish in an immense bowlful of soup, glistening with oil and chiles—the following version is on a more modest scale.

Serves 6–8 at the end of a Chinese meal, 4 as a Western-style starter

1 whole carp or sea bass (about 1 3/4 pounds), cleaned, with head and tail intact	**2 teaspoons Shaoxing rice wine or medium-dry sherry**
salt and pepper to taste	**6 cups everyday stock (see page 318) or chicken stock**
	a 2-inch piece of fresh ginger

2 cloves of garlic
1/2 cup pickled mustard
  greens
2 Sichuanese pickled chiles or
  5 Thai pickled chiles

1 scallion, green part only
peanut oil
3 teaspoons cornstarch
1 tablespoon egg white

1 Using a cleaver or other sharp knife, carefully cut away the flesh from each side of the fish to make 2 fillets. Starting at the tail ends, cut the fillets at an angle into slices a bit more than 1/4 inch thick, each with a piece of skin. Place in a bowl and sprinkle with salt and 2 teaspoons Shaoxing rice wine. Leave to marinate while you prepare the other ingredients.

2 Pierce the fish head with a whack of the cleaver or a sharp knife to release its juices. Chop the tail from the backbone, and then cut the backbone into a few chunks. Set aside.

3 Bring the stock to a boil.

4 Peel and slice the ginger and garlic. Chop the pickled greens at an angle into slices to match the fish. Sichuanese pickled chiles should also be sliced at an angle—tiny Thai chilies are best used whole. Finely slice the scallion.

5 Heat 2 tablespoons of oil in a wok over a high flame. Add the ginger, garlic, and chiles and stir-fry for 10–20 seconds until they are fragrant. Add the pickled greens and stir-fry for another 30 seconds or so. Add the stock, return to a vigorous boil, and then throw in the fish head, tail, and bones. Fast boil for 5–10 minutes.

6 When the stock is nearly ready, add the cornstarch and egg white to the fish slices and stir in one direction to coat them.

7 When the soup is ready, remove and discard the fish head, tail, and bones if you wish to (a Chinese home cook would often leave them in). Turn the heat down to a simmer, season with salt and pepper to taste, and drop in all the fish slices separately so they don't stick together. When they are just cooked, pour the soup into a serving bowl. Sprinkle with scallion slices and serve.

OPTIONAL EXTRA STAGE FOR CHILE FIENDS

Before you start cooking the fish soup, make the following preparations:

1 Take a handful of dried chiles (8–10 chiles) and 2 teaspoons of Sichuan peppercorns. Using rubber gloves, snip the chiles in half and discard as many seeds as possible. Heat 3 tablespoons of oil in a wok over a medium flame until hot but not yet smoking. Add the chiles and Sichuan peppercorns and stir-fry until they are fragrant and the chiles are just beginning to brown (take care not to burn them). Then immediately remove the spices with a slotted spoon and set them aside to cool.

2 When the spices are cool, transfer them onto a cutting board and chop them finely with a gentle rocking motion, using a cleaver taken in both hands or a two-handled chopper.

3 When the fish soup has been cooked and poured into the serving bowl, swiftly rinse out the wok and dry it well. Then heat another 3–4 tablespoons of oil in the wok until smoking. Sprinkle the chopped chiles and peppercorns over the soup and drizzle with the hot oil, which will sizzle dramatically. You can finish with the scallion slices if you wish.

SWEET-AND-SOUR CRISPY FISH

tang cu cui pi yu

糖
醋
脆
皮
魚

This dish is a real party piece—a whole, delectably crunchy fish draped in a fragrant sweet-and-sour sauce, scattered with a garnish of brilliant red and green. It's a popular banquet dish in Sichuan and is often the centerpiece of a dinner out with friends. Sichuanese cooks will usually make it with grass carp, but I've successfully made the dish with the more readily available sea bass. The dish looks most splendid when a whole fish is used, but to do this you must have a wok or a deep-fryer large enough to immerse it completely. If this isn't possible, cut the fish in half and reassemble it on the serving plate, or use large boneless chunks of firm, white-fleshed fish (these can be simply dusted with dry potato flour or cornstarch).

Do make sure you deep-fry the fish twice according to the recipe, or it may become crisp and golden before the flesh is cooked through.

Serves 2 as a main dish with rice and a salad, 4 with two or three other dishes

1 carp or sea bass (1 3/4 pounds), gutted and cleaned, with head and tail intact

plenty of peanut oil for deep-frying

FOR THE MARINADE

1 tablespoon Shaoxing rice wine or medium-dry sherry

3/4 teaspoon salt

2 scallions, white and green parts

a 2-inch piece of fresh ginger, unpeeled

FOR THE SAUCE

1 tablespoon light soy sauce

4 1/2 tablespoons sugar

2 teaspoons Shaoxing rice wine or medium-dry sherry

1/4 teaspoon salt

4 teaspoons cornstarch

3 tablespoons cold everyday stock (see page 318) or chicken stock

FOR THE STARCH COATING

3/4 cup cornstarch, with a little extra on hand

OTHER INGREDIENTS

3 teaspoons finely chopped fresh garlic

3 teaspoons finely chopped fresh ginger

4 scallions, white and green parts, finely sliced, white and green parts separated

1 1/2 cups everyday stock (see page 318) or chicken stock

3 tablespoons Chinkiang or black Chinese vinegar

2 teaspoons sesame oil

FOR THE GARNISH

2 scallions, white and green parts cut into fine slivers, or a few sprigs of fresh coriander (cilantro)

3 Sichuanese pickled chiles or a 1/4 of a red bell pepper, finely slivered

1 If you are using a whole fish, you must make several deep cuts into the flesh to allow the deep-frying oil to penetrate it: lay the fish on its side and, using a sharp knife or cleaver, cut down into the thickest part of the fish near the backbone, about 2 inches from the base of the fish head and at right angles to the backbone itself. When the knife touches the bones of the spine, swivel the blade inside the flesh to face the head and continue cutting paral-

lel to the backbone and toward the head for about another 1 1/2 inches. This will create a thick flap of fish flesh. Make further, similar cuts at 2-inch intervals until you reach the thinner tail flesh, and then repeat on the other side of the fish, again cutting down to the spine and back toward the head. (When you have finished, if you hold the fish upside down by its tail, the flaps should all hang outward slightly.) Use the back corner of the cleaver to crack the head of the fish, making a small gash that will allow its flavors to emerge. Trim the tail into a tidy shape if desired.

2 Holding the fish by its tail, splash it with the Shaoxing rice wine and then rub it all over, including inside the flaps and the gut cavity, with the salt for the marinade. Smash the scallions and ginger with the side of a cleaver blade or a heavy object and roughly chop them. Stuff all the pieces into the gut cavity and the flaps. Leave the fish to marinate for about 30 minutes (about the time it takes to chop and measure out the other ingredients).

3 Combine the soy sauce, sugar, wine, salt, cornstarch, and cold stock in a small bowl for the sauce. In a separate bowl, mix 3/4 cup of cornstarch with enough water (a scant 1/2 cup) to make a fairly thick but still drippy paste. Assemble the other ingredients near the stove and make sure your serving dish is at hand.

4 When you are ready to begin cooking, heat plenty of deep-frying oil over a high flame to about 325°F. Discard the ginger and scallion pieces from the marinated fish and wipe it dry with paper towels. Smear it generously inside and out with dry cornstarch (about 3 tablespoons).

5 When the oil has reached the right temperature, hold the fish up by its tail and coat it with the cornstarch paste, using your fingers to push it into all the crevices. The flaps of flesh should hang outward slightly, laden with paste. Then, still holding the fish by its tail, lower the head into the oil and allow it to fry for a couple of minutes as you ladle hot oil over the body of the fish and into the flaps. When the oil has fixed the flaps in their open position, standing stiffly out from the body, immerse the fish totally in the oil and fry for another minute or two until the flesh is just cooked. Remove the fish carefully to your serving dish and lay it on its belly.

6 Reheat the oil to 400–425°F. Immerse the fish in the hot oil and fry for a few minutes more until the batter is crisp and golden. Carefully remove it to your serving dish. Cover your hand with a clean kitchen towel or paper towels and gently squash the fish—this will help the flavors of the sauce to penetrate. Keep the fish warm while you prepare the sauce.

7 Pour off the deep-frying oil, give the wok a quick rinse, and return it to a high flame. Add 3 tablespoons of peanut oil. When the oil is hot, add the garlic, ginger, and scallion whites and stir-fry until they are richly fragrant. Then add the stock.

8 Bring the liquid to a boil. Give the prepared sauce ingredients in the bowl a stir, add to the wok, and stir briskly until the liquid thickens. Finally, remove from the heat; throw in the scallion greens, vinegar, and sesame oil; stir in; and pour the sauce all over the waiting fish.

9 Sprinkle with the garnish ingredients and serve.

SICHUAN-STYLE STEAMED FISH

qing zheng xian yu

The queen of all the fish in Sichuan's many rivers is probably the *jiang tuan* catfish, a proud, scaleless creature that lurks in the deeper waters. It has long whiskers, a pointed snout, few bones, and plenty of tasty flesh. In the past it flourished in the rivers at Chongqing and Leshan, although these days it's rare to find it in the wild. The fish is prized all over China for its tender, tasty meat and relative lack of bones. In Sichuan, they like to steam it whole and serve it with a fine stock and a ginger-and-vinegar dip. The following recipe is created in homage to this famous banquet dish: the cooking method is traditional, although I've inevitably had to use a different kind of fish. I've chosen the grouper, which has firm, unbony flesh and looks splendid on the dinner table. You can buy it at many good fish markets.

To make this dish you will need a bowl large enough to take the fish, curled around if necessary, but not too large to fit into your steamer. You will also need a serving dish that will take the whole length of the fish and some of the stock (any extra stock can be served separately as a soup if necessary). I have given instructions for making the traditional vinegar dip, although my friends loved the flavors of the fish and stock alone. If you do make the dip, invite your guests to pull out pieces of fish with their chopsticks and then dip them in the vinegar. The stock can be drunk from the rice bowls at the end of the meal.

Serves 2–3 as a main dish with one vegetable and rice, 4 with three other dishes

1 whole grouper, rock cod, or
    sea bass (about 2 pounds),
    cleaned, with head and tail
    intact (or 2 smaller fish)

FOR THE MARINADE

1 tablespoon Shaoxing rice
    wine or medium-dry sherry
3/4 teaspoon salt

OTHER INGREDIENTS

3–4 Chinese dried
    mushrooms (about 1/3
    ounce)
1/3 ounce dried shrimp

1 ounce cooked ham
3 cups finest clear stock or
    rich chicken stock
a 1-inch piece of fresh ginger,
    unpeeled
1 scallion, white and green
    parts
salt and pepper

FOR THE DIP

a 1-inch piece of fresh ginger
2 tablespoons Chinkiang or
    black Chinese vinegar
1 teaspoon sesame oil

1 Set the dried mushrooms and shrimp to soak in very hot water for about 30 minutes.

2 Make several parallel cuts into the fleshy part of the fish, about 2 inches apart, 1 inch deep, and at right angles to the backbone. The cuts should be angled toward the head, not straight down toward the bones. Splash the fish inside and out with the wine, and rub it all over with the salt. Let marinate for 15–30 minutes.

3 If you wish to make the dip, cut the ginger into fine slivers and put it into a little dish with the vinegar and sesame oil.

4 Shake the fish dry and wipe it inside and out with paper towels. Drain the mushrooms and shrimp, reserving the soaking water. Finely slice the mushrooms, discarding any tough parts. Cut the ham into thin, rectangular slices. Then stuff a slice of ham, a slice of mushroom, and a couple of shrimp into each of the cuts in the sides of the fish. (You can put a few slices into the body cavity too.)

5 Bring the stock to a boil and add the reserved soaking water.

6 Carefully place the fish into a deep bowl that will fit into your steamer (you may have to curve it around the bowl). Crush the ginger and scallion slightly with the side of a cleaver blade or a heavy object and put them inside and around the fish. Pour the stock into the bowl, place it in a steamer, cover and steam over a high heat for about 12 minutes, until just cooked through.

7 Gently transfer the fish to a deep serving dish. Remove the bits from the stock with a slotted spoon and discard them. Then season the stock with salt and pepper to taste and pour it over the fish. Serve with the dip if desired.

FISH BRAISED WITH BEAN CURD
IN SPICY SAUCE

dou fu shao yu

When the Sichuanese eat a great hearty dish of fish or rabbit in lashings of spicy sauce, they often send any remaining sauce back into the restaurant kitchen to be reheated with some bean curd. The tender, slippery bean curd absorbs the flavors of the sauce, and another dish is instantly created. It's not the kind of practice you'd find in formal restaurants, but it's common in the rustic eateries that have become fashionable in recent years. The following dish combines both fish and bean curd in a single dish. It's a delightful combination of textures, and the sauce has a gentle, languid spiciness. Sichuanese people often make the dish with a few tiny crucian carp, which have a particularly lovely flavor. A couple of small trout could be substituted. You will need a large, deep platter to serve this dish.

Serves 4 as a main dish with one vegetable dish and rice

1 whole carp or sea bass
   (1 1/2 pounds), cleaned,
   with head and tail intact
1 block of bean curd (about 1
   pound)
peanut oil
FOR THE MARINADE
1/2 teaspoon salt
1 tablespoon Shaoxing rice
   wine or medium-dry sherry
FOR THE SAUCE
4 tablespoons Sichuanese chili
   bean paste
1 1/2 tablespoons finely
   chopped fresh ginger
1 tablespoon finely chopped
   garlic

2 scallions, white and green
   parts separated and finely
   sliced
2 cups everyday stock (see
   page 318) or chicken stock
1 teaspoon dark soy sauce
3 teaspoons Sichuanese sweet
   wheaten paste or sweet
   bean sauce mixed with 3
   teaspoons cold water
2 tablespoons Shaoxing rice
   wine or medium-dry sherry
6 teaspoons cornstarch mixed
   with 3 tablespoons cold
   water

1 Use a sharp knife to make shallow slashes at 1 1/2-inch intervals across the fattest part of the fish, at right angles to the backbone. These will help the flavors to penetrate its flesh. Rub the fish inside and out with the marinade ingredients and leave it while you prepare everything else.

2 Cut the bean curd into slices about 1/2 inch thick (the slices should ideally be about 2 1/2 inches by 2 inches). Place in a panful of lightly salted boiling water and leave to refresh over a very gentle heat—for best results do not let the water bubble.

3 Season the wok, then add one-third cup oil and return the wok to a high heat. Add the fish and fry for about 2 minutes on each side until the skin is crisp and golden. Remove and set aside.

4 Discard oil, rinse the wok, and then return it to a medium heat with 1/4 cup oil. When the oil is hot but not smoking, add the chili bean paste and stir-fry for 20–30 seconds, until the oil is red and richly fragrant. Add the ginger, garlic, and scallion whites and stir-fry for about 20 seconds more, until they are fragrant. Then add the stock and soy sauce. Place the fish in the wok, bring the liquid to a boil, then turn the heat down and simmer for about 6 minutes, spooning over the sauce from time to time. Turn the fish and continue to simmer for another 4–5 minutes. Then add the sweet bean sauce mixture and the Shaoxing rice wine and mix them in gently. Next add the bean curd and simmer everything for another couple of minutes.

5 Gently remove the fish from the sauce and lift it onto a large serving platter. Add the cornstarch mixture to the wok to thicken the sauce—you may need a little more or a little less than 4 teaspoons, depending on how much the sauce has reduced. You should end up with a gravy-like consistency. Finally, add the scallion greens, stir them in, and ladle the bean curd and sauce all over the waiting fish.

DRY-BRAISED FISH WITH PORK IN SPICY SAUCE

gan shao xian yu

Dry-braising is a peculiarly Sichuanese version of a cooking method used all over China. All braised dishes are first heated over a high flame and then left to simmer gently in a stock-based sauce. With dry-braising, however, the sauce is left to reduce naturally, until all the seasonings have been absorbed by the main ingredients or cling to them in a delicious sticky coating. Starch is never added to thicken the sauce. The following dish is a local specialty and one of my favorites. By the time you serve it, the sauce will have entirely disappeared, and the fish lies in a small pool of glossy red oil, with a scattering of scarlet chiles, pale scallions, crispy pork, and dark salted mustard greens. It is not excessively hot, especially if you use the real Sichuanese pickled chiles (the whole chiles are added mainly for color, so you could even use a little red bell pepper for a milder dish). If they can, Sichuanese cooks use rock carp (*yan li*), one of the most esteemed local fish, but sea bass is sensational.

The fish tends to disintegrate slightly with the slow cooking, so a little care is needed in transferring it to the serving dish. If you follow the Sichuanese practice and let your guests use their chopsticks to help themselves to pieces of fish, most of the cooking oil will be left on the plate, but it's still a rich dish and is best served with plain rice and one or two simple stir-fried vegetables.

Serves 2–3 as a main dish with rice and a vegetable, 4 with three other dishes

1 whole carp or sea bass (1 1/2 pounds), cleaned, with head and tail intact
1/2–2/3 cup peanut oil

FOR THE MARINADE
1/2 teaspoon salt
1 tablespoon Shaoxing rice wine or medium-dry sherry

FOR THE PORK GARNISH
1/3 pound boneless, fresh pork belly
1 teaspoon light soy sauce
3/4 teaspoon dark soy sauce
1/4 teaspoon salt
1 teaspoon Shaoxing rice wine or medium-dry sherry

OTHER INGREDIENTS
5 scallions, white parts only
3 Sichuanese pickled chiles or 5 tiny Thai pickled chiles

1 tablespoon pickled chili paste
2 teaspoons finely chopped fresh ginger
2 teaspoons finely chopped garlic
1 1/3 cups everyday stock (see page 318) or chicken stock
2 tablespoons fermented rice wine, Shaoxing rice wine, or medium-dry sherry
1 teaspoon light soy sauce
1 teaspoon dark soy sauce
1/4 teaspoon salt
1 1/2 teaspoons sugar
2 tablespoons Sichuanese *ya cai* or Tianjin preserved vegetable

TO FINISH
2 teaspoons sesame oil

1 Use a sharp knife to make shallow slashes at 1 1/2-inch intervals across the fattest part of the fish, at right angles to the backbone. These will help the

flavors penetrate its flesh. Rub the fish inside and out with the marinade ingredients and leave it while you prepare everything else.

2 Cut the scallion whites and Sichuanese chiles (if using) into 2 1/2-inch sections. Finely chop the pork and mix it with the soy sauces, salt and Shaoxing rice wine.

3 Season the wok, then add 1 tablespoon of oil and return it to a high heat. Add the pork and stir-fry for a couple of minutes, until it is a little crispy. Remove and set aside. Rinse and dry the wok.

4 Dry the fish with clean paper towels. Heat 1/3 cup of oil in the wok until smoking hot. Add the fish and fry each side for a couple of minutes until golden and crisp. Remove and set aside. (The fish can be briefly deep-fried instead if you have the oil on hand.)

5 Turn off the heat and allow the oil to cool slightly until it stops smoking. Then return the wok to medium heat, add the pickled chili paste, and stir-fry for about 30 seconds until the oil is a deep orange-red. Add the ginger, garlic, scallions, and Sichuanese chiles (if using) and stir-fry for another 20 seconds or so until they are richly fragrant. Then pour in the stock and bring to a boil.

6 Add the fish to the wok and season with the Shaoxing rice wine, soy sauces, salt, and sugar. When the liquid has returned to a boil, turn the heat down to medium and simmer for 10 minutes, spooning the sauce over the fish from time to time. Turn the fish, add the precooked pork, *ya cai*, and Thai chiles (if using), and continue to simmer for about 10 minutes more, until the water in the sauce has evaporated, leaving only the cooking oil.

7 Using 2 slotted spoons, carefully remove the fish to a shallow serving dish. Spoon the remaining contents of the wok over the fish. Use a pair of chopsticks to pluck out some pieces of pickled chile and scallion and arrange them prettily along the top of the fish. Drizzle with the sesame oil. Serve at once.

SPICY BRAISED FISH WITH WHOLE GARLIC

da suan shao yu

The Sichuan region is known for its *du suan*, or "single garlic," which produces round, purple-skinned bulbs that are not divided into cloves. This garlic is often used whole in braised dishes, where its little round bulbs are sometimes arranged around the edge of the plate like a string of pearls. The Sichuanese like to make the following dish with a type of small, whiskered catfish. These fish have a delightfully slippery texture and are always eaten absolutely fresh. The amount of garlic used may sound excessive, but the cooking method makes it mellow and delicious, nothing to be feared.

Serves 3 as a main dish, 4 with two or three other dishes

1 carp or sea bass (1 1/2 pounds), cleaned, with head and tail intact

FOR THE MARINADE

1/2 teaspoon salt

1 tablespoon Shaoxing rice wine or medium-dry sherry

OTHER INGREDIENTS

3 heads of garlic with nice fat cloves

peanut oil

4 tablespoons Sichuanese chili bean paste

2 tablespoons finely chopped fresh ginger

2 cups everyday stock (see page 318) or chicken stock

3/4 teaspoon dark soy sauce

1 teaspoon sugar

1 tablespoon cornstarch mixed with 3 tablespoons cold water

2 scallions, green parts only, finely sliced

1 teaspoon Chinkiang or black Chinese vinegar

1 Use a sharp knife to make shallow slashes at 1 1/2-inch intervals across the fattest part of the fish, at right angles to the backbone. These will help the flavors to penetrate its flesh. Rub the fish inside and out with the marinade ingredients and leave it while you prepare everything else.

2 Peel all the garlic cloves.

3 Heat 1/3 cup of oil in a wok over a gentle flame until it is hot but not smoking. Add all the garlic and stir-fry for about 5 minutes until the cloves have slightly wrinkled skins and are just tender; they should remain white. Remove and set aside. Drain the fish and pat it dry with paper towels. Then turn the heat up to high and fry the fish until its skin has tightened. Remove and set aside.

4 Turn off the heat, pour off all but about 3 tablespoons of oil, and allow it to cool slightly until it has stopped smoking. Then add the chili bean paste and stir-fry over a medium flame for about 30 seconds until the oil is red and richly fragrant. Add the ginger and stir-fry for another 20 seconds or so until it smells delicious. Pour in the stock, turn up the heat, and bring to a boil.

5 Stir in the soy sauce, sugar, and salt to taste, and then add the fish. When the liquid has returned to a boil, turn the heat down to medium and simmer for about 6 minutes. Turn the fish over in the sauce, add the garlic, and continue to simmer for another 6 minutes until the fish is cooked and the sauce is much reduced. Transfer the fish to a serving plate. Remove the garlic from the sauce with a slotted spoon and arrange the cloves around the fish. Turn up the heat to reduce the sauce a bit more if necessary, then add the cornstarch mixture in a couple of stages, stirring as the liquid thickens (you can add a bit more cornstarch and water if necessary to achieve a good gravy-like consistency).

6 Finally, turn off the heat, stir in the scallions and vinegar, and pour the sauce over the waiting fish. Serve immediately.

FISH STEW IN AN EARTHEN POT

sha guo xian yu

Lift the lid on this earthy stew and you will be soothed by its rich, subtle aromas and delicate colors. Thin slices of mushroom, ham, and chicken drift in a clear stock, their gentle pinks and browns setting off the blue-gray skin of the gently curving fish. This dish is usually made in a heavy earthenware pot (*sha guo*, literally "sand-pot") that retains heat well and is thought to be good at preserving the original, essential flavor of the raw ingredients.

This fish stew is traditionally made with *ya yu*, a kind of carp named after Ya'an, the place in western Sichuan where it is a local specialty. It can also be made with bean curd: just blanch the bean curd in lightly salted boiling water and then put it into the casserole dish instead of the fish. Prepare the other ingredients as in the following recipe, and simmer everything together for 10–15 minutes, until the bean curd has absorbed the flavors of the sauce.

You can serve this dish Sichuan-style, toward the end of a Chinese meal, but it also makes a great lunch with crusty bread and a salad.

Serves 4–6 people as a Sichuan-style final soup or a Western-style starter

I whole sea bass (about 2 pounds), cleaned, with head and tail intact

3/4 cup peanut oil

FOR THE MARINADE

a I 1/2-inch piece of fresh ginger, unpeeled

I scallion, white and green parts

1/2 teaspoon salt

I tablespoon Shaoxing rice wine or medium-dry sherry

OTHER INGREDIENTS

1/2 ounce (I tablespoon) dried shrimp

3 dried Chinese mushrooms

1/4 pound oyster mushrooms

1/3 pound cooked chicken meat

2 ounces Smithfield ham or bacon

3/4 pound firm bean curd

I whole bamboo shoot (2–2 1/2 ounces)

5 cups chicken stock

salt and ground pepper

1 Set the shrimp and Chinese mushrooms to soak separately in hot water for about 30 minutes.

2 Make shallow cuts into the fleshy part of the fish at 1 1/2- to 2-inch intervals—6 or 7 cuts in total. The cuts should be at right angles to the backbone. Partially crush the ginger and scallion with the side of a cleaver blade or a heavy object, and cut the scallion into a few sections. Rub the fish all over with the salt and wine, inside and out, including the slits you have made. Place the ginger and scallion into the cavity and leave to marinate for about 30 minutes. Put your casserole dish into a 200°F oven to warm up.

3 Cut the oyster mushrooms into 2 or 3 pieces lengthwise (so they are easy to eat with chopsticks). Thinly slice the cooked chicken. Cut the ham into thin rectangular slices. Cut the bean curd into rectangular slices about 1/2 inch thick and leave them to soak in very hot, lightly salted water for 5 minutes or so. Blanch the bamboo shoot in lightly salted boiling water for a minute or two and then slice thinly. In all this cutting, try to make sure the pieces are all roughly on the same scale—the soup will look much prettier if all the ingredients are cut in harmony.

4 Thinly slice the reconstituted dried mushrooms.

5 Discard the ginger and scallion from the marinade and dry the fish with paper towels. Heat the oil in a wok until smoking. Add the fish and fry for a minute or two on each side to tighten the skin. Drain it and place it in the warmed casserole dish, curving its spine so it will fit.

6 Pour off all but about 3 tablespoons of the oil in the wok. Return it to a medium flame, add the oyster mushrooms and bamboo shoot, and stir-fry for about 30 seconds, until the mushrooms smell delicious. Pour in the stock, and then add the shrimp (with their soaking water), ham, chicken, dried mushrooms, and bean curd. Season lightly with salt and pepper. Bring the soup to a boil, skim if necessary, and then pour everything into the casserole dish with the fish. Set the soup to simmer gently for 15–20 minutes, until the fish is cooked and has absorbed all the flavors of the sauce. Serve in the cooking pot.

FISH WITH CHILES AND SICHUAN PEPPER

la zi yu

This dish has all the hallmarks of Chongqing cooking—the lavish use of chiles and Sichuan pepper and the final sousing of spicy oil that makes it sizzle fragrantly. The fish remains tender and succulent in its protective clothing of starch and water. The following recipe is based on one served at the Converging Rivers Fish Restaurant (*hui chuan yu guan*) in Chengdu. Though this may be hard to believe, I have actually toned down the amounts of chiles and Sichuan pepper used—the restaurant typically fries up 3 or 4 ounces of dried chiles and 2–3 tablespoons Sichuan pepper for a similar amount of fish. The lavish dressing of oil is what gives the dish its fragrance: do remember that you are not expected to eat it (just pull out pieces of fish from the bowl with your chopsticks and let most of the oil fall away before you eat them). The whole spices are also usually left in the bowl.

Serves 2 as a main dish with one vegetable dish and rice, 4 with three other dishes

1 pound filleted carp, sea bass, or other white-fleshed fish

FOR THE MARINADE
a 1-inch piece of fresh ginger, unpeeled
1 scallion, white and green parts
1/2 teaspoon salt
2 teaspoons Shaoxing rice wine or medium-dry sherry
4 tablespoons cornstarch mixed with 3 tablespoons cold water

FOR THE BASE FLAVORINGS
6 dried Sichuanese chiles
a 1-inch piece of fresh ginger

3 cloves of garlic
5 scallions, white and green parts
3 tablespoons peanut or corn oil
1 tablespoon Sichuanese chili bean paste
1/2 teaspoon Sichuan pepper

FOR THE SPICY OIL
3/4 cup peanut or corn oil
1 1/2 tablespoons chili bean paste
1–2 ounces dried red chiles, preferably Sichuanese
2 teaspoons whole Sichuan pepper

1 Slightly crush the ginger and scallion for the marinade with the flat side of a cleaver or a heavy object. Cut the scallion into 3 or 4 sections. Lay the fish fillets on a cutting board and, holding your knife at a shallow angle to the board, cut them into slices 1/4 to 1/2 inch thick. Place the slices in a bowl, add the salt, wine, ginger, and scallion, and leave to marinate while you prepare the other ingredients.

2 Snip all the chiles in half with a pair of scissors and shake out as many seeds as possible.

3 Prepare the base flavorings: peel and thinly slice the ginger and garlic. Discard the coarse outer leaves of the scallions, crush them slightly with the flat side of a cleaver blade or a heavy object, and then cut them into 2- to 3-inch sections. Heat 3 tablespoons of oil in a wok over a high flame. When it is just beginning to smoke, turn the heat down a little, add the chili bean paste, and stir-fry until the oil is red and fragrant. Then throw in the ginger, garlic, scallions, dried chiles, and Sichuan pepper and continue to stir-fry until they all smell delicious and the scallions are tender. The oil should be hot enough to keep them sizzling, but take care not to burn them. When they are ready, transfer them into a deep serving bowl.

4 Bring a pot of water to a boil over a high flame. Discard the ginger and scallion from the fish marinade, add the cornstarch mixture, and stir well to coat all the fish slices. When the water is boiling, drop in all the slices. (Do not stir them before the water has returned to a boil or the starch coating will fall away.) Allow the water to return to a boil. When the fish slices are just cooked, remove them with a slotted spoon and scatter them over the base flavorings in the serving bowl.

5 Working quickly, heat 3/4 cup of oil over a high flame until it is just beginning to smoke. Add the chili bean paste and stir-fry until the oil is red and fragrant. Add the remaining chiles and Sichuan pepper and stir-fry until they are crisp and fragrant—the longer you fry them, the more fragrant and spicy the oil will become. Again, the oil should be hot enough to keep everything sizzling, but the spices must not burn—remove the wok from the stove for a few seconds if it seems to be overheating. Finally, pour the oil with the spices all over the fish. Serve immediately, while it is still sizzling.

HOT-AND-NUMBING TINY FISH

ma la zi yu

At many riverside towns and villages in the Sichuan countryside, tiny fish and freshwater shrimp are deep-fried, spiced, and then sold as a delicious, crunchy snack. In Leshan, where the world's largest statue of the Buddha presides over the sweeping brown waters of the Min River, I remember buying them from a tiny stall on the riverbank. They were fresh and crisp, and they left the tingling traces of chili and Sichuan pepper on my lips.

The following recipe is splendidly easy and, served hot, makes a wonderful nibble for a cocktail party. I've suggested using frozen whitebait as the fish, because they are relatively easy to find, but you can also use the tiny frozen shrimp sold in some Asian supermarkets or the more familiar large prawns. The advantage of the tiny fish and shrimp is that you can eat them whole. You can add salt to the final seasoning if you wish, but I don't find it necessary with whitebait.

Serves 4 as a starter, 6 as a nibble with drinks

1 pound frozen whitebait or tiny frozen shrimp
3/4 cup all-purpose flour
peanut oil for deep-frying
FOR THE MARINADE
1/2 teaspoon salt
1 tablespoon Shaoxing rice wine or medium-dry sherry
a 2-inch piece of fresh ginger, unpeeled

2 scallions, white and green parts
FOR THE SEASONING
2 tablespoons peanut oil
1–3 Sichuanese ground chiles, to taste, or 1/2 teaspoon cayenne pepper
1/2–1 1/2 teaspoons ground roasted Sichuan pepper (see page 74)

1 Defrost the fish.

2 Rub the fish all over with the salt and wine. Slightly crush the ginger and scallions with the side of a cleaver blade or a heavy object and roughly chop them. Add them to the fish. Leave to marinate for about 15 minutes.

3 Heat the oil for deep-frying over a high flame to about 375°F. While it is heating up, remove the ginger and scallion pieces from the marinade and shake the fish dry in a colander. Toss them in the flour, making sure they are evenly coated.

4 Fry the fish in 2–3 batches until they are crisp—this will take 2–3 minutes per batch. Remove and drain.

5 When the fish are all ready, heat 2 tablespoons of oil in a clean wok over a moderate flame. Add the ground chiles (if using) and stir-fry briefly, until the oil is red and fragrant, taking great care not to let it burn. Add the Sichuan pepper and mix well. Then throw in all the fish and toss briskly to distribute the spices evenly. Serve immediately.

VARIATIONS

Crispy shrimp with salt and Sichuan pepper—*jiao yan su xia*: deep-fried shrimp or prawns can simply be served with a sprinkling of salt and ground roasted Sichuan pepper (see page 74). If you use prawns, you must de-vein them first. This dish can be eaten hot, but it is also served as part of a cold appetizer course.

You can use the same method to make delicious potato chips: deep-fry them as usual, and then toss them in a hot wok with salt, ground chiles, and Sichuan pepper, as in the fish recipe above.

6
vegetables and bean curd

ALTHOUGH THE MOST FAMOUS SICHUANESE DISHES ARE virtually all made with meat or fish, most of the local population actually live on a diet dominated by legumes, grains, and vegetables. This is partly an economic necessity, for meat is still a luxury for the poor, but it is also related to ideas about health and longevity in traditional Chinese culture. Early medical texts describe the health benefits of largely vegetarian eating, and many members of the ruling classes and literati have throughout history expressed a preference for frugal living and the simple peasant diet. These days, many educated people still eat very little meat at home, and everyone knows that it's better to "eat more vegetables, eat less meat" (*duo chi shu cai*, *shao chi rou*). A typical home-cooked dinner in Sichuan might consist of a few dishes of vegetables stir-fried with tiny pieces of meat, some bean curd perhaps, a simple stock-based soup and plenty of rice: extravagant consumption of meat and fish is usually associated with dining out and entertaining.

Despite this widespread acceptance of a diet based largely on grains and vegetables, total vegetarianism is still rare in China. Most people find it hard to imagine abstaining from all meat products, all the time, and the only places where you're likely to find strict vegetarians are the monasteries. One of the most important precepts of Buddhism is the ban on killing, but the religion doesn't explicitly forbid the consumption of meat. In the original Indian Buddhism, monks were expected to eat almost all the food that was placed in their begging bowls: this included meat, as long as they didn't suspect an animal had been killed specifically for their benefit. But after Buddhism entered China during the early Han period, a distinct tradition of vegetarian eating developed, partly because begging was never culturally acceptable in China, so Chinese Buddhist monasteries had to produce their own food. The idea of vegetarian eating wasn't completely alien: periods of abstention from meat had been part of Chinese ritual life since ancient times. But the establishment of the tradition is credited to Emperor Wu Di of the sixth-century Liang Dynasty, whose own conversion to Buddhism led him to adopt a vegetarian diet on compassionate grounds. He banned the use of meat in state sacrifices and enforced a rule of strict vegetarian eating in Buddhist monasteries all over the southern Yangtze region.

The daily diet of Buddhist monasteries is very simple, but the food offered to their guests and patrons is anything but. In the centuries since the time of the Emperor Wu Di, when monasteries began to hold feasts, Buddhist vegetarian cooking has become extraordinarily sophisticated. Over the last century its development has been fostered by specialist Buddhist restaurants, which grew out of the lay Buddhist associations of the 1920s and 1930s. The really distinctive feature of Chinese Buddhist cooking is the practice of using all the culinary arts to transform vegetarian ingredients into dishes—called *fo zhai cai*—that resemble meat or fish in their appearance, taste, and texture. At the Wenshu Monastery in central Chengdu, a special restaurant offers feasts that mirror the banquets of classic Sichuanese cuisine but are made entirely without meat and without the pungent spices that are traditionally frowned on in Buddhist monasteries (these include garlic and scallions). The "beef slivers with sesame seeds" served there as a starter are actually made from mushroom stalks, chosen because of their chewy, meaty texture and rich taste—the finished dish, drizzled with sweet chili oil and scattered with seeds, looks and tastes remarkably like the real thing. The "spare ribs" are made from pieces of chewy bean curd, colored pink like pork, each impaled on a "bone" made from a stalk of quite hard bamboo shoot; the "fish in spicy bean sauce" from a fish-shaped pile of mashed potato wrapped in bean curd skin, deep-fried, and then draped in a lustrous red sauce. Other key ingredients in this kind of Buddhist vegetarian cooking include wheat gluten, various soybean and bean curd products, and imitation meat made from the konnyaku yam (*mo yu*), a Sichuan specialty.

Ordinary Sichuanese vegetable cooking may not be this elaborate, but it is also colorful, exciting and richly varied. The markets of Sichuan, "the land of plenty," are overflowing with fresh, seasonal vegetables all year round. Some of the local produce is familiar to Westerners, like tomatoes, potatoes, onions, and sweet peppers, as are certain Asian breeds of vegetables: long, thin, sweet-fleshed eggplants; red-skinned radishes the size of parsnips; tight-fleshed, prickly cucumbers; loosely gathered heads of slender celery; huge Sichuanese white cabbages. You'll also find the produce strongly associated with Chinese cooking: winter melons, silk gourds, and bitter melons; water spinach; lotus rhizomes; green, yellow, and flowering chives; fresh ginger and single-cloved garlic; long green Chinese onions; shelled green soybeans; and yard-long beans. Fresh bamboo shoots, quite unlike the stale-flavored canned varieties available outside China, are available in several varieties, including bitter bamboo shoots (*ku sun*), spring bamboo shoots (*chun sun*), and winter bamboo shoots (*dong sun*).

Chinese leeks, also known as "green garlic" (*suan miao* or *qing suan*), which are longer, thinner, and more tender than their Western equivalent, are widely used in Sichuanese cooking. Another ubiquitous vegetable is a type of bolted lettuce with a swollen stem and sparse leaves (*wo sun* or *qing sun*), which has a subtle and quite marvelous flavor. The stems of this lettuce are peeled, and their jade-like flesh is used as a secondary ingredient in all kinds of salads, stir-fries, and braised dishes; the leafy tips are sliced and stir-fried as a vegetable. Daylily flowers (*huang hua*) are sometimes added to soups and stir-fries, and you can also find unusual seasonal greens like purple amaranth leaves (*han cai*), which are wonderful stir-fried with garlic; sour ze'er gen (*Houttuynia cordata*), which is used in soups and salads; and the tender green shoots of the Chinese toon tree (*chun ya*), which are often mixed with duck eggs and made into a kind of omelet with an intriguing herby taste. Delicate pea leaves (*dou miao*), sometimes known as "dragon's whiskers" because of their curling tendrils, are sometimes added to soupy banquet dishes.

Many parts of Sichuan also have their own local specialties. Around the holy Daoist (Taoist) mountain Qing Cheng Shan, small restaurants serve the famous local black bacon stir-fried with *jue cai*, a purplish fiddlehead fern. No visit to the Bamboo Sea (*zhu hai*) in southern Sichuan is complete without a banquet of local exotica: bamboo pith fungus (*zhu sun*), many types of fresh bamboo shoot, and the rich, gelatinous "ox liver mushroom" (*niu gan jun*).

The following chapter contains a selection of Sichuanese vegetable dishes. Not all are entirely vegetarian, although those that do contain meat can easily be adapted for vegetarians by the simple omission of the meat and the substitution of vegetable oil for any stock or animal fat. My Chinese friends might laugh at me for including some of the following dishes in a book that is intended to show some of the glories of Sichuanese cooking. Most of them are very simple home-cooked dishes that don't appear in serious cookbooks and aren't taught in cooking schools. They are, however, quick to make, delicious to eat, and very healthy eaten with a generous bowl of rice. Including a few simple stir-fries in a home-cooked Chinese dinner also takes much of the stress away from the cook. Especially when you are beginning to experiment with Chinese cooking, it's best to make only one or two of the more complex dishes at a time and accompany them with a couple of simple vegetable dishes. Practicing a few of these dishes should also help you to look into your refrigerator or pantry with a new, Sichuanese eye. Odds and ends of vegetables can be transformed into a delicious feast—a couple of zucchini cut into slivers and stir-fried with garlic; two eggs cooked with a couple of tomatoes; a bag of spinach stir-fried with a few dried chiles and Sichuan peppercorns. It doesn't take long to learn to make a meal this way.

FISH-FRAGRANT EGGPLANTS

yu xiang qie zi

The following recipe is a Sichuan classic and one of my personal favorites. More than any other dish, for me it sums up the luxuriant pleasures of Sichuan eating: the warmth of its colors and tastes, the rich subtlety of its complex flavors. Like other fish-fragrant dishes, it is prepared with the flavorings used in traditional Sichuanese fish cooking: pickled chiles, garlic, ginger and scallion. But unlike the more illustrious fish-fragrant pork slivers, this dish derives its color not from pickled chiles alone, but from pickled chiles mixed with fava beans in the famous Pixian chili bean paste.

The sauce is sweet and sour and spicy, with a reddish hue and a visible scattering of chopped ginger, garlic, and scallion. The dish is equally delicious hot or cold. I usually serve it to guests with a meat or bean curd dish and a stir-fried green vegetable, but it makes a fine lunch simply with brown rice and a salad. The eggplants, deep-fried to a buttery tenderness, are delectable. I have eaten this dish in restaurants all over Sichuan and recorded numerous different versions of the recipe. The following two will, I hope, make you sigh with delight.

Serves 4 with three other dishes

1 1/3–1 2/3 pounds eggplants (2 decent-sized eggplants or a generous handful of slender Asian eggplants)
salt
peanut or corn oil for deep-frying
1 1/2 tablespoons Sichuanese chili bean paste
3 teaspoons finely chopped fresh ginger
3 teaspoons finely chopped garlic

1/2 cup everyday stock (see page 318) or chicken stock
1 1/2 teaspoons white sugar
1/2 teaspoon light soy sauce
1 1/3 teaspoons cornstarch mixed with 1 tablespoon cold water
1 1/2 teaspoons Chinkiang or Chinese black vinegar
4 scallions, green parts only, sliced into fine rings
1 teaspoon sesame oil

METHOD 1

1 Cut the eggplants in half lengthwise and then crosswise. Chop each quarter lengthwise into 3 or 4 evenly sliced chunks. Sprinkle with 1 1/2 teaspoons of salt and leave for at least 30 minutes to draw out some of the juices. If you are using Asian eggplants, simply slice them in half lengthwise and then into 3-inch sections—there is no need to salt them.

2 In your wok, heat oil for deep-frying to 350–400°F (at this temperature it will just be beginning to smoke). Add the eggplants in batches and deep-fry for 3–4 minutes until slightly golden on the outside and soft and buttery within. Remove and drain on paper towels.

3 Drain off the deep-frying oil, rinse the wok if necessary, and then return it

to a high flame with 2–3 tablespoons of oil. Add the chili bean paste and stir-fry for about 20 seconds until the oil is red and fragrant; then add the ginger and garlic and continue to stir-fry for another 20–30 seconds until they are fragrant. Take care not to burn the flavorings—remove the wok from the heat for a few seconds or turn down the heat if necessary.

4 Add the stock, sugar, and soy sauce and mix well. Season with salt to taste if necessary.

5 Add the fried eggplants to the sauce and let them simmer gently for a few minutes to absorb some of the flavors. Then sprinkle the cornstarch mixture over the eggplants and stir in gently to thicken the sauce. Next, stir in the vinegar and scallions and leave for a few seconds until the onions have lost their rawness. Finally, remove the pan from the heat, stir in the sesame oil, and serve.

METHOD 2

1 Follow steps 1–4 of the recipe above, but lay the fried eggplants neatly onto a warmed serving dish.

2 When the sauce has returned to a boil, add the cornstarch mixture and stir as it thickens. Throw in the vinegar and scallions and stir until the scallions have just lost their rawness. Remove from the heat, stir in the sesame oil, and pour over the waiting eggplants.

The advantage of the first method is that you can, if you wish, fry the eggplants some time in advance, because they will be warmed up by the final braising in the sauce.

VARIATIONS

The fish-fragrant sauce made according to the second method can be poured over stuffed eggplant fritters (see page 301) or seafood such as prawns or squid. The seafood can be simply boiled or steamed, or deep-fried, perhaps with a light tempura-style batter. Some restaurants serve the sauce in a bowl as a dip for deep-fried prawns. These variations are recent innovations—they have only been served in upscale restaurants since fresh seafood began to be flown in from the coast.

TIGER-SKIN GREEN PEPPERS

fu pi qing jiao

虎
皮
青
椒

This dish is so-called because the frying method makes the skins of the peppers slightly wrinkled and golden in places, so they look streaky "like a tiger's skin." After the frying, the peppers are seasoned with salt and then dressed on the serving dish with a little aromatic vinegar, a delicious contrast to their rich, buttery flesh. The Sichuanese use small, thin-skinned green chiles that are generally 2 1/2–3 1/2 inches long, but you can use any kind of green pepper that is available. (I've used thin-skinned Turkish peppers, the long, thin green peppers used for pickling, and ordinary green bell peppers. Do not use the green chiles available in the West, which are much too hot.) Ordering this dish in a Sichuan restaurant is a bit of a gamble because you never know what kind of chile will be used—sometimes they are as sweet and mild as bell peppers, others so hot they'll leave you gasping.

Serves 4 with three other dishes

3/4 pound green bell peppers
1 cup peanut oil
1/4–1/2 teaspoon salt to taste

1–2 teaspoons Chinkiang or
black Chinese vinegar

1 Wash the peppers. If you are using bell peppers, quarter them and discard their seeds and stems. If you are using small, thin-skinned peppers, just squash them slightly with the palm of your hand or the side of a cleaver and leave the stems intact.

2 Heat the oil in a wok until just smoking, then add the peppers and fry over medium heat for 5–6 minutes, stirring constantly. Keep pressing the skins of the peppers onto the surface of the wok as you fry. The peppers are ready when their flesh is absolutely tender and their skins are streaky. Don't cook at too high a temperature or they'll burn before they are soft—you can always turn the heat up at the end to color them slightly if you need to.

3 Pour most of the oil off into a heatproof dish. Sprinkle the peppers with salt to taste and stir and toss until they are evenly seasoned. Pile them

onto a serving dish and drizzle with the vinegar. (The vinegar flavor should be light—don't souse the peppers in it.) Mix gently with chopsticks and serve. This dish also tastes good cold.

DRY-FRIED GREEN BEANS I
gan bian si ji dou

This is one of Sichuan's most famous vegetable dishes. The green beans are traditionally dry-fried over a medium heat until they are tender and slightly wrinkled, although these days most restaurants deep-fry them to reduce the cooking time. If you want to minimize the oiliness, you can steam or boil the beans to cook them through instead of frying them, and then follow the rest of the recipe (from step 3) according to the instructions given below. This method is not authentic, but the results are delicious, particularly for the vegetarian version of the dish.

Serves 4 with three other dishes

10 ounces haricots verts or
 green beans
peanut oil
3 ounces ground pork (about
 2/3 cup)
2 teaspoons Shaoxing rice
 wine or medium-dry sherry

2 teaspoons soy sauce
2 tablespoons Sichuanese *ya
 cai* or Tianjin preserved
 vegetable, finely chopped
salt to taste
1 teaspoon sesame oil

1 Remove any strings from the edges of the beans and trim off the tops and tails. Break them into short sections (about 2 inches long).

2 Heat 2 tablespoons of oil in a wok, add the beans, and stir-fry over a medium flame for about 6 minutes, until they are tender and their skins are a little puckered. Remove from the wok and set aside. (If you want to save time, deep-fry the beans at about 350°F until they are tender and puckered.)

3 Heat another 2 tablespoons of oil in the wok over a high flame, add the pork, and stir-fry for 30 seconds or so until it's cooked, splashing in the Shaoxing rice wine and the soy sauce as you go.

4 Add the *ya cai* or Tianjin preserved vegetable and stir-fry briefly until hot, then toss in the beans. Stir and toss, adding salt to taste (remember that the *ya cai* is already very salty).

5 Remove from the heat, stir in the sesame oil, and serve.

VARIATION

One restaurant I know in Chengdu cooks a similar dish with bitter melon, which is sensational. The melon is deseeded and cut into thin strips and then fried in the same way as the beans, until the strips are tender and slightly wrinkly. The final frying is exactly the same as in the recipe above, although they do add a few dried chiles and a couple of lengths of scallion, white and green parts.

DRY-FRIED GREEN BEANS 2

gan bian si ji dou (VEGETARIAN VERSION)

This vegetarian version of dry-fried beans is almost nicer than the classic dish with its scattering of ground pork. The recipe is my own recreation of a dish from a tiny restaurant near the Sichuan Conservatory of Music in Chengdu. The spices and flavorings are all toasty and fragrant, the beans tender and juicy.

Serves 4 with three other dishes

10 ounces haricots verts or
   green beans
2 scallions, white parts only
peanut oil

8 dried chiles, snipped in half,
   preferably Sichuanese
1/2 teaspoon Sichuan pepper

3 cloves of garlic, thinly sliced, and an equivalent amount **of fresh ginger, thinly sliced**
salt to taste

1 Remove any strings from the edges of the beans and trim off the tops and tails. Break them into short sections (about 2 inches long). Cut the scallions at a steep angle into thin "horse ear" slices, 1 1/2 inches long.

2 Heat 2 tablespoons of oil in a wok over a low to medium flame. Add the green beans and stir-fry over a medium flame for about 6 minutes, until they are cooked and tender with slightly puckered skins. Remove and set aside. (You can deep-fry them to save time—see previous recipe.)

3 Heat 2 tablespoons of fresh oil in the wok over a high flame. Add the chiles and Sichuan pepper and stir-fry very briefly until they are fragrant. Quickly add the garlic, ginger, and scallions and stir-fry until they are all fragrant. Throw in the beans and stir and toss the ingredients together, adding salt to taste. Serve.

FLOWERING CHIVES WITH SMOKY BACON
la rou chao jiu cai hua

腊
肉
炒
韭
菜
花

One of my favorite Sichuanese stir-fries is a simple mix of garlic stems (*suan tai* or *suan hao*) and slivers of smoky bacon. The garlic stems, which come from one of a number of varieties of garlic used in Sichuan, have a crisp texture and a fresh, chive-like flavor, and are usually sold doubled up into long green skeins. Their taste is perfectly complemented by the meat. You can sometimes find garlic stems in Chinese supermarkets, but flowering chives seem to be more readily available, which is why I have made them the subject of this recipe. Flowering chives have slender, dark green stems, each topped by a miniature garlic bulb. Sometimes they are sold as "onion flowers." The following recipe is delicious and delightfully easy to make. Some Sichuanese cooks steam the bacon until it is cooked before they begin.

291

Serves 2 with one other dish and rice for a simple supper, 4 with three other dishes and rice

8 ounces flowering chives or garlic stems	2 tablespoons peanut oil
3 1/2 ounces slab (unsliced) bacon or pancetta (preferably in one piece)	salt to taste
	1 teaspoon sesame oil

1 Chop the chives into 1 1/2- to 2-inch sections, discarding the bulbs at the end of each stalk. Cut the bacon across the grain into strips of a similar length and thickness to the chive sections.

2 Heat the oil in a wok over a high flame. Add the bacon and stir-fry until it is cooked and smells delicious (30–60 seconds), then throw in all the chives and stir and toss for about 3 minutes until they are tender (garlic stems take a little longer to become tender). Season with salt to taste and stir in the sesame oil off the heat, just before serving.

STIR-FRIED MIXED MUSHROOMS

shan zhen hui

When I paid a late summer visit to the Wolong Nature Reserve in western Sichuan, I discovered that one of the local cooks was, like me, a former student of the Sichuan Institute of Higher Cuisine in Chengdu. In China this "same-school" (*tong xue*) bond is an important one, and I was immediately taken in as one of the family. My *tong xue* Peng Rui and I pottered around in the kitchen while his mother smoked bacon over a smoldering fire in the shed at the back. The highlight of the visit, however, was a trip we made up the valley in search of wild food plants.

We chugged up the road on a borrowed moped, the immense, pine-clad mountains rising steeply on either side, their peaks shrouded in drifting mists. Through the center of the valley wound a rushing peacock-blue river, tumbling over a mass of boulders. Small-scale farmers were carving out their livings on the steep lower slopes, creating a beautiful patchwork of tiny plots. Dark leaves flowered out around the hearts of cabbages, pinky-white radish tops swelled out of the earth, yellow corn cobs and scarlet chiles dangled in enormous bundles from the wooden eaves of scattered stone cottages. At one point we left the road and went on foot up a craggy gorge where cataracts spilled down into a mountain stream. Here, the changing seasons brought wild walnuts and crabapples, tiny wild strawberries, and an abundance of wild fungi.

The following recipe is created in homage to a dish of stir-fried wild mushrooms that Peng Rui made that night. The fungi are cooked with chicken fat, a Chinese luxury that gives them an exquisite richness without actually recalling the taste of chicken. The other flavorings are simple and colorless, allowing you to appreciate the variety and natural subtlety of the fungi. You can vary the mushrooms as you will—just try to bring together a few contrasting colors and textures.

Serves 4 with three other dishes

about a pound of mixed mushrooms: shiitake, oyster, Chinese golden needle, Japanese enoki, or button	**3 tablespoons chicken fat or lard**
2 plump cloves of garlic	**1/3 cup chicken stock**
2 tablespoons peanut oil	**1/2 teaspoon salt to taste**
	3/4 teaspoon cornstarch mixed with 2 teaspoons water

1 If you are using enoki mushrooms, make sure you pull them gently apart so they don't stay in one clump. Cut all the other mushrooms into thickish slices (about 1/4 inch). Thinly slice the garlic.

2 Heat the oil and chicken fat or lard in a wok over a high flame until just smoking. Add the garlic and stir-fry briskly until it is fragrant and on the verge of browning. Throw in all the mushrooms except for the enoki and stir-fry for about 2 minutes. Then add the enoki and continue to stir-fry until all the mushrooms are tender—another minute or so.

3 Pour in the stock and season with salt to taste. Bring to a boil, simmer for a few seconds, and then add the cornstarch mixture and stir until it has gently thickened the sauce. Transfer onto a plate and serve.

STIR-FRIED AMARANTH LEAVES OR SWISS CHARD WITH GARLIC

chao han cai

 This spring and summer vegetable—*han cai*—is the tender young leaves and stems of a species of amaranth. The leaves have purple hearts and green edges and can have rounded or pointed ends. The Sichuanese traditionally eat this vegetable on the fifth day of the fifth lunar month, *Duan Wu Jie* (the Dragon Boat Festival).

Han cai can be stir-fried with chiles and Sichuan pepper, as in the recipe for water spinach on page 295, or blanched, cooled, and then dressed with the hot and garlicky sauce on page 146. Best of all, however, I love the tender leaves stir-fried with garlic as in the recipe below. As they cook, their purple pigments come out and stain the juices and the garlic a beautiful pink, a lovely contrast to the wilted, dark green leaves. This vegetable isn't easy to find, but pops up seasonally in some Chinese and Vietnamese food shops. You can cook the more readily available red Swiss chard the same way, to similarly delicious effect.

Serves 2 with a main dish and rice

3/4 pound fresh, tender amaranth (*han cai*) leaves or red Swiss chard	**2 teaspoons finely chopped garlic**
2–3 tablespoons peanut oil	**1/4 teaspoon salt to taste**

1 Wash the *han cai* thoroughly. Discard the coarser stalks and break the tender ones into 4-inch lengths. Shake dry.

2 Heat the oil over a high flame until just smoking. Add the garlic and stir-fry briskly until it is fragrant. Throw in all the *han cai* and mix well, making sure you scoop the garlic up from the base of the wok and toss it in with the leaves. Continue to stir-fry until the leaves have wilted and the stalks are tender, seasoning with salt to taste.

VARIATIONS

Many other leafy vegetables are delicious stir-fried with garlic. I've encountered, among others, Chinese water spinach, Chinese milk vetch (*shao cai* or *chao cai*), and various wild Sichuanese vegetables. Ordinary spinach is delicious cooked this way, too. Always use very tender young leaves and stalks, discarding fibrous bits.

STIR-FRIED WATER SPINACH WITH CHILE AND SICHUAN PEPPER
qiang kong xin cai

Water spinach is grown in most parts of Sichuan and is a very common stir-fried vegetable. There are two main varieties, with different-shaped leaves, but both have the same round, hollow stems, which is why their common Sichuanese name, *kong xin cai*, means "hollow-heart vegetable." The Cantonese like to cook this vegetable with fresh red chiles and fermented bean curd, but in Sichuan it is usually fast-fried with dried chiles and Sichuan peppercorns, as in the following recipe, or with finely chopped garlic. Water spinach is known in Mandarin Chinese as *weng cai* and *tong cai*; it is sold as *ong choy* or *tong choy* in Cantonese supermarkets.

Serves 2 with a main dish and rice, 4 with three other dishes

3/4 pound fresh water spinach
   or ordinary spinach
a small handful of dried
   chiles, preferably
   Sichuanese

3 tablespoons peanut oil
1/2 teaspoon whole Sichuan
   pepper
1/4–1/2 teaspoon salt to taste
1 teaspoon sesame oil

1 Thoroughly wash the water spinach, discarding any wilted leaves and coarser stalks. Tear or cut into 4-inch sections. Wearing rubber gloves, snip the chiles in half or into 1-inch sections, discarding as many seeds as possible.

2 Heat the oil in a wok until hot but not smoking. Add the chiles and Sichuan pepper and stir-fry for 10–20 seconds until the oil smells spicy and the chiles are just beginning to turn a darker red—take care not to burn them. Throw in all the spinach and stir-fry for about 3 minutes until the leaves have wilted and the stems are tender and juicy, seasoning with salt to taste. Finally, remove from the heat and stir in the sesame oil. Serve.

VARIATION

Water spinach is also delicious stir-fried with garlic and seasoned with a little salt. Simply substitute minced or slivered garlic for the spices in the recipe above.

DRY-FRIED BITTER MELON

gan bian ku gua

   In Chinese, bitterness (*ku*) is the universal metaphor for suffering. Chinese people remember the famine years of the late 1950s and the grim banishments of the Cultural Revolution as a time when they "ate bitterness," *chi ku*. But despite its association with sorrow, bitterness also has its benefits. Bitter words spoken by an emperor's adviser were a token of his loyalty, and bitterness in food is seen as useful in Chinese medical theory. In Sichuan, in the sultry summer months, bitter foods are thought to cool the body and drive out perspiration. The undisputed queen of bitter foodstuffs is *ku gua*, the bitter melon or gourd, a long, gnarled, bright green vegetable with a withering bite. It's a common feature on Sichuanese dinner tables whenever the weather's hot and humid, particularly prepared according to the following easy recipe, which is a local specialty. The extremely bitter flavor of this vegetable is definitely an acquired taste, but one adored by those who grow to like it.

Serves 2 with one other dish and rice, 4 with three other dishes

1 bitter melon (about 1 pound)	**1–2 tablespoons peanut oil**
1 green bell pepper	**salt to taste (about 3/4 of a teaspoon)**

1 Cut the bitter melon in half lengthwise. Scoop out the seeds and pith and throw them away. Chop each half into 2-inch sections, and cut these lengthwise into very thin slices. Halve the pepper, discard the seeds, stalk, and pith, and cut it into thin slices about as long as the melon slices.

2 Smear a wok with a very little oil and heat it over a medium hot flame. Add the bitter melon and pepper slices and stir-fry them for about 5 minutes, until they are cooked but still a little crunchy. Toward the end of the cooking time, add the oil and season with salt to taste (Sichuanese cooks would use more oil—I like this dish with just a tablespoonful or so). Then just turn onto a dish and serve.

STIR-FRIED POTATO SLIVERS WITH CHILES AND SICHUAN PEPPER

qiang tu dou si

The Chinese approach to potatoes is radically different from the Western one. They're not seen as a staple food, but as a vegetable that is cooked as an accompaniment to rice. In Chinese, they are known as "earth beans" or as "foreign taro," the latter a reference to their New World origins and comparatively recent introduction to China. Sometimes potato chunks are simmered with beef or lamb in slow-cooked stews. More often in Sichuan they are cut into fine slivers and simply stir-fried. This cooking method keeps them crunchy and lends them a very different character from the mashed, boiled, deep-fried, and roasted potatoes popular in the West. You can make this dish with any kind of potato, but it works best with those with a waxy rather than a floury texture. The finer and more even your chopping, the better the result—good Sichuanese cooks slice them so finely they look almost like skeins of wool when they are cooked, languidly entwined on the plate. Take care not to burn the spices.

Some Sichuanese friends of mine jokingly called this dish yang *yu chao tu dou*, which roughly translates as "spud-fried potatoes"—a way of sending up a very economical and simple dish by giving it an over-elaborate name.

Serves 4 with 3 other dishes

1 1/2 pounds potatoes	**1 teaspoon whole Sichuan**
peanut oil	**pepper**
6 dried chiles, preferably	**salt**
Sichuanese	**sugar**
	1–2 teaspoons sesame oil

1 Peel the potatoes and cut them as evenly as possible into very thin slices. Then lay these slices flat and cut them into very fine matchstick slivers. Soak for a few minutes in plenty of cold, lightly salted water to remove excess starch. You can also use a mandoline or the coarse grater in a food processor to slice the potatoes.

2 Just before cooking, drain the potatoes in a colander, shaking out as much water as possible.

3 Season the wok, then add 2 tablespoons of oil and swirl it around over a medium flame until hot but not smoking. Add the chiles and Sichuan pepper and stir-fry briefly until the oil is fragrant and spicy. Add the potatoes, turn the heat up, and stir-fry vigorously for 4–5 minutes, seasoning with salt and maybe a pinch of sugar to taste (about 1/2 teaspoon will do). When the potatoes are hot and cooked but still al dente, remove from the heat, stir in the sesame oil, and serve.

VARIATIONS

This method of quick-frying with chiles and Sichuan pepper (known as *qiang* in Chinese) can be used with several different vegetables. Typical variations include the following:

Mung bean sprouts: follow the method above, but stir-fry for a shorter time, until the bean sprouts are just cooked.

Chinese cabbage (also known as Chinese leaves) or Western green cabbage: cut into 1/2- to 1-inch slices and cook as above. Add a good slosh of Chinkiang vinegar just before serving for a fabulous extra kick of flavor.

Broccoli: cut into florets and blanch in lightly salted water with a splash of cooking oil until just tender, then fry as above.

Potato and green bell pepper slivers (*qing jiao tu dou si*): omit the chiles and Sichuan pepper and use 1 green bell pepper (or a mixture of different colored peppers for a lovely effect), very finely slivered, instead. To cook, simply season the wok, then heat the cooking oil and add the potatoes with the peppers. Stir-fry and season as above. You can throw in a few scallion slivers at the end if you like.

SWEET CORN KERNELS WITH GREEN PEPPERS

qing jiao yu mi

Sweet corn has a poetic name in Chinese—it literally means "jade rice"—but it is not considered a prestige food. In Sichuan, it's associated with subsistence eating in the poor mountain areas of the province. Cornmeal is made into some snacks and sweets, for example a type of coarse, conical steamed bun known as *wo wo tou*, which is still a peasant staple but has recently appeared in some fashionable restaurants as a pseudo-rustic novelty snack. Fresh sweet corn kernels are often stir-fried, as in the following recipe.

This is the kind of everyday dish that doesn't appear in recipe books, but it's a regular on the menus of informal Sichuanese restaurants and a popular home-cooked dish. You can use frozen corn or a can of unsweetened sweet corn instead of corn on the cob, but of course you won't get the delicious juicy crunch of the fresh kernels if you do it this way. The sweet corn can be first boiled and then tossed briefly in the wok with the green peppers, but I prefer it fried. In Sichuan the corn is usually cooked with small, thin-skinned green peppers, but you can use other types or a mixture of red and green sweet peppers instead. This dish definitely tastes best with plenty of salt—maybe a little more than you would put into other dishes.

Serves 4 with three other dishes

2 or 3 small green bell
    peppers (enough to give a
    pretty scattering of green
    amid the yellow)

2 ears of fresh corn (about 14
    ounces corn kernels)
peanut oil
sea salt

1 Chop the peppers into tiny chunks to complement the small, squarish sweet corn kernels. Slice the kernels from the corn cob.

2 Heat 3 tablespoons of oil in a wok, add both vegetables, and stir-fry them for about 5 minutes over a medium flame until the sweet corn kernels are tender, adding sea salt to taste. Serve.

DRY-FRIED EGGPLANTS

gan bian qie zi

干
煸
茄
子

The dry-frying method is a Sichuan specialty. When it's applied to vegetables, they are stir-fried in a dry wok over a medium flame until just cooked. Then a little oil is added and they are seasoned with salt to taste. This cooking method brings out their fragrance and gives them a nice, slightly toasty taste—rather like Western grilled vegetables. It's important to keep them moving in the wok and not to work at too high a temperature lest the vegetables burn before they are ready. You can vary the proportions of eggplant and green pepper in the recipe according to your desires or the leftover vegetables in your refrigerator, but don't overload the wok or they won't cook evenly. The bright green peppers should taste fresh and slightly crunchy, livening up the languid flesh of the eggplants.

Serves 2 with one other dish, 4 with three other dishes as part of a Chinese meal

about a pound of eggplant
1 1/2 teaspoons salt
1/2 of a green bell pepper

peanut oil
1 teaspoon sesame oil

1 Cut the eggplant(s) in half lengthwise, and then slice them thinly at an angle (ideally the slices should be 1/8 inch thick). Sprinkle with the salt and leave for at least 30 minutes to draw out some of the juices (this step is not necessary for the slender Asian eggplants, which can simply be sliced and cooked). Cut the pepper into thin slices.

2 Smear a wok lightly with peanut oil and heat it over a fairly hot flame until smoking. Add the eggplants and stir and toss for about 3 minutes to "break their rawness." Then add the pepper slices and 1–2 more tablespoons of oil. Continue to stir-fry for another 2 minutes or so until the pepper is just cooked. Season with more salt if necessary. Finally, remove from the heat, stir in the sesame oil, and serve.

STUFFED EGGPLANT FRITTERS WITH SICHUAN PEPPER

jiao yan qie bing

These substantial snacks offer a tantalizing combination of textures: crisp batter and buttery eggplant flesh surrounding a succulent meat center. They are often served with a fish-fragrant sauce just like the one used to drape simple deep-fried eggplants (see page 285), but here I've suggested an easier version, offered simply with a dip of ground roasted Sichuan pepper, and salt if you need it. The recipe can be prepared in advance right up to the final frying. In Chengdu, the fritters are made with long, thin Asian eggplants, which don't need salting. The eggplants are peeled then chopped into "sandwich slices" (*lian jia pian*), where the knife blade stops short of the cutting board on alternate cuts, so the final result is lots of pairs of slices that are still joined together at one end. The filling is simply stuffed between these "sandwich slices" before they are dipped into the batter.

Serves 4 as a starter or as part of a Chinese meal

301

1 large eggplant (about 10 ounces)
salt
1/2 cup ground pork
about 3/4 cup cornstarch
1/2 teaspoon soy sauce
1/2 teaspoon Shaoxing rice wine or medium-dry sherry

2 medium eggs
oil for deep-frying

TO SERVE

1 tablespoon ground roasted Sichuan pepper (see page 74)
1/2 tablespoon salt

1 Peel the eggplant and slice it thinly (at 1/8-inch intervals). Sprinkle with 3/4 teaspoon salt and leave for at least 30 minutes to draw out the bitter juices.

2 Put the ground pork in a small bowl. Add 3/4 teaspoon of cornstarch, 2 pinches of salt, the soy sauce, Shaoxing rice wine, and 4 teaspoons of cold water, and mix to give a soft paste.

3 Beat the eggs, and gradually mix in the rest of the cornstarch to yield a thick batter.

4 When the eggplant slices are ready, drain them well and squeeze gently to get rid of as much water as possible. Place a small blob of meat stuffing on each slice and fold the slice in half to enclose it, pushing the edges together.

5 Heat oil for deep-frying to about 300°F.

6 Use chopsticks to dip each stuffed eggplant slice into the eggy batter, and then drop into the deep-frying oil. Fry gently for about 5 minutes, until the meat stuffing is cooked through (cut one fritter in half to make sure). The batter should still be pale in color. Make sure the oil doesn't overheat or the fritters will brown before the meat is cooked. As they are ready, remove the fritters from the oil with a perforated spoon, drain well on paper towels, and set aside.

7 Just before you want to eat the fritters, reheat the deep-frying oil until smoking. Add all the fritters and fry for about a minute until crisp and golden brown. Serve immediately with dips of salt and Sichuan pepper.

VARIATION

Vegetarians can stuff their fritters with the following mixture: a generous handful of any type of mushrooms, very finely chopped; 1 teaspoon light soy sauce; 1 1/2 teaspoons cornstarch; 2 teaspoons cold water; and a little salt to taste. The first time I made this vegetarian version, for some friends in Chengdu, the fritters were so popular that I never even managed to sample them—by the time I emerged from the kitchen my eager friends had devoured all of them! Even meat-eaters said they were as good as—if not better than—the real thing.

ZUCCHINI SLIVERS WITH GARLIC

chao nan gua si

One of my favorite simple stir-fries is made with a small, round zucchini-like vegetable that the Sichuanese call southern gourd (*nan gua*). The flesh is cut into fine slivers and stir-fried with garlic as a delicious side dish. I have found no exact equivalent to this gourd, but zucchini are fairly similar and taste good cooked the same way.

Serves 2 with one main dish, 4 with three other dishes

a generous pound zucchini
salt

1 1/2 teaspoons finely
   chopped garlic
2 tablespoons peanut oil

1 Cut the zucchini into thin slices and then into very fine slivers. If you have time, sprinkle them with about half a teaspoon of salt and leave them for about 30 minutes to draw out some of their water—this improves their final texture and reduces the cooking time.

2 Heat the oil in a wok over a high flame until just beginning to smoke. Add the garlic and stir-fry briskly until it is fragrant. Then add all the zucchini and mix well, making sure you scoop the garlic up from the base of the

wok and toss it in with the slivers. Continue to stir-fry over a high heat for 3–4 minutes until the zucchini are just tender, seasoning with salt to taste. Turn onto a serving plate.

CAULIFLOWER WITH SMOKY BACON

la rou shao hua cai

Cauliflower is thought to be native to the eastern Mediterranean and has only been used in China for a couple of hundred years. In Sichuan you occasionally see it blanched and cold-dressed in stock and sesame oil, but it's more commonly cooked with a little smoky bacon, as in the following recipe. The pink, strong-tasting bacon is an appealing contrast to the pale, bland cauliflower, and it tastes even better if you use a little lard or chicken fat in the cooking. You can blanch the cauliflower first, until it is almost cooked, if you wish to cut down on the last-minute cooking time.

Serves 2 with one other dish, 4 with three other dishes

1/2 a cauliflower (about 2/3 pound)
3 ounces slab (unsliced) bacon or pancetta
2 cloves of garlic
2 tablespoons peanut oil or lard

1 cup everyday stock (see page 318) or chicken stock
salt and white pepper to taste
2 1/4 teaspoons cornstarch mixed with 3 teaspoons cold water

1 Cut the cauliflower into florets small enough to be picked up with chopsticks. Slice the stem thinly. Cut the bacon into thin strips. Peel and thinly slice the garlic.

2 Heat the oil or lard in a wok over a high flame. When it is smoking, add the bacon and stir-fry for about 30 seconds until it is cooked and smells delicious. Add the garlic and continue to stir-fry for another 20 seconds or so until it, too, is fragrant. Throw in all the cauliflower and mix it into the fragrant oil. Add the stock and bring it to a boil, season with salt to taste, then cover the wok with a lid and cook for about 5 minutes until the cauliflower is just tender.

3 Remove the lid to allow the liquid to reduce slightly and adjust the seasoning, adding pepper to taste. Then add the cornstarch mixture, stirring as the liquid thickens. Serve immediately.

FRIED EGGS WITH TOMATOES

fan qie chao dan

This dish is not peculiar to Sichuan, as it is eaten all over China. It does, however, frequently appear on Sichuanese menus, and it's so simple and delicious that I thought I would include it in this book. Like many simple stir-fries, this dish can be made into a soup simply by reducing the quantities and adding a bit of stock (see instructions below).

Serves 4 with three other dishes

4 medium eggs
1/2 pound ripe, fleshy
   tomatoes (about 2)

2 scallions, green parts only
salt and pepper
peanut oil

1 Beat the eggs together and season with salt and pepper to taste. Cut the tomatoes in half and slice them fairly thinly. Finely slice the scallions.

2 Season the wok, then add 3 tablespoons of oil and heat over a high flame until smoking. Pour in the egg mixture. As soon as the egg has formed a skin over the base of the wok, add the tomatoes. Then wait until the egg is half-cooked and mix everything together. Stir-fry gently until the egg is just cooked and the tomatoes just hot. (Don't overcook the egg: it should remain light and fluffy.) Add the scallions, stir once or twice, and then slide onto a serving dish.

VARIATION

Fried egg and tomato soup (*fan qie jian dan tang*): Use only 3 eggs and a single tomato. Season the wok as above, add 1–2 tablespoons of peanut oil, and heat until smoking. Then add the beaten eggs and slide them around the base of the wok. Do not break up the omelet: allow it to become slightly golden on the bottom, then flip it over and cook the other side. Add about 1 quart of stock and bring to a boil. (You can break up the omelet at this stage or let your guests serve themselves from it with chopsticks at the table.) Adjust the seasoning, add the tomatoes and, when they are just cooked, add a few green leaves for color (romaine lettuce, baby bok choy, or pea shoots will all do). Pour into a soup bowl and serve with a scattering of scallions if desired. This soup is often eaten at the end of a Sichuanese meal.

PICKLED STRING BEANS WITH GROUND PORK

rou mo jiang dou

This simple dish is typical of Sichuanese home cooking, but it is also served in restaurants. The string beans are steeped briefly in a brine, which gives them a gentle salty-sourness and preserves their crunchy texture. They are then stir-fried with just a little meat and a few spices. Because of the pickling, you must plan this dish a day or two before you wish to eat it.

Serves 4 as part of a Chinese meal with two or three other dishes

1/2 pound string beans
pickling solution (see page 71)
1/4 pound ground lean pork
1/2 teaspoon Shaoxing rice
   wine or medium-dry sherry
1/2 teaspoon light soy sauce
salt

peanut oil for cooking
3–4 Sichuanese dried chiles,
   snipped in half, seeds
   discarded
1/2 teaspoon whole Sichuan
   pepper

1 Wash and trim the beans and then dry them thoroughly. Immerse them in the pickling solution and leave the pickling jar in the refrigerator or a cool place for 1–3 days.

2 Shortly before cooking, place the pork in a bowl with the Shaoxing rice wine, soy sauce, and 3 generous pinches of salt; mix well and set aside.

3 Chop the beans into 1/8-inch slices to complement the small grains of the ground pork.

4 Season the wok, then add 1 tablespoon of oil and heat over a high flame until smoking. Add the pork and stir-fry until it is dry and a little crispy. Then tip the meat back into the marinating bowl.

5 Return the wok to the flame with 1 tablespoon of fresh oil. When the oil is hot but not yet smoking, add the chiles and Sichuan pepper and stir-fry briefly until they are fragrant, taking great care not to let them burn. Throw in the beans and pork and stir-fry for another minute or two until the beans are hot and fragrant. Turn out onto a serving plate.

STIR-FRIED MIXED VEGETABLES
si zhong shu cai

When I was a student in Chengdu, this was one of my favorite vegetable dishes—a fresh and colorful medley of contrasting tastes and textures. It was a specialty of a little restaurant called the Bamboo Bar. The sliced lotus root, as always, looks beautiful and exotic and has a fabulous crunchy feel in the mouth. This dish is very easy to cook and makes a refreshing contrast to some of the more highly flavored Sichuanese dishes. The quantities of individual vegetables are entirely flexible—just try to use a good balance of colors.

Serves 4 with two or three other dishes and rice

1/2 a smallish cucumber
  (about 1/3 pound)
1 section of lotus root (about
  1/3 pound)
a 2-inch piece of fresh ginger
1 large tomato (about 1/2
  pound)

a handful or two of snow peas
  or haricots verts or green
  beans (about 1/4 pound)
4 tablespoons peanut oil
salt to taste

1 Cut the cucumber in half lengthwise and scoop out the seedy part (I like to eat this as I prepare the rest of the food). Cut each half into sections about 2 inches long and cut these lengthwise into fairly thin rectangular slices. Sprinkle with 1/4 teaspoon of salt, mix well, and leave to drain while you prepare the other vegetables.

2 Scrub the lotus root thoroughly, scraping off the outer skin if it's really grubby. Then cut into thin, round slices—each one will have a beautiful pattern of holes in it. Place in a bowl of lightly salted cold water for a few minutes to remove any excess starch and prevent discoloration. Peel and thinly slice the ginger.

3 Cut the tomato in half and slice fairly thinly. Wash the beans, trim off the tops and tails if necessary, and cut into 2-inch sections.

4 Heat the oil in a wok over a high flame until smoking. Add the beans and stir-fry until just tender. Remove with a slotted spoon and set aside. Return the wok to a high flame, add the ginger, and stir-fry until you can smell its fragrance. Then add the lotus root slices and stir-fry for a minute or two until they are hot and just cooked. Add the cucumber and stir-fry some more until piping hot. Finally, add the prefried beans and the tomatoes and cook until hot, seasoning with 1/2–3/4 teaspoon of salt to taste. When the tomatoes are just cooked but still intact, turn everything onto a plate and serve.

LOTUS ROOT IN SWEET-AND-SOUR SAUCE
tang cu ou pian

This is a colorful, fun dish that my friends and I used to enjoy eating in Chengdu. The patterned slices of lotus root are piled up on the serving dish and draped in a rich sweet-and-sour sauce scattered with bright red tomato and brilliant green scallion leaves. The lotus slices themselves look so extraordinary that cooking them is always a slightly surreal experience.

Serves 4 with two or three other dishes

2 sections of lotus root (about 2/3 pound)
2 ripe tomatoes (about 1/3 pound)
peanut oil for deep-frying

FOR THE SAUCE
3 scallions, green parts only
1/4 teaspoon salt
2 tablespoons white sugar

1 tablespoon Chinkiang or black Chinese vinegar
3 3/4 teaspoons cornstarch
3/4 cup everyday stock (see page 318) or chicken stock
2 teaspoons finely chopped fresh ginger
2 teaspoons finely chopped garlic
2 teaspoons sesame oil

1 Scrub the lotus roots thoroughly and cut them into slices 1/8 inch thick.

Each round slice will have a beautiful pattern of holes in it. Put the slices into a bowlful of lightly salted water to soak for a few minutes while you prepare the other ingredients.

2 Cut the tomatoes into slices just under 1/2 inch thick and then cut these into small cubes. Thinly slice the scallion greens.

3 Combine the salt, sugar, vinegar, and cornstarch with a spoonful or so of stock in a small bowl.

4 Drain the lotus slices and pat dry with a paper towel. Heat the deep-frying oil over a high flame until beginning to smoke. Add all the lotus root slices and fry them for 30–60 seconds until they are cooked and about to start going brown. Remove with a slotted spoon, drain well, and pile up on a serving plate.

5 Pour all but about 3 tablespoons of the oil into a heatproof container for later use. Return the wok to the heat, add the ginger and garlic, and stir-fry for 20–30 seconds until they smell delicious. Pour in the rest of the stock and bring to a boil. Add the tomatoes and cook for a few seconds, then give the sauce a stir and add it to the wok. Mix as the liquid thickens. Finally, stir in the scallion greens, remove from the heat, and mix in the sesame oil. Pour the sauce over the waiting lotus slices and serve immediately.

BRAISED SILK GOURD

bai you si gua

The long silk or loofah gourd (*si gua*) has a thick, coarse skin and pale, spongy flesh. Because of this texture, it is best cooked with plenty of stock or water. In the following everyday Sichuan dish, which is almost soupy, the slices of gourd are beautifully tender in their garlic-flavored sauce. There are two main varieties of silk gourd. The Sichuanese use the plump, pale *Luffa cylindrica*, which can be found in some Southeast Asian grocers; most Cantonese food shops stock the thinner *Luffa acutangula*, which has sharp ridges in its dark green skin (the Cantonese call it *see-gwa*).

Serves 4 with three other dishes

2 1/2 pounds silk gourd (3–4 gourds)	3/4 cup everyday stock (see page 318) or chicken stock
5 cloves of garlic	salt to taste
3 tablespoons peanut oil	3 teaspoons cornstarch mixed with 6 teaspoons water

1 Remove the thick outer skin from the silk gourds using a vegetable peeler or a sharp knife. Cut them in half lengthwise. Cut each half into 2 1/2-inch sections and then into slices about 1/8 inch thick. Peel and thinly slice the garlic.

2 Heat the oil in a wok over a high flame until it is just beginning to smoke. Add the garlic and stir-fry for about 20 seconds until it smells delicious. Add the sliced gourds and stir-fry for another minute or two, and then pour in the stock. Simmer for 3–4 minutes until tender, seasoning with salt to taste.

3 Finally, give the cornstarch mixture a stir and add it to the wok. Stir briskly as the liquid thickens, and then turn out onto a serving dish.

BEAN CURD

Bean curd (*dou fu*, more commonly transliterated as tofu) is one of the most nutritious and versatile of all Chinese foods. When Westerners think of bean curd, they usually think only of the thick, white blocks of bean curd, or perhaps of the smoked or flavored varieties that are sometimes available in health food stores or Asian supermarkets. These, however, are just two of the many varieties of bean curd enjoyed in China. In most Chengdu markets, the standard white bean curd is available in several consistencies; there is also smoked bean curd in thin, firm slabs with a honey-brown surface (*dou fu gan*); glossy chunks of firm bean curd that have been simmered in "five-spice" broth (*wu xiang dou fu*); large brown squares of "bean curd skin" (*dou fu pi*); sausage-shaped rolls of bean curd with an Edam-like texture (*su dou ji*); tender "flower" bean curd (*dou hua*); and ripe-smelling fermented bean curd in chili sauce (*dou fu ru*).

Bean curd is made from soybeans, which are an exceptionally rich source of protein. The raw beans, however, are not easily digestible, so they are usually made into bean curd before they are eaten. The basic method is as follows: dried soybeans are soaked in plenty of cold water for several hours or overnight. They are then ground with fresh water to make "bean curd milk" and strained through a double layer of cheesecloth to remove the solid beany residue (the residue—*dou zha*—can be used as animal feed, but it is also sometimes cooked, as in the Sichuanese dish "duck with bean curd residue," *dou zha ya zi*). The strained milk is boiled, and then a coagulant is added, either bittern or gypsum. The liquid is finally poured into a wooden mold lined with cheesecloth and left to set. For the ordinary white bean curd, the setting curd is squeezed beneath a weight in a special bean curd press to expel excess water; for "flower bean curd" it is left to set naturally and then returned to a wokful of water to simmer gently until it is required. Smoked bean curd is made by laying slices of set curd onto a wooden rack above the dying embers of a wood fire until they are golden-yellow.

Chinese legend has it that bean curd was the invention of a second-century king of Huainan, Liu An. This legend, however, originates in a much later text, Li Shizhen's encyclopedia of medicinal plants (*ben cao gang mu*), which was written during the Ming Dynasty in the sixteenth century. According to Chinese scholars, the earliest written reference to bean curd is a tenth-century work by Tao Gu, long after its supposed invention by the Huainan king. All that is known for certain is that by the Song Dynasty (960–1279 A.D.) it had become a popular food.

Bean curd can be eaten in any number of ways. Smoked bean curd can be eaten directly, as a snack, and various types of "dry" bean curd are chopped up and dressed in spicy sauces. Fermented bean curd, the Chinese equivalent of ripe blue cheese, is eaten as a relish or used in marinades. The common white bean curd in all its manifestations can be braised, sometimes after an initial deep-frying, or added to soups. Before it is used in cooking, this kind of bean curd is usually left to soak for a few minutes in very hot, lightly salted water, which heats the curd and removes any lingering taste of the coagulant.

Gourmets insist that the quality of the water used to make the bean curd is a crucial determinant of its flavor. For this reason, some places in Sichuan with particularly fine water sources are celebrated for their bean curd, like Xiba county in the south of the province. In nearby Leshan, where the giant

Buddha draws many visitors, there are specialist "Xiba bean curd restaurants" that offer thirty or forty different dishes made with fresh Xiba bean curd.

POCK-MARKED MOTHER CHEN'S BEAN CURD

ma po dou fu

Ma po dou fu is named after the smallpox-scarred wife of a Qing Dynasty restaurateur. She is said to have prepared this spicy, aromatic, oily dish for laborers who laid down their loads of cooking oil to eat lunch on their way to the city's markets. It's one of the most famous Sichuan dishes and epitomizes Sichuan's culinary culture, with its fiery peasant cooking and bustling private restaurants. Many unrecognizable imitations are served in Chinese restaurants worldwide, but this is the real thing, as taught at the Sichuan provincial cooking school and served in the Chengdu restaurants named after Old Mother Chen. The Sichuan pepper will make your lips tingle pleasantly, and the tender bean curd will slip down your throat. It's rich and warming, a perfect winter dish.

This recipe traditionally uses a scattering of ground beef, which is unusual in Sichuan cooking, where pork is the most common meat. Sometimes the beef is precooked and added to the main dish at the last minute to preserve its crispness. Vegetarians may omit the meat altogether and still enjoy the dish. The traditional vegetable ingredient is *suan miao*, the long, narrow Chinese leeks, but scallions are often used as a substitute if no leeks are available. You can reduce the amount of cooking oil if you wish (as little as 3 tablespoons will work), although it's traditional to serve this dish with a good layer of chile-red oil on top. For the deepest ruby-red color, use real Sichuan chili bean paste and ground Sichuanese chiles. *Ma po dou fu* is usually served heartily in a bowl, rather than on a plate.

Serves 2–3 as a main course with one vegetable dish and rice, 4 with three other dishes

1 block bean curd (about 1 pound)

4 baby leeks or 2 leeks

1/2 cup peanut oil

6 ounces ground beef

2 1/2 tablespoons Sichuanese chili bean paste

1 tablespoon fermented black beans

2 teaspoons ground Sichuanese chiles (only for chile fiends)

1 cup everyday stock (see page 318) or chicken stock

1 teaspoon white sugar

2 teaspoons light soy sauce

salt to taste

4 tablespoons cornstarch mixed with 6 tablespoons cold water

1/2 teaspoon ground roasted Sichuan pepper (see page 74)

1 Cut the bean curd into 1-inch cubes and leave to steep in very hot or gently simmering water that you have lightly salted. Slice the leeks at a steep angle into thin "horse ear" slices 1 1/2 inches long.

2 Season the wok, then add the peanut oil and heat over a high flame until smoking. Add the minced beef and stir-fry until it is crispy and a little brown, but not yet dry.

3 Turn the heat down to medium, add the chili bean paste and stir-fry for about 30 seconds, until the oil is a rich red color. Add the fermented black beans and ground chiles and stir-fry for another 20–30 seconds until they are both fragrant and the chiles have added their color to the oil.

4 Pour in the stock, stir well, and add the drained bean curd. Mix it in gently by pushing the back of your ladle or wok scoop gently from the edges to the center of the wok—do not stir or the bean curd may break up. Season with the sugar, a couple of teaspoons of soy sauce, and salt to taste. Simmer for about 5 minutes, until the bean curd has absorbed the flavors of the sauce.

5 Add the leeks or scallions and gently stir in. When they are just cooked, add the cornstarch mixture in two or three stages, mixing well, until the sauce has thickened enough to cling glossily to the meat and bean curd. Don't add more than you need. Finally, pour everything into a deep bowl, scatter with the ground Sichuan pepper, and serve.

HOMESTYLE BEAN CURD

jia chang dou fu

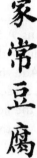

Homestyle is the name given to a particular type of Sichuanese flavor, which is salty-savory and moderately hot, with a hint of sweetness in the sauce. It is usually based on Sichuan chili bean paste, although there are dozens of variations in the additional flavorings used. Some recipes call for fermented black soybeans or sweet soybean paste, others pickled chiles. As the name suggests, this style of cooking is inspired by the hearty simplicity of Sichuanese home cooking, although it can be used to cook extravagant ingredients like sea cucumber. In this recipe, the puffy bean curd becomes juicy and flavorsome in the hot, beany sauce. The vegetables give an attractive splash of green. Although Sichuanese restaurants generally cook this dish with meat, the pork can easily be omitted to give a delicious vegetarian dish. (I almost always cook the vegetarian version myself.) If you fry the bean curd in advance or buy bean curd that has been deep-fried, it is extremely quick to make. And do remember that it also tastes good cold.

Serves 4 with two or three other dishes as part of a Chinese meal

1 block of bean curd (about 1 pound)

optional: 1/4 pound lean bacon

peanut oil for deep-frying

2 tablespoons chili bean paste

3 cloves of garlic, sliced, plus an equivalent amount of fresh ginger, also sliced

3 baby leeks or scallions, white and green parts, sliced diagonally into "horse ears"

1 1/3 cups everyday stock (see page 318) or chicken stock

1/2 teaspoon sugar

1/2–1 teaspoon light soy sauce

3/4 teaspoon cornstarch mixed with 1 1/2 teaspoons cold water

1 Cut the bean curd into square slices 2 inches long and about 1/2 inch thick. Thinly slice the pork if you are using it.

2 Heat oil for deep-frying to a very high temperature.

3 Add the bean curd slices in batches of 7 or 8, and deep-fry for a few minutes until puffy and golden (they should still be white and juicy inside). Drain well and set aside.

4 Season the wok, then heat 2 tablespoons of oil over a moderate heat. If using the pork, add it to the wok and stir-fry until it smells delicious. Add the chili bean paste and stir-fry until the oil is red and richly fragrant. Add the garlic and ginger and fry until they, too, are cooked and fragrant. Add the stock and bean curd and bring to a boil. Turn the heat down slightly, season with sugar and soy sauce to taste, and simmer for 3–4 minutes until the liquid is reduced and the bean curd has absorbed some of the flavors of the sauce. Add the leeks or scallions and stir briefly until just cooked. Finally, scatter the cornstarch mixture into the center of the wok, stir until the sauce thickens, and turn out onto a serving plate.

VARIATION

Bear's paw bean curd: this exotic-sounding dish is so named because the bean curd is not deep-fried but fried in a little oil on the surface of the wok until it is toasty and golden in places, lending it a puckered appearance "like a bear's paw" (bear's paw is a legendary Chinese delicacy, now banned for conservation reasons). Cooking the bean curd this way takes longer than deep-frying, unless you do it in a very wide, flat frying pan.

FISH-FRAGRANT BEAN CURD

yu xiang dou fu

The following recipe is my recreation of a wonderful dish served by a former student of the Sichuan cooking school in his restaurant: juicy, tender chunks of bean curd infused with the teasing flavors of the classic "fish-fragrant" ingredients: pickled chile, ginger, garlic, and scallion. We ate it as a cold starter, but it's equally, if not more, delicious eaten hot. The gentle simmering allows the bean curd to absorb all the richness of the sauce. You can cut the bean curd chunks in half before you begin so they draw in even more juice and flavor.

Serves 2 as a main dish, 4 as part of a Chinese meal

peanut oil
3 teaspoons finely chopped
  fresh ginger
3 teaspoons finely chopped
  garlic
3 scallions, white parts only,
  sliced at a steep angle into
  slices 1 1/2 inches long
  ("horse ears")
2 tablespoons pickled chili
  paste

1 package deep-fried bean
  curd (about 1/2 pound)
*(if you wish to deep-fry the bean
  curd yourself, follow the
  instructions in the preceding
  recipe)*
3/4 cup everyday stock (see
  page 318) or chicken stock
2 teaspoons light soy sauce
1 teaspoon sugar
1/4 teaspoon salt

1 Heat 3 tablespoons of peanut oil in a wok over a high flame until just
  smoking. Add the ginger, garlic, scallion, and pickled chili paste and stir-fry
  for a minute or so until the oil is red and richly fragrant, taking care it does
  not burn. Turn the heat down if necessary.

2 Add the bean curd and the stock, bring to a boil, and season with soy
  sauce, sugar, and salt. Mix well, turn down the heat, and simmer gently for
  about 10 minutes, stirring from time to time until the stock has mostly
  evaporated and the sauce is reduced to a little red oil. You can tell when
  the time is right because the oil will begin to sizzle as the last of the stock
  disappears.

3 Pile the bean curd chunks on a serving dish and sprinkle with the bits of
  chile, garlic, ginger, and scallion from the wok. Serve hot or cold.

7
stocks and soups

STOCKS

You will need stock to make all the soups in this book. A good stock will also enrich the sauces of all kinds of other dishes, although water can be used instead if you only need small quantities. The finer the stock, the more delicious the final dish. In testing most of the recipes in this book I have used an everyday stock made from pork bones and chicken—I make it in large quantities and freeze it in small containers of various sizes.

Most Sichuanese cooks use the simple everyday stock (*xian tang*, *gu tou tang*) for general purposes. Some recipes require the use of a stock made with only one main ingredient, such as pure chicken stock (this is called *yuan tang*, "original stock"). Vegetarians use a stock made by boiling up soybean sprouts, which are thought to have a good (*xian*) taste.

EVERYDAY STOCK
xian tang

This is the Sichuanese all-purpose stock, used for all kinds of soups and sauces. It's not good enough for banquet cooking—for that you'll need the superior recipe below—but it is inexpensive, nourishing, and easy to make. If you use good bones, from traditionally reared or organically produced animals and fowl, all the better. Good butchers will probably give you the bones free of charge or for a nominal fee. Make the stock in large quantities and then freeze it in smaller batches, which can be quickly defrosted when you wish to use them. In restaurants a whole chicken is often used, but I generally just toss in what's left of the carcass when I've removed the breast and leg meat to use in other dishes. You can add some duck or duck bones too if you have them.

about 2 pounds of pork bones	**2-inch piece of fresh ginger,**
about 1 pound of chicken	**with peel, crushed**
parts (wings, backs)	**a couple of scallions**

Smash the chicken carcass and larger bones. Put all the meat and bones into a large pot. Fill with enough water to cover, bring to a rapid boil, and skim. Then add the ginger and scallions, turn down the heat, and simmer gently for 2–3 hours. Strain the liquid and let cool. Cover, keep refrigerated, and use it within a few days, or freeze. Skim off the fat each time you use it.

FINE BANQUET STOCK
te zhi qing tang

特製清湯

Some of Sichuan's most expensive banquet dishes rely on the superb quality of their stocks, which are traditionally made with chicken, duck, pork bones, and ham. The following recipe is adapted from one in the textbook of the Sichuan Culinary Institute. For best results, you should use mature, female chickens and ducks, free-range or organically reared.

NOTE
Sichuanese cooks clarify their stocks by adding pastes made from raw meat, which rise to the surface, collecting the scum. The classic method is first to use a "red paste" made from minced pork mixed with an approximately equal quantity of water, and then a "white paste" made from chicken breasts, again pummeled to a paste and mixed with an approximately equal quantity of water. The cooked pork paste is discarded, but the

cooked chicken breast mixture can be tied up with cheesecloth and left in the clarified stock for another hour, at 200°F, to improve the clarity of the liquid and its flavor. Straining the cooked stock through cheesecloth, however, gives a perfectly respectable result and is the method I use at home.

1 pound chicken pieces (drumsticks, thighs, necks, wings, etc.), preferably from free-range or organically reared birds	**5 quarts water**
	a 2-inch piece of fresh ginger, unpeeled
	1 scallion, white and green parts
1 pound duck pieces	**1 teaspoon Shaoxing rice wine or medium-dry sherry**
1 pound pork spare ribs	
1 pound ham, preferably Smithfield, without rind	**salt and white pepper**

1 For best results, begin by blanching all the meats and poultry pieces (except for the ham) in boiling water to remove any remaining blood and impurities, and then rinse them under the tap. Discard the blanching water.

2 Place all the meats and poultry pieces in a large pot, cover with water, and bring to a boil over a high flame. Skim off any scum that rises to the surface. Crush the ginger slightly with the flat side of a cleaver blade or a heavy object and add it to the stockpot along with the scallion and Shaoxing rice wine. Then cover the pot and simmer very gently over a low flame for about 3 hours. Skim off any fat that gathers on the surface from time to time.

3 When the stock is ready, strain it into a clean pot, using cheesecloth or a very fine sieve. Season with about a teaspoon of salt and a couple of pinches of white pepper (do not use black pepper, which will damage the clear appearance of the stock).

SOUPS

In Guangdong and other parts of southern China, soup is eaten at the start of a meal, to "open the stomach" (*kai wei*) and refresh the appetite. In Sichuan, however, soup is served at the end of the meal, and its function is to cleanse the palate after the intense, heavy flavors of a typical Sichuanese meal. For this reason, Sichuanese soups tend to be clear and delicately flavored. Little effort goes into preparing them in the home and in everyday restaurants—most recipes begin with a simple stir-frying, followed by the addition of stock and "white" seasonings (salt and white pepper). The final soup should be pale and under-salted. Common examples include pickled vegetable and noodle soup, bean curd soup with a few leafy greens and tomato slices, and fried egg and tomato soup (see page 306). Dinner guests pluck the solid pieces from the soup bowl with chopsticks and eat them with rice—when they have eaten their fill of rice, they fill the rice bowls with soup, which they eat with china spoons or simply drink from the bowl. The soup washes down any stray rice grains, ensuring that nothing is wasted. The Chinese always speak of "drinking soup," not eating it. For grander meals, the soup has the same character, although the ingredients used may be exotic and the stock is of a finer quality.

Some soups are more substantial, including perhaps a whole fish or duck, but again the solid ingredients tend to be eaten separately and the clear soup on its own at the end. One notable exception is the hot-and-sour type of soup that is so popular in the West. Hot-and-sour soups are thick with sliv-ered meat and vegetables and intensely flavored. This type of thick soup is known by a distinctive term, *geng*, which dates back to the Zhou Dynasty, when it referred to a mixed meaty soup or stew.

SIMPLE CHICKEN STEW

qing dun quan ji

This is a Sichuanese version of that universal tonic, chicken soup, which brings comfort to the mind and body. The cooking method is designed to bring out and enhance the chicken's natural fla-vors—the ginger, scallions, and wine are merely used to dispel any lingering rankness. Salt is added cautiously at the end, just before the dish goes to the table. The soup can be eaten Sichuan-style, at the end of the meal, or with bread in the Western fash-ion. If you wish to be Chinese about it, serve the chicken in the soup, either in one large bowl or spooned into individual bowls: your guests can pluck out the flesh with their chopsticks and then drink the soup directly from their bowls. Any leftovers are a wonderful base for a simple noodle soup (just cook the noodles separately in boiling water, and then add them to a bowlful of seasoned chicken stock, with a few blanched vegetables and some chicken meat if you like).

1 whole chicken, preferably an organically reared bird (about 4 pounds)	**2 scallions, white and green parts**
a 1-inch piece of fresh ginger, unpeeled	**2 teaspoons Shaoxing rice wine or medium-dry sherry**
	salt and pepper to taste

1 Optional first step: plunge the chicken into a pot of boiling water and return to a boil. Remove and drain (this is done to remove the bloody juices, which improves the flavor of the finished stew).

2 Slightly crush the ginger with the side of a cleaver or a heavy object. Wash and trim the scallions and break them into a few long sections.

3 Place the chicken in a pot or casserole dish with just enough water to cover it (2 1/2–3 1/2 quarts). It's best to use a pot just large enough to accommodate the chicken: this way you won't have to add excessive amounts of water, so the final soup will be richly flavorful. Bring the liquid to a boil over a high flame and skim off any scum that rises to the surface. Add the ginger, scallions, and wine, then turn the heat down and simmer gently, half-covered, until the chicken is very tender and comes easily away from the bone (this will take a couple of hours).

4 Season the soup with salt and pepper to taste (it should be very gently salted), simmer for another 5–10 minutes, and then serve.

PORK AND WHITE RADISH SOUP

lian guo tang

This soup is served at the end of the meal, to wash away the rich flavors of the main dishes: because of this, it is usually under-salted. The radish slices are clear and crunchy even when cooked, the pork slices soft and tender. Dinner guests should use their chopsticks to lift out slices of pork and radish and dip them into the relish. Finally, they should drink the refreshing liquid, either using a china spoon or directly from their rice bowls. The name lian guo tang literally means something like "even the soup in the cooking pot," which may refer to the fact that even the cooking pot was brought to the table with the final soup, marking a thorough conclusion to the meal.

Serves 4 as a Western-style starter, 4–6 as a final soup, Sichuanese-style

FOR THE SOUP
1 pound boneless pork, in one piece (traditionally a mix of fat and lean meat, with skin)
a 1-inch piece of fresh ginger, unpeeled
2 scallions, white and green parts
1 teaspoon whole Sichuan pepper
about 1 pound Asian white radish (daikon)

salt and white pepper
FOR THE RELISH
1 generous handful of dried chiles, preferably Sichuanese
4 tablespoons peanut oil
2 teaspoons whole Sichuan pepper
3 tablespoons Sichuanese chili bean paste
1 tablespoon light soy sauce
1 tablespoon dark soy sauce

1 Bring 2 quarts of water to a boil over a high flame and add the pork. Return the liquid to a boil, skim, and then add the ginger, scallions, and Sichuan pepper. Turn the heat down to a moderate flame and simmer for about 20 minutes, until the pork is just cooked. Remove the pork and set

aside to cool. Remove the remains of the ginger and scallions with a slotted spoon and discard them, reserving the cooking liquid.

2 Wearing rubber gloves, snip the chiles in half and discard as many seeds as possible. Heat the oil in a wok over a moderate flame. Add the chiles and Sichuan pepper and stir-fry briefly until they are crisp and fragrant, taking great care not to burn them (add a little cool oil or remove the wok from the stove if the cooking oil is overheating). Remove the spices with a slotted spoon and set them aside to cool. Return the oily wok to the stove, add the chili bean paste, and stir-fry over a moderate heat for 30–60 seconds, until the oil is a deep red and richly fragrant. Turn the cooked paste with the oil into a bowl.

3 When the chiles and Sichuan pepper have cooled down, chop them finely with a cleaver or in a food processor. Add them to the chili bean paste with the light and dark soy sauces. Mix the relish well and divide into 4 tiny dishes, one for each person.

4 Cut the pork into the thinnest possible slices. Peel the radish, chop it into 2-inch sections, and then cut these lengthwise into very thin slices.

5 Return the soup liquid to a boil, add the radish slices, and simmer for a few minutes, until they are tender. Then add the pork and simmer for another couple of minutes, seasoning to taste with salt and pepper. Turn into a soup bowl and serve.

VARIATIONS

The dishes of relish can be varied as you please. One quick version is simply to mix soy sauce, chili oil with its chile flakes, and sesame oil to taste.

Chinese cabbage or winter melon may be used instead of the white radish.

CHICKEN SOUP WITH PICKLED MUSTARD GREENS

suan cai ji si tang

This soup is extremely easy to make and most delicious. The pickled leaves lend it a delicate sourness and a pale jade color; the chicken slivers are cooked so briefly they're tender and velvety. The Sichuanese would always serve this soup at the end of the meal, to cleanse and refresh the palate, but it makes a fine European-style starter.

In Sichuan this soup is a dish for a special occasion. A more everyday version, which is probably the most common after-dinner soup in Sichuan, is pickled vegetable soup with bean thread noodles (*suan cai fen si tang*). To make this soup, just soak a few dried bean thread noodles in hot water for 20–30 minutes before you begin, and add them to the soup instead of the chicken. Pork slivers can also be used instead of the chicken, for a less refined dish.

Serves 4 as a Western-style starter, 4–6 as a final soup, Sichuanese-style

2 small boneless, skinless chicken breasts (about 1/2 pound)

FOR THE MARINADE

2 teaspoons Shaoxing rice wine or medium-dry sherry
1/2 teaspoon salt
1 1/2 tablespoons egg white

3 3/4 teaspoons cornstarch

OTHER INGREDIENTS

1/4 pound Sichuanese pickled mustard greens
1 quart good chicken stock
salt and white pepper to taste

1 Cut the breasts as evenly as possible into very fine slivers (preferably less than 1/4 inch thick). Place them in a bowl, add the marinade ingredients, and mix well, stirring in one direction. Leave to stand in a cool place for about 15 minutes. Drain the pickled mustard greens and cut them into fine slivers to match the chicken.

325

2 Heat the chicken stock in a wok or saucepan. When it has come to a boil, add the pickled leaves and simmer gently for a couple of minutes until they have lent their flavor to the broth. Season with salt and pepper to taste (if you are serving the soup at the end of the meal, you may wish to follow the Sichuanese practice and keep it slightly undersalted).

3 Add the chicken slivers, using chopsticks to separate them. As soon as they are cooked, pour the soup into a deep bowl and serve immediately.

PLAIN STEWED OXTAIL SOUP

qing dun niu wei tang

清燉牛尾湯

This wonderful winter soup is a specialty of Chongqing. A whole oxtail is simmered gently for many hours, until it is beautifully tender and the fat melty and delicious. The tail is served in a bowl of clarified stock, with a dip of red, spicy, salty relish on the side. It's perfect for a soothing, refreshing end to a Sichuanese meal. The dish is closely associated with Muslim cooking, although these days it is popular outside the Muslim community. The most acclaimed oxtail soup is made by the Old Sichuan (*lao si chuan*) restaurant in central Chongqing, which serves extraordinarily good Sichuanese food with an unusual emphasis on beef dishes.

The cooking method that gives the dish its name, *qing dun*, is a way of stewing meat and poultry, gently, in their own juices, without the addition of salt or other flavorings. The ginger, Sichuan pepper, and Shaoxing wine don't really count as flavorings: they are just used to suppress the strong, rank taste of beef, which is much disliked by Chinese gourmets. The chicken, similarly, is not used to give the dish a chicken flavor, but cunningly to enhance the natural, essential taste of the beef. Salt is never added until the end, just before the dish goes to the table. This method of stewing is often used in the medicinal, curative dishes that are a specialty of Sichuan. They, like this oxtail stew, are about extracting the essences of things, not about the thrill of complex flavors.

One closely related dish is plain stewed beef soup (*qing dun niu rou tang*) made with a good chunk of beef leg and served with strips of crisp daikon (Asian radish). Another is called ox whip soup with Chinese wolfberries (*gou qi niu bian tang*) and comes with a scattering of brilliant scarlet berries. I devoured this with enormous pleasure on my first visit to the Old Sichuan restaurant, relishing the tender meat, the sumptuous stock, and the spicy sauce. It was only later that I discovered "ox whip" was not, as I had assumed, a fancy name for oxtail, but actually a euphemism for ox penis. The dish, another Old Sichuan specialty, is predictably thought to enhance masculine vitality and boost the yang energy of the body. If you are ever lucky enough to visit this marvelous restaurant, you have been warned.

Serves 4–6

1 large oxtail (2–3 pounds) or 2 1/2 pounds thick chunks of oxtail	**1/4 cup Shaoxing rice wine or medium-dry sherry**
2 chicken legs	**salt**
a 3- to 4-inch piece of fresh ginger, unpeeled	**FOR THE RELISH**
2 teaspoons whole Sichuan pepper	**1 tablespoon peanut oil**
	4 tablespoons Sichuanese chili bean paste
	1–2 teaspoons dark soy sauce
	2 teaspoons sesame oil

1 Remove any remnants of skin from the oxtail. Use a sharp knife to cut through to the center of the tail at each joint, all the way around, taking care not to actually sever the joints. You should end up with a series of rings of flesh that are still attached to the central line of bone. Leave the tail to soak for 20 minutes in cold water to remove some of the bloody juices. Then discard the soaking water and rinse the tail.

2 Bring 2 1/2 quarts of water to a boil in a large pan. Add the oxtail and bring to a boil over a high flame. When the water has boiled, use a perforated spoon to skim off as much of the scum that gathers on the surface as possible. Then add the chicken, return to a boil, and skim again. Crush the ginger

with the side of a cleaver blade or a heavy object and throw it into the pan. Add the Sichuan pepper and Shaoxing rice wine. Then half-cover the pan, reduce the heat to a simmer and let the soup bubble away gently for several hours, giving the meat a stir from time to time. The meat should be stewed until it is really tender and comes away easily from the bone—3 hours will do it, although one of my sources suggests simmering it for 7 1/2.

3 Toward the end of the cooking time, remove the tail and the chicken pieces from the pan. Discard the chicken or set it aside to be eaten later. Strain the soup through a piece of muslin in a sieve or colander lined with a double layer of cheesecloth to remove the ginger, pepper, and any remaining scum, and then return it to the pan. Replace the oxtail and continue to simmer until it is beautifully tender.

4 To make the relish, heat the peanut oil in a wok until hot but not smoking. Add the chili bean paste and stir-fry for about 30 seconds until it smells delicious and the oil has turned red. Pour into a small bowl. When the paste has cooled down, add the soy sauce and the sesame oil.

5 When you are ready to eat, transfer the oxtail to a big china bowl or soup tureen. Season the soup lightly with salt to taste, and then pour it over the tail. Serve the soup with the relish. If you want to be really Sichuanese, let everyone pluck pieces of meat from the tail with their chopsticks and dip them into the relish. They can then drink the soup from their rice bowls. Otherwise, you can divide the tail and the soup and serve it individually, Western-style.

VARIATIONS

Plain stewed beef soup—*qing dun niu rou tang*: choose a good chunk of beef rump on the bone. Soak it for 20 minutes in water to cover, drain, and then stew it with chicken, ginger, Sichuan pepper, and wine, as in the recipe above. Toward the end of the cooking time, remove the beef from the soup and cut it against the grain into finger-sized strips, discarding bones, skin, or gristly bits. Strain the soup, discarding the chicken, and then return the beef to the pan and continue to simmer. Peel a daikon (Asian radish) or two and chop them into chunky strips to match the beef. Boil the radish strips until soft in fresh water and add them to the beef stew for a few minutes to absorb some of the flavors. To serve, place the radish strips at the bottom of the soup bowl, add the beef, and then pour over the beef soup. Scatter with fresh coriander (cilantro) if desired. Serve with the chili bean relish described above.

HOT-AND-SOUR SOUP

suan la rou si tang

The combination of hot-and-sour flavorings in soup dishes is popular all over Southeast Asia. But whereas in Thai cooking the hot taste comes from fresh chiles, in this Sichuanese version it is derived from ground pepper. The classic Sichuanese hot-and-sour soup is a banquet dish made from expensive ingredients like a kind of pig's foot tendon (*ti jin*) or dried sea cucumber, but these can be varied at will, because the essence of the dish lies mainly in its combination of flavors. The hot pepper tingles over the lips and warms the heart, while the sour vinegar provides a deep and satisfying contrast. What is also notable is the combination of textures that make it a treat for the mouth, teeth, and tongue.

The following recipe is made with pork slivers and a number of other contrasting ingredients. Vegetarians can substitute thin strips of bean curd, or a few other kinds of mushroom, thinly slivered. Some cooks add beaten egg whites, drizzled into the hot soup after it has been thickened, and allowed to set into "flakes." This kind of thick soup is usually served in the middle of a Chinese meal, unlike the more watery soups that tend to be served at the end. It also works well as a Western-style starter.

The hot-and-sour flavoring style is unusual in Sichuanese cooking because it relies so heavily on pepper instead of the more common chile hotness. When we learned how to make a version of this soup at the Sichuan cooking school, my classmates were shocked at the amount of pepper our teacher added—rather amusing considering their vast capacity for chile eating.

Serves 6–8 (makes enough to fill about 8 small Chinese rice bowls)

1/3 pound boneless, tender,
    lean pork

FOR THE MARINADE

1 teaspoon Shaoxing wine
1/4 teaspoon salt
2 1/4 teaspoons cornstarch
2 teaspoons cold water

OTHER INGREDIENTS

4–5 Chinese dried
    mushrooms
5 ounces fresh or canned
    bamboo shoots
a 1-inch piece of fresh ginger
4 button mushrooms (about 3
    ounces)
4 ounces cooked ham,
    preferably Smithfield,
    thickly cut
3 scallions, green parts only

1 teaspoon sesame oil
1 tablespoon lard or peanut
    oil
1 1/4 quarts everyday stock
    (see page 318) or chicken
    stock
1 tablespoon Shaoxing rice
    wine or medium-dry sherry
1 teaspoon light soy sauce
1 teaspoon dark soy sauce
salt to taste
ground white or black pepper
    to taste
6 tablespoons cornstarch
    mixed with 6–9 tablespoons
    cold water
3–4 tablespoons Chinkiang or
    black Chinese vinegar

1 Place the dried mushrooms in plenty of hot water to soak (they need about 30 minutes). Refresh the canned bamboo shoots by blanching them in lightly salted boiling water for a couple of minutes.

2 Cut the pork into very fine strips and place in a small bowl. Add the marinade ingredients and mix well. Peel and thinly slice the ginger. Thinly slice the button mushrooms and cut the ham into thin strips. Cut the bamboo shoots into very fine strips. When the dried mushrooms are reconstituted, slice them thinly too.

3 Thinly slice the scallion greens and scatter them in a large serving bowl. Drizzle with the sesame oil.

4 Heat the lard or peanut oil in a saucepan or wok over a high flame. Add the ginger and stir-fry for about 30 seconds until it is fragrant. Toss in the bamboo shoots, ham, and dried and fresh mushrooms and stir a few times. Then pour in the stock and bring to a boil.

5 When the liquid is boiling vigorously, skim away any scum with a perforated spoon and discard. Add the Shaoxing rice wine and soy sauces, and season with salt and pepper to taste. The soup should be well salted, and the pepper should give it a really spicy kick without overwhelming the other flavors.

6 Add the pork strips and use a pair of chopsticks to separate them. When they are just about cooked, give the cornstarch mixture a stir and add it to the soup in a couple of stages, mixing well and allowing the liquid a few seconds to thicken before you add a little more. Add just enough cornstarch to give the soup a nice heavy, glossy consistency without making it gloppy. You will probably need just over three-quarters of the mixture, depending on the exact volume of the stock.

7 Finally, turn off the heat and add the vinegar—enough to give the soup a delicious, mellow sourness without making it taste actually vinegary. Pour the soup on to the scallions and sesame oil in the serving bowl, and serve immediately.

JADE WEB SOUP WITH QUAIL EGGS AND BAMBOO PITH FUNGUS

yu wang zhu sun tang

玉
网
竹
蓀
湯

The bamboo pith fungus (*Dictyophora* species) grows in the bamboo forests of southern Sichuan. Here, the landscape is miraculous, beautiful. The bamboo grows lavishly and intensely green, arching over isolated farmhouses, quivering in the gentle breeze. Within the forest the thin, smoke-green bamboo trunks rise smooth and unadorned, exploding overhead into a lushness of leaves. Cataracts spill down the rocky hillsides, over red earth and boulders. The air buzzes with the chatter of birds and insects. Everything is damp and moss-grown, moist and oozing.

The Bamboo Sea isn't only a place to wonder at the scenery—it's also a source of natural medicines and exotic foodstuffs. Several different varieties of bamboo are regarded as delicacies, and there's also the bamboo flower lichen, which grows on the bamboo itself (*zhu hua*); tender bamboo frogs, which can be braised with wild mountain chiles; the famous "ox-liver" mushroom, with its heavy, gelatinous texture; and numerous other wild fungi. According to Sichuanese gourmets, however, the "king of mountain treasures," the "empress of all the fungi," is the magnificent bamboo pith fungus (*zhu sun*).

The fungus has a phallic-looking central section, which is overhung by a delicate lacy white parasol and topped by a darker cap with a forbidding smell. The main part of the plant, including the parasol, has a delicate fragrance and can be eaten fresh, but it is also dried and packed off to other parts of the province and the country. It is most commonly served in soup dishes based on fine clear stocks, where its slithery, crunchy texture and lovely appearance can be most appreciated, but I've also had it stir-fried with chiles and Sichuan pepper to delicious effect. Wild bamboo pith fungus, which grows on the fallen leaves of the bamboo forest, is sold at a premium, but the plant is also cultivated by local farmers. The plant grows in some other parts of China, but the Sichuanese fungus is regarded as particularly fine. Bamboo pith fungus has been eaten in China since at least Tang Dynasty times.

If you visit the Bamboo Sea in springtime, you can sample the extraordinary volvae of the unripe plant, which are known as its "eggs" in Chinese (*zhu sun dan*). These plump mushroom balls, through which the mature fungus eventually bursts, are a pale, pinky brown and usually about the size of a small tangerine. When sliced, they reveal unexpected treasures: a rainbow of layers of pink, white, and gray gelatinous flesh, with a lacy, embryonic fungus curled up within. Local cooks stir-fry these slices with the palest of flavors—salt, chicken stock, and a little garlic, nothing to detract from the main ingredient. The dish, a visual and textural delight, is unforgettable.

Dried bamboo pith fungus can be bought for a reasonable price in Chinese supermarkets. The individual fungi are bundled together, but after soaking they extend to their original form. The quail's eggs are poached in the following recipe, but they can be hard-boiled instead if you prefer.

Serves 6

15 whole dried bamboo pith fungi (about 1/2 ounce)

12 quail eggs

1 1/4 quarts good chicken stock

salt and white pepper to taste

1 Soak the fungi in lightly salted hot water for about 15 minutes, until they become soft and silky. Then rinse them well under the tap, washing away any gritty bits. Snip off and discard the bases of the fungi with a pair of scissors, then cut them into 2-inch sections. Cut the frilly parasol sections of the fungi into smaller pieces if necessary.

2 Bring the stock to a boil and season with salt and pepper to taste (Sichuanese cooks would tend to undersalt it). Add the bamboo fungus and simmer gently for 10–15 minutes until it has absorbed the flavors of the stock.

3 Bring some water to a boil in a shallow pan, add a little salt, and then turn the heat down to a gentle simmer and break the eggs into the water to poach to your liking. When the eggs are done, trim off any raggy bits if you wish and place the eggs in a serving bowl. Top with the prepared bamboo pith fungi, pour over the seasoned stock, and serve.

CHICKEN "BEAN CURD" SOUP

ji dou hua

The elaborate culinary trick has long been a part of Chinese food culture and is a measure of the great sophistication of Chinese cuisine. Vegetarian dishes that look and taste like meat or fish are a notable feature of cooking in Buddhist monasteries and restaurants, but in the following Sichuanese specialty, an apparently plain vegetarian dish turns out to be made from expensive chicken breast. The chicken is pummeled to a purée and then set into a kind of curd that looks exactly like the inexpensive "flower" bean curd that is a popular peasant snack. As they say, it's "flower bean curd without the beans; chicken without the appearance of chicken" (*dou hua bu yong dou, chi ji bu jian ji*). Apart from being witty, this gentle soup is most delicious, with its fine stock, dainty garnish of leafy greens, and scattering of dark pink ham.

Serves 6–8

about 1 ounce cooked ham, preferably Smithfield

a few tender green leaves of baby bok choy, cabbage, or bibb lettuce

2 boneless, skinless chicken breasts (about 1/2 pound)

1 3/4 quarts chicken stock

5 large egg whites (about 1/2 cup)

2 tablespoons cornstarch mixed with 2 tablespoons cold water

1 teaspoon Shaoxing rice wine or medium-dry sherry

salt and white pepper

1 Finely chop the cooked ham and set aside. Blanch the green leaves in boiling water and then refresh immediately under the tap. Set aside.

2 Remove as much fat and tendon as possible from the chicken breasts. Place them in a food processor with about 1 cup of cold chicken stock and whizz to a very fine paste. Transfer the paste to a large bowl. Use your hand to mix in another half-cup of cold stock. Combine the egg whites and cornstarch mixture and add them to the chicken a little at a time. Use your hand to whip everything together thoroughly after each batch, before the rest is added. Stir in the Shaoxing rice wine and about 3/4 teaspoon of salt.

3 Bring the stock to a boil. Give the chicken mixture another good stir and then pour it all into the stock. Give it one good mix to prevent it from sticking to the bottom of the pan and then leave it alone. Bring the pan back to a very gentle simmer and leave it for about 5 minutes, until the chicken "curd" has set and is thoroughly cooked.

4 Put the blanched green leaves into your serving bowl. Then gently scoop the chicken curd into the bowl, taking care not to let it disintegrate too much. Strain over some of the clear stock, and then scatter with the chopped ham.

5 Serve immediately.

CHICKEN BALLS IN CLEAR SOUP

qing tang ji yuan

  A bowl of clear soup, with pale chicken balls floating, wisps of green leaves drifting—this is a favorite Sichuanese banquet soup. The chicken balls are made from white breast meat, with a little seasoning and some egg white and cornstarch to help them keep their shape. Sichuanese chefs usually beat the chicken breast to a paste using only the back of their cleaver blades. It's a little laborious, but helps to make the final chicken balls wonderfully smooth. If you use a food processor, the recipe is much quicker and easier to make, but still unusual and delicious. For those who'd like to try the traditional method, I've given instructions below. Please note that the chicken balls can be cooked a little in advance, kept in cold water in the refrigerator, and then reheated when you wish to serve them. They freeze very well too.

Serves 4–6 as a Western-style starter, 6 as a final soup, Sichuanese-style

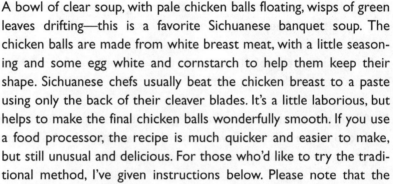

2 skinless, boneless chicken breasts (about 1/2 pound)
1–1 1/4 quarts clear chicken stock
3–4 egg whites (1/2 cup)
1 tablespoon chicken fat or lard

salt and white pepper
1 1/2 tablespoons cornstarch mixed with 2–3 teaspoons cold water
a handful of bok choy leaves or napa cabbage leaves

1 Remove and discard the large tendons in the chicken breasts and any visible wisps of fat or smaller tendons. Put the meat into a food processor with 1/4 cup of the stock and whizz to a really smooth paste.

2 Transfer the chicken paste to a decent-sized mixing bowl and add the egg whites in several stages, mixing in one direction. Take care to blend in each batch of egg white thoroughly before you add the next. It is best to stir the mixture by hand, separating your fingers so they work like a kind of whisk, but you can use a wooden whisk if you'd rather not get mucky. When the egg whites are all incorporated, add the chicken fat or lard and 1/4–1/2 teaspoon of salt. Mix well, still stirring in one direction. Finally, add the cornstarch mix-

ture and stir for 3–5 minutes more until the mixture has stiffened slightly. You should end up with a mixture about the consistency of cake batter.

3 Blanch the green leaves in a little boiling water and then refresh them in cold water to keep their color.

4 Bring a large pot of clean water to a boil on one burner, and heat up the remaining stock on another.

5 When the stock is hot, dip the green leaves into it for a few seconds to absorb some chicken flavors and then lay them in the bottom of a deep serving bowl. Leave the stock to simmer gently.

6 When the water has boiled, turn it down to a gentle simmer. Then use your hands to make the chicken balls: take a small handful of chicken paste in one hand and make a gentle fist, thumb side up. Gently squeeze the paste up through the hole between your thumb and index finger until you have a blob about the size of a cherry tomato. Use your other hand, palm up, to scoop the blob from the top of your fist and drop it very gently into the simmering water. It is best to hold this hand very close to the surface of the water so the chicken ball holds its shape. Repeat until you have used up all the chicken paste. Simmer the chicken balls for about 3 minutes until they are just cooked, and then transfer them to the serving bowl with a perforated spoon. You may wish to cook them in two or three batches.

7 Finally, season the stock to taste with salt and pepper and pour it over the chicken balls and green leaves in the bowl. Serve immediately.

VARIATION

Meatball soup—*jiu zi tang*: for more everyday soup, make the meatballs from pork instead of chicken, use an egg or two instead of egg white only, and add a little finely chopped ginger to the paste. Cook the meatballs in the stock itself, taking care to skim off any scum that rises as they cook. Finally, add a few pretty vegetables to the soup: perhaps bok choy leaves or pea shoots, soaked lily buds (*huang hua*), soaked cloud ear mushrooms, or sliced tomatoes. When you have gently poured the soup into the serving bowl, you may wish to scatter over a few slices of green scallion.

TO MAKE THE CHICKEN PASTE BY HAND

Pummel the chicken breasts with the blunt side of a cleaver blade, or use two cleaver blades held side by side, until they are really pulpy. Keep turning the pile of paste to ensure an even pummeling, removing any visible wisps of stringy white tendon. When you have made a pretty smooth paste, lay the cleaver blade almost parallel to the cutting board and draw the blade across the pulp, smearing the paste to the board so you can see and remove every last tendon. The reason for using this laborious method rather than a food processor or the sharp side of the cleaver blade is that you won't chop up the tendons, so with a little patience you can remove them all whole, giving the final paste a superlatively smooth texture.

SIMPLE BEAN CURD SOUP

dou fu tang

This amazingly simple soup is typical of everyday Sichuanese cooking and is often drunk at the end of the meal.

Serves 4–6

1 large tomato (about 1/3 pound)	salt and pepper
1/2 pound bean curd	a generous handful of bok choy leaves or napa cabbage leaves
1 quart everyday stock (see page 318) or chicken stock	

1 Cut the tomato in half and then into thickish slices (about 1/8 inch thick). Cut the bean curd into squares of a similar thickness and leave in a pot of very gently simmering, lightly salted water to refresh for a few minutes. Wash the leaves, discarding any tough bits.

2 Bring the stock to a boil and season to taste with salt and pepper. Add the drained bean curd and simmer for a few minutes to let it absorb the flavors of the stock. Add the tomato slices and cook for 10–20 seconds until they are just tender. Add the leaves, stir once or twice and then pour everything into a serving bowl.

337

8

sweet dishes

UNUSUALLY AMONG THE WORLD'S GREATEST CULINARY
nations, the Chinese traditionally have little taste for sweetness. Although
sweets and candied fruits may be enjoyed as nibbles, especially around the
Chinese New Year, most meals are entirely savory, with sugar used just in
very small quantities as a seasoning. One or two sweet dishes, such as eight-
treasure wok pudding, do occasionally feature on banquet menus, but they
are always served as an intermediate course and rarely at the end of the
meal as in the Western dessert tradition. Various sugary dumplings and other
sweets are sold by Sichuanese street vendors: recipes for some of these can
be found in the chapter on street food (page 84).

SILVER EAR FUNGUS IN CRYSTAL SUGAR SOUP

yin'er geng

This exotic-sounding soup has a wonderful texture. The dried fungus, soaked and steamed until it is meltingly soft, lolls in the soup
in translucent, diaphanous waves. The liquid is heavy but not sickly
sweet. Sweet soups are a curious idea to Westerners, but they do
make a refreshing and intriguing conclusion to a meal. This one is
sometimes offered as a sort of final *digestif* after a banquet of
Sichuanese snacks, when it is served to each guest in a separate,

tiny bowl. I have also enjoyed it at the end of a more standard Chinese meal, when it is served in one large bowl and dished up at the table. According to Chinese medicine, silver ear fungus moistens the lungs and replenishes the yin energies of the body. This soup is seen as particularly nutritious for the elderly. Some restaurants add a few peeled tangerine segments or pineapple chunks, but I prefer the simplicity of the recipe below. Most cookbooks suggest steaming the soup, but you can also simmer it over a very low flame (stirring from time to time to prevent sticking) or do as my Sichuanese friend Peng Li does and leave it to stew gently in an electric crockpot.

Serves 4–6

1/2 ounce dried silver ear fungus

1 cup rock sugar, crushed
3 cups water

1 Soak the fungus in hot water for about 15 minutes until soft. Then pick out any hard bits and impurities with your fingers, and tear it into smaller pieces if necessary.

2 Dissolve the sugar in the water over a gentle flame. Add the fungus and then transfer to the top of a double boiler or to a bowl that you can place in your steamer. Bring the water at the bottom of the double boiler or steamer to a boil, cover, and steam over a medium flame for 2 hours. Remember to replenish the steaming water from a boiling kettle as necessary.

3 Serve hot (although it's also delicious cold).

EIGHT-TREASURE WOK PUDDING
ba bao guo zheng

This sweet dish, often served at Sichuanese banquets, has a moist cakey texture a little reminiscent of some Indian sweetmeats and is studded with delicious pieces of fruit and walnuts. In Sichuan it is served alongside savory dishes, but it can also be eaten as a Western-style dessert.

Serves 4–6

1 tablespoon walnut kernels
3/4 cup peanut oil or lard
about 3 ounces (6 tablespoons, total) dried or candied fruits, as varied as possible (perhaps 1/2 ounce dates, 1 ounce candied cherries, 1 ounce mixed candied peel, 1/2 ounce dried blueberries)
1 cup all-purpose flour
1 cup boiling water
1/2 cup sugar

1 Fry the walnuts in just enough oil to cover them (about 1/4 cup), over a medium flame, until they are golden and fragrant. Remove, drain, and chop into small pieces.

2 Finely chop all the dried and candied fruits.

3 Heat the rest of the oil in a wok over a medium flame. Add all the flour and stir-fry for about 10 minutes, stirring constantly and scraping the bottom of the wok. Turn the heat down if the flour is at risk of burning. When the mixture is turning a little yellow and smells cooked and cakey, stand back from the wok and pour in some of the boiling water (steam will whoosh up out of the wok). Stir well and add the rest of the water. Stir in the sugar, give it a few seconds to dissolve, and then mix in all the nuts and dried fruits. Mix well, adding a little more oil if necessary to moisten it, and then tip onto a serving plate. Eat while hot.

EIGHT-TREASURE RICE PUDDING
ba bao fan

When this sticky rice pudding is turned out of its steaming bowl, the white mound of rice is inlaid with a mosaic of dried and candied fruits and seeds. The rice is sweet and succulent, steaming hot. "Eight-treasure" refers to the selection of fruits and seeds, which may include dried lily buds, Chinese dates, and candied peel. The most important thing is just to have a nice mixture of colors and tastes, so feel free to be creative with whatever's in your pantry. Slivered almonds and pine nuts would make a fine addition, and candied angelica could also be used. Sichuanese cooks make this recipe with lard, but I don't much like the taste of it in sweet dishes and have substituted peanut oil—it works just as well and tastes much lighter. For grander meals this pudding is doused with a clear sugar syrup, but cooks often sprinkle it with a little white sugar instead. Sushi rice can be used instead of glutinous rice.

Serves 4 as a dessert, 6 with a selection of savory dishes as part of a Chinese meal

1 1/4 cups white glutinous rice
a colorful selection of dried and candied fruits: for example, 10 dried Chinese dates, 2 tablespoons dried blueberries, 6 candied cherries, 2 tablespoons cut mixed citrus peel, 2 tablespoons large, pale sultanas (yellow raisins)
1/2 cup white sugar
3 tablespoons peanut oil

FOR THE SYRUP
2/3 cup white or crystal sugar
2 tablespoons water

1 Rinse the rice thoroughly under the cold tap, then leave it to soak in plenty of cold water for about 2 hours. Put the Chinese dates, blueberries, or any other dried fruits to soak in hot water.

2 When the rice has been soaked, drain it well and put it into a bowl with 1 cup water. Place the bowl in your steamer and steam over a high flame

341

for 20–25 minutes. Then remove from the heat and stir in the sugar and peanut oil.

3 Cut the cherries and Chinese dates in half and remove the stones from the dates. Oil a shallow bowl that will fit into your steamer (I use a bowl that is 8 inches in diameter and 2 inches deep). Arrange all the dried and candied fruits in an attractive pattern on the base of the bowl. The Chinese usually arrange them in 6 lines radiating from a piece of fruit in the center, with a few colorful bits and pieces in between, but you can be as inventive as you like. When the pattern is finished, carefully add a layer of rice mixture to the bowl, taking care not to move the pieces of fruit. Mix the remaining rice with any leftover fruits, and press it gently into the bowl. You should end up with a full bowl of rice.

4 Place the bowl in the steamer and steam over a high flame for another 15 minutes.

5 When the pudding is nearly ready, make the syrup. Dissolve the sugar in the water over a gentle heat and let it simmer until it reduces to a heavy syrup.

6 Finally, remove the pudding bowl from the steamer and cover it with a serving plate. Working swiftly, invert the plate and bowl, turning the beautifully patterned rice onto the serving dish. Pour the syrup over it and serve immediately.

9

hotpot

IF YOU WANDER AROUND CHENGDU ON A SUMMER'S
evening, you'll find the streets filled with diners, their tables scattered across
the sidewalks in the shade of leafy trees. Many will be gathered around bubbling hotpots, in which dozens of dried chiles bob up and down in an oily red
broth. There they'll while away the hours, chatting, sipping beer, and dipping
morsels of food into the soup to cook. Hotpot—literally "firepot"—is one of
Sichuan's most popular dishes and a favorite excuse for a get-together with
family or friends. Untold thousands of restaurants across the region are
devoted to it, and in its hometown of Chongqing there is even a "Hotpot
Street." Fancy restaurants lavish with marble and chandeliers serve it up, while
beneath the steel supports of city overpasses, workers hunker down to eat it,
paying a few *jiao* at a time for a skewer of food to plunge into the spicy broth.

The "hotpot" itself, a wok or saucepan filled with a dark, rich soup, sits on
a stove, whether it's a charcoal brazier on the sidewalk, a gas burner in a specially cut-out restaurant table, or just a portable burner on the floor at home.
Around it, "like stars around the moon," are arrayed dozens of small plates,
each piled high with a different ingredient. Slender bean sprouts, crisp green
leaves, air-dried sausages, all kinds of innards, and many varieties of mushroom
are often favored, but elegant restaurants also serve exotic seafood and
whole little fish. Guests select pieces of food from this tempting array and
drop them into the soup to cook. Then, after a few minutes' chat and a few
sips of beer, they lift them out with their chopsticks and dip them into a delicious mixture of seasoned sesame oil and chopped garlic. This style of eating

is found in various parts of China, but the deep-red "hot-and-numbing" hotpot is unique to Sichuan.

The Sichuanese love to spend whole days or evenings eating hotpot, sitting around the simmering wok for hours on end. The end of the meal is comfortably undefined: you just cook, and eat, and eat, and cook for as long as you fancy. The pace ebbs and flows, with bursts of enthusiastic gobbling followed by gentle lulls of inactivity. Even when the meal is naturally drawing to a close, there is usually someone still exploring the soup for a forgotten tidbit.

Hotpot makes a fiery winter dish, potent at expelling the creeping dampness of the Sichuan winter. But the Sichuanese are peculiar among the Chinese in eating their spicy hotpot all year round. Even at the height of summer, hotpot restaurants are overflowing with customers who fan themselves in the sweltering heat even as they swallow another mouthful of chile-laden food.

Eating Sichuan's "hot-and-numbing" hotpot produces the most delicious physical sensation, a warmth and relaxation that begins in the belly and radiates out to all the extremities of the body, soothing away tension and anxiety, calming the mind and spirit. Early in the twentieth century, opium was thrown into the broth to enhance this effect, and used by devious restaurant owners to make sure their customers came back for more. Today, this practice is illegal under China's strict drugs laws, but it still crops up occasionally, and in recent years a number of Chengdu restaurateurs have been fined the equivalent of thousands of dollars for slipping opium into their soup. Amazingly, however, opium poppy heads can still sometimes be found in the markets of Sichuan, nestling innocently among the cinnamon bark and star anise as though they were any other spice. I encountered them once during a summer lunch party in a small town near Chengdu. Some friends set up a hotpot on their kitchen floor and we all sat around it on little stools to eat. There was a perceptible change of mood as the meal progressed. Conversation at the beginning was animated, with wit and laughter, but gradually an intoxicated stupor overcame us all and we just fell asleep, on armchairs, sofas, anywhere. Only later, after a long, blissful siesta had restored me to my senses, did I notice the enormous poppy heads bobbing around in the pot.

Chinese scholars trace the origins of this kind of eating back thousands of years. People in China were cooking food in a soup over a fire, an embryonic form of hotpot, before the time of Confucius, who lived in the fifth century B.C. Lin Hong, a Song Dynasty (960–1279) writer, describes a group of people cooking broth on a tabletop stove and sitting around it to eat pieces of a rabbit they'd caught, with each person using a skewer to cook their own meat. But the practice is thought to have gained popularity only in the Ming and Qing periods (1368–1644 and 1644–1911), and the famous eighteenth-century gourmet Yuan Mei declared that "when entertaining guests on winter days, it is customary to serve hotpot." During the Qing Dynasty, the hotpot was adopted by the imperial court and appeared on the emperor's winter menu. The fashion reached ludicrous heights of extravagance at the feast held to mark the enthronement of the Emperor Jia Qing in 1796, when the imperial kitchen staff laid on no fewer than 1,550 hotpots for the guests!

Sichuan hotpot, with its characteristic spicy broth, has more humble origins. It was born on the banks of the river at Chongqing, where bamboo pole–bearing peddlers sold their wares. Meat dealers would haul a load of water buffalo innards in from the countryside and wash, chop, and parboil it. Then a pot of chiles, Sichuan pepper, and broth would be set up on a stove by the river, and workers would gather round to eat, each paying a few *jiao* for a skewer of meat to warm them up. This original "beef tripe hotpot" (*mao du huo guo*) is the grandfather of today's more elaborate dish.

Only in the 1930s did a Chongqing restaurateur elevate the Sichuan hotpot to a restaurant table. Now, more than sixty years later, the dish is enjoyed wherever there are Sichuanese people. It has shed its reputation as a poor man's dish and has become extremely fashionable. Beef tripe is still a popular dipping ingredient, but the original riverside menu has expanded wildly since the early days, with the addition of ever more exotic meats, vegetables, and seafoods. One restaurant I visited recently offered the following hotpot menu: beef tripe, cow's throat tendons (*huang hou*), squid, crucian carp, hairtail fish (*dai yu*), eels, loaches (*ni qiu*), poultry gizzards, sliced pig's kidneys, smoked bacon, Sichuanese cured sausage (*xiang chang*), rabbit's kidneys, rabbit's stomachs, fatty beef, goose intestines, pig's intestines, pig's brains, luncheon meat, crispy pork, meatballs, tender beef, "chicken-leg" mushrooms (*ji tui gu*), fragrant mushrooms (*xiang gu*), button mushrooms (*mo gu*), oyster mushrooms (*ping gu*), golden needle mushrooms (*jin zhen gu*), white seaweed (*hai bai cai*), lettuce stems (*qing sun*), lotus roots, winter melon, bamboo shoots, potatoes, sheet seaweed (*hai dai*), konnyaku yam jelly (*mo yu*), sweet potato noodles (*fen tiao*), cauliflower, jellied duck's blood, wood ear fungus, bean curd skin, Chinese cabbage, bean sprouts, Chinese leeks (*suan miao*), water spinach, lily buds, rice jelly, celery, tomatoes, various types of fish, duck tongues, frogs, and chicken kidneys.

On the streets, an inexpensive version of hotpot, known simply as "hot-and-numbing scalding broth" (*ma la tang*), is still immensely popular. Here, customers help themselves to tiny morsels of food impaled on bamboo skewers, which they dip into the spicy soup. A single skewer might hold a spinach leaf, a slice of bean curd, a strip of eel, or a rabbit's kidney. The final bill is calculated simply by adding up the number of empty skewers each customer has acquired. There are many other types of hotpot, too, from the spicy fish-head hotpot served with dips of crushed nuts and coriander, to the fabled "chrysanthemum flower pot," which includes a plate of white chrysanthemum blossoms with stems and stamens removed—a banquet dish of the highest order.

The original Chongqing hotpot is the fieriest of them all—a response to the oppressively humid climate of this "furnace city." Chongqing people make their hotpot with small, pointed chiles that are much hotter than the popular Chengdu varieties, and they use them with a reckless abandon. The last time I ate hotpot in Chongqing, the early summer heat was already so intense that the air was almost soupy and people were walking around in slow motion, fanning themselves and mopping their brows. We sat, my friends and I, by the banks of the river where the workers used to gather, fighting the steamy atmosphere with the searing heat of chiles. In Chengdu, eating hotpot doesn't have to be such an intense experience. Most restaurants offer hotpots with a central partition in a "yin-yang" design, so you can have one half filled with the traditional spicy broth and one half filled with a mild soup made from fish and chicken.

SICHUAN HOTPOT
si chuan huo guo

四川火鍋

Making a Sichuan hotpot is a wonderfully easy and delightful way to entertain. You can make the hotpot broth in advance, and preparing the dipping ingredients doesn't take long. It's also a relaxed way of eating, and particularly enjoyable alfresco on a warm summer's evening.

To make this dish, you will need a portable burner that can sit in the center of your dining table, within reach of all your guests. The hotpot itself can be a wok or an ordinary saucepan. If you have two cooking rings or a special hotpot wok with a central partition, you can serve a spicy and a mild soup at the same meal and allow people to use them according to their tastes. You can also provide, if you wish, a slotted spoon, a little wire net, or even a tea strainer for catching elusive morsels of food.

SPICY HOTPOT BROTH (*hong tang lu*)

The amounts of chiles and Sichuan pepper used in this broth are very much a matter of personal taste. In Chongqing they use even larger quantities of very hot chiles (often a thin variety from Yunnan called the *xiao mi jiao*). In the following recipe, I've suggested using an amount that I find pleasantly spicy but not overwhelming: you can adjust it if you wish. The dipping ingredients served with this kind of hotpot usually include several different types of innards. Many are simply unavailable in the United States, and unless you have a real appreciation of texture as the Chinese do, you won't see the point of eating them anyway. For these reasons, I have offered a list of suggested dipping ingredients that are both appealing to Western tastes and in keeping with the Sichuanese tradition. You can vary them as you will.

Serves 4–6

1/4 cup fermented black beans

1/3 cup Shaoxing rice wine or medium-dry sherry

a 3-inch piece of fresh ginger, unpeeled

1/4 cup dried Sichuanese chiles

1/2 cup peanut or vegetable oil

2/3 cup beef dripping or lard

1/2 cup Sichuanese chili bean paste

about 3 quarts good beef stock or everyday stock (see page 318)

1 tablespoon rock sugar

optional: 1/3 cup Sichuanese fermented glutinous rice wine

salt to taste

1 teaspoon whole Sichuan pepper

1 Mash the black beans with 1 tablespoon of the Shaoxing wine, either with a

mortar and pestle or in a food processor, until you have a smooth paste. Wash the ginger and cut it into slices about the thickness of a coin.

2 Snip all the chiles into halves or into 1-inch sections with a pair of scissors, and discard as many seeds as possible. Heat 3 tablespoons of the peanut or vegetable oil in a wok over a medium flame until it is hot but not smoking. Add all the chiles and stir-fry them briefly until they are crisp and fragrant, taking great care not to burn them (the oil should sizzle gently around the chiles). Remove them with a slotted spoon and set aside. Pour the cooking oil into a separate container and set aside. Give the wok a quick rinse and dry it thoroughly.

3 Place the beef dripping and the rest of the peanut or vegetable oil into a wok and heat over a gentle flame until the dripping has melted completely. Then turn the heat up to medium. When the oils are just beginning to smoke (250–300°F), add all the chili bean paste and stir-fry for a minute or so until the oil is richly red and fragrant. The paste should sizzle gently—take care not to burn it (you can switch off the heat for a few seconds if it is in danger of overheating). When the oil has reddened, add the mashed black beans and the ginger and continue to stir-fry until they are fragrant. Then pour in about 1 1/2 quarts of the stock and bring it to a boil. (The rest of the stock will be used for topping up the hotpot as you eat—see page 352.)

4 When the liquid has come to a boil, add the rock sugar and the rest of the Shaoxing rice wine, with the fermented rice wine if you have it, and salt to taste.

5 Finally, add the prepared chiles and Sichuan pepper according to taste and leave the broth to simmer for 15–20 minutes, until it is wonderfully spicy.

PLAIN HOTPOT BROTH (bai tang lu)

There are a number of ways of making this kind of broth. The most elaborate is to follow the instructions for making fine banquet stock on page 319, but if you don't feel like being so extravagant, you can use the recipe below. Many Sichuanese cooks would enhance the chicken stock by adding some stock made from little crucian carp, which have a wonderful flavor.

Serves 4–6

2 tablespoons Shaoxing rice wine or medium-dry sherry	**salt to taste**
about 3 quarts rich chicken stock	**1 ripe red tomato, halved**
	2 scallions, white parts only, cut into 2 or 3 sections

Stir the wine into the chicken stock and season it with salt to taste. Pour about 2 quarts of stock into your hotpot and use the rest to top it up as the meal progresses. Shortly before you place the hotpot before your guests, add the tomato and scallions.

DIPPING INGREDIENTS

What you dip into your hotpot is very much a matter of personal taste. The greater the variety in flavors, colors, and textures, the more enjoyable the hotpot will be. Preparing the dipping ingredients is also very easy, so buy as many different kinds as you can. Aim for at least 8–12 different ingredients for a party of 4–6 people. Buy enough of each ingredient to pile high a small plate. In Sichuan it is customary to serve each dipping ingredient on a separate plate, but you can pile them up on one great platter if you wish.

The following foods are all recommended as dipping ingredients, but do feel free to improvise!

Chinese air-dried sausages, cut into short sections

chicken breasts, very thinly sliced

pork tenderloin, very thinly sliced

lean beef or lamb, very thinly sliced

cooked meats of all kinds, sliced

smoked bacon, thickly sliced

firm bean curd, thickly sliced

dry bean curd skin, soaked until soft

shiitake mushrooms, whole

oyster mushrooms, whole

button mushrooms, whole

enoki mushrooms, whole

large flat mushrooms, cut into chunky slices

any other kind of fresh mushroom

wood ear or cloud ear mushrooms, presoaked in hot water for at least 30 minutes

Chinese dried mushrooms, presoaked in hot water for at least 30 minutes

Asian radishes or turnips, peeled and thickly sliced

lotus roots, scraped clean, sliced, and soaked in lightly salted water

potatoes, peeled, thickly sliced and soaked in lightly salted water

water spinach, cut into lengths

soybean sprouts, whole

cauliflower, cut into florets

broccoli, cut into florets

winter melon, deseeded, peeled, and cut into thick slices

fresh coriander (cilantro)

Less traditional ingredients include:

fresh squid, cut into bite-size pieces

shelled prawns

FOR THE SEASONING DIPS

sesame oil

peanut or vegetable oil

plenty of garlic, finely chopped (at least one head of garlic for every 4 people)

salt

EATING THE HOTPOT

You can serve your hotpot broth in a wok or an ordinary saucepan—if you use a wok, make sure you have a wok stand to keep it stable. Place the pot on a portable burner in the middle of your dining-table. Arrange all the raw dipping ingredients on plates around the cooking ring. Give each guest a small rice bowl and a pair of chopsticks and allow them to mix their own seasoning dips: suggested quantities for each person are 2 tablespoons of peanut or vegetable oil, 2–3 teaspoons of sesame oil, 1–2 tablespoons of finely chopped (not crushed) garlic, and salt to taste. Leave the oils and salt with a bowlful of chopped garlic on the table so people can top up their dips as they need to.

Bring the hotpot to a boil and allow the beef drippings to melt if you are heating them from cold. When it is bubbling away merrily, you can begin to cook and eat. Just encourage everyone to tip pieces of prepared food into the hotpot at their leisure and allow the food to cook. When the food is ready, it can be fished out with chopsticks, dipped into the seasonings, and eaten. The whole Sichuan pepper and chiles are not meant to be eaten. Some kinds of food, such as bean sprouts, will be ready very quickly; others, such as potatoes, will take several minutes.

As the liquid in the hotpot evaporates, top it up with fresh stock, adding more salt if necessary. Allow the stock to return to a boil before you continue cooking.

If you have any food left over, the same hotpot broth can be reheated the following day!

the 23 flavors of Sichuan

Here follows a brief explanation of the twenty-three complex flavors which are at the heart of the Sichuanese culinary canon. The first four are the most famously associated with Sichuanese cookery, and most of the following seven are also typically local. The remainder overlap more significantly with the tastes of China's other cooking regions.

1 **Homestyle flavor** (家常味型 *jia chang wei xing*): This uniquely Sichuanese taste is based on the hearty flavors of domestic cooking. Homestyle dishes are described as salty, savory, and a little bit hot (*han xian wei la*). The basic seasonings used are typically local: chili bean paste, salt, and soy sauce. Pickled red chiles, fermented black beans, and sweet fermented paste can also have a role to play. Examples: twice-cooked pork, salt-fried pork, homestyle bean curd, Tai Bai chicken.

2 **Fish-fragrant flavor** (魚香味型 *yu xiang wei xing*): Another celebrated Sichuanese invention, based on the seasonings used in traditional fish cookery, this flavor combines salty, sweet, sour, and spicy notes, with the heady fragrance of garlic, ginger, and scallions. The core seasoning is pickled red chiles, either on their own or mixed with fava beans in Sichuanese chili bean paste, which give fish-fragrant dishes their distinctive orange-red hue. Examples: fish-fragrant sauce for cold chicken, fish-fragrant pork slivers, fish-fragrant eggplants.

3 **Strange-flavor** (怪味味型 *guai wei wei xing*): Also uniquely Sichuanese, this type of flavor is based on the harmonious mixing of salty (*han*), sweet (*tian*), numbing (*ma*), hot (*la*), sour (*suan*), fresh-savory (*xian*), and fragrant (*xiang*) notes. No individual flavor should clamor for the attention at the expense of any other; each should be equally stressed. Examples: strange-flavor chicken, strange-flavor peanuts.

4 **Hot-and-numbing flavor** (麻辣味型 *ma la wei xing*): This is the flavoring style most strongly associated with Sichuanese food, particularly with hearty peasant cooking. It is based on a delicious double whammy of chiles and Sichuan pepper, backed up with salt and other secondary seasonings, such as sugar, sesame oil, and occasionally five-spice powder. The level of fieriness varies widely from place to place: the people of Chongqing have a fabled appetite for extremely hot-and-numbing dishes, a consequence, they say, of the city's oppressively warm and humid climate. Examples: hot-and-numbing dried beef, pock-marked Mother Chen's bean curd (*ma po dou fu*), boiled beef slices in a fiery sauce, dry-fried beef slivers, Sichuan hotpot.

5 **Red-oil flavor** (紅油味型 *hong you wei xing*): This describes a delicious mixture of ruby-red chili oil, soy sauce, and sugar, perhaps with a little sesame oil thrown in for extra fragrance. It combines salty (*han*), savory (*xian*), hot (*la*), and fragrant (*xiang*) tastes with a hint of sweetness in the aftertaste and is used in cold dishes. Example: chicken chunks in red-oil sauce.

6 **Garlic paste flavor** (蒜泥味型 *suan ni wei xing*): A scrumptious combination of mashed garlic, chili oil, and sesame oil with a special soy sauce that has been simmered with brown sugar and spices until it is dense and fragrant. This gently spicy sauce is used on cold meat and vegetable dishes. Example: cold pork in hot and garlicky sauce.

7 **Scorched chili flavor** (煳辣味型 *hu la wei xing*): As its name suggests, this type of flavor is derived from frying dried chiles in a wok until they are crisp, fragrant, and just turning color; other ingredients are then added and tossed in the chili-flavored oil. Sichuan pepper is typically used in conjunction with the chiles, and soy sauce, vinegar, sugar, ginger, scallions, and garlic are often added to create a complex flavor that is fragrant, hot, salty, and savory, with a slightly sweet aftertaste (*xiang la han xian, hui wei lue tian*). The tricky thing about making scorched-chile dishes is that the cooking oil must be hot enough to make the chiles fragrant, but must not burn them. I find that the safest way to achieve this is to throw the chiles into the wok before the oil is smoking hot—you can then continue heating the oil until they sizzle, but you don't run the risk of burning them immediately. Examples: Gong Bao (Kung Pao) chicken with peanuts, spicy cucumber salad.

8 Tangerine-peel flavor (陳皮味型 *chen pi wei xing*): Dried tangerine peel gives this flavor its distinctive fragrance, but always against a background of hot-and-numbing chiles and Sichuan pepper. You might also find a subtly sweet aftertaste. All Sichuanese cooks warn that you mustn't exaggerate the amount of tangerine peel you use or the food will taste bitter. This type of flavor is generally used for cold dishes made from meat and poultry. Example: spicy beef slices with tangerine peel.

9 Sichuan pepper flavor (椒麻味型 *jiao ma wei xing*): This curious-tasting flavor derives, oddly enough, from raw Sichuan pepper, which is mashed with green scallions and salt, and then mixed with a little soy sauce and sesame oil. The Sichuan pepper should give the sauce an amazing numbing quality—it's not worth making if your Sichuan pepper isn't fresh and bursting with fragrance. Used for cold meat, poultry and offal dishes. Example: chicken slices in Sichuan pepper and sesame oil sauce.

10 Sichuan pepper and salt flavor (椒鹽味型 *jiao yan wei xing*): A simple combination of ground dry-roasted Sichuan pepper and salt, which is typically used as a dip for hot, deep-fried foods. The Sichuan pepper is best roasted the day you wish to use it; it loses its fragrance if you keep it for too long. Example: stuffed eggplant fritters with Sichuan pepper.

11 Hot-and-sour flavor (酸辣味型 *suan la wei xing*): This type of flavor typically combines the mellow taste of Chinese vinegar with a gentle kick of ground white pepper against a background of plenty of salt. Some local versions use chili pastes or chili oil instead of pepper; others derive their sour flavors from pickled vegetables. Most food experts stress that sourness is the base of this type of flavor; the spicy seasonings play an "assisting" role. The standard hot-and-sour dish is a thick soup (*geng tang*) made with meat, seafood, or eggs, although the same tastes can be used in dressing some cold dishes. Example: hot-and-sour soup.

12 Fragrant fermented sauce flavor (醬香味型 *jiang xiang wei xing*): This flavor is created by cooking main ingredients like meat, poultry, or bean curd in a dense brown sauce based on sweet wheaten paste (*tian mian jiang*) and soy sauce. It combines sweet and salty tastes. Example: stir-fried pork slivers with sweet fermented paste.

13 **Five-spice flavor** (五香味型 *wu xiang wei xing*): As its name suggests, five-spice flavor is created through the use of several spices, either whole or ground together as five-spice powder. Five-spiced foods, which may include all kinds of meat and poultry, as well as eggs and bean curd, are often simmered in a rich broth flavored with ginger, scallion, Shaoxing rice wine, and spices, and then served cold (example: stewed aromatic meats). They can also be braised in a spiced liquid which is finally reduced to a delicious sticky sauce (example: five-spiced "smoked" fish), or steamed with a spicy marinade (example: fragrant and crispy duck). The spices can be varied at will, but often include star anise, cassia bark, and Sichuan pepper (see "fragrant things" in the ingredients section on page lxiii).

14 **Sweet fragrant flavor** (甜香味型 *tian xiang wei xing*): This flavor is used in hot, sweet dishes made using a variety of cooking methods. It derives its sweetness from white or crystal sugar, sometimes with the addition of fruit juices or candied fruits. Examples: eight-treasure wok pudding, silver ear fungus in crystal sugar soup.

15 **Fragrant wine flavor** (香糟味型 *xiang zao wei xing*): This type of flavor is based on fermented glutinous rice, which has a delicious, alcoholic smell and taste, with perhaps the addition of salt, sugar, sesame oil, and other spices. It is typically used with meat, poultry, and some vegetable ingredients like bamboo shoots. Example: cold chicken with fragrant rice wine.

16 **Smoked flavor** (煙香味型 *yan xiang wei xing*): This flavor is created by smoking salted meat or poultry over smoldering wood and leaves. The Sichuanese famously use tea-leaves to smoke their duck; other meats can be smoked over bamboo leaves, pine needles, rice straw, peanut husks, or sawdust. Examples: tea-smoked duck, homemade bacon with Sichuanese flavorings.

17 **Salt-savory flavor** (咸鲜味型 *han xian wei xing*): A very simple type of flavor that is designed to bring out the natural, fresh, delicious taste (*xian wei*) of the raw ingredients. Salt is the base flavoring; other seasonings, such as sugar, soy sauce, and sesame oil may be added, but their effects should be subtle and they should not overwhelm the taste of the main ingredient. This flavor is used in hot and cold dishes. Examples: stir-fried pig's liver, fresh fava beans in a simple stock sauce, chicken "bean curd" soup.

18 Lychee flavor (荔枝味型 *li zhi wei xing*): This flavor does not use any actual lychees, but is actually a sort of sweet-and-sour in which the sour notes stand out a little more than the sweet, rather like the fruit. The sour and sweet tastes are always played out over a background of gentle saltiness. Example: pork in lychee sauce with crispy rice.

19 Sweet-and-sour flavor (糖醋味型 *tang cu wei xing*): The Sichuanese have their own version of this famous Chinese flavor. It usually relies heavily on sugar and vinegar against a salty background, and when used for hot dishes, it is also flavored with ginger, garlic, and scallions. Examples: sweet-and-sour red peppers, sweet-and-sour pork, sweet-and-sour crispy fish.

20 Ginger juice flavor (姜汁味型 *jiang zhi wei xing*): Fresh ginger, salt, and vinegar give this flavor its distinctive taste and fragrance; soy sauce and sesame oil are also added. Ginger juice sauces are used with some cold meats and green vegetables and, occasionally, on hot dishes. Examples: fine green beans in ginger sauce, steamed pork knuckle in ginger sauce.

21 Sesame paste flavor (麻醬味型 *ma jiang wei xing*): Another type of flavor used for cold dishes, this one relies on toasted sesame paste, sesame oil, salt, and chicken stock, sometimes with the addition of soy sauce. It is used with various types of innards, as well as one or two different vegetables. Example: crisp lettuce in sesame sauce.

22 Mustard flavor (芥末味型 *jie mo wei xing*): This type of flavor is used with some cold dishes on summer and autumn menus. It is based on the salty-savory flavor, but with a hint of vinegar sourness and a burst of hot mustard.

23 Salt-sweet flavor (咸甜味型 *han tian wei xing*): A combination of saltiness and sugar sweetness, it is used in varying proportions in some hot meat and poultry dishes. Shaoxing rice wine and pepper are usually added, perhaps with other spices. Example: braised chicken with chestnuts.

the 56 cooking methods of Sichuan

The following are the fifty-six cooking methods of the Sichuanese culinary canon, as listed in the 1998 Sichuan culinary encyclopedia published by the Chongqing Publishing House.

1 chao 炒 : a general term for stir-frying food cut into small pieces in a wok, usually with oil as the heating medium (*you chao*), but occasionally using salt (*yan chao*) or even sand (*sha chao*).

2 sheng chao 生炒 : "raw-frying," stir-frying as above, where the food is raw when it enters the wok.

3 shu chao 熟炒 : "cooked-frying," stir-frying in which the meat is cooked when it enters the wok.

4 xiao chao 小炒 : "small-frying" (see explanation on page 43).

5 ruan chao 軟炒 : "soft-frying," in which ingredients such as fresh fava beans or chicken breast are mashed to a pulp, mixed with water, egg, and starch, and then stir-fried in hot oil over a high flame until cooked.

6 bao 爆 : "explode-frying," fast stir-frying cross-hatched pieces of crisp animal foods like kidney and poultry gizzards in hot oil at a very high temperature.

7 liu 熘 : a type of frying in which small pieces of food (often fish) are first cooked in oil or steamed and then tossed in a wokful of sauce. Sometimes the sauce is simply poured over the precooked food on the serving dish.

8 *xian liu* 鮮熘: a variation of *liu* in which soft pieces of fish or poultry are draped in an egg white batter and prefried in plenty of gently heated oil. Excess oil is then drained off and the sauce ingredients added to the wok. This method keeps the main ingredients beautifully tender.

9 *zha liu* 炸熘: "deep-fry *liu*," a variation of *liu* in which the food is first deep-fried and then added to a wokful of sauce, or turned out onto a serving dish to receive the sauce.

10 *gan bian* 干煸: "dry-frying" (see explanation on page 43).

11 *jian* 煎: shallow-frying over a medium heat in a flat-bottomed pan until the food, usually flatbreads, pastries, or fried eggs, is golden on both sides.

12 *guo tie* 鍋貼: "pot-sticking," shallow-frying over a gentle heat in a flat-bottomed pan. The food is not moved, so it develops a golden toasty crust on one side but remains soft on top.

13 *zha* 炸: deep-frying food in plenty of oil, usually over a high flame, until it is crisp.

14 *qing zha* 清炸: "clear deep-frying," deep-frying once only in hot oil over a high flame until the outside of the food is crisp and fragrant. The food is not coated in any kind of starch or batter.

15 *ruan zha* 軟炸: "soft deep-frying," deep-frying of small pieces of food coated in an egg white batter, first at a lower temperature and then at a higher, so the outside of the food is crunchy but the inside tender.

16 *su zha* 酥炸: "crisp deep-frying," in which the food is coated in flour or batter or rolled up in some kind of skin, deep-fried briefly in hot oil to fix its shape, and then fried in even hotter oil until it is crisp and golden.

17 *jin zha* 浸炸: "soak deep-frying," in which the food is put into a wokful of warm oil and allowed to heat up very slowly until it is cooked through.

18 *you lin* 油淋: "oil-drenching," in which the food, often whole, precooked poultry, is held over a wokful of hot oil and drizzled with the oil until it is crisp and deeply, glossily red on the outside but still tender within.

19 *qiang* 熗: another type of frying (see explanation on page 44).

20 *hong* 烘: frying gently in a little oil until the food, usually some kind of omelet or eggy pancake, is crisp and fragrant on the outside but fluffy and bubbly within.

21 *cuan* 汆: boiling slices or strips of food, or meatballs and fishballs, in water until they are cooked, either as a soup or as part of a more complex cooking process.

22 *tang* 燙: cooking small pieces of food briefly in boiling water until just done, often as a stage in a longer cooking process.

23 *chong* 沖: cooking runny pastelike foods in oil or water, until they are cooked and can hold their shape.

24 *dun* 燉: stewing large pieces of food or whole fowl in water, perhaps with a little ginger and scallion, over a very low flame and for a very long time, until they are extremely soft. Brings out the original, essential flavor (*yuan wei*) of the main ingredient.

25 *zhu* 煮: boiling large chunks of food in plenty of water until they are done, either as a primary stage of cooking or to make simple vegetable soups.

26 *shao* 燒: one of the most universal Chinese cooking methods, which involves bringing food to a boil in a seasoned liquid and then simmering it over medium or gentle heat until the food is soft and the sauce is reduced and glossy. The sauce can also be thickened with starch just before serving. The main ingredients are usually precooked by any one of a number of methods.

27 *hong shao* 紅燒: "red-braising," a type of braising in which the sauce includes soy sauce or caramel color to give the ingredients a deep red hue.

28 bai shao 白燒："white-braising," a type of braising in which the sauce does not contain strongly colored seasonings, so the pale natural color of the main ingredient, often fish, chicken, or vegetables, is emphasized.

29 cong shao 葱燒："scallion braising," a type of braising that begins with the frying of a few scallion pieces in oil; then the stock and other ingredients are added. The final dish has a strong scalliony flavor.

30 jiang shao 醬燒："braising with fermented sauce," a type of braising that begins with the frying of a little sweet fermented paste before the addition of stock and seasonings. The main ingredients are usually deep-fried before they are added to the braising pan.

31 jia chang shao 家常燒："homestyle braising" (see explanation on page 43).

32 sheng shao 生燒："raw braising," braising tougher ingredients, which are simmered slowly with seasonings until soft, at which point the heat is increased to reduce the liquid; or tender ingredients, which are cooked by a similar method but usually prefried.

33 shu shao 熟燒："cooked braising," a faster type of braising used to cook small pieces of food.

34 gan shao 干燒："dry-braising" (see explanation on page 43).

35 du 熠：a Sichuanese folk method of cooking (see explanation on page 44). Chef Xiao Jianming of Piaoxiang Restaurant says the term *du* is an onomotopoeia, derived from the bubbling sound—*gu-du-gu-du-gu-du*—made by the liquid in the wok!

36 ruan du 軟熠："soft *du*," also known as "soft-braising" (*ruan shao*). Like *du* except that the food is not prefried but is either directly added to the simmering sauce or briefly dunked in warm, not hot, oil.

37 hui 燴：similar to white-braising, but with a shorter cooking time and more liquid. Used to cook two or more ingredients together in a pale, gentle sauce.

38 men 燜: stewing prefried ingredients in a tightly closed pot, over a low or medium flame. The liquid—not as much as for other stewing methods—is added at the start of the cooking and not reduced. It can be thickened with starch before serving.

39 wei 煨: stewing chunks of food with stock, flavorings, and caramel color or dark soy sauce over an extremely low flame, until they are cooked and beautifully brown and the liquid much reduced.

40 kao 㸁: another kind of stewing, in which large chunks of rather tough food (like bear's paw or shark's fin) are simmered gently with stock, flavorings, and perhaps a few supplementary ingredients.

41 zheng 蒸: steaming.

42 qing zheng 清蒸: "clear steaming," in which pale foods are steamed with pale-colored flavorings like ginger, scallion, salt, and wine, and also some fine stock.

43 han zheng 旱蒸: "dry-steaming," steaming food wrapped in paper or in a covered dish, with seasonings but no surrounding liquid.

44 fen zheng 粉蒸: "rice-meal steaming," in which various meats and poultry are mixed with marinade ingredients and a coarse rice meal and then steamed.

45 kao 烤: roasting meat, poultry, or fish before a radiating heat source, usually whole, and sometimes filled with stuffing or wrapped in leaves or clay.

46 gua lu kao 掛爐烤: "hanging-oven roasting," roasting fowl by hanging them in a closed oven.

47 ming lu kao 明爐烤: roasting meat, poultry, or fish over an open-topped stove.

48 kao xiang kao 烤箱烤: "oven-roasting," roasting in a closed oven.

49 tang zhan 糖粘 : encrusting food in a seasoned sugary paste or a sugar syrup.

50 zha shou 炸收 : "deep-fry and receive," simmering deep-fried foods in a seasoned broth until they absorb or "receive" all the flavors of the surrounding liquid.

51 lu 鹵 : stewing foods in a spiced broth.

52 ban 拌 : tossing raw or cooked foods in a seasoning sauce, like a salad.

53 pao 泡 : pickling in brine.

54 zi 漬 : steeping in a flavored liquid.

55 zao zui 糟醉 : steeping in liquor (zao means wine-pickled, zui means drunken).

56 dong 凍 : jellying or freezing.

That's it.

glossary of Chinese characters with definitions

巴　*ba* – the name of the ancient kingdom based in eastern Sichuan

八角　*ba jiao* – star anise (literally "eight horns")

巴蜀　*ba shu* – the ancient Ba and Shu kingdoms in the area that is today called Sichuan, and a poetic name for Sichuan

白酒　*bai jiu* – strong vodka-like wine

白味　*bai wei* – "white-flavored"

本草綱目　*ben cao gang mu* – sixteenth-century encyclopedia of medicinal plants

包子　*bao zi* – steamed bun with filling

冰糖　*bing tang* – rock or crystal sugar

菜刀　*cai dao* – cleaver

菜墩　*cai dun* – cutting board

菜油　*cai you* – rapeseed oil

蠶豆　*can dou* – fava bean (literally "silkworm bean")

草果　*cao guo* – *Amomum tsao-kuo* (a type of "false cardamom")

草魚　*cao yu* – grass carp (*Ctenopharyngodon idellus*)

長江鱘　*chang jiang xun* – Yangtze sturgeon (*Acipenser dabryanus*)

炒　*chao* – to stir-fry

炒鍋　*chao guo* – wok

朝天椒　*chao tian jiao* – "facing-heaven" chile (a variety of chile)

炒香　*chao xiang* – to "fry-fragrant" (see page 42)

陳皮　*chen pi* – dried tangerine peel

成都　*cheng du* – Chengdu

吃醋　*chi cu* – to be cuckolded (literally "to eat vinegar")

吃苦　*chi ku* – to "eat bitterness" (to suffer)

蟲草　*chong cao* – caterpillar fungus (*Cordyceps sinensis*)

重慶　*chong qing* – Chongqing

川北涼粉　*chuan bei liang fen* – North Sichuan pea jelly

川鹽　*chuan yan* – Sichuanese well salt

捶　*chui* – to pound with the back of a cleaver blade

春筍　*chun sun* – spring bamboo shoot

椿芽　*chun ya* – the tender shoots of the Chinese toon tree (*Toona sinensis* according to Chinese sources)

蔥　*cong* – Chinese scallions (*Allium fistulosum*)

蔥花　*cong hua* – scallion "flowers" (thin slices)

醋　*cu* – vinegar

攢盒　*cuan he* – decorative hors d'oeuvre box

脆　*cui* – a type of crispness (see page 31)

大蔥　*da cong* – large scallions

大蒜　*da suan* – garlic

大頭菜　*da tou cai* – preserved turnip-like vegetable (*Brassica juncea* var. *napitormis*)

大象便餐　*da zhong bian can* – "convenient dish for the masses"

帶魚　*dai yu* – hairtail fish (*Trichiurus haumela*)

燈籠椒　*deng long jiao* – "lantern peppers" (sweet peppers)

燈盞窩形　*deng zhan wo xing* – "lamp-dish" slices

電飯鍋　*dian fan guo* – electric rice-cooker

丁　*ding* – a cube

丁丁糖　*ding ding tang* – ding ding candy

丁配丁，絲配絲　*ding pei ding, si pei si* – "cubes with cubes, slivers with slivers"

丁香　*ding xiang* – cloves

冬菜　*dong cai* – "winter vegetable" (a kind of preserved mustard green)

冬筍　*dong sun* – winter bamboo shoot

豆瓣醬　*dou ban jiang* – chili and fava bean paste

豆豉　*dou chi* – black fermented soybeans

豆腐　*dou fu* – bean curd

豆腐乾　*dou fu gan* – dry bean curd

豆腐腦　*dou fu nao* – "bean curd brain" (standard Chinese name for flower bean curd)

豆腐皮　*dou fu pi* – bean curd skin

豆腐乳　*dou fu ru* – fermented bean curd

豆花　*dou hua* – flower bean curd

豆花不用豆，吃雞不見雞 *dou hua bu yong dou, chi ji bu jian ji* – "flower bean curd without the beans, chicken without the appearance of chicken"

豆苗 *dou miao* – pea leaves (also known as "dragon's whiskers")

豆渣 *dou zha* – soybean residue

熠 *du* – a Sichuanese cooking method (see page 44)

獨蒜 *du suan* – Sichuanese single-cloved garlic

斷生 *duan sheng* – to "break the rawness" of food

端午節 *duan wu jie* – the Dragon Boat Festival (fifth day of the fifth lunar month)

燉雞湯 *dun ji tang* – simple chicken soup

多吃蔬菜，少吃肉 *duo chi shu cai, shao chi rou* – "eat more vegetables, eat less meat"

鵝腸 *e chang* – goose intestines

二姐兔丁 *er jie tu ding* – "second-sister rabbit cubes" (a cold dish)

二金條 *er jin tiao* – "two golden strips" (a variety of chile)

番椒 *fan jiao* – "barbarian peppers" (Ming Dynasty name for chiles)

肥而不膩 *fei er bu ni* – richly fat without being greasy

粉條 *fen tiao* – a type of thick, transparent starchy noodle made from various legumes or sweet potatoes

鳳尾條 *feng wei tiao* – "phoenix tail" strips

佛齋菜 *fo zhai cai* – Buddhist vegetarian food

複合味 *fu he wei* – compound flavors

斧楞片 *fu leng pian* – "axe-blade" slices

蓋碗茶 *gai wan cha* – lid-bowl tea (Sichuanese style of tea drinking)

甘 *gan* – sweet

乾杯 *gan bei* – Cheers! Bottoms up!

乾煸 *gan bian* – to "dry-fry"

甘草 *gan cao* – licorice root (*Glycyrrhiza uralensis*)

乾海椒 *gan hai jiao* – dried chiles

乾菌 *gan jun* – dried fungi

擀麵杖 *gan mian zhang* – rolling pin

乾燒 *gan shao* – to "dry-braise"

高良姜 *gao liang jiang* – galangal

割烹 *ge peng* – to cut and to cook

羹 *geng* – a kind of thick soup

工夫茶 *gong fu cha* – southeastern Chinese tea-drinking ritual

勾芡 *gou qian* – to thicken a sauce with starch

骨牌片　*gu pai pian* – "domino" slices

骨頭湯　*gu tou tang* – pork bone stock

刮　*gua* – to scrape

光杆青菜　*guang gan qing cai* – type of mustard green used to make *ya cai* (q.v.)

桂皮　*gui pi* – cassia bark (*Cinnamomum cassia*)

鱖魚 or 桂魚　*gui yu* – Chinese perch (*Siniperca chuatsi*)

鍋巴　*guo ba* – rice crust

鍋鏟　*guo chan* – wok scoop

過油　*guo you* – to "pass through the oil" (preliminary deep-frying of ingredients)

果汁味　*guo zhi wei* – "fruit-juice flavor"

海白菜　*hai bai cai* – white seaweed (*Ulva lactuca*)

海帶甘　*hai dai gan* – dried sheet seaweed

海椒　*hai jiao* – "sea peppers" (Sichuan dialect for chiles)

海椒面　*hai jiao mian* – ground chiles

咸　*han* (Sichuan dialect) or *xian* (Mandarin) – salty

莧菜　*han cai* – Sichuan dialect for amaranth leaves (*Amaranthus tricolor*)

好辛香　*hao xin xiang* – liking for hot and fragrant tastes

耗子洞張鴨子　*hao zi dong zhang ya zi* – Mr. Zhang's Mousehole Duck
　　　　(restaurant in Chengdu)

紅白茶　*hong bai cha* – "red-and-white tea" (see page 27)

烘爆雞丁　*hong bao ji ding* – fast-fried chicken cubes (see page 238)

紅油　*hong you* – chili oil (literally "red oil")

胡豆　*hu dou* – Sichuanese dialect for fava bean (literally "foreign bean")

胡椒面　*hu jiao mian* – ground white pepper

煳辣雞丁　*hu la ji ding* – chicken cubes with seared chiles (see page 238)

花茶　*hua cha* – "flower tea" (jasmine blossom tea)

花椒　*hua jiao* – Sichuan pepper (*Zanthoxylum simulans*)

花生米　*hua sheng mi* – peanuts

黃喉　*huang hou* – cow's throat tendons

黃花　*huang hua* – lily buds

黃酒城　*huang jiu cheng* – City of Yellow Wine

黃臘丁　*huang la ding* – yellow catfish (*Pseudobagrus fulvidraco*)

黃鱔　*huang shan* – yellow eel (see *shan yu*)

茴香　*hui xiang* – fennel seeds

火爐　*huo lu* – furnace

雞腿菇　*ji tui gu* – chicken-leg mushroom

鯽魚　*ji yu* – crucian carp (*Carassius auratus auratus*)

家常燒　*jia chang shao* – to "homestyle braise" (a type of braising)

箭杆青菜　*jian gan qing cai* – type of mustard green used to make *dong cai* (q.v.)

江團　*jiang tuan* – Sichuanese dialect name for a type of catfish (*Leiocassius longirostris*)

醬油　*jiang you* – soy sauce

角　*jiao* – unit of currency

椒房　*jiao fang* – "pepper houses"

餃子　*jiao zi* – boiled crescent dumplings

錦江　*jin jiang* – Brocade River

金針菇　*jin zhen gu* – golden needle mushrooms

韭菜葉麵條　*jiu cai ye mian tiao* – chive-leaf noodles

韭黃　*jiu huang* – yellowed Chinese chives (*Allium tuberosum*)

丸子　*jiu zi* – meatballs

蕨菜　*jue cai* – fiddlehead ferns

開花　*kai hua* – to burst into flower

開水白菜　*kai shui bai cai* – "white cabbage in boiling water"

開胃　*kai wei* – to "open the stomach" (whet the appetite)

砍　*kan* – to chop

烤箱烤　*kao xiang kao* – to roast in an oven

顆　*ke* – a tiny cube

孔雀開屏　*kong que kai ping* – "peacock spreading its tail"

空心菜　*kong xin cai* – water spinach (*Ipomoea aquatica*)

口感　*kou gan* – "mouth-feel"

苦　*ku* – bitter

苦瓜　*ku gua* – bitter melon (*Momordica charantia*)

苦筍　*ku sun* – bitter bamboo shoot

塊　*kuai* – a chunk

筷子　*kuai zi* – chopsticks

筷子條　*kuai zi tiao* – "chopstick" strips

辣　*la* – hot, spicy

辣椒　*la jiao* – standard Mandarin Chinese for chile

辣妹子　*la mei zi* – hot, spicy girls

辣中有鮮味　*la zhong you xian wei* – "*xian* flavors in the midst of spiciness"

老　*lao* – overcooked, tough (literally "old")

老四川　*lao si chuan* – Old Sichuan restaurant in Chongqing

醪糟　*lao zao* – fermented glutinous rice wine

冷淡杯　*leng dan bei* – "a few cold dishes and a glass of beer" (Sichuanese "tapas")

粒 *li* – a grain of chopped food

禮記 *li ji* – The Book of Rites

鯉魚 *li yu* – carp (*Cyprinus carpio carpio*)

荔枝街 *li zhi gai* – Lychee Lane

連夾片 *lian jia pian* – "sandwich slices"

蓮花白 *lian hua bai* – Sichuanese white cabbage (*Brassica oleracea* var. *capitata*)

蓮子 *lian zi* – lotus seeds

料酒 *liao jiu* – cooking wine

靈活 *ling huo* – spirited, flexible

龍抄手 *long chao shou* – Long Chao Shou snack restaurant in Chengdu

漏瓢 *lou piao* – perforated ladle

滷水 *lu shui* – aromatic broth (see page 179)

麻 *ma* – the numbing taste of Sichuan pepper

馬耳朵 *ma 'er duo* – "horse ear" slices

麻花 *ma hua* – deep-fried dough twists

碼芡 *ma qian* – to coat raw ingredients in a runny starch paste before cooking

碼味 *ma wei* – to marinate

饅頭 *man tou* – steamed bun

蠻頭 *man tou* – "barbarian head" (archaic name for steamed bun filled with meat)

毛肚火鍋 *mao du huo guo* – beef tripe hotpot

毛峰茶 *mao feng cha* – Mao Feng tea

眉毛 *mei mao* – eyebrows

梅子 *mei zi* – plum

蒙頂甘露 *meng ding gan lu* – Meng Ding sweet dew tea

麵條 *mian tiao* – noodles

蘑菇 *mo gu* – button mushrooms

魔芋 *mo yu* – konnyaku yam jelly (made from *Amorphophallus rivieri*)

木耳 *mu'er* – "wood ear" or "cloud ear" fungus (genus *Auricula*)

南瓜 *nan gua* – "southern gourd" (a type of pumpkin)

內部發行 *nei bu fa xing* – "for internal circulation only"

嫩 *nen* – tenderness, delicacy (of meat, fish, etc.; see page 31)

泥鰍 *ni qiu* – loach or weatherfish (*Misgurnus anguillicaudatus*)

鯰魚 *nian yu* – Amur catfish (*Silurus asotus*)

牛鞭 *niu bian* – ox penis

牛肝菌 *niu gan jun* – ox-liver mushroom (*Boletus spp.*)

牛舌片 *niu she pian* – "ox-tongue" slices

濃　*nong* – strong, dense, concentrated (e.g., of flavor)

炟　*pa* – the texture of food that has been cooked until it is very soft
（Sichuan dialect, see page 31）

怕辣　*pa la* – "fear chile-hotness"

泡　*pao* – to pickle, pickled

泡菜罈子　*pao cai tan zi* – Sichuanese pickle jar

袍哥肉　*pao ge rou* – "Secret Society Meat" (a nickname for twice-cooked
pork)

泡海椒　*pao hai jiao* – pickled chiles

片　*pian* – a slice

片　*pian* – to cut horizontally

飄香　*piao xiang* – "Drifting Fragrance" (the name of a restaurant in Chengdu)

瓢子　*piao zi* – ladle

平地一聲雷　*ping di yi sheng lei* – "a sudden clap of thunder"

平菇　*ping gu* – white oyster mushrooms (*Pleurotus ostreatus*)

七星椒　*qi xing jiao* – "seven-star" chile (a variety of chile)

芡粉　*qian fen* – white starch (pea, corn, or potato flour)

熗　*qiang* – a type of stir-frying (see page 44)

切　*qie* – to cut vertically

茄汁味　*qie zhi wei* – "tomato sauce flavor"

青城雪芽　*qing cheng xue ya* – Qing Cheng Mountain snow shoot tea

青岡樹　*qing gang shu* – oriental white oak (*Cyclobalanopsis spp.*)

青蒜　*qing suan* – "green garlic" (another name for *suan miao*)

青筍　*qing sun* – another name for *wo sun* (q.v.)

曲酒　*qu jiu* – generic term for strong vodka-like wines

全興大曲酒　*quan xing da qu jiu* – a Sichuanese sorghum liquor

肉豆蔻　*rou dou kou* – nutmeg

三生面　*san sheng mian* – a type of hot-water dough

三蒸九扣　*san zheng jiu kou* – "Three steamed dishes and nine steamed bowls"
(folk name for rural banquet)

臊味　*sao wei* – foul odour

澀味　*se wei* – astringent taste

色香味形　*se xiang wei xing* – "color, fragrance, flavor, and form"

砂鍋　*sha guo* – earthenware pot

沙姜　*sha jiang* – "sand ginger" (see *shan nai*)

山城小湯圓　*shan cheng xiao tang yuan* – Mountain City little glutinous rice balls

山奈　*shan nai* – a type of ginger (also known as *sha jiang*) (*Kaempferia galanga*)

膻味　*shan wei* – muttony odor

鱔魚　*shan yu* – yellow or swamp eel (*Monopterus albus*)

山珍海味　*shan zhen hai wei* – "treasures from the mountains and the seas"

尚滋味　*shang zi wei* – enjoyment of taste

燒　*shao* – to braise

苕菜　*shao cai* – Chinese milk vetch

筲箕　*shao ji* – bamboo basket

紹興酒　*shao xing jiu* – Shaoxing rice wine

生　*sheng* – raw

生姜　*sheng jiang* – ginger

石爬魚　*shi pa yu* – a type of catfish (*Euchiloglanis kishinouyei*)

食在中國，味在四川　*shi zai zhong guo, wei zai si chuan* – "China is the place for food, but Sichuan is the place for flavor"

食豬肉　*shi zhu rou* – "Eating Pork" (a poem by Su Dongpo)

熟　*shu* – cooked (as opposed to raw)

蜀　*shu* – the name of the ancient kingdom centred on today's Chengdu (and a poetic name for the Chengdu area)

蜀犬吠日　*shu quan fei ri* – "Sichuan dogs bark at the sun"

梳子背　*shu zi bei* – roll-cut chunks

絲　*si* – "silken thread" (sliver)

絲瓜　*si gua* – "silk gourd" (*Luffa cylindrica* or *Luffa acutangula*)

飼料　*si liao* – manufactured animal feed

酥　*su* – a type of crispness (see page 31)

素豆雞　*su dou ji* – sausage-shaped roll of bean curd (literally "vegetarian bean chicken")

酸　*suan* – sour

酸菜　*suan cai* – pickled mustard greens

蒜毫　*suan hao* – garlic stems

蒜苗　*suan miao* – Chinese leeks, scallions, green garlic

蒜薹　*suan tai* – garlic stems

燙面　*tang mian* – a type of dumpling dough made with hot water

特點　*te dian* – distinguishing characteristics

蹄筋　*ti jin* – a type of tendon from a pig's foot

甜　*tian* – sweet

天府之國　*tian fu zhi guo* – the land of plenty

甜面醬　*tian mian jiang* – sweet fermented wheat paste

田席　*tian xi* – rural banquet (literally "field feast")

條　*tiao* – a strip

通菜　*tong cai* – Mandarin Chinese for water spinach

同學　*tong xue* – "same-school," classmate

土　*tu* – rustic, earthy, free-range (literally "earth")

團圓　*tuan yuan* – reunion

剜　*wan* – to gouge

味精　*wei jing* – monosodium glutamate, MSG (literally "the essence of flavor")

圍棋　*wei qi* – the game Go

蕹菜　*weng cai* – Mandarin Chinese for water spinach

萵筍　*wo sun* – a type of lettuce with a thick stem (*Lactuca sativa* var. angustata)

窩窩頭　*wo wo tou* – a type of steamed bread

烏骨雞　*wu gu ji* – black-boned chicken

無咸不成菜　*wu han bu cheng cai* – "you can"t make a dish without saltiness"

五花肉　*wu hua rou* – pork belly meat (literally "five-flower meat")

五糧液　*wu liang ye* – Sichuanese "five-grain wine"

勿談國事　*wu tan guo shi* – "do not discuss national affairs"

五香粉　*wu xiang fen* – five-spice powder

稀飯　*xi fan* – plain rice porridge

下飯菜　*xia fan cai* – "send-the-rice-down" dishes

鮮　*xian* – (see explanation on page 28)

莧菜　*xian cai* – Mandarin Chinese for amaranth leaves

鮮美　*xian mei* – delicious *xian* flavor

香　*xiang* – fragrant

香菜　*xiang cai* – common Sichuanese name for coriander (cilantro) (literally "fragrant vegetable")

香腸　*xiang chang* – air-dried sausage

香菇　*xiang gu* – "fragrant mushrooms" (shiitake — *Lentinus edodes*)

香料　*xiang liao* – "fragrant things" (generic name for spices)

象牙條　*xiang ya tiao* – "elephant tusk" strips

香油　*xiang you* – sesame oil

小炒　*xiao chao* – to "small-fry" (a type of stir-frying)

小吃　*xiao chi* – "little eats" (snacks)

小蔥　*xiao cong* – small scallions

小茴　*xiao hui* – fennel seeds

小籠　*xiao long* – small steamer

小米椒　*xiao mi jiao* – a type of chile

辛　*xin* – hot, pungent

腥味　*xing wei* – fishy odour

醒園錄　*xing yuan lu* – the earliest Sichuanese cookbook, the work of Li Huanan

熊貓戰竹　*xiong mao zhan zhu* – "panda fighting bamboo"

雪豆　*xue dou* – "snow beans" (butter beans)

芽菜　*ya cai* – a type of preserved mustard green

雅魚　*ya yu* – a type of carp (*Schizothorax prenanti*)

鹽都　*yan du* – "Salt Capital" (Zigong City)

岩鯉　*yan li* – "rock carp" (*Procypris rabaudi*)

芫荽　*yan sui* – Mandarin Chinese name for coriander

洋芋炒土豆　*yang yu chao tu dou* – "spud-fried potatoes"

野山椒　*ye shan jiao* – wild mountain chile

一菜一格，百菜百味　*yi cai yi ge, bai cai bai wei* – "one dish, one style; one hundred dishes, one hundred different flavors"

異味　*yi wei* – peculiar smell

銀耳　*yin'er* – silver ear fungus (also known as white wood ear; *Tremella fuciformis*)

銀針絲　*yin zhen si* – "silver needle" sliver

魚眼蔥　*yu yan cong* – "fish-eye" scallion slices

原湯　*yuan tang* – stock made with only one main ingredient

側耳根　*ze'er gen* – *Houttuynia cordata* (a salad vegetable)

炸　*zha* – to deep-fry

榨菜　*zha cai* – preserved mustard tuber

炸收　*zha shou* – to "deep-fry and draw in" (see page 363)

斬　*zhan* – to chop

樟　*zhang* – camphor

漳州　*zhang zhou* (place name)

蒸　*zheng* – to steam

蒸籠　*zheng long* – steamer

炙鍋　*zhi guo* – to season the wok

痣鬍子龍眼包子　*zhi hu zi long yan bao zi* – "Hairy Mole" dragon's-eye steamed buns (name of a Chengdu restaurant)

指甲片　*zhi jia pian* – "thumbnail" slices

芝麻　*zhi ma* – sesame seeds

芝麻醬　*zhi ma jiang* – sesame paste

中國　*zhong guo* – China (literally "Middle Kingdom")

中國食經　*zhong guo shi jing* – *The Chinese Classic of Food*

竹海　*zhu hai* – the Bamboo Sea
竹花　*zhu hua* – bamboo flower lichen
竹刷　*zhu shua* – bamboo wok brush
竹蓀　*zhu sun* – bamboo pith fungus (*Dictyophora spp.*)
竹蓀蛋　*zhu sun dan* – volvae of the bamboo pith fungus
竹葉青　*zhu ye qing* – green bamboo leaf tea

sources and resources

Shopping for Chinese ingredients and equipment needn't be as intimidating—or as challenging—as it once was. Many supermarkets now carry a wide selection of fresh and packaged Asian foods. However, your best bet is often to visit your local Chinatown: most cities have at least a small Asian neighborhood filled with the most authentic (and least expensive) ingredients and equipment such as woks, steamers, and tableware. You may want to bring this book on your shopping trip and show vendors the Chinese characters for the items you're seeking. Language barriers can be difficult to surmount but most shopkeepers will be delighted to help you once they understand what you'd like.

The following ingredients require a bit more description, and may necessitate a trip to a Chinese grocery store:

Bean curd: The best bean curd to use in these recipes is the fresh curd soaked in water that is available in most Chinese food shops, as well as in many grocery stores. Soft silken tofu, which is available in health food stores, can be substituted for "flower" bean curd.

Bamboo pith fungus: Look for the feather-light, pale, lacy dried fungus in Chinese supermarkets (sometimes sold as "bamboo fungus").

Black fermented beans: I use the Pearl River Bridge brand, "Yang Jiang Preserved Beans with Ginger," which is sold in Chinese stores in cylindrical cardboard cartons.

Dried spices and dried fruit: Most Chinese shops (as well as many better supermarkets) will carry all the spices used in this book, including cassia bark, star anise, fennel seeds, cau guo, "sand ginger," etc. Dried fruit such as jujubes (Chinese dates) and Chinese wolfberries, as well as some of the other ingredients used in some "eight-treasure" dishes, can be found in larger Chinese supermarkets or spice shops in your local Chinatown.

Dried lotus leaves: Available at most Chinese groceries, including those listed in the Sources section (see page 377).

Frozen plantain leaves: Available at larger Chinese grocery stores and in most Chinatowns.

Pickled chili paste: The Sichuanese simply pound their pickled chiles to a paste, without adding garlic or any other flavorings. Look out for brands that list chiles, water, and salt as their main ingredients (not vinegar). If you can't find this, a good substitute is the Indonesian product sambal olek.

Sichuan chili bean paste: Look for pastes made with fava beans rather than soybeans. I use Lee Kum Kee's chili bean sauce (Toban Dijan).

Sichuanese dried chiles: Look for Sichuanese "facing heaven" chiles (*chao tian jiao*). Other types of dried chiles can be used instead, although they won't have a comparable favor. The larger dried chiles sometimes sold in Chinese supermarkets are a reasonable substitute, but beware of using the much hotter tiny dried chiles from India or Thailand.

You can use the chili flakes sold in Chinese shops to make Sichuanese chili oil, but if you can find real Sichuanese ground chiles they will yield a better fragrance and color.

Sichuan pickled chiles: Very difficult to find. I've suggested using a mixture of pickled chili purée and red bell pepper as a substitute for Sichuanese chiles in some recipes.

Sichuan pepper: Can be hard to find in Chinese grocery stores, but it can be ordered from both Adriana's Caravan and the CMC Company (see below).

Soybeans, frozen in the pod: Also known as *edamame*, these can be found at most large grocery and health food stores.

Soy sauce: I use Pearl River Bridge brand dark and light soy sauces: they make two different kinds (in both light and dark), one of which is traditionally brewed without the addition of MSG or food coloring.

Sweet bean paste: Used as a substitute for Sichuanese sweet fermented paste; I use Mong Lee Shang brand from Taiwan.

Vinegar: I use Gold Plum brand of Chinkiang vinegar, which has a complex, mellow taste, very reminiscent of Sichuanese Baoning vinegar.

LOCAL SOURCES

The **99 Ranch Market** chain is a rapidly expanding group of Asian supermarkets featuring produce, meat, seafood, and packaged foods. Many stores in California and across the West, with more and more throughout the country—check the yellow pages or their Web site, www.99ranch.com, to find a local branch.

NEW YORK
Chinese American Trading Company
91 Mulberry Street
New York, NY 10013
212-267-5224
Fax: 212-619-7449
No fresh ingredients, but a wide variety of spices and dried food, as well as cooking equipment. English spoken.

Kam Man Food Products
200 Canal Street
New York, NY 10013
212-571-0330
Fax: 212-766-9085
Asian produce and a large selection of the packaged foods described above. English spoken.

Mon Fung Company
208 Grand Street
New York, NY 10013
212-925-5111

For general information and directions to New York's Chinatown:
www.chinatown-online.com/nychinatown.htm

BOSTON
Ming's Supermarket Inc.
1102 Washington Street
Boston, MA 02118
617-338-1588
In the heart of Boston's Chinatown; features both fresh and packaged foods. English spoken.

WASHINGTON, D.C.
Mee Wah Lung Co.
608 H Street, N.W.
Washington, DC 20001
202-737-0968
Fresh produce and most of the packaged goods described above. English spoken.

ATLANTA
Ranch Market
5150 Buford Highway, N.E.
Doraville, GA 30340
770-458-8955
Part of the Asian Square Marketplace development, which features a variety of Asian shops and restaurants and is a good source for dishes and serving pieces.

CHICAGO
Dong Kee Co.
2252 S. Wentworth Avenue
Chicago, IL 60616
312-225-6340
Full range of fresh Asian produce and packaged goods described above.

For general information on Chicago's Chinatown, including directions
and an extensive directory of markets and grocery stores:
www.chicago-chinatown.com

CLEVELAND
Asia Grocery and Gift
4825 Pearl Road
Cleveland, OH 44109
216-459-8839
Asian produce, meat, seafood and packaged goods. English spoken.

HOUSTON
Hong Kong Supermarket
5708 South Gessner Drive
Houston, TX 77036
713-995-1393
A good selection of produce, meat, seafood, and packaged goods. Limited English spoken.

LOS ANGELES
Far-East Supermarket
758 New High Street
Los Angeles, CA 90012
213-628-8708
In the heart of Los Angeles's Chinatown. Limited English spoken, but wide range of fresh produce and packaged goods.

AB Market
711 New High Street
Los Angeles, CA 90012
213-617-1229
Just down the street from the Far-East Supermarket, another spot to try if they don't have the ingredients you need.

For fresh produce, try the Asian Farmer's Market held every Thursday afternoon from 3 to 7 P.M. in the public parking lot in Chinatown at 727 N. Hill between Alpine and Ord.

For information, directions, and a comprehensive list of markets in Los Angeles's Chinatown, check www.chinatownla.com

SAN FRANCISCO
May Wah Supermarket
547 Clement Street
San Francisco, CA 94118
415-668-2583
Extensive selection of fresh Asian produce and packaged ingredients, in addition to seafood and meat. Large supply of equipment at low prices, and a bit less hectic than the stores in Chinatown.

Chong Kee Jan Co.
838 Grant Street
San Francisco, CA 94108
415-982-1432
In the heart of San Fransisco's Chinatown. If they don't have what you're looking for, they'll direct you—in English—to a neighboring store that does. National delivery via UPS.

SEATTLE
Uwajimaya
600 5th Avenue S., Suite 100
Seattle, WA 98104
800-889-1928
206-624-6248
Fax: 206-624-6915
email: Hiroshi@uwajimaya.com
www.uwajimaya.com
Although primarily known as a Japanese store, this large store also stocks some Chinese ingredients and a variety of Asian produce and cooking equipment. National delivery via UPS.

Chinatown Grocery
676 S. Jackson Street
Seattle, WA 98104
206-621-8499

For directions, information, and an extensive business directory, check www.internationaldistrict.org

ONLINE AND MAIL ORDER SOURCES

There are several good online and mail-order sources, especially for spices and cooking equipment:

The Oriental Pantry
423 Great Road (Route 2A)
Acton, MA 01720
978-264-4576
www.orientalpantry.com
Equipment and ingredients; a good selection of spices and soy sauces (including my preferred brand, Pearl River Bridge). National delivery.

Pacific Rim Gourmet
email: customerservice@pacificrim-gourmet.com
www.pacificrim-gourmet.com
An excellent equipment source, including a wide variety of woks and steamers. Some ingredients, though not an exceptionally large Chinese selection. National delivery.

The CMC Company
P.O. Drawer 322
Avalon, NJ 08202
800-262-2780
Fax: 609-861-3065
Email: sales@thecmccompany.com
www.thecmccompany.com
With "hard to find ingredients for the serious cook," this site offers many of the ingredients described above (as well as an impressive assortment of ingredients for other ethnic cuisines). National delivery.

Adriana's Caravan
409 Vanderbilt Street
Brooklyn, NY 11218
800-316-0820
718-436-8565
www.adrianascaravan.com
Wide variety of spices and herbs, including the elusive Sichuan peppercorn. National delivery.

bibliography

Very little has been written about Sichuanese food in the English language, so I have drawn mainly on Chinese written sources in my research for this book. The following have been particularly useful:

Liu Xuezhi, *Chengdu's Distinctive Local Snacks* (*cheng du feng wei xiao chi*), Sichuan Dictionary Publishing House, Chengdu, 1993.

Luo Changsong, *Sichuanese Home Cookery* (*jia ting chuan cai*), Sichuan Science and Technology Publishing House, Chengdu, 1985.

Ren Baizun (ed.), *The Chinese Classic of Food* (*zhong guo shi jing*), Shanghai Cultural Publishing House, Shanghai, 1999.

Xiong Sizhi, *Famous Sichuanese Snacks* (*si chuan ming xiao chi*), Sichuan Science and Technology Publishing House, Chengdu, 1986.

Xiong Sizhi (ed.), *The Mysteries of Sichuanese Food* (*chuan cai ao mi*), Sichuan People's Publishing House, Chengdu, 1993.

Zhang Furu, *Appreciation of Sichuanese Food* (*chuan cai shang xi*), Sichuan Science and Technology Publishing House, Chengdu, 1987.

Zhang Furu (ed.), *Encyclopaedia of Sichuanese Cuisine* (*chuan cai peng ren shi dian*), Chongqing Publishing House, Chongqing, 1999.

Zhang Mu (ed.), *Sichuanese Cuisine* (*chuan cai*), Shandong Science and Technology Publishing House, 1996.

Cookery Textbook (*jiao xue cai*), Sichuan Provincial Labor Department Office for Technical Education and Research, Sichuan Science and Technology University Publishing House, Chengdu, 1991.

A Guide to Sichuan's Distinctive Local Products (*si chuan te chan feng wei zhi nan*), Sichuan People's Publishing House, Chengdu, 1984.

Sichuanese Cookery Book (*si chuan cai pu*), Chengdu Food and Drink Company, Center for Training and Research in Sichuanese Cookery, Chengdu, 1988.

Sichuanese Cooking Techniques (*chuan cai peng tiao ji shu*), Sichuan Institute of Higher Cuisine, Sichuan Education Publishing House, Chengdu, 1993.

Sichuanese Snack-Making Techniques (*chuan dian zhi zuo ji shu*), Sichuan Institute of Higher Cuisine, Sichuan Education Publishing House, Chengdu, 1992.

The account of the history of chiles in China in the introduction, pages 14–15, is derived with kind permission from a conference paper by Professor Jiang Yuxiang of the Sichuan University Museum: "A study on chiles" (*la jiao kao*). I am also much indebted to Gwenaële Chesnais's *Les Maisons de Thé de Chengdu* (unpublished MS, Institut National des Langues et Civilisations Orientales, Paris), and to Francesca Tarocco of the School of Oriental and African Studies in London for sharing with me her research on Buddhist vegetarian food.

The following English-language books have been invaluable in my research into Chinese ingredients and my efforts to create recipes that work in a Western kitchen:

Chang, K. C. (ed.), *Food in Chinese Culture*, Yale University Press, New Haven, 1977.

Cost, Bruce, *Foods from the Far East*, Century, London, 1990.

Davidson, Alan, *Oxford Companion to Food*, Oxford University Press, Oxford, 1999.

So, Yan-kit, *Classic Chinese Cookbook*, Dorling Kindersley, London, 1984.

So, Yan-kit, *Classic Food of China*, Macmillan, London, 1992.

acknowledgments

The most important ingredient in this book has been the generosity of my friends and teachers in China and in England. I cannot begin to explain how much I owe to Professor Feng Quanxin and his wife Qiu Rongzhen of the Sichuan Institute of Higher Cuisine, who have been tireless in their support for this project. Professor Xiong Sizhi, China's leading authority on Sichuanese food culture, has been extremely generous with his time and his library. Fan Shixian, the head chef of the Long Chao Shou restaurant in Chengdu, has been an unforgettable teacher. Special-grade chef Zhang Shechang has been endlessly patient in answering my questions.

I would also like to thank my other teachers at the Sichuan Institute of Higher Cuisine, Gan Guojian, Lu Maoguo, Long Qingrong, and Li Daiquan, for their inspiring lessons and their kindness to the only foreigner among their students. Du Li, Huang Weibing, Lu Yi, and Li Yunyun have also been most supportive. At Sichuan University Museum, I am much indebted to Professor Jiang Yuxiang, and at the Sichuan Minorities Institute, to Qin Heping. Wang Xudong of *Sichuan Cookery* (*si chuan peng ren*) magazine has given me many extremely useful books. The veteran journalist Che Fu and food critic Zhang Changyu also helped me on my way.

Chefs and restaurant owners all over Sichuan have been incredibly kind, welcoming me into their kitchens and letting me try my hand at the wok or cutting board. In Chengdu, I would particularly like to thank Manager Li Lin and the staff of the Shufeng Restaurant, Manager Yu De and the staff of the Chengdu Restaurant, Feng Rui and his family at the Bamboo Bar, Xiao Jianming and Xiao Ming of Piaoxiang, everyone at Long Chao Shou (especially waiter Xu Gang), and everyone at the Mousehole. In Chongqing, I am much obliged to Mao Xinning, the manager of Old Sichuan, and to the head chef at Xiao Dongtian. It is impossible to name individually all the other chefs, bean curd makers, market vendors, snack sellers, and restaurateurs who have contributed to this book.

Liu Yaochun and Xu Jun of Sichuan University have been fantastic friends

384

and have helped me immeasurably in every respect—I couldn't have written the book without them. Yu Weiqin, Zhou Xiaowei, Kou Caijun, Zhou Yu, Tao Ping, Li Shurong, Peng Rui, Liu Chun, and Zeng Bo have all contributed recipes, ideas, and contacts. Shang Meng kindly helped me with some of my translations.

Francesca Tarocco has, as always, been a splendid and inspirational friend, a formidable critic, and an exacting taster. I hope that this book will always remind her of our many shared adventures in Sichuan and in Europe. Seema Merchant has been passionate about this project since the beginning and has been a wonderful friend and indispensable critic. Mara Baughman has sustained me with herbs and affection in equal measure. Special thanks also to Lipika Pelham for all her moral support and enthusiastic tasting. My mother, Carolyn Dunlop, has tested recipes and given me invaluable advice. Non Shaw has been a mentor in many ways, and her guidance as a seasoned writer has been particularly useful.

I would also like to thank heartily all the other *lao wai* in Chengdu and at home in England who have spurred me on, especially Penny Bell and Simon Linder, Louise Beynon, Gwenaële Chesnais, Ian Cumming, Volker Dencks, Jo Forkin, Jari Grosse-Ruyken, Rachel Harris, Jakob Klein, Angie Knox, Marianne Bek Phiri, Pietro Piccoli, Davide Quadrio, Maria af Sandeberg, Monica de Togni, Clemens Treter, Elena Valussi, and Alessandro Zelger. In London, I would like to thank Yan-kit So for her support and encouragement and for giving Chinese cookbook writers something to aspire to with her excellent books; Norman Fu, for sharing with me some of his culinary expertise; Alan Davidson and Helen Saberi for their advice on naming ingredients; Huw Prendergast at Kew Gardens for his advice on trees; and Nick Wilson, Lindsey Jordan, Sara Marafini, Tom Weldon, and the rest of the team at Michael Joseph for taking this project on with such great enthusiasm. Many, many thanks also to Tara Fisher for her photographs, and to Qu Lei Lei for his beautiful calligraphy. Jeremy Carpenter, Martin Toseland, Sue Bale, Ann Barr, and Angela Atkins all provided me with valuable advice in the early stages. I am also much indebted to Alan Le Breton and Larry Jagan at the BBC World Service, who helped me to pursue this project while continuing to work at the BBC.

Finally, I would like to thank my parents, Bede and Carolyn Dunlop, for bringing me up in a house full of extraordinary food and for giving me the run of the kitchen from a very early age.

index

a note about the author

Fuchsia Dunlop studied Sichuanese cooking as a full-time student at the Sichuan Institute of Higher Cuisine in Chengdu, China, where she lived from 1994 to 1996. She was the first foreigner to enroll as a regular student in the institute's professional training course. She now lives in London, works for the BBC World Service, and writes about Chinese food and current affairs for the *Economist*, the *Guardian Weekly*, *China Review*, *The Observer*, *The Asian Wall Street Journal*, *Food and Travel*, and Radio 4's *The Food Programme*. Fuchsia was educated at Magdalene College, Cambridge; Westminster University; and the School of Oriental and African Studies. The British edition of this book won the Guild of Food Writers' Jeremy Round Award for best first book of 2001.